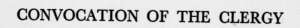

CONVOCATION OF THE CLERGY

CONVOCATION OF THE CLERGY

A STUDY OF ITS ANTECEDENTS AND ITS RISE
WITH SPECIAL EMPHASIS UPON ITS GROWTH
AND ACTIVITIES IN THE THIRTEENTH AND
FOURTEENTH CENTURIES

BY

DOROTHY BRUCE WESKE, A.M., Ph.D.

Published for the Church Historical Society

LONDON
SOCIETY FOR PROMOTING
CHRISTIAN KNOWLEDGE
NORTHUMBERLAND   AVENUE,   W.C.   2
NEW YORK :   THE   MACMILLAN   COMPANY

First published 1937

Made in Great Britain

MATRI MEÆ

A thesis submitted in partial fulfilment of the requirements for the degree of Doctor of Philosophy at Radcliffe College, March, 1934.

PREFACE

In the preparation of this study I have placed myself in the debt of many. To Radcliffe College and to the Wellesley College Alumnæ Association I am deeply grateful for fellowships which enabled me to go abroad and to remain there during two years for the writing of this thesis. I wish to render thanks to the University of London for the privileges and opportunities accorded me there, especially at King's College and the Institute of Historical Research.

To the custodians and their assistants of the British Museum, the Public Record Office and the Harvard College Library for their courteous help in facilitating the use of manuscripts and books my indebtedness is beyond measure. To his Grace, the Archbishop of Canterbury, I wish to express my gratitude for the privilege of access to the archiepiscopal registers at Lambeth Palace. To the Lord Bishop of Winchester and the Diocesan Registrar for the privilege of access to the episcopal archives at Winchester, and to the Very Reverend the Dean and Chapter of Winchester for the privilege of access to the archives in the Chapter Library, I tender my thanks.

Among those whose interest and advice have been a spur to me I would mention Professors W. E. Lunt, F. M. Powicke, and Elisabeth Hodder, Dr. Rose Graham, Mr. C. R. Cheney, Mrs. B. E. R. Formoy, Mr. H. G. Richardson, and Mrs. A. W. Goodman. To my friend, Dr. I. J. Churchill, Assistant Lambeth Librarian, I am greatly indebted for her infinite help and encouragement during the writing of this study. I would express special thanks also to Mr. Hilary Jenkinson, Maitland Lecturer in the University of Cambridge and Reader in Diplomatic and Archives in the University of London, for giving generously of his time for consultation and comment on this study.

But above all I would acknowledge my greatest debt to two—the Rev. Dr. Claude Jenkins, then Professor of Ecclesiastical History in the University of London and Lambeth Librarian, under whose guidance this study was written, and who has given abundantly of his time both for direction and for the reading of the manuscript, and to Professor C. H. McIlwain, Eaton Professor of the Science of Government in Harvard University, without whose stimulus this thesis would never have been launched, and who has given helpful advice as to its presentation in the final form. Whatever value this study may possess is a direct result of the privilege of working under them. For its errors I alone am to blame.

To the librarians of the Cleveland Public Library I would express my gratitude for their unfailing courtesy in putting at my immediate disposal their excellent collection of printed English source materials while I was correcting the final proof. I desire also to thank the Librarian of Kenyon College, Gambier, Ohio, for her kindness in facilitating the use of certain volumes. To my friends, Miss Elima A. Foster and Dr. Eva Matthews Sanford for their aid and advice concerning the proof and to Miss Arlene Jermyn and Miss Margaret Nace for their untiring help in reading the proof I tender my thanks. To Dr. Claude Jenkins, Regius Professor of Ecclesiastical History in the University of Oxford, and to my husband, John R. Weske, I am especially indebted for their interest and encouragement in the publication of this study. Finally I wish to express my appreciation to the Church Historical Society and to the Society for Promoting Christian Knowledge of their acceptance of this book and of the kindness and patience of the latter during the period of its preparation for publication.

DOROTHY BRUCE WESKE

Cleveland, Ohio
March 5, 1937

CONTENTS

NOTE

THE name of the manuscript placed first in a footnote indicates that I have actually examined it. If the manuscript has been transcribed in a printed work, the reference to the latter follows the name of the manuscript. When the printed work appears first and is followed by the name of the manuscript and its folios in brackets, the latter has been inserted for the convenience of the reader who may wish to go direct to the manuscript. When arranged thus, it indicates that I have not examined the manuscript. In quoting transcribed documents, the manuscript references have been kept in the form in which the editor or transcriber gave them. The transcription also has been left in the form in which it was given. The rules for transcription laid down in Volume I of the *Bulletin of the Institute of Historical Research* have been followed in the transcription of documents for this study.

ABBREVIATIONS

Add. Ch.	Additional Charter.
Add. MS.	Additional Manuscript.
Anc. Cor.	Ancient Correspondence.
Cal. C. R.	*Calendar of Close Rolls.*
Cal. P. R.	*Calendar of Patent Rolls.*
C. and Y. Soc. ...	Canterbury and York Society.
Const. Hist. ...	Constitutional History.
E. H. R.	*English Historical Review.*
H. & S.	Haddan & Stubbs's *Councils and Ecclesiastical Documents.*
Hist. MSS. Com. ...	Historical Manuscripts Commission.
Int. Rep.	*Interim Report of the Committee on House of Commons Personnel and Politics.*
K. R. Mem. Roll	King's Remembrancer's Memoranda Roll.
L. T. Mem. Roll...	Lord Treasurer's Memoranda Roll.
Parl. Writs ...	*Parliamentary Writs*, edited by Palgrave.
Rec. Com. ...	Record Commission.
Reg.	Register or Registrum.
Rep. Dig.	*Reports brought from the Lords on the Dignity of a Peer.*
Rot. Parl.	*Rotuli Parliamentorum.*
Sur. Soc.	Surtees Society.
Vet. Reg. Sar. ...	*Vetus Registrum Sarisberiense.*
Wor. Epis. Reg. ...	*Worcester Episcopal Registers.*
✕	Indicates a date somewhere between the two given dates.

A date in brackets such as 1369(–70) gives the year according to the Old Style and New Style Calendars.

Appendix

    (A) indicates that the convocation assembled.

    (S) indicates that the convocation was summoned but that the certainty of its having met is not known.

CHAPTER I

THE DEVELOPMENT OF ECCLESIASTICAL ASSEMBLIES IN ENGLAND (597—1295)

PART I

Ecclesiastical Assemblies in England before the Norman Conquest (597—1066)

An intensive study of the Convocation of the Clergy demands that we first investigate its roots. The earliest traces that we have of ecclesiastical gatherings in England date from the period of Augustine. Britain, though christianized during the Roman occupation, on the withdrawal of the Roman legions soon fell a prey to the Anglo-Saxon invasions. The adherents of Christianity were then either destroyed or driven into the north and west. When Augustine, therefore, came to England in 597 at the instance of Pope Gregory the Great, he found wide opportunities for his mission.

Augustine's problem, however, was not merely one of winning the Angles and Saxons to Christianity. He also had to confront the leaders of the vestiges of that earlier Christianity which had been planted in Britain. These were Britons, whose teachings he found differed considerably from those of the Church at Rome. It was with the purpose then of persuading the Britons to some sort of reconciliation that they might carry forward together the work of christianizing the pagan Angles and Saxons that Augustine about 602 summoned a gathering in the west of England at a place known to tradition as "Augustine's Oak." Hither came Augustine and his followers and the leaders of British Christianity. Augustine stressed the need of the Britons' accepting the Roman practice of celebrating Easter. [1] When

[1] Haddan and Stubbs (edd.), *Councils and Ecclesiastical Documents relating to Great Britain and Ireland*, III, 38.

Augustine successfully worked a miracle upon a blind man, the Britons, we are told, conceded the validity of his claims, but said that they could not depart from the traditions of their forefathers without consulting the rest of their people.[2] It was decided that another conference should be held.[1] When this conference assembled, probably the same year, at a place of which we do not know the name, there were present besides Augustine and his group, seven bishops and many very learned men from the monastery of Bangor.[2] Augustine demanded reconciliation on only three points: the manner of baptism, the celebration of Easter, and their union with his group in preaching the word to the Angles and Saxons.[3] The Britons were again recalcitrant and thus failed to make possible a harmonious settlement.

Pope Gregory had great dreams for the development of the Church in Britain. In 601 he sent the pallium to Augustine, accompanying it with a letter in which he outlined a plan whereby Britain was to be divided into two provinces of twelve dioceses each with an archbishop presiding over each province.[4] He made it clear that Augustine was to have authority over both provinces during his lifetime (a concession granted personally to him in reward for his services[5]), but that on his death precedence should go to whichever archbishop had been consecrated first.[4] Gregory named the archiepiscopal Sees as London and York.[4] Gregory's plan was never really carried out. The East Saxons soon abandoned the faith and made it impossible to have the archiepiscopate established at their capital, London.[5] Christianity was not taken to York by any of the representatives of the Roman mission until 625, when

[2] H. & S., III, 39.
[3] Ibid., III, 40.
[4] Venerabilis Baedae Opera Historica, ed. C. Plummer, I, 63—4.
[5] Ibid., II, 52.

Paulinus, one of those who had brought the Pope's letter to Augustine in 601, and who since then had been ordained bishop by Justus, went north in 625 as chaplain to the Queen of Edwin, King of Northumbria. [6] After Edwin accepted Christianity, Paulinus was made Bishop of York, but all authorities admit that he was never *de facto* Archbishop of York. [7] In 633, upon the death of Edwin in battle, Paulinus fled from York and established himself at Rochester. [7] It was there that he received the pallium sent to him by Pope Honorius who, sending one at the same time to Archbishop Honorius of Canterbury, [7] evidently designed to carry out Gregory's plan.

Christianity was carried on in the north after the departure of Paulinus by James the deacon. [8] It received a decided impetus under King Oswald, who was followed by his brother Oswiu. Both kings were adherents of British Christianity. During the reign of Oswiu in 664 a conference was held at Whitby, known sometimes as the " Synodus Pharensis." [9] The chief questions of discussion were the date for the celebration of Easter and the form of the tonsure. [9] There were present supporters of both the Roman and the British ways of thinking. [9] Finally Oswiu, convinced of the weight of the Roman arguments, gave his decision in

[6] H. & S., III, 75.
[7] W. Hunt, *The English Church from its Foundation to the Norman Conquest*, p. 69.
[8] *Ibid.*, p. 70.
[9] H. & S., III, 100—6.
J. C. Ayer, " Church Councils of the Anglo-Saxons," *Papers of the American Society of Church History*, second series, VII, 93—4.
Dr. Ayer writes, " The gathering at Whitby in 664, the so-called *Synodus Pharensis*, was not a church council. It had, indeed, to do with religious matters of grave importance to the life of the Church, but it was a gathering of lay and clerical notables under the presidency of the king. It can hardly be regarded as strictly a witenagemot of the Northumbrian kingdom, as Agilbert, a West Saxon bishop, was present and took part as did also Tuda, a bishop from South Ireland. It was rather an extraordinary conference called by Oswy for an extraordinary occasion and for his own guidance. There is no type of church council under which it can be brought."

favour of following the teachings of the Church at
Rome.[9] Thus unity was brought about between the
north and the south. Not long after this Wilfred, who
had played a prominent part at the council, was elected
to the See of York.[10]

In 668 Theodore of Tarsus was sent to Britain as
Archbishop of Canterbury.[11] Though he doubtless
knew of Pope Gregory's letter, he seems to have received no instructions for the carrying out of the dual
system, but assumed immediately metropolitical authority over the whole of England. Bede says that
Theodore was the first of the archbishops to whom the
whole Church of the English agreed to give the right
hand of fellowship.[12]

Theodore created a number of new dioceses. In East
Anglia he gave the See of Elmham to the north folk,
leaving Dunwich to the south folk.[13] He established
the See of London on a firmer basis than ever before
by putting a strong bishop in charge.[13] Mercia he
divided into five dioceses: Worcester, Leicester, Lichfield, Sidenaceaster or Stow, and Dorchester.[14] Later
he made a sixth see at Hereford.[14] In the north,
without attempting to get in touch with Wilfred, who
had gone to the Continent to be consecrated, Theodore
carved Northumbria into four sees, making two new
dioceses in Deira and Bernicia, another at Lindsey, and
leaving York as the fourth.[15]

Under Theodore there were definite strides forward
in conciliar development. Among notable instances is
the Council of Hertford[16] in 673 which, in the words

---

[10] H. & S., III, 106.
[11] *Ibid.*, III, 115.
[12] Baeda, *op. cit.*, I, 204: "*Isque primus erat in Archiepiscopis, cui omnis Anglorum ecclesia manus dare consentiret.*"
[13] Hunt, *op. cit.*, p. 139.
[14] *Ibid.*, 141—2.
[15] *Ibid.*, p. 146.
[16] H. & S., III, 118—22.

of Mr. William Hunt, is significant in being " the first occasion on which the English Church deliberated and acted as a single body." [17]   He further adds that this synod " was the first English national assembly, and as such was the forerunner of the witenagemots and parliaments of a unified and indivisible nation, which had yet to be formed out of the discordant elements of the heptarchic kingdoms." [18]   Present at the council were all the bishops of the Anglo-Saxon Church, with the exception of Wini, the simoniacal Bishop of London. [19] The list includes Theodore, Archbishop of Canterbury; Bisi, Bishop of the East Anglians; Wilfred, Bishop of the Northumbrians (by deputy); Putta, Bishop of Rochester; Leutherius, Bishop of the West Saxons; and Winfred, Bishop of Mercia. [20]   The purpose of the council was to treat concerning " the necessary business of the Church." [20]   Moreover, they were to treat concerning their faith that they might preserve incorruptibly whatever had been defined and decreed by the holy fathers. [20]

Of particular interest is this synod, for from the account of it we gain some knowledge of the procedure followed. When Theodore had completed his speech, he questioned each one of them, according to rank, as to whether he would consent to guard those things which had been decreed by the fathers of old. [20]   To which all the bishops replied that it was pleasing to them all to preserve whatever the canons of the fathers defined. [20]   Thereupon, Theodore immediately read aloud ten chapters from the book of canons concerning things which he considered necessary for them. [20] These canons dealt with the celebration of Easter, the control of bishoprics, monasteries, the clergy, questions

[17] Hunt, op. cit., p. 138.
[18] Ibid., p. 139. Cf. Ayer, infra, p. 7, n. 30.
[19] H. & S., III, 121, n. b.
[20] Ibid., III, 119.

of marriage and divorce, etc.[21] One canon called for
the assembling of a synod twice a year.[22] It was,
however, agreed that the synod should be held annually
in August at Clovesho,[22] a place most probably in
Mercia.[23] After a proper definition and discussion of
the canons, each bishop subscribed to them with his
own hand.[24] Theodore then dictated the substance of
the definition to Tititlus, the notary.[24] Each then
realized that whoever should go against these canons
would know himself to be separated from every episcopal[25] office *(officio sacerdotali)* and their society.[24]

In 680 Theodore held another important council—
that of Hatfield (sometimes called Heathfield).[26] To
this council came John the Precentor from Rome, bringing with him the canons of the Lateran Council of 649,
which were adopted by the present gathering.[27] We
do not know definitely who were in attendance at this
council. The only mention of it alludes to Theodore
and other bishops of Britain.[28] Archbishop Theodore
presided.[29] Unanimous consent was given to the
Catholic Faith.[29] Besides the canons of the Lateran
Council of 649 the faith of the first five general councils was accepted.[29]

The ecclesiastical councils of the early period are
particularly important. As Bishop Stubbs brings out,
the Church was the one unifying note in the centuries
when there were many small kingdoms.[30] Politically a

---

[21] H. & S., III, 119—21.
[22] *Ibid.*, III, 120.
[23] Hunt, *op. cit.*, p. 137.
[24] H. & S., III, 121.
[25] In early documents " sacerdotalis " is translated " episcopal."
[26] H. & S., III, 141—4.
[27] *Ibid.*, III, 143.
[28] *Ibid.*, III, 142.
[29] *Ibid.*, III, 142.
[30] W. Stubbs, *Constitutional History of England,* I (sixth edition). Cf.
Ayer, *op. cit.*, 106.
    Dr. Ayer, while admitting that " the fact that the Anglo-Saxons readily

man was a Northumbrian, a Mercian, or a West Saxon, but in his relationship to the Church he was English. [30] The Council of Hertford (673), where there were representatives from East Anglia, Kent, Wessex, Mercia and Northumbria, well illustrates this point. [31] There were probably as many sections of the country represented at Hatfield (A.D. 680) as at Hertford, though there exists no definite list of those who were in attendance.

As we pass on to the eighth century, we find it to be a period of marked growth in the number of councils. It is also noteworthy for the establishment in 734 or 735 of the archiepiscopate of York *de jure* and *de facto*. [32] At this time Egbert, Bishop of York, received the pallium from Rome. [32] From this point there was a definite head of the Church in the north. It is difficult to say anything in regard to the regularity with which the councils were held. We have seen that in Theodore's time it was provided that a council should be held annually at Clovesho, but this does not seem always to have been fulfilled. [33] Sometimes there was a council in Wessex as in 705 [34] or 710 × 716 [35]; at other times one in Northumbria as in 765 × 774 [36] or in 787. [37] The most frequent places of meeting were Clovesho, [38] and Celchyth or Chelsea. [39] The composition of these synods was elastic. Generally an archbishop and at

accepted Christianity added one more bond of union between the various nations in England," declares that "when the actual circumstances of the union of the kingdoms are examined, there seems very little room for profound church influence."

[31] H. & S., *op. cit.*, III, 118ff.
[32] *Ibid.*, III, 335.
[33] *Ibid.*, III, *passim*.
[34] *Ibid.*, III, 268ff.
[35] *Ibid.*, III, 295ff.
[36] *Ibid.*, III, 433ff.
[37] *Ibid.*, III, 443ff.
[38] *Ibid.*, 300, 340, 360, 483, 512. The dates of the councils were 716, 742, 747, 794, 798.
[39] *Ibid.*, 464—5. The dates of the councils were 788, 789.

least one king were present. As for the other constituents present, our information is culled from such
general expressions as *ecclesiastici patres*,[40] *omnes
Saxonicæ gentis archimandritæ*,[41] and *omnis sena-
tus et universus clericorum ordo*,[42] or from the more
specific data found in the subscriptions of conciliar acts
and charters, which may not always include all who
were present. The councils at Clovesho and Celchyth
had the largest attendance. In Clovesho in 716 there
were present the Archbishop of Canterbury, thirteen
bishops, seven priests, one dean, one abbot, three
præpositi, one count, and twenty-one persons without
description.[43] Again, at Clovesho in 747, there were in
attendance the King of Mercia, the Archbishop of
Canterbury, eleven bishops,[44] and at Chelsea in 787
the papal legates, Offa, King of Mercia, the Archbishop of Canterbury, twelve bishops, four abbots,
three " duces," one " comes."[45] From these lists we see
that these councils were rarely purely ecclesiastical in
composition.[46] Very often the chief lay magnates were
present. Indeed, sometimes it is difficult to decide
whether a gathering was primarily an ecclesiastical
council or a witenagemot. There seems to have been
no consciousness of early rivalry on the part of the ecclesiastical and secular, or any overlapping of powers that
was repugnant to either group.[47] The bishops wel-
comed the attestation and confirmation of their acts by
the secular powers, and likewise, the secular powers the
support of the ecclesiastical.[47]

---

[40] H. & S., III, 275.
[41] *Ibid.*, III, 276. " Archimandrita " is a term used in the Eastern
Church.
[42] *Ibid.*, III, 295.
[43] *Ibid.*, III, 300ff.
[44] *Ibid.*, III, 360.
[45] *Ibid.*, III, 460ff.
[46] *Ibid.*, III, *passim.*
[47] Stubbs, *Constit. Hist.*, I (sixth edition), 143—4, 252—3.

There is a wide range in the business treated by the assemblies of the eighth century. Space does not allow a detailed account, but here are a few of the topics with which these gatherings were concerned: the confirmation of the privileges granted by past kings, episcopal elections, the establishment of new sees, the Catholic Faith, the reformation of abuses, acts dealing with monastic life, ritual, the complaint of injuries, and grants of land. [48]

The synods of the ninth century are very similar in character to those of the eighth. There is, however, one significant difference: they are much more concerned with land grants and suits in regard to land. This marks a step on the part of the clergy towards a rapid increase of interest in secular affairs. Of fifteen synods about which we have information in the ninth century, nine are concerned in whole or in part with land questions, and three with questions of inheritance. [49]

The Synod of Clovesho in 803 is of particular note as its list of subscriptions seems to foreshadow a definite development in the system of representation. [50] Besides the Archbishop of Canterbury there were twelve bishops present. [50] Under the names of the archbishop and the several bishops, which are separately spaced, are lists of representatives presumably from the various dioceses. [50] These generally include several abbots and priests. In the case of Canterbury there is the archdeacon. [50] In many instances there are deacons. The fact that, under the dioceses of London and Selsey there are names of persons without description, gives rise to the possibility that there may have been lay delegates. [50] As we have no other instance in these early centuries of so orderly a representation, it does not follow that this scheme was for the time being permanently adopted.

[48] H. & S., III, *passim.*
[49] *Ibid.,* III, 530—630, *passim.*
[50] *Ibid.,* III, 546—7.

Parallel with the growth of the synod in the seventh, eighth and ninth centuries was the development of the witenagemots, hardly to be distinguished from the synods. The place of assemblage for the greater part of the seventh century is indefinite in the records— merely the general location being given, such as Mercia,[51] Wessex[52] or Northumbria.[53] The character of their composition, apart from the fact that the king of the particular district was always present, is also vague. One finds generalizations such as *principes*,[54] *consilarii*[54] and *sapientes suæ gentis*.[55] Towards the end of the seventh century (688 × 693) two bishops are specifically mentioned.[56] Thenceforth there are lists of bishops who definitely constitute part of the witan.[57] In the witenagemot at Baccanfeld (Bapchild, Kent) 696 × 716 there were abbots and priests, as well as deacons, *duces* and *satrapi* present.[58] The seventh century witenagemot was predominantly concerned with religious or ecclesiastical subjects.[59] In the matters treated may be found business such as the foundation of an abbey, an episcopal election, the division of bishoprics, the reading of communications from the apostolic see, ecclesiastical laws.[59]

Our knowledge for the witenagemots of the eighth century is much more definite, both as to the place of assemblage, and the character of the composition.[60] Those witenagemots, of which we have records, were held under the kings of Mercia. In general, the gatherings included the Archbishop of Canterbury, bishops numbering from two to nine, abbots and priests, and of the laity—*principes, duces* and *præfecti*.[60] In addition, we frequently find persons without descrip-

---

[51] H. & S., III, 127.
[52] *Ibid.*, III, 214.
[53] *Ibid.*, III, 106.
[54] *Ibid.*, III, 80.
[55] *Ibid.*, III, 106.

[56] *Ibid.*, III, 214.
[57] *Ibid.*, III, 232—659, *passim.*
[58] *Ibid.*, III, 238ff.
[59] *Ibid.*, III, 80—238, *passim.*
[60] *Ibid.*, III, 250—529, *passim.*

tion.[60] With few exceptions the matters treated are the grants of land to laymen and ecclesiastics.[60]

In the ninth century there are records of witenagemots, not only under Mercian kings, but under the kings of Kent and Wessex.[61] The composition is similar to that of the preceding century.[61] In many cases the attendance is greater. Again the subjects treated are mostly land questions.[61] Frequently during the century the grants are made " cum consensu et communi consilio Episcoporum et principium meorum et omnium seniorum gentis nostræ," or with some similar expression.[62] The idea of a definite limitation on the royal power was beginning to be voiced.

When we approach the latter part of the ninth century our problem becomes a much more difficult one. In the first place, records are fewer in number. In the second place, for a great deal of our information we have to draw henceforth upon cases of law. Finally, with the fluidity of institutions in the period, the distinction becomes less and less between a synod and a witenagemot. The statement has been made that the practice of holding church councils " had fallen into disuse " in the centuries immediately preceding the conquest.[63] We must go deeper than this assertion. If there was a cessation of purely church councils—and this we acknowledge, was there a cessation on the part of the clergy in the transacting of church business? We declare that there was not. The clergy were not lacking in energy. The laws extant for the latter part of the ninth century, the tenth century, and the first quarter of the eleventh century embrace a liberal

[61] *Ibid.,* III, 530—659, *passim.*
[62] *Ibid.,* III, 633.
[63] Z. N. Brooke, *The English Church and the Papacy,* p. 101.
Dr. Macdonald puts the lapse of conciliar activity even earlier: " A prominent feature in the Norman reformation was the revival of conciliar action. After the time of Theodore, the national assemblies of the church fell into disuse." A. J. Macdonald, *Lanfranc,* p. 95.

amount of ecclesiastical legislation.[64]   The affairs of
the Church certainly were not dead issues.   The name
synod may have disappeared, but the matters that used
to be discussed in synods continued to be settled, even if
they were settled in the witenagemots.

We know that among the members of the witan
were ecclesiastics.   As the latter generally possessed
whatever learning there was, it is probable that
they played a prominent role in formulating legislation.
So long as the ecclesiastical group had a strong voice in
the government, it is extremely doubtful that they were
even conscious of any cessation in the usual form of
church government.

In days when there was danger continually from the
marauding Danes, it is most natural to find the ecclesiastical and secular powers standing together out of
common interest.

The outstanding set of laws for the latter part of the
ninth century is that of Alfred.[65]   We do not know
where they were issued.   The date of promulgation is
unknown.   Professor Liebermann favours 892—93,[66]
while Mr. Attenborough thinks perhaps that the date
was earlier.[67]   These laws, which were formulated by
Alfred, and were approved by all his councillors, who
declared that they should be observed, are definitely
ecclesiastical in tone.   Emphasis is put upon respect for
the Church, whether it be a question of sanctuary,[68] or
of weapons being drawn in the presence of an archbishop or bishop, who are both ranked with the ealdor-

[64] F. L. Attenborough (ed.), *The Laws of the Earliest English Kings,
passim.*

A. J. Robertson (ed.), *The Laws of the Kings of England from
Edmund to Henry I, passim.*

[65] Attenborough, *op. cit.,* pp. 62—93.

[66] F. Liebermann (ed.), *Die Gesetze der Angelsachsen,* III, p. 34.

[67] Attenborough, *op. cit.,* p. 35.

Mr. Attenborough gives as his reason Alfred's description of himself
as " West Seaxna cyning."   Later Alfred used another title.

[68] *Ibid.,* p. 67 (Alfred, 4).

man. [69] Where the questions are not distinctly ecclesiastical, they deal with moral problems—slaying, adultery, assault, arson, stealing. [70] We may conclude that the ecclesiastics gave their support on the condemnation of these offences.

In contrast to these laws, there exists the Peace between King Alfred and King Guthrum (880 × 890), in the making of which we are told that all the councillors of the English nation played a part. [71] This was specifically secular legislation; it dealt with boundaries, trade and suits. There is nothing to indicate ecclesiastical participation, except the knowledge that there were always ecclesiastics among the king's councillors.

The Peace which was made some years later (900? × 925?) between King Edward and King Guthrum [72] is widely different from the Peace noted above, for ecclesiastical influence is very apparent in it. The love of one God and the renunciation of all heathen practices are enjoined. [73] There is condemnation for those who fail to pay the amends of the Church, which were determined by the bishops. [74] A great section is given to tithes, and there are certain rulings in regard to Sunday bargaining, fasts, wizards, [75] etc. The bishop figures prominently throughout, and in one instance is classified with the king or earl of the province. [72]

Of the groups of laws under King Edward, both the one issued in the period 900? × 925? [76] and that of 921? × 925? [77] handle the administration of justice and the public peace.

In King Athelstan's reign (925? × 939?) the eccle-

[69] *Ibid.*, p. 73 (Alfred, 15).
[70] *Ibid.*, pp. 62—93 (Alfred), *passim*.
[71] *Ibid.*, pp. 98—101 (Alfred and Guthrum).
[72] *Ibid.*, p. 103 (Edward and Guthrum).
[73] *Ibid.*, p. 103, paragraph 1 (Edward and Guthrum).
[74] *Ibid.*, p. 103, paragraph 2 (Edward and Guthrum).
[75] *Ibid.*, pp. 103—9 (Edward and Guthrum).
[76] *Ibid.*, pp. 115—17 (Edward and Guthrum, I Edward).
[77] *Ibid.*, pp. 119—21 (II Edward).

siastical influence is again strongly apparent.[78] This period produced six issues, besides a special ordinance concerning charities and one concerning ordeals.[79] In five of the series bishops are mentioned as taking part in the legislation.[80] In two cases only an archbishop is mentioned.[81] With one exception all the groups include ecclesiastical provisions. A hint is given, too, as to methods of procedure: In *I Athelstan,* the king, archbishop and other bishops issue instructions to the reeve in every borough.[82] The bishops and reeves are to give these orders to their subordinates.[82] Certainly this would indicate no lack of ecclesiastical activity in legislation, though it must be admitted that the meetings were evidently held under the king's summons and under his presidency. In general there seems to have been no desire for independent action on the part of the bishops. Even in a local gathering in Kent, bishops, thegns, nobles and commoners met together with councillors sent by the king.[83] A meeting such as this seems to have been summoned at the king's instance, for we learn that he had sent special injunctions about titles, etc., and had advised them concerning the peace of the land.[84] The legislation at this council had to do with tithes, the proclamation of measures enacted at the Council of Grately, punishments and sureties.[83] The tone of the conclusion is humble, almost abject, in which they request the king to make alterations if the legislation contains too much or too little.[85]

II Athelstan[86] (issued at Grately) and *VI Athel-*

---

[78] Attenborough, pp. 123—73, *passim* (Athelstan I—VI).
[79] For some of the series we know the places of meeting: Grately, Exeter, Kent, Thunresfeld, London.
[80] I, II, III, VI Athelstan and Ordinance.
[81] I, II Athelstan.
[82] Attenborough, *op. cit.,* p. 123 (Preamble I Athelstan).
[83] *Ibid.,* pp. 143—7 (III Athelstan).
[84] *Ibid.,* p. 143 (Preamble III Athelstan).
[85] *Ibid.,* p. 147 (Conclusion III Athelstan).
[86] *Ibid.,* pp. 127—43 (II Athelstan).

stan [87] (issued at London) are perhaps the fullest groups of the laws, and comprise in one or the other generally the subjects touched upon in the remaining groups. In *II Athelstan* the questions treated are justice, theft, ordeal, exchange of cattle, coinage, fasts, fines, burial in consecrated ground. [86] In *VI Athelstan* theft, cattle, slaves, meetings of officials, of the kindred, punishments are found among the subjects for legislation. [87]

While we have not been able to find here any legislation so purely ecclesiastical as that which we found in the seventh and eighth centuries and the first part of the ninth century, at least the clergy could express their opinions and assert their authority through the law promulgated by the king.

In the next set of laws, the three series of Edmund (945 × 946), bishops or ecclesiastical councillors are also specifically mentioned. [88] The subjects are similar to those of preceding times—the promotion of Christianity and the preservation of the public peace. [88] Again, in the series of laws under Edgar [89] the measures are of like character, with perhaps more definite regulations in regard to the administration of justice and special emphasis upon Church dues, and the establishment of uniformity of payment of them throughout the kingdom. *IV Edgar* stresses obedience to bishops. [90] The regulations, in general, were to be enforced throughout the realm.

Ethelred's reign covers the latter part of the tenth century and the beginning of the eleventh. There are ten series of laws, [91] and in all but one [92] the councillors are mentioned as taking part in the making of them.

[87] *Ibid.*, pp. 157—69 (VI Athelstan).
[88] Robertson, *op. cit.*, pp. 7—15 (I, II, III Edmund).
[89] *Ibid.*, pp. 17—39 (I, II, III, IV Edgar).
[90] *Ibid.*, p. 33 (IV Edgar, 1, paragraph 8).
[91] *Ibid.*, pp. 53—133 (I—X Ethelred).
[92] IV Ethelred, X Ethelred.

Of the ten, one is a treaty of peace,[93] another contains certain regulations in force in London in regard to trade.[94] *VI, VII, VIII, IX, X* are distinctly ecclesiastical in tone. Five series lay particular emphasis on the promotion of the Christian life, or the fulfilment of Christian duties.[95] *VI* and *VIII* give regulations for the ecclesiastics themselves, such as the proper discharge of their duties, the grading of churches, the division of tithes and the trials of members of the clergy. Here are instances, therefore, of functions being fulfilled in a witan that one might have considered the special province of ecclesiastical councils.

In addition to the laws issued towards the latter part of Canute's reign, we find three councils mentioned by Roger of Hoveden. The first of these was in London in 1016.[96] Here the king, all the bishops, *principes* and *optimates* gathered. The main business was the exclusion of the brothers of Edmund from the succession. The other two councils were held in 1018[97] and 1020[97] at Oxford and Cirencester respectively. The former was concerned with the keeping of the law of Edgar by both the English and the Danes. We are not told the purpose of the latter.

Canute's laws issued either in 1027[98] or from 1029—1034[98] are in two parts—the first dealing with ecclesiastical affairs, the second with secular, though even these embrace many moral questions. These laws were made by Canute and his councillors.[99] They reflect the laws of the preceding periods. The dominance of ecclesiastical power is apparent in such clauses as " the bishops are God's heralds and teachers, and they shall

---

[93] II Ethelred.
[94] IV Ethelred.
[95] V, VI, VII, IX, X Ethelred.
[96] Roger de Hoveden, *Chronica,* Ed. W. Stubbs (Rolls Series) I, 85.
[97] *Ibid.,* I, 87.
[98] Robertson, *op. cit.,* pp. 137—9.
[99] *Ibid.,* pp. 155, 175 (Preamble I Canute, Preamble II Canute).

proclaim and zealously give example of our duty towards God " ;[100] or " he who disdains to hearken to the messengers of God shall have to settle his case with God Himself." [101] An important clause in *II Canute* provides that ecclesiastical amends be settled in accordance with the directions contained in the canon law and secular amends in accordance with the secular law. [102] This shows that gradually there was growing up, most probably quite unconsciously, the assignment of certain matters to the ecclesiastical province, the assignment of others to the secular province. This was to deepen and foreshadow the cleavage between the ecclesiastical and secular, which had its fulfilment under William I when he separated the Church courts. [103] Before the Conquest the definite division between the two groups of affairs did not come. Ecclesiastical activity had by no means lapsed as some would have us think. On the contrary, it was so strong that it furnished the backbone of the legislation issued in the name of the temporal authority.

PART II

Ecclesiastical Assemblies in England after the Norman Conquest (1066—1295)

WHEN we approach the reign of William I, we naturally wonder in what way the position of the Church in England was affected by his coming. Did conditions remain the same, or was there a drastic change? A document, called by Davis a diploma, issued in 1068 to the Church of S. Martin (le Grand), London, confirming the grants of Ingelric, priest in

[100] *Ibid.*, p. 173 (I Canute 26).
[101] *Ibid.*, p. 175 (I Canute, paragraph 4).
[102] *Ibid.*, p. 195 (II Canute 38, paragraph 2).
[103] *Ibid.*, p. 235 (William I : Episcopal Laws 2).

Essex, [104] is one of many similar instances which lead us to think that at the outset conditions were largely the same as in the pre-Conquest period. The subscriptions to this diploma reveal the composition of the assembly wherein it was granted. This body included the king and queen and their son, the two archbishops of England, four bishops of English sees and three bishops of French sees, nine abbots of English abbeys, eight chaplains, various earls and *principes*. Here was a question of a grant of land being settled as in pre-Conquest days by a mixed gathering.

A document, called also by Davis a diploma, restoring land to Giso, Bishop of Wells, seems to have been granted in a somewhat similar assembly. The subscriptions include those of the king and queen, of two archbishops, of two bishops of French sees, of seven bishops of English sees, and of four English abbots (one undesignated). [105]

It is interesting to note that there are extant letters of citation from the cardinal legates to the Bishop of Worcester to the council that was to be held at Winchester at Easter 1070. [106] The bishop is commanded to be present and to show the letters to all abbots of his diocese [106] This council illustrates a definite transition movement. Although there were papal legates in England in 1062, [107] it does not appear that a papal legate had been present at a council there since 787. [108] At the Council of Winchester in 1070 there were three legates present—Ermenfridus, Bishop

---

[104] H. W. C. Davis, ed., *Regesta Regum Anglo-Normanorum*, I, 6, no. 22.

[105] *Ibid.*, I, 7, no. 23.

[106] D. Wilkins, ed., *Concilia Magnæ Britanniæ et Hiberniæ*, I, 323 (Ex. mss. Fr. Junii, n. 99 inter codices mss. Bodlej).

[107] Florence of Worcester, *Chronicon ex Chronicis*, ed. B. Thorpe (English Historical Society) I, 220.

[108] Stubbs, *Constit. Hist.*, I (sixth edition), 267: "An envoy of Eugenius II, bearing an English name, attests the acts of the council of Clovesho in 824."

of Sion, and two cardinals. We are told that they were in England at King William's request. [109] Although the king presided over this council, the presence of the papal legates at it was certainly a step towards bringing England into closer relations with Rome.

The main business of this council was the degrading of Stigand, Archbishop of Canterbury. His brother, Agelmarus, Bishop of the East Angles, was also degraded. [110] Other bishops and abbots were deprived of their honours. To this council modern scholars attribute the set of sixteen canons, which Wilkins attributed to a later date. [111] The canons dealt with plurality, simony, letters of commendation, ordinations, altars, celebration of Holy Communion and baptism, masses, burial of the dead, punishment, monks, annual synods, titles, chastity of clerks, chalices. [112] It is also thought that the penitential, for those who should fall in war, was passed at this council. [113] Wulfstan, Bishop of Worcester, came forward at this time with claims against the See of York for certain lands. [114]

Another council where Ermenfridus was also present was held at Windsor the same year at Pentecost. [114] The cardinal legates had returned. We are told specifically that Ermenfridus held this synod. At this time another bishop was degraded—Angelricus, Bishop of the South Saxons. [114] Another person by the name of Stigand was given the See of Selsey, which was transferred to Chichester. [114]

[109] Ordericus Vitalis, "Historia Ecclesiastica," *Patrologia Latina,* ed. J. P. Migne, CLXXXVIII, 321.

[110] Florence of Worcester, *op. cit.,* II, p. 5.

[111] H. Böhmer, *Kirche und Staat in England und in der Normandie im XI und XII Jahrhundert,* pp. 62—4, n. 3.

Macdonald, *op. cit.,* pp. 96—7, n. 1. The page reference to Wilkins here cited is incorrect.

[112] *Ibid.,* I, 365. (One set of canons is quoted: Ex. MSS. Cotton, Tiber, c. I, n. 3.)

Wilkins, *op. cit.,* I p. 366. Wilkins assigns the acts to 1076.

[113] *Ibid.,* I, 366 (Ex vetusto libro Saxonico, ad Wigorn. eccl. quondam spectante, citante Spelm).

[114] Florence of Worcester, *op. cit.,* II, 6.

Not very long afterwards, Lanfranc, Abbot of Caen, was appointed to the See of Canterbury. He was consecrated on August 29th, 1070.[115] This marks a significant moment for the English Church. Here we find a man of cosmopolitan background, one schooled in Italy, who had contributed much to creating Bec a centre of learning, under whom Pope Alexander II had sat as a student, coming into control of the metropolitical See of England, where the Church was notably national from its very insular position. Would Lanfranc, who was accustomed to the practice of the Church on the Continent, be content to have ecclesiastical business transacted in the witans as had been the national custom for some two hundred years? From the first, it was evident that Lanfranc was bent upon some sort of reorganization of the Church along definite lines. This was apparent when Thomas of Bayeux, Elect to the See of York, came to Lanfranc shortly after the latter's consecration to be consecrated.[116] Lanfranc demanded a written profession of obedience, with the addition that he should swear the oath of profession. Thomas refused. At first he was supported in his refusal by the king,[117] but later Lanfranc convinced the king of the wisdom of his demand. William, therefore, commanded Thomas to submit.[117] Thomas for a while held out and then at last yielded, promising to submit himself to Lanfranc in all precepts which pertained to the Christian religion.[117] The question as to the necessity for Thomas's successors to make a profession was left to a future council.[117]

A council took place in 1070 after the consecration of Lanfranc, where in the presence of the king, the

[115] Florence of Worcester, II, 7. The date in brackets in the text is given incorrectly. The feast of S. John Baptist mentioned, was the feast of the Decollation, not of the Nativity.

[116] William of Malmesbury, *De Gestis Pontificum Anglorum,* ed. N.E.S.A. Hamilton (Rolls Series), p. 39.

[117] *Ibid.,* p. 41ff.

Archbishop of Canterbury and the primates of all England, the claims of Wulfstan against York were settled.[118]

When Lanfranc and Thomas went to Rome to receive the pallia, the question of the supremacy of Canterbury was broached by Thomas to Pope Alexander.[119] The outcome was that the pope declared that the case should be settled by the bishops and abbots in England.

At Winchester in 1072 at Easter the case of the supremacy of Canterbury over York was opened in the presence of the king, the bishops and abbots.[120] It was shown and proved by the authorities of different writings that the Church of York should be subject to that of Canterbury, and should obey her in all things that pertained to the Christian religion.[120] The boundaries of the dioceses subject to the Archbishop of York were discussed. It was pointed out that Durham should be subject to York, and all the regions from the boundaries of the bishopric of Lichfield and the river Humber to the extreme boundaries of Scotland.[121] The continuation in Latin of MS. A of the *Saxon Chronicle*, which Plummer entitles *The Later Acts of Lanfranc*, gives an account of this council.[122] The chronicler states that at this time Lanfranc instituted many things that should be preserved concerning the worship of the Christian religion.[122] Modern scholars attribute to this council a set of thirteen canons listed by Wilkins under another date.[123] The canons dealt with simony, ordinations, celebration of councils twice a year, the powers

---

[118] Florence of Worcester, *op. cit.*, II, 8.
[119] William of Malmesbury, *op. cit.*, pp. 40—1.
[120] *Ibid.*, p. 42.
[121] *Ibid.*, p. 43.
[122] *Two of the Saxon Chronicles Parallel*, ed. C. Plummer, I, Appendix B, p. 288.
[123] Böhmer, *op. cit.*, pp. 62—4, n. 3.
  Macdonald, *op. cit.*, pp. 96—7, n. 1. The page reference to Wilkins, here cited, is incorrect. *Vide infra*, p. 22, n. 124.

of bishops, penitence, apostate clerks and monks, titles, the checking of the invasion of ecclesiastical possessions, the bearing of arms by clerks, and reverence to clerks and monks.[124] Anathema was proclaimed against those who failed to observe these canons.

At this time the abbot of the new monastery was deposed.[122] The case of the supremacy of Canterbury was settled temporarily at Windsor at Pentecost in 1072.[125] We know this from the accord extant to which those present subscribed their names.[125] Freeman calls this assembly " a general gemot of the whole realm."[126] Since the subscriptions, apart from that of the king, are those of ecclesiastical persons, one is led to think that the accord was made in an ecclesiastical council. Those subscribing were the king, the legate, Hubert, the two archbishops, the bishops of London, Sherborne, Worcester, Hereford, Wells, Dorchester, Winchester, Elmham, Chichester, Rochester and Exeter, and the abbots of Ramsey, Glastonbury, Ely, Chertsey, Evesham, St. Albans, S. Peter's (Westminster), S. Edmunds, Burgh, Abingdon and Winchester.[125] Either at Windsor or at the preceding Council at Winchester it was decided that if the Archbishop of Canterbury should call a council, the Archbishop of York and all his subject bishops should come.[121] York was released from making his profession by oath, with no prejudice to the successors of the Archbishop of Canterbury who should wish to exact it.[121] He made his profession in writing. The procedure in the case of the death of either the Archbishop of Canterbury or that of the Archbishop of York was determined.[121]

These Councils of Winchester and Windsor are interesting to us not only for the subject matter, which

---

[124] Wilkins, op. cit., I, 365 (" e libro Saxonico Wigornensis ecclesiæ, etiamque e libro Excestrensis ecclesiæ deprompta (citante Spelmanno) ").
[125] Davis, op. cit., I, 17, n. 64.
[126] E. A. Freeman, The Norman Conquest, IV (second edition), 356.

they discussed, but as examples of the gradual reshaping of Church administration under the guidance of Lanfranc. When emphasis begins to be made upon procedure, it is apparent that there is a trend towards nice distinctions. But in the next council a still further advance is noticeable. Certain very definite problems in the Church were to be attacked. This council was held in 1075 at S. Paul's, London.[127] There were present the two archbishops and the bishops of eleven other sees. Lanfranc is mentioned as ordering and presiding (*jubente atque idem concilio præsidente*). It is specifically noted that the Bishop of Durham did not attend, but sent a canonical excuse.[128] The very mention of this shows that the regulations were beginning to be precise in regard to attendance. The account of the council begins with the statement that " since for many years back the use of councils had been obsolescent, some things were renewed which were known to have been defined in ancient canons."[129] References were made in the canons issued to specific councils of the past. The canons dealt with the transference of episcopal sees to cities, the seating plan in synods, letters of commendation, permission to speak in council, marriage, prohibition of the purchase and sale of sacred orders, prohibition of bishops, abbots and clergy taking part in the sentencing of a man to death or maiming.[130] In these canons may be noted several progressive moves. The transference of sees to the cities was in accord with continental custom. It meant that there would be in the future definite centres of episcopal activity. The desire to have it stated in black and white where each

[127] Milo Crispin, *Vita Lanfranci, Beati Lanfranci Opera Omnia,* ed. J. A. Giles, I, 305.
[128] *Ibid.,* I, 306.
[129] *Ibid.,* I, 306 : " Et quia multis retro annis in Anglico regno usus consiliorum obsoleverat, renovata sunt nonnulla quæ antiquiis etiam noscuntur canonibus definita."
William of Malmesbury, *op. cit.,* p. 67. A similar statement is made.
[130] *Ibid.,* pp. 67—8.

bishop should sit, shows again the tendency of Lanfranc
to have precise organization, and to build up a definite
hierarchy in the Church. Emphasis is again laid upon
rank, when it is declared that permission to speak in
councils must be obtained from the archbishop, bishops
and abbots being excepted. A line of cleavage is struck
between the clergy and the laity in the prohibition of
the clergy from taking part in judgments which
involved death or maiming.

The following year (1076) in April, a council was
held at Winchester.[131] At this council the case of
Ailricus, Bishop of Chichester, was defined and brought
to an end.[132] Furthermore, a series of canons was
passed.[132] Several of these canons dealt with the
question of clerical marriage.[132] No " canonicus " was
to marry. Priests, who lived in fortresses or villages,
and had wives, were not to be compelled to give them
up.[132] Those, who did not have them, were not to take
them.[132] Bishops were to take care not to ordain priests
and deacons unless they professed that they had no
wives.[132] Other canons dealt with letters of commendation, the rendering of service, the summoning by the
bishop of laity accused of crime, and the priestly benediction in marriage.[132]

The chapter dealing with excommunication and in
the last event forfeiture for those accused of crime, who
failed to answer the summons of the archbishop,
alludes to a decree that had been issued by the king.[133]
The date of issue of this decree was (according to
Dr. Liebermann) some time between 1070 and 1076.[134]
Dr. Liebermann prefers April 1072;[134]   Dr. Böhmer

[131] Plummer (ed.), *Two of the Saxon Chronicles Parallel*, I, Appendix
B, 289.
[132] Mathew Parker, *De Antiquitate Britannicæ Ecclesiæ et Privilegiis
Ecclesiæ Cantuariensis* (ed. 1729), p. 173. Parker quotes *Liber Constitu-
tionum Wigornensis*, p. 101.
Wilkins, *op. cit.*, I, p. 367. Wilkins quotes Parker, *op. cit.*, p. 173.
[133] Robertson, *op. cit.*, p. 235.
[134] Liebermann, *op. cit.*, I, 485.

gives 1076.[135] The earlier date seems the more likely, as the description of the decision of the decree at the beginning reflects the customary manner of decision in the pre-Conquest days. Here is a translation of the king's words: " Be it known to all of you and the rest of my loyal subjects who dwell in England, that I have decided, in full council and with the advice of my arch-bishops, bishops, abbots and all the magnates of my kingdom, upon the improvement of the conditions of episcopal jurisdiction which, up to my time, has not been of a proper character in England, or in accordance with the precepts of the holy Canon Law." [136] It seems to have been issued in a great council of the realm rather than in an ecclesiastical synod. There is, of course, the possibility of the motion having come first from a synod, and of its then having been taken to the Great Council for ratification and enforcement. It is not difficult to see the influence of Lanfranc behind it. This decree, which separated the ecclesiastical and secular courts, marked a progressive step for the ecclesiastical power. It set the clergy very much apart. It dealt a decided blow to the old order of Anglo-Saxon times when the spiritual and lay magnates sat side by side in the secular court for the common weal. Hence-forth, no bishop or archdeacon was to hold in the hundred court pleas affecting episcopal jurisdiction.[136] They were not to bring forward for the judgment of laymen any case affecting episcopal jurisdiction.[136] The accused was to come to the place appointed by the bishop and was to make amends to God and the bishop according to the Canon Law.[136] If the person summoned refused to obey the summons, the authority and power of the king and sheriff were to be used.[136] No sheriff or baron was to interfere with the jurisdiction of the bishop.[136]

[135] Böhmer, *op. cit.*, pp. 62—4, n. 3.
[136] Robertson, *op. cit.*, p. 235. Miss Robertson's translation is here quoted.

Thus was the Church given a definite sphere of administrative activity. Once she had obtained it, she was to treasure it, and to be willing to fight for it even to the death as in the time of Becket. The Church became more and more an entity set apart. It was the exclusiveness that took its rise in the separation of the ecclesiastical courts that was probably responsible two centuries later for the clergy's desire to meet separately for the making of their grants rather than to vote them in the general parliaments.

While King William granted privileges to the clergy, he was very careful to provide that ultimate authority rested with himself.[137] No pope was to be acknowledged until the king had given his consent.[137] No papal letters were to be received until they had first been shown to him.[137] No one was to be excommunicated even for heinous crimes unless the king had given his permission.[137] Matters to be discussed in the councils presided over by the archbishop had first been accepted by the king.[137] In this way William strengthened his own authority, and prevented any check that the clergy might have been able to have on the secular authority through their very solidarity.

We know of three more ecclesiastical councils held in William's reign by Lanfranc, though there is little record of their business. At a council in London in 1076, Ælnodus, Abbot of Glastonbury, was deposed.[138] In 1081 there was a council at Gloucester. The presence of the bishops there offered an opportunity for the consecration at that time of William (of S. Carilef) to the See of Durham.[138] For three days after the meeting of the Great Council at Gloucester in 1085(-6) Lanfranc held a council. The Abbot of Croyland was

---

[137] Stubbs, *Const. Hist.*, I (sixth edition), 309—10.
[138] Plummer, *Two of the Saxon Chronicles Parallel*, I, Appendix B, 289.

deposed.[139] The king's clerks, Robert, William and Maurice, were appointed to the Sees of Chester,[140] Norfolk (i.e. Thetford), and London.[139]

The reign of William I was of the utmost importance to the Church. While the early councils of his reign were similar in character to those of pre-Conquest days, we find that after the appointment of Lanfranc to the See of Canterbury, great vigour was instilled into the Church, and a series of purely ecclesiastical councils were held. The prestige of the archbishopric of Canterbury was heightened by the definite settlement as to its precedence over the archbishopric of York. Ecclesiastical solidarity was strengthened by the royal decree for the separation of lay and ecclesiastical courts. Under William, the tie with Rome was made stronger. Whereas this tie might have its dangers when the king was weak, it could not help at the same time infusing a certain consciousness among churchmen as to the separate entity of the Church, and a desire for independence of lay control.

Conciliar activity in the reign of William II (1087–1100) had a lull. In 1093 the bishops assembled for the consecration of Anselm as Archbishop of Canterbury, but there is no record that any other business was carried on by the bishops at this time.[141] It is interesting to note that the bishops of Worcester and Exeter sent messengers to explain their absence on account of infirmity.[141]

A further testimony to the cessation of councils in this reign is the ardent speech with which Anselm in 1094 urged the king to renew councils in accordance

---

[139] *Ibid.*, I, Appendix B, 290. I, 216.

[140] Chester was at one time included with the See of Coventry and Lichfield. W. Stubbs, *Registrum Sacrum Anglicanum* (second edition), p. 226.

[141] Eadmer, *Historia Novorum in Anglia,* ed. Martin Rule (Rolls Series), p. 42.

with ancient usage.[142]   He declared to him that no council had been held since the king had ascended the throne and that many crimes had broken forth, and through becoming customary, had grown to great strength.[142] This attempt, however, was repulsed by the king, who considered that the settlement of such things should be in accordance with his wish, not in accordance with that of the archbishop.[143] We hear later of a council held at Rockingham on February 25th, 1095.[144] There were present bishops, abbots, *principes,* and a numerous multitude of monks, clerks and lay-men.[145] Anselm addressed them, asking for counsel as to whether he could maintain his fidelity to the king, and at the same time preserve his obedience to the apostolic see.[146] The council was prolonged for days, the bishops acting as intermediaries between Anselm and the king.[147] Finally a temporary truce was reached.[148] After this, Anselm continued to have trouble with the king. The archbishop at last obtained permission to leave the country,[149] and did not return to England until the reign of Henry I.[150] From this it is evident that the Church was not yet strong enough to make herself heard under an unruly king. Councils had not yet become a part of the year's routine. The king's support of them or acquiescence in them was needed to make them effective.

After his return to England, Anselm held a council at Lambeth in 1100 in regard to the marriage between King Henry and Matilda of Scotland.[151] Among those present were two archdeacons.[152] This mention of archdeacons is of importance, as we have not found any archdeacons specifically mentioned as present hitherto

[142] Eadmer, *op. cit.*, p. 48.
[143] *Ibid.*, pp. 48—9.
[144] *Ibid.*, p. 53.
[145] *Ibid.*, pp. 53—4.
[146] *Ibid.*, pp. 54—5.
[147] *Ibid.*, p. 56ff.

[148] *Ibid.*, p. 66.
[149] *Ibid.*, p. 87.
[150] *Ibid.*, p. 119.
[151] *Ibid.*, pp. 122—3.
[152] *Ibid.*, p. 123.

at any of the post-Conquest councils. In 1102 Anselm held a general council at the Abbey of S. Peter, Westminster.[153] Besides the archbishops there were present eleven bishops and one bishop-elect. Anselm presided.[153] We are told that the council was held " with the common consent of the bishops, abbots and *principes* of the whole realm." A number of canons were passed in regard to such subjects as simony, celibacy, etc.[154] Certain abbots were deposed.[154]

In August 1107 there was a *conventus* of bishops, abbots and *proceres* in the palace of the king at London.[155] During the first three days Anselm was absent.[155] The king discussed the question of investitures with the bishops.[155] At last when Anselm appeared, the terms of the final settlement in regard to investitures were made. In addition to this, ecclesiastical vacancies in England and Normandy were filled at the advice of Anselm and the *proceres*.[155] Anselm brought forward a demand of profession from the Archbishop of York.[155] It was agreed that the Archbishop of York should give his hand to the Archbishop of Canterbury, declaring that he would preserve the same subjection in the archiepiscopate that he had professed in the bishopric of Hereford.[156] Though the business of this gathering seems to have been definitely ecclesiastical, it has the character of a mixed council rather than that of a purely ecclesiastical one.

Because many priests were violating the statutes of the Council of London, held earlier in the reign to enforce the celibacy of the clergy, King Henry assembled all the *majores* of the realm at London in 1108 at Pentecost, and treated concerning this question with the Archbishop of Canterbury and all the other

---

[153] *Ibid.*, p. 141.
[154] *Ibid.*, p. 142ff.
[155] *Ibid.*, p. 186.
[156] *Ibid.*, p. 187.

bishops.[157]   There, in the presence of the king " with
the assent of all his barons," the bishops passed canons
in regard to the celibacy of priests, deacons and archdeacons, and in regard to other allied subjects.[158]

For the election of an Archbishop of Canterbury, the
king summoned the bishops and *principes* of England
to Windsor on April 26th, 1114.[159]   He also invited the
prior and some of the brothers of Canterbury.[159]
Though the matter treated was ecclesiastical in
character, this gathering seems to have been a meeting
of the king's council rather than a purely ecclesiastical
council.   The fact that the meeting was held at the
king's court at Windsor is one indication of this.   The
candidate upon whom the bishops finally fixed their
mind, was the one who became Archbishop of Canterbury, but it must be acknowledged that they had first
to gain the consent of the king before the election was
valid.[160]   The fact that the king was willing to change
his mind in favour of Richard of Rochester from
Fabrricius of Abingdon, whom he had first sponsored,
shows the value and authority he conceded to episcopal
judgment.[160]

A gathering, somewhat similar in composition, held
the following year (1115) on September 16th at the
palace of Westminster and spoken of as a *conventus,*
was also probably a meeting of the king's council.[161]
The bishops and *principes* of the whole realm were
present.[161]   Anselm, the papal legate, read letters which
he had brought from the apostolic see.[161]

In 1123 the king summoned all ecclesiastical persons
of the kingdom to a council at Gloucester for the election of an Archbishop of Canterbury.   Though the

---

[157] Eadmer, *op. cit.,* p. 193.
[158] *Ibid.,* pp. 194—5.
[159] *Ibid.,* p. 222.   The see was vacant for five years after the death of
Anselm.
[160] *Ibid.,* p. 222.
[161] *Ibid.,* p. 231ff.

chronicler calls it a *Concilium magnum*,[162] there is no record of any business other than the election being transacted at this time. One hardly knows how to classify such a gathering. At least, the habit of assembling *ad hoc* was being fostered by a meeting of this kind.

John of Crema, papal legate, came to England in 1125 and held a synod at the Abbey of S. Peter, Westminster, on September 9th.[163] There were present the Archbishops of Canterbury and York, twenty bishops, about forty abbots and a "multitude of clergy and people."[163] A number of canons were passed dealing with merely ecclesiastical subjects, such as the prohibition of fees for the fulfilment of priestly offices, the celibacy of the clergy, etc.[164] John of Crema presided.[163]

It is of special interest that we have a record of the Archbishop of Canterbury's mandate for this council. The bishops, abbots, priors and archdeacons of each diocese were summoned.[165] In this mandate we have the first use, so far as we know, of the word *convocatio* for an ecclesiastical council[165] in England.

The next council was two years later (1127) and was

---

[162] *The Historians of the Church of York*, ed. James Raine (Rolls Series), II, 198.

[163] Florence of Worcester (Continuation), *op. cit.*, II, 81.

[164] *Ibid.*, II, 80—3.

[165] H. Hody, *A History of English Councils and Convocations*, Pt. IV, 34, quotes the following passage, which Sir Henry Spelman transcribed from the MS. Codex Landavensis:

"Willelmus Cantuariensis Archiepiscopus Urbano Landavensi Episcopo salutem. Literis istis tibi notum facere volumus, quod Johannes Ecclesie Romanæ Presbyter Cardinalis atq; Legatus, Ordinatione nostra; coniventia Concilium celebrare disposuit Lundoniæ in Nativitate beatæ semper Virginis Mariæ. Propterea præcipimus, ut in præfato termino in eodem loco nobis occurras cum Archdeaconibus et Abbatibus et Prioribus Tuæ Dioceseos, ad difiniendum super negotiis Ecclesiasticis et ad informandum seu corrigendum quæ informanda vel docenda seu corrigenda docuerit sententia convocationis nostræ."

Concilia, Decreta, Leges, Constitutiones in Re Ecclesiarum Orbis Britannici (1066—1531) compiled by Sir Henry Spelman, I, 33.

For the reference in Hody, I am indebted to G. Trevor, *The Convocations of the Two Provinces*, p. 24, n. 33.

again held at the Abbey of S. Peter, Westminster.[166]
Apart from the Archbishop of Canterbury and the
twelve bishops who were specified, the composition of
the gathering was covered by the vague expression,
" great multitudes of clerics and laymen."[167]   Canons
similar to those passed at the Legatine Council of 1125
were again instituted.[168] The chronicler adds that some
secular business was discussed.[169]   As a point of order,
it is interesting to note that the Archbishop of York
sent letters explaining his absence, and the Bishop of
Durham, who was overcome by illness on the way, was
careful to send explanations by the prior and clerics of
Durham.[166] The decrees of this council were further
strengthened by the consent and confirmation of the
king.[170] From this, we gather that the Church was not
yet strong enough to stand alone in legislation.

The very close tie that existed between the secular
and spiritual powers was well illustrated in 1129, when
the king summoned a council to enforce the prohibition
against priests having wives.[171]   The Archbishops of
Canterbury and York were present and the bishops of
ten other sees.[172] Four sees were vacant at the time.[173]

We cannot call this a meeting of the king's council
as there is no mention of lay lords being present.   At
the same time, it does not represent a typical ecclesiastical council in that the abbots were not summoned.
It is simply another example of the fluidity of medieval
institutions.

[166] Florence of Worcester, *op. cit.*, II, 85.

[167] *Ibid.*, II, 86 : " Confluxerant quoque illuc magnæ multitudines
clericorum, laicorum."

[168] *Ibid.*, II, 86ff.

[169] *Ibid.*, II, 86: " Acta sunt ibi de negotiis secularibus nonnulla,
quædam quidem determinata, quædam dilata, quædam vero propter
nimium æstuantis turbæ tumultum, ab audientia judicantium profligata."

[170] *Ibid.*, II, 88.

[171] *Annales Monastici (Annales de Waverleia)*, ed. H. R. Luard (Rolls
Series), II, 221.

[172] Henry of Huntingdon, *Historia Anglorum*, ed. Thomas Arnold
(Rolls Series), pp. 250—1.

[173] *Ibid.*, p. 251.

Henry I's reign brought about a revival of councils which were made up of ecclesiastics and which dealt with purely ecclesiastical subjects. In mixed councils, however, such as the conventions of 1107, it still was possible for ecclesiastical matters to be discussed. Though the clergy were mentioned vaguely as being present at some of the councils of the reign, the chroniclers do not state whether they were there in a representative capacity. A tendency towards development in procedure is indicated by the letters from the Bishop of Durham explaining his absence. Ecclesiastical legislation still demanded the royal confirmation. The churchmen had not yet reached a point where they wished to draw aside to themselves.

In April of the opening year of his reign (1136), King Stephen met the clergy in London and commanded the ancient customs to be observed.[174] This gathering can hardly be designated as an ecclesiastical council, but it indicates that the clergy were strong enough to insist upon their rights, and to demand that they be confirmed.

Two councils followed in 1138. The first was at Northampton. We are told that the king held the council.[175] The composition of the gathering was not entirely ecclesiastical, as there were earls, barons and nobles present, besides the Archbishop of York, the bishops and abbots.[175] The business consisted of the appointment of a bishop to the See of Exeter and an abbot to Winchcombe.[175]

The second council of the year was presided over by Alberic, papal legate, and was held on December 13th

---

[174] *Chronicles of the Reigns of Stephen, Henry II and Richard I (Gesta Stephani)*, ed. Richard Howlett (Rolls Series), III, 17.
Symeon of Durham, *Opera Omnia* (John of Hexham, Continuation), ed. Thomas Arnold (Rolls Series), II, 288.
[175] Florence of Worcester (Continuation), *op. cit.*, II, 105.

at the Abbey of S. Peter, Westminster. [176, 177] It was
similar in character to the Legatine Council of 1125.
There were eighteen bishops and thirty abbots in
attendance, besides a "multitude of clergy and
people." [176] Again canons were passed—some dealing
with subjects handled before, some touching upon new
topics, such as the limitation of the reservation of the
Host. [178] An important chapter protected the clergy
from the usurpation by violence of movables or im-
movables. [179] In this, the clergy were making a stand
for the protection of their property—a principle which
they were to develop later to the point of asserting their
independence of being dictated to in the matter of
grants of money.

In the following year (1139) at a council which
assembled at Winchester, the Archbishop of Canterbury and almost all the other bishops were present.
Those who laid hands on the clergy, or on the possessions of the Church, were again severely denounced. [180]
This time, of course, it was done with special reference
to the capture of the Bishops of Salisbury and
Lincoln. [181] A decree of the pope announcing the
appointment of the Bishop of Winchester, brother of
the king, as papal legate, was read.

Two years later, on April 7th, 1141, at Winchester,
Henry, Bishop of Winchester, exercised his legatine
powers and presided at a council at Winchester com-
posed of the Archbishop of Canterbury, all the bishops

---

[176] *Chronicles of the Reigns of Stephen, Henry II and Richard I*
(Richard of Hexham, *De Gestis Regis Stephani*), III, 172.
[177] Florence of Worcester (Continuation), *op. cit.*, II, 114.
[178] *Chronicles of the Reigns of Stephen,* etc. (Richard of Hexham),
III, 173—5.
[179] *Ibid.*, III, 174.
[180] Symeon of Durham, *op. cit.* (John of Hexham, Continuation), II,
301.
William of Malmesbury, *Historia Novella*, ed. William Stubbs (Rolls
Series), II, 550.
[181] *Ibid.*, II, 551.

of England and many abbots. [182] It is particularly noteworthy that if any were absent they sent excuses, and
their excuses for absence were read. [182] The legate held
a secret conference with the bishops; later he summoned the abbots, and lastly, the archdeacons. [182]
These separate consultations with the bishops, the
abbots and the archdeacons are significant, as they
foreshadow the times in the latter part of the thirteenth
century and in the fourteenth century when in convocation the various degrees of clergy withdrew apart
for separate discussion.

In the following December, Henry of Winchester
presided over another council at Westminster, where
the papal letters were read, and the king declared his
complaints.

Again the English legate held a council—this time
in London in 1142 with the Archbishop of Canterbury,
many bishops and abbots present. [183] The question of
protection for the clergy was still a critical issue. Excommunication was declared against plunderers of
monks and clerks, and against other malefactors. [184]
" Actores, preceptores, executores " and founders of
castles were also excommunicated. [184] The inclusion of
the latter persons was probably an attempt on the part
of the Church to curb in whatever way possible the
anarchy that was rife in the reign of Stephen. A council
in 1143 at Winchester, presided over by the legate, at
which bishops, abbots and men of religion were

---

[182] *Ibid.*, II, 574.
[183] Gervase of Canterbury, *Historical Works,* ed. William Stubbs (Rolls
Series), I, 122.
Chronicon Angliæ Petriburgense, ed. J. A. Giles (Caxton Society),
p. 91.
Roger of Wendover, *Chronicon: sive Flores Historiarum,* ed. Henry
O. Coxe (English Historical Society), II, 232—3.
In the following chronicles the date of this council is given as 1143:
Chronicles of the Reigns of Stephen, etc. (Wm. of Newburgh, *Historia
Rerum Anglicarum*), I, 43; Hoveden, *op. cit.,* I, 206.
[184] Gervase of Canterbury, *op. cit.,* I, 122.

assembled, settled a dispute between the Archbishop of Canterbury and the Abbot of S. Augustine's. [185]

There were two more councils before the close of Stephen's reign. In 1151 the Archbishop of Canterbury celebrated a council at London in the middle of Lent in the presence of the king and his son. [186] The new and unjust appeals were discussed. [186] The year after (1152) there was another council held at London, which it is difficult to designate as purely ecclesiastical. [187] The king, the Archbishop of Canterbury, the bishops and the *proceres* of England were in attendance. The king there made an appeal for the coronation of his son Eustace. The bishops met it with refusal, the archbishop having received letters from the pope prohibiting the crowning of Eustace. [188]

In a reign as anarchical as was that of Stephen, it speaks well for the Church that she was able to hold any councils. The only council, however, for which there is a record of legislation was the Legatine Council of 1139. During this reign the procedure of excuses for absence was again used. The appearance of archdeacons yet another time is a note in the development of a systematic representation of various grades of the clergy.

The period of Henry II's reign is marked by fairly frequent assemblies in which the higher clergy appear. These assemblies varied in character. Many of them were mixed councils, with both nobles and prelates in attendance. Such councils were the one at Northampton in 1157, when the question of the Abbot of S. Augustine's profession to the Archbishop of Canterbury was considered, [189] the council in 1164 at Claren-

[185] Wilkins, *op. cit.*, I, 422—3. (Ex. Chron. W. Thorn. in ann.)
[186] Gervase of Canterbury, *op. cit.*, I, 147.
[187] *Ibid.*, I, 150.
[188] *Ibid.*, I, 150.
[189] *Ibid.*, I, 163.

don wherein the king demanded that the bishops subscribe to certain constitutions,[190] and that in 1170 at London in regard to the coronation of Prince Henry.[191] For examples of other councils which were solely ecclesiastical, we may take those at London and at Westminster in 1162[192] and 1173[193] for the election of an Archbishop of Canterbury; that at Oxford in 1166[194] for the expulsion of heretics; that at Westminster in 1175[195] when certain ecclesiastical decrees were promulgated, and the Legatine Council at Westminster in 1176,[196] which disbanded shortly after it had assembled, because of the contentions between the Archbishops of Canterbury and York. Several other ecclesiastical councils of minor importance may be named, such as those at Marlborough in 1182[197] Windsor in 1184,[198] and Eynsham in 1186.[199]

The composition of the mixed councils consisted of the king, the earls, barons, *proceres*, the bishops, abbots and priors. In one instance we find the phrase —" the clergy and people consenting and assenting."[200] In the greater ecclesiastical councils the bishops were always present. Sometimes there were abbots and priors, and occasionally the description of the attendance holds the vague term " many clergy."[201]

[190] *Ibid.*, I, 176.
Hoveden, *op. cit.*, I, 221—2.
Wendover, *op. cit.*, II, 299—302.
[191] *Ibid.*, II, 354.
Hoveden, *op. cit.*, II, 4.
[192] Gervase of Canterbury, *op. cit.*, I, 169.
[193] Ralph de Diceto, *Opera Historica*, ed. William Stubbs (Rolls Series), I, 368.
[194] Wendover, *op. cit.*, II, 315.
[195] Hoveden, *op. cit.*, II, 72—8.
Gervase of Canterbury, *op. cit.*, I, 251—5.
[196] *Ibid.*, I, 258.
Hoveden, *op. cit.*, II, 92—3.
[197] Wendover, *op. cit.*, II, 409.
[198] Gervase of Canterbury, *op. cit.*, I, 313—18.
[199] *Ibid.*, I, 335.
[200] Hoveden, *op. cit.*, II, 4—5. " Clero et populo consentientibus et assentientibus."
[201] *Ibid.*, II, 92.

D

We know practically nothing of the procedure of these councils. Sometimes there is a hint such as that indicating that the bishops had to put their seals to the Constitutions of Clarendon,[202] or that there was a dispute as to where the bishops should sit.[203]

There is no indication as to the development of representation among the lower clergy as yet, nor of their actual participation in any decisions.

The bishops met a number of times during the ten years' reign of Richard I. On some of these occasions the earls and barons were present too. Such an assembly was probably a meeting of the Great Council. As instances of this type may be cited the council of 1191[204] at London, those of 1194[205] at Nottingham and Northampton, and that of 1197[206] at Oxford. Two important purely ecclesiastical councils were those of Pipewell in 1189,[207] when a number of ecclesiastical vacancies were filled, and of York in 1195,[208] when the Archbishop of Canterbury, who was also papal legate, published a series of decrees concerning such matters as ritual, the Sacraments, the dress of priests, ecclesiastical suits, tithes and the morals of the clergy. Among other ecclesiastical councils there were two for the election of an Archbishop of Canterbury,[209] and two at Gloucester and Westminster, presided over by William of Ely, who was papal legate.[210]

The composition of these Church councils was made up for the most part of bishops. In several instances abbots and priors were mentioned as being in attend-

---

[202] Hoveden, I, 222.
[203] Gervase of Canterbury, *op. cit.*, I, 258.
[204] *Chron. of Reigns of Stephen,* etc. (Wm. of Newburgh), I, 344. Diceto, *op. cit.*, II, 99.
[205] Hoveden, *op. cit.*, III, 240—1, 244.
[206] Gerv. of Canterbury, *op. cit.*, I, 549.
[207] Hoveden, *op. cit.*, III, 15—16.
[208] *Ibid.*, III, 294—7. *Chron. of Reigns of Stephen,* etc. (Wm. of Newburgh), II, 442.
[209] Diceto, *op. cit.*, II, 102—3, 108.
[210] *Ibid.*, II, 83, 85.

ance. At the Legatine Council for the diocese of York in 1195 two archdeacons were present. [211] In accordance with their privilege, the monks of Canterbury took part in the election of the Archbishop of Canterbury. Not yet do we find any account of activity on the part of the lower clergy, or any call for their representation in clerical assemblies.

During John's reign (1199—1216) there were councils of various kinds. The bishops, abbots and priors continued to meet in great councils, such as that at Oxford on January 2nd, 1204, [212] those at London in January 1207, [213] and in late August or the beginning of September 1210, [214] and the one at St. Albans in 1213. [215]

Because of John's refusal to comply with the wishes of Pope Innocent III as to his appointment of Stephen Langton to the See of Canterbury, difficulties ensued, and due to these, legatine councils were more frequent in this reign. We may note the following: that held by John of Ferentino at Reading in October 1206 [216] before King John's break with the Papacy, and those at Northampton in 1211, [217] at Wallingford [218] and Reading [219] in 1213, and at S. Paul's, London, in 1214. [220] Other important ecclesiastical assemblies were held at Westminster on September 19th, 1200, [221]

---

[211] Hoveden, *op. cit.*, III, 294.

[212] Wendover, *op. cit.*, III, pp. 174—5.

[213] *Ann. Monast. (Waverleia)*, II, 258.

[214] Wendover, *op. cit.*, III, 234—5.
Wilkins, *op. cit.*, I, 531 (Ex Johanne de Rupescissa Cottonius, in Posthumis, p. 209).

[215] Wendover, *op. cit.*, III, 262.

[216] *Ibid.*, III, 187—8. Cf. C. R. Cheney, "The Papal Legate and English Monasteries in 1206," *English Historical Review*, XLVI (1931), 443—52.

[217] *Ann. Monast. (Annales de Margan)*, I, 30—1.

[218] Wilkins, *op. cit.*, I, 540—1 (Chronicon Dunstaplensis prioratus in MS. Cott. Tiberius A.x.).

[219] *Ann. Monast. (Waverleia)*, II, 278.
Wendover, *op. cit.*, III, 276.

[220] *Ibid.*, III, 283.

[221] Hoveden, *op. cit.*, IV, 128—37.

when decrees similar to those published at York in
1195 were promulgated, and at St. Albans on
May 26th, 1207.[222] The latter council, which King
John forbade to continue in session, is particularly
notable, as it appears to be the most representative
council which had been held up to this point. The
king's letter forbidding it to remain in session was
addressed to the " archbishops, bishops, abbots, archdeacons and all the clergy." Apparently this was a
national synod, and from the king's letter we learn that
they were considering a subsidy imposed on the clergy
of England by the pope. In no purely ecclesiastical
council before this date have we found that the clergy
met together to consider a financial matter. We have
had mention of tithes, but those have been incidental
in the decrees. Here, too, we find all gradations of the
clergy mentioned. In the phrase " omni clero " is it
possible to find representatives of the lower clergy?

The king's letter to the prior and convent of Glaston-

[222] *Rotuli Litterarum Patentium*, ed. T. D. Hardy (Record Commission), I, 72 (Patent Roll 8 John, m. 1):
  " Rex archiepiscopis, episcopis, abbatibus, archidiaconis et omni clero
apud sanctum Albanum ad concilium convocato salutem. Conquerente
universitate comitum baronum militum et aliorum fidelium nostrorum
audivimus quod non solum in laicorum gravem perniciem sed etiam in
tocius regni nostri intollerabile dispendium super Romscoto præter
consuetudinem solvendo, et aliis pluribus inconsuetis exactionibus
auctoritate Summi Pontificis consilium inire et consilium celebrare
decrevistis. Nos vero licet ob honorem fidei nostre et debitum reverentie
quod sancte Romane ecclesie impendere tenemur voluntati eiusdem
patris nostri domini Pape Innocentii obtemperare cupiamur: tantum
omittere non possumus quin querelas fidelium et subditorum nostrorum
clamancium et de jactura sua sibi timencium prout necesse est sub-
veniamur et emergentibus causis quæ indempnitati pacis et unitatis
regni nostri obviare possunt: qua decet celeritate et diligentia occur-
ramus. Vobis igitur præcise mandamus et expresse prohibemus ne
super predictis vel aliquibus aliis concilium aliquod autoritate aliqua in
fide qua nobis tenemini: teneatis vel contra regni nostri consuetudinem
aliquid novum statuatis, sed sicut nos et honorem nostrum et communem regni tranquillitatem diligitis a celebracione hujus concilii et a
predictis tractatibus ad presens supersedeatis quousque cum universitate
vestra super hoc colloquium habuimus scientes pro certo quod expediet
honori sancte Romane ecclesie et domino Pape et nobis et vobis: quod
istud ad presens negocium differatur donec generalem conferenciam
quomodo possit commodius et honestius explicare. . . . Teste me ipso
apud Eboracum. XXVI. die Maii."

bury, issued October 30th, 1214,[223] summoning them to
a council at Reading fifteen days after Christmas, is of
significance. He not only asked the prior's attendance,
but he requested him to bring with him five or six of
the more discreet and more mature members of his
chapter—" quinque aut sex de discretioribus et maturi-
oribus Capituli vestri." We think we may consider this
one of the initial steps in the experimentation which
was to develop towards a wider clerical representation.

Henry III's reign witnessed an increase in the importance of the clergy as a whole, and a growing consciousness on their part of a right to attach conditions
to their grants, as well as an insistence on the principle
that those providing the money for a grant should
participate in the actual voting of it. The king's ex-
travagant policy made him resort more frequently to
demands for money. In opposition to these, the clergy
were stirred to more activity. Henry III was also in
close touch with the various popes. Accordingly legatine councils were held from time to time.

The extent of the power of the lower clergy in regard
to their consent to taxation in the reign of Henry III
has been discussed by Professor Lunt.[224] He has shown
quite conclusively that at the end of the reign of
Henry III the pope might force the payment of taxes
by the lower clergy on their spiritualities without their
consent, but when the request came from the king
without the papal mandate, the lower clergy were
always consulted before the royal council, or in convocation.[225] " The claim of the lower clergy, made in
1255, that the prelates could not rightfully pledge them
to the payment of taxes without consultation, seems to

[223] *Rotuli Litterarum Clausarum,* ed. T. D. Hardy (Record Commission), I, 176.
[224] W. E. Lunt, " The Consent of the English Lower Clergy to Taxation during the Reign of Henry III," *Persecution and Liberty. Essays in
Honor of George Lincoln Burr,* pp. 117—69.
[225] *Ibid.,* p. 169.

have been observed in practice by the prelates thereafter. Against the papal *plenitudo potestatis* the claim could not hold good. If the pope authorized the bishops or other prelates to decide on behalf of the lower clergy, the decision was binding on the lower clergy."[225]

Let us examine the character of the assemblies during the reign of Henry III. This period was essentially an experimental time when those in authority (entirely unconsciously) were trying out ways of government—both ecclesiastical and lay. Convocation had not yet fallen into the routine grooves to which it was to adapt itself in the fourteenth century.

Early in the reign there was a Legatine Council at Bristol for the swearing of fealty to Henry and the putting of Wales under an interdict.[226] Here were present the papal legate Guala, eleven bishops, prelates of inferior rank, earls, barons, knights.[226] There is no mention here of representatives of the lower clergy. In 1222 a provincial council took place at Oxford,[227] but nothing is said as to its composition. On February 2nd, 1225, at Westminster, parliament met.[228] Earls, barons and prelates were present, and granted a fifteenth on movables. Roger of Wendover mentions the clergy and people as being there, but we can regard this only as a vague generalization. The following year on January 13th, 1226, the papal legate, Otho, was present in a council when the apostolic letters were

---

[226] *Ann. Monast. (Waverleia)*, II, 286.

H. Tillmann, *Die päpstlichen Legaten in England bis zur Beendigung der legation Gualas* (1218), p. 107ff.

[227] Matthew Paris, *Chronica Majora*, ed. H. R. Luard (Rolls Series), III, 73—4.

Chron. Angliæ Petriburg., pp. 124—5.

Wilkins, I pp. 585+—97 (Ex. MS. Cotton., Otho A XV).

Ann. Monast. (Annales Monasterii de Theokesberia), I, 66. *(Waverleia)*, II, 296.

[228] *Ibid. (Annales, Prioratus de Dunstaplia)*, III, 93.

Wendover, *op. cit.*, IV, 99.

Walter of Coventry, *Memoriale*, ed. W. Stubbs (Rolls Series), II, 256.

read.[229]   Those present included bishops, abbots, priors, deans of cathedral churches and archdeacons. The summons to this council is important, as it is the first known instance of the mandate being sent by the Archbishop of Canterbury to the Bishop of London, and thence to the various bishops.[230] No decision was reached, the ecclesiastics giving as their excuse the absence of the king, the archbishops and certain bishops.[231] The national council held May 3rd, 1226, in London, is of special significance, for it foreshadows a tendency to greater representation among the clergy. The representation did not extend to the parochial clergy, but it did include cathedral and collegiate churches and religious houses. Our information comes from a Salisbury register, which includes the Archbishop's summons sent through the Bishop of London.[232]   Another council was held October 14th, 1226.[233]   This is of even greater importance, as the same Salisbury register gives us some of the details in regard to the preparation for it.[234] The king had hoped to have the grant made locally in each diocese, and the archbishop had carried out his request to promote this.[235]   But the canons of Salisbury, realizing the advantage of unity of action, requested the archbishop to have a common discussion, to which he should summon the several proctors of the various chapters.[236] The archbishop complied, and ordered that they send a proctor to London on October 14th.[237]   The Salis-

[229] Wendover, *op. cit.*, IV, pp. 114—15.
Vetus Registrum Sarisberiense alias dictum registrum S. Osmundi Episcopæ, ed. W. H. Rich Jones (Rolls Series), II, 45.
[230] J. Armitage Robinson, "Convocation of Canterbury. Its Early History," *Church Quarterly Review*, LXXXI (1915), 86—7.
[231] Wendover, *op. cit.*, IV, 115—16.
[232] *Vetus Registrum Sarisberiense*, II, 46—7.
[233] *Ibid.*, II, 66.
[234] *Ibid.*, II, 55ff.
[235] *Ibid.*, II, 55—9.
[236] *Ibid.*, II, 61—2.
[237] *Ibid.*, II, 62—3.

bury canons elected two proctors and stipulated certain conditions as to their making a grant.[238] They were to make a grant if it was pleasing to the proctors of the other chapters.[239] They favoured a grant smaller than a fifteenth.[239] The money was to be collected by worthy men appointed by the chapters, and not by the bishop's officials, or his archdeacons.[239] Their instructions included still other items of a similar nature.[240] The council which met on October 14th, 1226, comprised prelates, deans of cathedral chapters or their proctors, men of religion or their proctors, and archdeacons.[241] Not yet were the parochial clergy represented. It may be possible, as Professor Lunt suggests,[242] that the archdeacons were vested by the lower clergy with powers similar to those given to the cathedral proctors, but we have no definite information as to this. The council granted a sixteenth.[243]

The council of October 1226 has just been noted as apparently a marked advance for the distinctly ecclesiastical council. If the record of the composition of the Great Council at Westminster on April 29th, 1229,[244] can be trusted, a step forward in the relations of the clergy and laity had taken place. Roger of Wendover gives as present at this assembly archbishops, bishops, abbots, priors, templars, hospitallers, earls, barons, and rectors of churches (*ecclesiarum rectores*). If it is true that the rectors of churches were present, we have then the first instance of the participation of the parochial clergy in a lay assembly. But even then there tends to be a cleavage between the ecclesiastical and the lay. The laity refused to make a grant. The

---

[238] *Vet. Reg. Sar.*, II, pp. 63—4.
[239] *Ibid.*, II, p. 64.
[240] For a fuller treatment of the powers entrusted to the Salisbury proctors, *vide infra*, Chapter VII, pp. 202—3.
[241] *Vet. Reg. Sar.*, II, 66.
[242] Lunt, *op. cit.*, p. 123.
[243] *Vet. Reg. Sar.*, II, 66.
[244] Wendover, *op. cit.*, IV, pp. 200—1.

bishops, abbots, priors and other prelates, after three or four days of deliberation, gave their assent.[245] The very fact that the ecclesiastics are mentioned separately tends to indicate that they deliberated apart from the laity. Whether the rectors of churches took an active part in the discussion is not stated; they are not mentioned as deliberating with the other ecclesiastics. The separation of the clergy and laity for deliberative purposes at this time, foreshadows the period when all clerical decisions in regard to grants would be taken out of lay councils and dealt with in convocation.

The next decade produced legatine councils, which were all held at London. In the first of these which met November 19th, 1237, and lasted for three days, the clergy presented their grievances.[246] This marks an important step, as later the yielding of a grant was to be made conditional on the redress of grievances similarly presented. At the second of the legatine councils which was held in May 1238, besides the legate, the Archbishop of York, and the bishops, the clergy are mentioned as having been present.[247] This vague term, however, does not point out any systematic representation of the clergy. The council of the summer of 1239[248] under the same legate, Otho, presents no further evidence.

In 1240 Otho held a council in May at Reading, which was later adjourned until the latter part of June at London.[249] The subject for discussion both times was the papal mandate for a grant. In the first, a

[245] *Ibid.*, IV, 201.
[246] *Ann. Monast.* (*Theokesberia*), I, 105. (*Annales Monasterii de Burton*), I, 253—6.
Mat. Paris, *Chron. Maj.*, III, 416—42.
[247] *Ibid.*, III, 484.
[248] *Ibid.*, III, 567.
[249] *Ibid.*, IV, 10—11.
Calendar of the Manuscripts of the Dean and Chapter of Wells (Hist. MSS. Com.), I, 403.
Lunt, *op. cit.*, pp. 127—32.

decision was delayed, with the excuse that counsel must
first be taken. [250]   At the second council there was considerable opposition, but a grant was made. [251]   In the
following autumn, however, Otho was still having diffi-
culty at a council held early in November to force payment. [252] According to Professor Lunt, the lower clergy
had no part in these councils. [253] "The lower clergy were
not convened in a single assembly by means of representatives.   The amount of the aid to be paid by the
lower clergy of each diocese was settled locally." [254]

The question of grants in the next ten years was discussed by the papal collector with the prelates at
sessions of the Great Council and met with refusal. [255]
At last they formulated a list of objections. [256]   But
the opposition was of no avail.   Six English bishops at
the Council of Lyons pledged 6,000 marks from English churches. [257]   At a parliament in Lent, 1246, protests were expressed by earls, barons, *proceres,* magnates, the noble inhabitants of the seaports, the whole
people and the whole clergy, [258] but again it is not

[250] Mat. Paris, *Chron. Maj.,* IV, 10—11.
[251] *Ibid.,* IV, 37—8. *Cal. of MSS. of the Dean and Chapter of Wells,*
I, 403.
[252] *Ibid.,* pp. 130—1.
Lunt, *op. cit.,* p. 130, n. 63 : "The annalist of Tewkesbury says consent was refused, though he adds that the abbot of his house paid Otto
50 marks on 7 November: pp. 115, 116." This date is incorrect. It
should be November 8. Cf. *Ann. Monast. (Theokesberia),* I, 116.
[253] *Ibid.,* p. 131.
[254] *Ibid.,* p. 132.
[255] *Ibid.,* pp. 132, 133.   In 1245 the bishops refused to answer at a
great council because several bishops and other prelates were absent.
No word was said of the rights of the lower clergy. *Ibid.,* p. 133.
W. E. Lunt (ed.) *Valuation of Norwich,* p. 31, n. 8.
Mat. Paris, *Chron. Maj.,* IV, 362, 368, 371, 375, 376. No legate
present in 1244. *Ibid.,* p. 362.
[256] *Ann. Monast. (Dunstaplia),* III, 167.
Mat. Paris, IV, 375—6.
[257] Lunt, *Consent,* p. 133.
[258] Mat. Paris, IV, 533 : "devoti filii sui comes Cornubia R(icardus),
S(imon) de Monte Forti comes Legrecestriæ, (Humfridus) de Boun comes
Herefordiæ et Esexiæ, R(ogerus) le Bigod comes Northfolckiæ,
R(icardus) comes Gloverniæ et Hertfordiæ, R(ogerus) comes Wintoniæ,
W(illelmus) comes Albemarliæ, H(ugo) comes Oxoniensis, et alii totius
regni Angliæ barones, proceres, et magnates, ac nobiles portuum maris
habitatores, necnon et clerus et populus universus. . . ."

known whether the lower clergy were here included. On December 1st, 1246, the clergy drew up objections to the payment of the papal taxes. [259] It is significant that the king summoned to a parliament on February 3rd, 1247, especially the archdeacons to sit with the magnates and a part of the clergy. [260] A remonstrance was sent to the pope. [261]

There were minor meetings of bishops at Dunstable [262] and Winchcombe in 1251. [263] In the same year there was a convocation at Reading. [264] On October 13th, 1252, the prelates in parliament granted a tenth for three years. [265] In 1253 the bishops were again active at the sessions of parliament in January [266] and May, [267] but there is no mention of the lower clergy. At the parliament in January 1254, [268] the prelates refused to make a grant from their clergy without their assent, but promised to discuss the matter with them. By a royal writ under date of February 5th, each bishop was to convene the abbots and priors of his diocese and induce them to give an aid. [269] By another royal writ of February 11th, [270] each bishop was asked to assemble his cathedral chapter, archdeacons, men of religion and clergy, and urge them to give an aid. On April 26th at Westminster certain discreet men from each of the local ecclesiastical assemblies of the latter type were to certify to the council " concerning the method and the

[259] *Ibid.*, IV, 581—5.
[260] *Ibid.*, IV, 590, 594.
[261] *Ibid.*, IV, pp. 595—6.
[262] *Ibid.*, V, p. 225.
[263] *Cal. of MSS. of Dean and Chapter of Wells*, II, 563.
[264] *Chronicle of the Monastery of Abingdon*, ed. J. O. Halliwell, Berkshire Ashmolean Society, p. 7.
[265] Mat. Paris, *Chron. Maj.*, V, 324—8.
[266] *Ibid.*, V, 359—60.
John of Oxenedes, *Chronica*, ed. Sir H. Ellis (Rolls Series), p. 194. *Ann. Monast.* (Burton), I, 305ff.
[267] Mat. Paris, *Chron. Maj.*, V, 373—8.
[268] *Calendar of Close Rolls* (1253—1254), p. 107.
[269] *Ibid.* (1253—1254), p. 112.
[270] *Ibid.* (1253—1254), p. 115.

amount of the said subsidy." [270-271] Professor Lunt has shown that these representatives of the lower clergy who met on April 26th, 1254, did more than merely " certify." [272] The Durham memorandum,[273] which he quotes, [274] shows clearly that they " exercised true representative functions."[275] This council, therefore, indicates definite progress in the development of fuller clerical representation in a royal assembly.

The prelates, who were with Rostand in October 1255, adjourned their convocation until January 13th, 1256.[276] This convocation is noteworthy because as in the lay assembly the lower clergy were having representation, so in convocation the composition was being extended to include them. The summons issued by the Bishop of Lincoln in his diocese for this convocation, requested that the dean bring with him " certain discreet canons," and that the archdeacons bring " three or four of the more discreet men of their archdeaconries." [277]

In the convocation which met in Lent 1257 the archdeacons were assembled to hear from Rostand, the pope's *nuncio*, the papal demands. The legate concluded with the statement that the deans, prelates, regulars (men of religion) and archdeacons should treat with their chapters and clergy (concerning the grant) and that they should return proctors in the month after Easter, who would be instructed to respond fully, or to come to an agreement.[278] It is known that Archbishop Boniface summoned a convocation after Easter. [279] At

---

[271] This translation is Professor Lunt's; Lunt, *Consent,* p. 142.

[272] *Ibid.,* pp. 142—4.

[273] British Museum, Stowe MS. 930, fols. 57 v., 58.

[274] Lunt, *Consent,* pp. 142—3.

[275] *Ibid.,* p. 144.

[276] Mat. Paris, *Chron. Maj.,* V, 524—7, 532, 539—44.

[277] *Ibid.* (Additamenta), VI, 314.

[278] *Ann. Monast. (Burton),* I, 384, 386—9. *(Annales Monasterii de Oseneia),* IV, 114—5.

Mat. Paris, *Chron. Maj.,* V, 621—3.

[279] *Ibid.,* V, 632, 637—8; VI, 353—65. *Ann. Monast. (Burton),* I, 389. Lunt, *Consent,* p. 148.

this session, or in a session of parliament, the clergy agreed to give the king a composition of 52,000 marks provided he would observe " Magna Carta." [280] The clergy listed their grievances in a number of articles, which they drew up, and presented to the king. [281]

Convocation was summoned to meet again the following August. [282] At this meeting the lower clergy were not to send special proctors from their numbers, but to vest their archdeacons with letters of proxy. [283] Though the king forbade it to be held, the convocation met. [284]

The convocation, which assembled at Merton the next year (1258) on June 6th, had a similar composition as that of August 1257, with the same arrangement for letters of proxy to be brought by the abbots, priors, deans and archdeacons from their subordinates. [285] This

[280] Mat. Paris, *Chron. Maj.*, V, 623—4.

[281] *Ibid.*, V, 637—8; VI, 353—65. *Ann. Monast. (Burton)*, I, 402.

[282] *Ibid. (Burton)*, I, 401—2; *(Annales Monasterii de Wintonia)*, II, 96.

It is worthy of remark that in a document issued in preparation for this ecclesiastical assembly the word " convocatio " was used. *Ann. Monast. (Burton)*, I, 402—3. Dr. J. Armitage Robinson *(op. cit., p. 91)* writes, " This is the first time that we have found *convocatio* thus used to describe the meeting of a representative assembly of the whole of the clergy of the province." It has, however, been noted above *(supra, p. 31)* that the term " convocatio " occurred in the Archbishop of Canterbury's mandate for 1125. The document quoted by the Burton annalist is nevertheless significant. It was probably sent out by the Archbishop of Canterbury some days after the issue of his mandate. It begins with the following words, " cum in ultima convocatione." The closing item in the document alludes to the king's having forbidden that they should come to this convocation ("ad hujusmodi convocationem") which had been summoned. Wilkins *(op. cit., I, 724)* quotes without stating the source, the king's writ to the Bishop of Lincoln in regard to the prohibition. The writ also used the word " convocatio ": " archiepiscopus Cantuar. quandam convocationem episcopum fieri fecerit London in Octav. assumptionis beatæ Mariæ, ut audivimus—inhibemus districte præfato archiepiscopo, in dictam convocationem faciat, sed convocationem illam, olim fuerimus in exercitu nostro, penitus revocet, et suspendat. . . . Teste me ipso apud Wodes. 19 die Julii." Dr. Armitage Robinson *(op. cit., p. 91)* calls attention to the fact that the Burton annalist " follows the lead of the documents which he quotes and uses the word more than once."

[283] *Ibid. (Burton)*, I, 402.

[284] *Ibid. (Burton)*, I, 403—5, 408; *(Wintonia)*, II, 96.

[285] *Ibid. (Theokesberia)*, I, 163; *(Burton)*, I, 411—12.

council drew up articles[286] concerning the grievances with which the clergy were burdened. A small council met at Oxford in 1258[287] and a provincial council at Lambeth in 1261.[288] Of the latter we do not know the exact composition. The council which met in London in May 1261, had the usual members—bishops, abbots, priors, archdeacons, with the addition of persons listed as " other ordinaries of churches." The papal *nuncio* was also present.[289]

The councils from 1263 through 1268 make no contribution to our knowledge of the development of convocation. It was in this period that the war between the king and the barons was taking place. Many of the councils that were called were presided over by the legate, Othobon, who hoped to establish peace between the two factions.[290]

On October 14th, 1269,[291] however, there was a convocation at the New Temple, London, at which we know definitely that the proctors of rectors and vicars were present. In this convocation the clergy drew up a list of grievances and made a strong appeal against making grants to laymen and being committed to such grants by their bishops.[291]

When Henry III's reign ended in 1272, the lower clergy surely must have been conscious of having then far more opportunity to assert themselves than their

[286] *Ann. Monast. (Burton)*, I, 412—25.
[287] Mat. Paris, *Chron. Maj.*, V, 707.
[288] Wilkins, *op. cit.*, I, 746. (Ex MSS. Cott. Otho A XVI et Vitell. A ii. collat. cum Lambeth N. 17 et MS. Elien. n. 235.) Wilkins's reference has been given in a corrected form.
[289] *Flores Historiarum*, ed. H. R. Luard (Rolls Series), II, 468—9.
[290] Flor. of W., *op. cit.* (Continuation), II, 199.
" Letters of Cardinal Ottoboni," ed. R. Graham, *English Historical Review*, XV (1900), 102, 110.
Wilkins, *op. cit.*, I, 762—3 (Ex MSS. Cotton. Tiberius A.X. et Chron. Hemingford in ann.).
C-J. Hefele and Dom H. Le Clercq, *Histoire des Conciles*, VI, Pt. I, 121.
Lunt, *Consent*, p. 156—9.
[291] Wilkins, II, *op. cit.*, 19—20 (Ex. MS. C. C. Christi, Oxon., num. 154).
Lunt, *Consent*, pp. 160—1.

predecessors had had in 1216. They had been represented at the great councils of 1229 and 1254. They
had presented their grievances in 1237 and 1257. They
had sent special proctors to convocation in 1256 and
1257, and on two occasions they had been able to
designate the archdeacons as their particular spokes-
men. As to what had been their gains in regard to
their consent to taxation we have quoted above from
Professor Lunt.[292]

Though there were councils in the period 1269—
1272,[293] not until 1273 is there again mention in them
of representatives of the lower clergy. This was in the
summons of the Archbishop of Canterbury to his
suffragan bishops to a convocation at the New Temple,
London, in which he requested them to bring with
them three or four persons of the greater, more discreet
and prudent men of their churches and dioceses.[294]
The abbots and priors were not summoned. This convocation was called independently by the archbishop
" to treat, provide and ordain what shall have seemed
fitting to further for the honour of God and His Holy
Church."[295] The proctors of the whole clergy were
again summoned by the same archbishop to a convocation on January 14th, 1277(–8), for the welfare and
honour of the Church.[296]

Under Archbishop Pecham councils became more
frequent. To his council at Reading, July 29th,

---

[292] *Supra*, pp. 41—2.
[293] *Royal and other Historical Letters,* ed. W. W. Shirley (Rolls Series),
II, 336.
    Calendar of Patent Rolls (1266—1272), pp. 508—9, 536.
    Ann. Monast. (Wigornia), IV, 460.
    Lunt, *Consent*, p. 162.
[294] Wilkins, II, (Ex reg. Giffard. Wigorn, fol. 41): "3 vel 4
persones de majoribus, discretioribus et prudentioribus suæ ecclesiæ et
diœceseos."
    Calendared in *Wor. Epis. Reg.* (Reg. Giffard), ed. J. W. Willis Bund,
II, 58.
[295] Wilkins, *op. cit.*, II, 26 (Ex Reg. Giffard, fol. 41).
[296] *Ibid.*, II, 30 (Ex Reg. Giffard, fol. 71).
    Calendared in *Wor. Epis. Reg.* (Reg. Giffard), II, 93.

1279,[297] and to his succeeding councils at London, January 20th, 1279(–80),[298] May 12th, 1280,[299] and May 4th, 1281,[300] only bishops were called. Two of these councils were summoned for the purpose of grants.[301] To the Council of Lambeth, October 7th, 1281, bishops, abbots, priors, deans of cathedral and collegiate churches, archdeacons and proctors of chapters were summoned.[302] This marked a decided advance in representation. In the council, in spite of the royal prohibition against doing anything to the prejudice of the crown,[303] the archbishop proposed to cancel certain liberties of the crown.[304] Though he had been forced in the Michaelmas parliament of 1279 to repeal various measures passed in the Council of Reading that same year,[305] it has been clearly shown by Professor Hilda Johnstone that Archbishop Pecham was able in the Council of Lambeth 1281 to regain his lost ground.[306] To the next two councils, those of

[297] The Register of John Pecham, Archbishop of Canterbury (1279–92) preserved in the archives at Lambeth Palace, fol. 10. Printed in Wilkins, *op. cit.*, II, 32—3.
Wilkins, *op. cit.*, II, 33—6 (Ex MSS. Digby Bodlej., n. 170 ; et Cotton. Otho A. 15. et reg. Giffard. Wigorn., n. ii, iii et iv et MS. Elien., n. 235).
Ann. Monast. (Waverleia), II, 391.
Chron. Mon. Abingdon, ed. Halliwell, p. 26.
[298] Reg. Pecham, fol. 165. Printed in Wilkins, *op. cit.*, II, 37.
Reg. Pecham, fol. 25. Printed in *Registrum Epistolarum Fratris Johannis Peckham, Archiepiscopi Cantuariensis*, ed. C. Trice Martin (Rolls Series), I, 145.
Cal. P.R. (1272—81), p. 359.
[299] Wilkins, *op. cit.*, II, 49 (" ex procuratorio episcopi Exon. quod in archivis illius ecclesiæ asservatur ").
[300] Reg. Pecham, fol. 99. Printed in Wilkins, *op. cit.*, II, 49—50.
[301] The Councils of January 20th, 1279—80, and May 4th, 1281.
[302] Reg. Pecham, fol. 175 v. — 176. Printed Wilkins, *op. cit.*, 50—1. *Reg. Epist., J. Peckham*, I, 211—12.
[303] Reg. Pecham, fol. 101—101 v. Printed Wilkins, *op. cit.*, II, 50.
[304] *Chron. Mon. Abingdon*, ed. Halliwell, p. 27.
Ann. Monast. (Chronicon Vulgo Dictum Chronicon Thomæ Wykes), IV, 285. This chronicle gives the date incorrectly as 1280.
[305] H. Johnstone, " Archbishop Pecham and the Council of Lambeth 1281." *Essays Presented to Thomas Frederick Tout*, n. 14, p. 172.
[306] *Ibid., passim.*

February 5th, 1281(-2),[307] and April 12th, 1282,[308] only bishops were summoned. The assembly, however, called by virtue of the king's writ at Northampton for the octave of Hilary (January 20th), 1282(-3),[309] had the same representation as that of the council which had assembled in October 1281.[310] Many of the clergy, however, were absent.[311] The subject for discussion was a grant.[310] This assembly refused to answer fully because of the absence of certain of the clergy who had not been duly summoned.[311] Hence it was decided that representatives of all the clergy should be called at a later date to another convocation.[311] They were summoned therefore to meet at the New Temple, London, in May 1283.[311] This convocation marks the initiation of the system that the diocesan clergy should be represented in convocation by two proctors from each diocese. When they assembled, the proctors of the clergy opposed the grant of a tenth for three years, which was the demand presented to them.[312] Articles were drawn up against a contribution.[312] Another convocation was summoned for October 20th, 1283, of the

---

[307] Reg. Pecham, fol. 64 v. Printed in *Reg. Epist., J. Peckham*, I, 256—7.

[308] Reg. Pecham, fol. 99. Printed in *Reg. Epist. J. Peckham*, I, 323.

Wor. Epis. Reg., II, 146—7 (Reg. Giffard, fol. 133): A list of "articles ordained by the Archbishop of Canterbury with the consent of his suffragans at Lambeth on Saturday before the Sunday on which is sung *Jubilate*" (Saturday was April 18th) leads one to infer that the place of meeting was changed.

[309] H. G. Richardson and George Sayles, "The Early Records of the English Parliaments," *Bulletin of the Institute of Historical Research*, V, n. 15, p. 149: "the name of parliament must be refused to the assemblies of clergy, knights, and burgesses at York and Northampton in January, 1283."

[310] Reg. Pecham, fol. 83 v.: Pecham speaks of it as "congregatione ad instantiam domini regis."

Wilkins, *op. cit.*, II, 91—2 (Ex regist. Giffard. Wigorn., fol. 166).

Calendared in *Wor. Epis. Reg.* (Reg. Giffard, fol. 166d), II, p. 187.

Cf. *supra* note 302.

[311] Reg. Pecham, fol. 83 v. Printed in *Reg. Epist. J. Peckham*, II, 508—9.

[312] *Ann. Monast. (Dunstaplia)*, III, 295—6.

E

same composition as that of the preceding council. [313] A grant was the business of this council, too. [314]

To the next four councils [315] of Archbishop Pecham only bishops were called. The council of October 13th, 1286, was summoned to deal with the state of the Church. [316] It has been suggested that the grievances listed in Giffard's register [317] are probably those that had been drawn up for consideration. [318] The business of the other three we do not know. Proctors of the whole clergy were also present at the convocation held at Ely on October 1st, 1290. [319]

For the clerical assembly of both provinces, which Edward I summoned to meet at Westminster on September 21st, 1294, it was requested that the lower clergy be represented by two proctors. [320] This is important, because it is the first instance since 1254 when we find the king calling the lower clergy definitely before him to take part in an assembly. The clause in regard to the coming of the lower clergy in the summons for this meeting to Henry, Prior of Canterbury, to whom the king wrote as the See of Canterbury was

[313] Reg. Pecham, fol. 84 v.—85, 86 v.—87.   Printed in *Reg. Epist. J. Peckham*, II, 536—7, 594—5.   Wilkins, *op. cit.*, II, 95.
The letter on fol. 84 v.—85 is inserted between two letters, the first dated "iiii Aprilis ordinationis nostræ anno quinto," the second dated "iii. Id. Maii." On the top margin of the folio the year of ordination is dated as the fifth. It is, therefore, to be inferred that the letter between belongs also to the year 1283.
[314] Reg. Pecham, fol. 86 v.—87.
[315] These councils were summoned for the following dates: October 13th, 1286; May 2nd, 1287; October 13th, 1287; May 2nd, 1289. For references *vide infra* Appendix A.
[316] Wilkins, *op. cit.*, II, 125–6 (Ex reg. Giffard. Wigorn., fol. 159). Wilkins gives wrong folio.
Calendared in *Wor. Epis. Reg.*, II, 295 (Reg. Giffard, fol. 258, 258d).
[317] Wilkins, *op. cit.*, II, 115—6. (Ex reg. Giffard.)
Calendared in *Wor. Epis. Reg.*, II, 298 (Reg. Giffard, fol. 260).
[318] E. B. Graves, "Circumspecte Agatis," *English Historical Review*, XLIII (1928), 7.
[319] Wilkins, *op. cit.*, II, 173 ("ex procuratorio Henrici de Estria, prioris Cantuar. . . . quod extat in registro ipsius," fol. 146).
This may not have been a council, but only a gathering for a consecration. Cf. *Ann. Monast. (Oseneia)*, IV, 325—6.
[320] William Stubbs, *Select Charters* (9th ed.), p. 476. (*Report on the Dignity of a Peer*, App. I, p. 59.)

vacant, is as follows: "Vocantes prius decanum et capitulum ecclesiæ vestræ, archdiacanos totumque clerum vestræ diocesis, facientesque, quod iidem decanus et archidiaconi in propriis personis suis, et dictum capitulum per unum, idemque clerus per duos procuratores idoneos, plenam et sufficientam potestatem ab ipsis capitulo et clero habentes, una vobiscum intersint modis omnibus tunc ibidem ad tractandum, ordinandum, et faciendum pro ipsis capitulo et clero ac eorundem nomine, quod de vestro, et aliorum prælatorum, decani archidiaconorum, procuratorum prædictorum communi consilio providebitur in præmissis." [320] It must be understood that this was not a meeting of the great council, nor of parliament. The king needed money, and decided that the best way to obtain it would be to call the clergy before him in an assembly made up solely of ecclesiastics.

In June 1295, Archbishop Winchelsey summoned his bishops and suffragans to a council on July 15th to treat in regard to certain "arduous articles" concerning the state of the Church and all ecclesiastical persons. [321] Here is a council for purely ecclesiastical matters summoned on the initiative of the archbishop, with no suggestion of which we know from the king, either by royal writ or otherwise.

It was in the following autumn (1295) that the king called for the first time diocesan clergy to parliament. [322] The clause which he used in regard to the premonishment of the clergy in his summons at this time to the Archbishop of Canterbury became, with occasional slight alterations, the official form for sum-

---

[321] The Register of Robert Winchelsey, Archbishop of Canterbury (1294—1313), preserved in the archives at Lambeth Palace, fol. 168 v.—169. Printed in *Registrum Roberti Winchelsey, archiepiscopi Cantuariensis*, ed. R. Graham (C. and Y. Soc.), pp. 30—1.

[322] *Parl. Writs*, I, 30. Wilkins, *op. cit.*, II, 215 (Ex rot. claus. 23 Ed. I, m. 3d.). Wilkins gives the wrong membrane. It should be 4d. *Cal. C.R.* (1288—96), 459.

moning the clergy to parliament in the future.   The
clause is as follows: " præmunientes priorum et capitulum ecclesiæ vestræ, archidiaconum, totumque clerum
vestræ dioeceseos: facientes, quod iidem prior et archidiaconus in propriis personis suis, et dictum capitulum
per unum, idemque clerus per duos procuratores
idoneos, plenam et sufficientem potestatem ab ipsis
capitulo et clero habentes, una vobiscum intersint,
modis omnibus tunc ibidem ad tractandum, ordinandum et faciendum nobiscum, et cum cæteris prælatis,
proceribus et aliis incolis regni nostri, qualiter hujusmodi periculis et excogitatis malitiis obviandum." [323]
It is interesting that the king asked for the same scale
of representatives which Archbishop Pecham had demanded for his convocation on May 9th, 1283. [324]   In
this writ the distinctive word " præmunientes " was
used for the first time.   This word was to be employed
henceforth to describe the clause which it introduced
concerning the clergy.

In the tracing of the development of representation
among the lower clergy, it has been noted that they
were in attendance at a great council in 1229, [325] and
that they were again present in a definitely representative capacity at a great council in 1254. [326]   Forty years
later (1294) they had been summoned by the king to
a special assembly to which no lay representatives were
called.   1295 marks the first inclusion, of which there is
a known record, of the representatives of the lower
clergy in the summons to the national assembly—the
parliament of the king.

[323] Wilkins, op. cit., II, 215.   Parl. Writs, I, 30.
[324] Reg. Pecham, fol. 83 v.   Printed in Reg. Epist. J. Peckham, II,
508—9.   Cf. supra, p. 53.
[325] Supra, pp. 44—5.
[326] Supra, pp. 47—8.

CHAPTER II

THE RELATIONS OF THE LOWER CLERGY AND PARLIAMENT
IN THE THIRTEENTH AND FOURTEENTH CENTURIES

THE question has often been discussed as to how long
the lower clergy continued to come to parliament. It
has been pointed out in the preceding chapter that the
lower clergy were first summoned to parliament in
1295,[1] when the " premunientes " clause was for the
first time included in the writ of summons to the archbishops and bishops. The scale of representation in
1295,[2] as has been stated, was that which had been
employed by Archbishop Pecham in 1283[3] when summoning his provincial council, and by the king when he
summoned the clergy before him to a purely clerical
assembly in 1294.[4] The lower clergy continued to be
summoned to parliament from time to time by the
" premunientes " clause, which was embodied in the
writ of summons to the archbishops and bishops. They
were called in 1296,[5] 1300,[6] and in Lent 1305.[7] For
the parliament which met on the octave of S. Hilary,
1307, we have a precise list of the proctors of the lower
clergy of various dioceses and archdeaconries.[8] The
clergy were again called in 1309[9] to a parliament to be
held a month after Easter.

For this meeting William of Occham, Archdeacon of

---

[1] *Supra*, p. 55.
[2] *Parl. Writs*, I, 30. *Cal. C.R.* (1288—96), 23 Edw. I, p. 459.
[3] Reg. Pecham, fol. 83 v. Printed in *Reg. Epist. J. Peckham*, II,
508—9.
[4] Stubbs, *Select Charters* (9th ed.), p. 476.
[5] *Parl. Writs*, I, 47.
[6] *Ibid.*, I, 83.
[7] *Ibid.*, I, 137.
[8] *Rotuli Parliamentorum ut et Petitiones et Placita in Parliamento*,
ed. J. Strachey and others (Record Commission), I, 189—91.
[9] *Parl. Writs*, II, ii, 24.

Stowe, gave power to three men to act alternately as
his proctor in this parliament.[10] An allusion is made in
this " procuratorium " to the proctors of the clergy.[10]

In 1314, however, instead of summoning the clergy
to a parliament, the king raised their ire by calling the
clergy of the province of Canterbury to Westminster,
and the clergy of the province of York to York before
his deputies in special clerical assemblies to be held on
the morrow of the Ascension.[11] They were called both
by diocesan writs through their bishops and by provincial writs through the archbishops.[11] The response
of the clergy of the province of Canterbury was a list
of articles.[12] The grounds of their complaint were the
form of citation. In the articles, which were presented
by the abbots, priors of cathedral churches, deans,
archdeacons, and proctors of the chapters and clergy of
the province of Canterbury, it was maintained that the

[10] P.R.O. Chancery, Parliam. and Council Proceedings, File 45, n. 2 :
" Vniuersis presentes Litteras inspecturis pateat per easdem quod ego
Willelmus de Occham—Archidiaconus Stowe in ecclesia Lincoln.
aduersa valitudine et impotencia corporis oppressus aliisque arduis
negociis prepeditus existens quominus in instanti congregacione prelatorum cleri procerum et magnatum Anglie apud Westmonasterium a
die Pasche proximo preterito in vnum mensem habienda personaliter
valeam comparere, ad comparend. pro me in dicta congregacione et
excusaciones meas Legitimas allegand. et proponend. et si necesse fuerint
proband. necnon ad faciend. nomine meo vna cum predictis Prelatis
magnatibus et proceribus Regni Anglie procuratoribusque cleri eiusdem
super negociis ibidem tractand. quod fuerit faciend. ac eciam ad con-
senciend. nomine meo hiis que tunc ibidem de communi consilio fauente
domino canonice contigerit ordinand. vel eciam pro vtilitate dicti Regni
prouideri Dilectos mihi in Christo Magistros Thom. de Langetoft de
Eston. Robertum Bernard de Carleton. et Hernen. (sic) de Luda de
Frysthorp ecclesiarum Rectores sub alternacione videlicet quemlibet
eorum in solidum procuratores et excusaciones meos facio ordino et con-
stituo per presentes. Promittens me ratum et firmum habiturum quic-
quid per dictos procuratores meos vel vnum ipsorum nomine meo factum
fuerit in premissis. In cuius rei testimonium sigillum meum presentibus est appensum. Dat. Lincoln. X Kalend. Maii. Anno domini
m^{o}ccc^o nono." Hernen is probably an error of the scribe for Henricum.
The *Register of John de Halton, Bishop of Carlisle.* Transcribed by
W. N. Thompson (C. and York Soc.), II, 234 : A transcription is given
of the " procuratorium " of the clergy of Carlisle for this parliament.
(P.R.O. Parliamentary Proxies, n. 29.)

[11] *Parl. Writs,* II, ii, 122—3. *Cal. Close Rolls* (1313—18), 7 Edw.
II, p. 96.

[12] Wilkins, *op. cit.,* II, 442—3. (Ex. reg. eccl. Cantuar. H., fol. 194
seq.)

clergy of the province or of the realm had not been accustomed to be convoked by royal authority. Another objection was that the royal writ had been inserted in the citation.[13] Alluding to a convocation held in the time of Archbishop Robert Winchelsey at which they had discussed this matter diligently, they declared that it had been there ordained that this kind of mandate should not pass. They also objected to the term " venire faciatis."[14] They further held that a metropolitan was not permitted to withdraw the subjects of his suffragans from their territories except for certain cases of which this was not one. Moreover, they were not accustomed to be called to Westminster, a place exempt (from any diocesan). There was danger, they feared, of this citation becoming a pernicious example. Furthermore, they contended that an aid could not be made unless it was done according to law, as was contained in the sacred canons. They, therefore, demanded the revocation of the writ, and appealed to the bishops that they would support them and deem their petition worthy of hearing.

An entry in the register of the prior of Canterbury shows that the archbishop gave a favourable ear to their requests.[15] In it they gave him thanks for promising to withdraw the citation, and also put in a plea against certain laymen, who had made threats concerning the aid. In order to obtain the grant for the king and at the same time not to offend the clergy, the Archbishop of Canterbury had to call a proper convocation of his province the following July.[16]

[13] This is interesting as in later years the archbishop usually inserted the king's writ as a ground for calling the convocation. Cf. Appendix A, *passim.*

[14] The king's writ contained the words " venire faciatis . . . suffraganeos vestros Decanos . . . ad tractandum." Cf. *Parl. Writs,* II, ii, 122.

[15] Wilkins, *op. cit.,* II, 444 (Ex reg. H. prior, Cant., fol. 195).

[16] The Register of Walter Reynolds, Archbishop of Canterbury (1313—1327) preserved in the archives at Lambeth Palace, fol. 105v.—106. Printed Wilkins, II, *op. cit.,* 444—5.

The king did not employ this method again, but in issuing a summons for the parliament to be held at Westminster on September 9th, 1314, he not only summoned the bishops individually and through them the clergy of their dioceses,[17] but he issued a provincial writ to the Archbishop of Canterbury to summon the bishops, deans and priors, archdeacons, and the clergy of each diocese of his province by proctors.[18] The question arises as to why a provincial writ was not issued at the same time to the Archbishop of York. It may be that the scribe omitted to record it.

The clergy were again summoned to the parliaments called to meet at Westminster on January 20th, 1314(–15),[19] and at Lincoln, January 27th, 1315(–16).[20] In each instance the provincial writ is recorded as having been issued to the Archbishop of Canterbury[21] and York.[21]

In 1315 in executing the " premunientes " clause of the diocesan writ and in carrying out the royal request in the provincial writ, which asked him to summon the clergy of his whole province to a parliament at Lincoln on January 27th, 1315(–16),[22] the archbishop summoned the clergy into his presence at the cathedral of Lincoln on the day before that appointed by the king for the parliament to be held there.[23] Whether this is to be considered an attempt on the part of the archbishop to appease the clergy, who objected to being summoned to lay assemblies, or a way of withdrawing business from parliament to convocation, it is difficult

---

[17] Parl. Writs, II, ii, 126. Cal. C.R. (1313—18), 8 Edw. II, p. 192.
[18] Parl. Writs, II, ii, 128. Cal. C.R. (1313—18), 8 Edw. II, p. 192.
[19] Parl. Writs, II, ii, 136—7. Cal. C.R. (1313—18), 8 Edw. II, p. 202.
[20] Parl. Writs, II, ii, 152. Cal. C.R. (1313—18), 9 Edw. II, p. 314.
[21] Parl. Writs, II, ii, 138, 154. Cal. C.R. (1313—18), 8 Edw. II, p. 202 ; 9 Edw. II, p. 314.
[22] Parl. Writs, II, ii, 152—4. Cal. C.R. (1313—18), 9 Edw. II, p. 314.
[23] W. Wake, The State of the Church, Appendix, pp. 41—2. (Transcript from Registrum Woodlock (Winton), fol. 197, Collat. cum Regist. Henr. Prior Cant., fol. 163b.)

to say. It is known, however, that the archbishop, many prelates, religious and clergy were absent, and that although the clergy present promised to aid the king, they said that they could define nothing definitely until those absent could be consulted.[24] The king later commanded the archbishop to summon a convocation for that purpose.[24] The archbishop, therefore, acted in accordance with the king's mandate and called a convocation.[25] The absence of the clergy at the Lincoln parliament would certainly indicate a laxity on their part in coming to parliament, and an unwillingness to make their decisions definitely in parliament.

The lower clergy continued to be summoned to the next three parliaments[26] by the " premunientes " clause.[27] In the last of these parliaments—that held at York on May 6th, 1319, the clergy made a grant of a twelfth on condition that this grant should be superseded if the pope should impose a tenth upon them.[28, 29] The grant of a tenth was at length superseded, as the pope complied with the king's request for

[24] Reg. Reynolds (Cant.), fols. 73—73v. Parl. Writs, II, ii, 158. Cal. C.R. (1313—18), 9 Edw. II, p. 325. It was at this parliament that the questions concerning the relation of the spiritual and temporal courts were rehearsed. Later at York the authoritative answers to these questions were incorporated by the king into a document, which was put upon the Statute Book, and which is known as the " Articuli Cleri." Statutes of the Realm (Record Commission) I, 171—4. Stubbs (Const. Hist., II (4th ed.), p. 356) thinks that the " Articuli Cleri " were probably published in consideration of the grant made by the clergy at York. Vide infra, n. 27.

[25] Wilkins, op. cit., II, 456 (Ex reg. Henr. prior, Cant., fol. 168).

[26] These parliaments were summoned for January 27th, 1317—18; October 20th, 1318; May 6th, 1319. A parliament was summoned for June 19th, 1318, but the writ was revoked.

[27] Parl. Writs, II, ii, 172; 182; 197. Cal. C.R. (1313—18), 11 Edw. II, p. 585; (1318—23) 12 Edw. II, p. 99; p. 131.

[28] Cal. C.R. (1318—23) 13 Edw. II, pp. 156, 203.

[29] Chronicles of the Reigns of Edward I and Edward II (Annales Paulini), ed. W. Stubbs (Rolls Series), I, 286. The clergy in their convocation in May 1319 had refused to make a grant of a third of their possessions for the Scottish war, for they thought the king had sent messengers to Rome to obtain papal consent to a grant.

a grant from the clergy, and imposed a tenth upon them. [30]

For the parliaments of January 20th, 1319(–20), [31] October 6th, 1320, [32] November 14th, 1322, [33] October 20th, 1324, [34] and June 25th, 1325, a writ with the " premunientes " clause was not issued. It was sent, however, for the parliaments of July 15th, 1321, [35] May 2nd, 1322, [36] February 23rd, 1323(–4), [37] November 18th, 1325, [38] January 7th, 1326(–7), [39] the great council [40] of September 15th, 1327, [41] and the parliaments of February 7th, 1327(–8), [42] April 24th, 1328, [43] the great council of July 31st, 1328, [44] and the parliaments of October 16th, 1328, [45] and March 11th, 1329(–30). [46] The provincial writ was issued to the Archbishop of Canterbury for the parliaments of July 15th, 1321 [47] and May 2nd, 1322. [48] It was sent to both archbishops for the parliament of February 23rd, 1323(–4). [49] Although a writ into which the " premunientes " clause was inserted was issued for the next

[30] *Cal. C.R.* (1318—23) 13 Edw. II, p. 203.

[31] *Parl. Writs,* II, ii, 215.

[32] *Ibid.,* II, ii, 219.

[33] *Ibid.,* II, ii, 261.

[34] *Ibid.,* II, ii, 317. The number of the membrane is given incorrectly in *Parl. Writs.* It should be m 33d. Cf. *Cal. C.R.* (1323—27) 18 Edw. II, p. 311.

[35] *Parl. Writs,* II, ii, 234.

[36] *Ibid.,* II, ii, 245.

[37] *Ibid.,* II, ii, 290.

[38] *Ibid.,* II, ii, 334.

[39] *Ibid.,* II, ii, 350.

[40] A distinction has been drawn by Mr. H. G. Richardson and Mr. G. O. Sayles between a parliament and a great council. Their decisions in regard to this have been followed here. H. G. Richardson and G. O. Sayles, " The Parliaments of Edward III," *Bulletin of the Institute of Historical Research,* viii (1930), 65—82.

[41] *The Lords' Report on the Dignity of a Peer,* IV, 376. " Et premuniatis " was used instead of " premunientes."

[42] *Ibid.,* IV, 378—9.

[43] *Ibid.,* IV, 381. " Et premuniatis was again used."

[44] *Ibid.,* IV, 384.

[45] *Ibid.,* IV, 386—7. " Et premuniatis was used."

[46] *Ibid.,* IV, 391—2.

[47] *Parl. Writs,* II, ii, 236.

[48] *Ibid.,* II, ii, 247.

[49] *Ibid.,* II, ii, 290.

two parliaments, the provincial writ did not appear again until the great council of July 31st, 1328, when it was issued to the Archbishop of York,[50] and to the keeper of the spiritualities of the archbishopric of Canterbury, the see being vacant. It was sent again for the Archbishop of York and the keeper of the spiritualities of Canterbury for the parliament of October 16th, 1328,[51] and to both archbishops for the parliament of March 11th, 1329(–30).[52] In summoning the clergy to the parliament of March 11th, 1329(–30), the Archbishop of Canterbury again called them to come into his presence,[53] as Archbishop Reynolds had done for the parliament at Lincoln on January 27th, 1315(–16).[54]

For some of these parliaments we have definite evidence that shows that the king's requests in the " premunientes " clause for representatives of the lower clergy were fulfilled. The " procuratoria " of the clergy of Carlisle for the parliaments of 1319,[55] 1322,[56] and 1324[57] show that the clergy of that diocese appointed proctors. The clergy of the dioceses of Lincoln[58] and of Lichfield[59] appointed proctors for the parliament to be held the Friday after Hilary, 1326(–7). We may assume, therefore, that other dioceses did the same for this parliament.

What, however, is of much more positive evidence for the presence of the lower clergy in parliament is

[50] *Rep. Dignity of Peer*, IV, 386.
[51] *Ibid.*, IV, p. 389.
[52] *Ibid.*, IV, pp. 390—2.
[53] Wilkins, *op. cit.*, II, 557—8. Wilkins does not give the source from which he obtained this mandate.
[54] *Supra*, p. 60.
[55] *Reg. John de Halton* (Carlisle), II, 235. Summary of P.R.O., Parliamentary Proxies, n. 264.
[56] *Ibid.*, II, 235. Summary of P.R.O., Parl. Proxies, n. 357.
[57] *Ibid.*, II, 235. Summary of P.R.O., Parl. Proxies, n. 450.
[58] Wake, *op. cit.*, p. 277. (Lib. Memorand., Henr. Burghersh (Linc.) fol. 152.)
[59] *Ibid.*, pp. 277—8. (Acta Capit. Eccl. Cath. Lichfield in Mus. Ashmol., 794.)

the records of payments for clerical proctors for parliament, which Mrs. Edith Clark Lowry has recently published from the bailiffs' accounts for the manors of Gamlingay in Cambridgeshire, and of Cheddington in Buckinghamshire. [60] These records comprise payments for proctors in parliament intermittently from 1280(-1 to 1373). [61] By an analysis in chart form, Mrs. Lowry has shown that in all these years for which payments were entered, there were parliaments or great councils to which the clergy were summoned. [62] In most of the cases where the payment for proctors is recorded, it is further identified by the words " ad parliamentum," and often the place of meeting of the parliament is added. When the payments are for proctors of convocation, there are distinguishing marks such as " ad consilium archiepiscopi," or " ad convocationem," or the place of meeting of the convocation where it is known that no parliament was being held at that time. [62] Mrs. Lowry concludes that if her " interpretation of the evidence from Gamlingay is correct, it seems clear that the diocese of Ely continued, though intermittently, to send clerical proctors to parliament in the thirty odd years after 1341. They probably attended," she adds, " not for financial reasons at all, but simply to keep in touch with what took place in parliament and to take part in whatever discussion might concern the clergy." [63]

[60] Mrs. Edith Clark Lowry, " Clerical Proctors in Parliament and the Knights of the Shire, 1280—1374," *Eng. Hist. Review*, vol. 48 (1933), 443—55.

[61] *Ibid.*, pp. 448—53, *passim*. The years in which payments were made were 1280(—1), 1295, 1296, 1307, 1309, 1318(—19), 1322, 1327, 1328(—9), 1329(—30), 1335, 1338 or 1339, 1346, 1351, 1366, 1371, 1373 and possibly for 1342. Although an instance is given of 1280(—1) the diocesan clergy were not summoned by proctors to parliament until 1295.

[62] *Ibid.*, pp. 448—53, *passim*.

[63] *Ibid.*, pp. 447, 454. Mrs. Lowry adds, " This does not necessarily alter the truth of the generally accepted position that the clerical proctors as a body had dropped out of parliament by the middle of the fourteenth century. It does, however, point to the fact that the usage did not cease all at once, but like many some-time constitutional practices fell gradually and almost imperceptibly into disuse."

In addition to the above instances, it is known that as late as 1379 the Lincoln diocese was taxed for the expenses of their proctors at both parliament and convocation. [64]

Apart from these records of payments for proctors, the summonses, and " procuratoria " giving the names of proctors appointed, there is little that can be found concerning the proctors of the lower clergy in parliament during the fourteenth century. There are, however, a few references to them in the *Rotuli Parliamentorum*. An allusion is made to the clergy in the roll for the parliament held March 16th, 1331(–2), wherein is recounted the fact that the prelates and proctors of the clergy withdrew to consult together. [65] During this parliament certain statutes which had been pronounced by the prelates and clergy at S. Paul's, and which are given in full in the parliament roll, were accorded and assented to by the king, prelates, earls, barons and other magnates and knights of the county, and the " Gentz du Commun." [66] No mention is made of the proctors of the clergy assenting to these statutes. The lower clergy's assent may have been given at a former time in a convocation at S. Paul's but there is no known record of a convocation at S. Paul's in the year 1332.

On the Saturday after the Monday on which the parliament opened, the knights of the counties, citizens and burgesses who had been summoned to the parliament and all the clergy had leave to go home, while the prelates, earls, barons and the " Gentz " of the council of the king remained. [67]

No writ with a " premunientes " clause was issued

---

[64] Wake, *op. cit.*, p. 311. (Lib. Jo. Bokingham (Linc.), fol. 184.)
[65] *Rot. Parl.*, II, 64, n. 5.
[66] *Ibid.*, II, 65, n. 5.
[67] *Ibid.*, vol. II, n. 11, p. 65b.

for the parliaments of September 9th, 1332,[68] December 4th, 1332,[69] and January 20th, 1332(-3),[70] but dating from the parliament of February 21st, 1333(-4), the clause became a part of the summons to parliament for all time.[71] There might occur the substitution of " Et premuniatis " for " premunientes,"[72] or the mere phrase " ad consentiendum "[73] instead of " ad faciendum et consentiendum," but apart from these slight variations the clause was identical and continuous. Such was not the case for the provincial writ. After its appearance for the parliament of March 11th, 1329(-30),[74] a writ to an archbishop to summon the clergy of his entire province to parliament did not appear again until the summons for the parliament of March 16th, 1331(-2).[75] Writs for summoning their provinces were then issued to both archbishops.[75] The writ went to the Archbishop of York and the keeper of the spiritualities of Canterbury for the parliaments of February 21st, 1333(-4),[76] and to both archbishops for the parliaments of September 19th, 1334,[77] May 26th, 1335,[78] March 11th, 1335(-6),[79] September 23rd, 1336[80] and March 3rd, 1336(-7).[81] It disappeared again for two years,[82] and then was employed for both archbishops for the parliaments of February 3rd, 1338(-9),[83] January 20th, 1339(-40),[84] and March 29th,

---

[68] *Rep. Dignity of a Peer,* IV, 411.
[69] *Ibid.,* IV, 416.
[70] *Ibid.,* IV, 418.
[71] *Ibid.,* IV, 423ff., *passim.*
[72] *Ibid.,* IV, 460—1, 479, 492—3, 515, 546.
[73] *Ibid.,* IV, pp. 470, 488—9, 500—1.
[74] *Ibid.,* IV, 394.
[75] *Ibid.,* IV, 411.
[76] *Ibid.,* IV, 425.
[77] *Ibid.,* IV, 430.
[78] *Ibid.,* IV, 446.
[79] *Ibid.,* IV, 456.
[80] *Ibid.,* IV, 463.
[81] *Ibid.,* IV, 473.
[82] *Ibid.,* IV, 479, 488, 492.
[83] *Ibid.,* IV, 506.
[84] *Ibid.,* IV, 509.

1340.[85] After this the provincial writ does not occur again. Instead of using this type of writ, the king was apt to request the archbishops to hold convocations near the time of parliament.[86]

In 1338 a sharp distinction was drawn between the prelates, abbots and priors in the parliament at Westminster, who made a grant that year of wool, and the clergy and other ecclesiastical persons, who granted a tenth for three years at S. Bride's Church, London, on October 1st the same year.[87] It was pointed out that those making the grant of wool were not held to pay a tenth for three years on their benefices, and those paying the triennial tenth on their benefices were not held for the grant on wool.[88] It is also evident from various letters that only those who were summoned individually to parliament were bound to pay the grant on wool.[89] The records indicate that the lower clergy were summoned both to the parliament that met February 3rd, 1338,[90] and to the great council that met July 26th, 1338,[91] wherein the grant of wool was made and the conditions formulated.[92] But we know that the grant of the tenth for three years was made in a convocation held some months later.[93] It is possible that the lower clergy were present in both of these assemblies, though we have no evidence of their presence in either. If they were present, it may be suggested that they were there only to listen to discussion, and to show the trend of the clerical mind in regard to business discussed.

[85] *Ibid.,* IV, 518.
[86] *Ibid.,* IV, 482, 553. For further examples see charts, Appendix A, Appendix B.
[87] P.R.O., Close Roll, 12 Edw. III, Pt. III, m. 2, m. 9.
[88] P.R.O., Close Roll, 12 Edw. III, Pt. III, m. 17.
[89] P.R.O., Close Roll, 12 Edw. III, Pt. III, m. 4d.
[90] *Rep. Dignity of a Peer,* IV, 488—9.
[91] *Ibid.,* IV, 492—3.
[92] P.R.O., Close Roll, 12 Edw. III, Pt. III, m. 4d.
[93] P.R.O., King's Remembrancer Memoranda Roll 115, 13 Edw. III, m. 13, "Brevia directa Barones."

In the roll for the parliament of the quindene of S. Michael (October 13th), 1339, mention was made that it was accorded by all the magnates and commons that letters be sent under the seal of the Archbishop of Canterbury and other prelates and barons to the Archbishop of York to make an aid, as the clergy of the province of Canterbury had done.[94] There is no indication in the roll that the proctors of the clergy of Canterbury were present in this parliament, though both they and the clergy of the province of York in the royal summons to the archbishops were to be premonished to come.[95] Evidently the grant made by the province of Canterbury referred to here, is that which was made the preceding year in the convocation at S. Bride's.[96]

In the parliament which met at Westminster in mid-Lent, 1340, a charter was given to the clergy in regard to presentation to benefices.[97] A grant was also made at this time by the prelates of churches, together with the earls, barons and " proceres."[98] The grant consisted of a ninth of fleece, lamb and sheaf.[99] It was expressly stated that no prelates nor clergy were to pay the ninth except those who held by barony and were accustomed to come to parliament.[100] Those of the clergy paying the ninth portion were not to be held to pay the tenth granted by the province of Canterbury.

[94] *Rot. Parl.*, II, 105, n. 16.
[95] *Rep. Dignity of a Peer,* IV, 503—4.
[96] P.R.O., K.R., Mem. Roll 115, 13 Edw. III, m. 13, " Brevia directa Barones."
[97] *Rot. Parl.*, II, 244, n. 58. An allusion is made to a charter granted in 14 Edw. III.
[98] *Ibid.*, II, 112.
[99] *Ibid.*, II, 112.
Thomas Walsingham, *Historia Anglicana,* ed. H. T. Riley (Rolls Series), I, 234.
[100] *Ibid.*, I, 234: " Quod nulli prælati, nec etiam aliquis de clero prædicto, ad hujus nonæ contributionem portionem tenerentur, nisi tantum illi qui per baroniam tenerent, et ad Parliamentum venire solent. Quodque ad solutionem decimæ ut præmittitur, concessæ, prælati et cæteri de clero nonam portionem prædictam solventes, nullatenus forent astricti."

Here again was a distinction made between two types of clergy.

In the following year at the parliament held April 23rd, 1341, petitions were presented by the Archbishop of Canterbury and other bishops of his province in regard to certain injuries done to the Church.[101] One of the special complaints was on account of the levy that was being made on those who paid the tenth and were not held to come to parliament.[102] In giving answers to their petitions, the king declared that the grants of the ninth and the tenth should be paid in the manner in which they were granted.[103] Though we do not hear of any activity of the lower clergy in parliament during this period, they were not disregarded. They were evidently making themselves felt, for in the parliament of June 7th, 1344, the Commons are found praying that no petition by the clergy to the damage of the Lords and Commons be granted until it had been tried by the king and council.[104] In this parliament, petitions were submitted to the king by the Archbishop of Canterbury and other prelates and clergy of his realm.[105] These petitions prayed against the arraignment or impeachment of an archbishop or bishop before justices in a criminal cause, against a clerk being impeached or arraigned before a lay justice in a question of marriage of which the justice had not cognizance, against the arraignment or impeachment of prelates, beneficed clerks or men of religion who have purchased land, against purveyance for the king from church estates, against prohibitions, against justices of the king having commissions to make inquests on the " juges " of Holy Church.[106] They made a plea against the use of

[101] *Rot. Parl.*, II, n. 129—30, nos. 18—26.
[102] *Ibid.*, II, 129, n. 25.
[103] *Ibid.*, II, 130, n. 32.
[104] *Ibid.*, II, 149, n. 8.
[105] *Ibid.*, II, 151—2, nos. 23, 24.
[106] *Ibid.*, II, 151—2, nos. 23, 24.

F

writs of " scire facias " to force the prelates and men of religion to answer in the Chancery in regard to tenths.[107]   The king's answers were given, and the prelates then prayed to have these answers put under seal, together with the terms of the tenth for three years granted to the king, and the cause for which it was granted.[108] A charter was then formulated and entered in the parliament roll.[109]   The grant was stated as having been made by the prelates and proctors of the clergy.[109]   In the charter the terms of the grant were stated, including the dates of payment for both the provinces of Canterbury and York.[109]   There were added the king's answers to the clergy's petitions, which were given with the assent of the Lords and Commons.[109]   Certainly the impression is not given here that the clergy were an integral part of the parliament. The answers to their petitions were something extraneous, which were granted by the king, the Lords and Commons. The proctors of the clergy took no part in this grant.

In 1351(–2) petitions were again brought forward by the archbishop and his suffragans for the clergy.[110] The first request was for the confirmation of the privileges of a charter conceded to them at mid-Lent, 1339(–40).[111] The other petitions were concerned with benefices, judgment of clerks, monks, etc. by the king's justices, the challenge of a clerk's clergy in his arrest, the statute " Circumspecte Agatis," presentation to benefices, vacancies of benefices, commissions of purveyance, temporalities of bishops in the hands of the king, a plea for the examination of the case of the Bishop of Exeter, the oppressions of and extortions

---

[107] *Rot. Parl.*, II, 152.
[108] *Ibid.*, II, 152. This charter was incorporated in the Statute Book. *Statutes of the Realm*, I, 302—3.
[109] *Ibid.*, II, 152—3, n. 24.
[110] *Ibid.*, II, 244—5, nos. 57—69.
[111] *Ibid.*, II, 244.

from prelates of Holy Church, benefices.[112] As in the past the king's answers were given, but there is found no activity of the lower clergy in parliament. One is led to infer that the petitions were formulated in the convocation held the preceding May 1351, when the clergy granted one tenth outright, and another tenth on the condition that their grievances should be redressed.[113]

At the parliament which met at Westminster on April 28th, 1376, petitions were presented to the king in the name of " sui humiles et devoti Oratores Clerus totius Cantuariensis Provincie."[114] The clergy begged that their grievances, which they presented in writing, be reformed, and that measures be taken in the present parliament to prevent such things being attempted again.[114] These petitions were concerned with the tithe of the forest, with royal prohibitions in cases of canonical punishment, with payments from the Church to the Church, with payment of tenths, with the seizure by royal servants of possessions of ecclesiastics for royal provisions, cases in regard to tenths under the name of chattels, with the impeding of ecclesiastical jurisdiction, with the seizure of ecclesiastics while they were occupied in divine offices, or were in churches or cemeteries.[115] The king gave answers to these petitions, as it was his custom to do.[115]

The petitions presented by the clergy at the parliament held in the quindene (October 13th) of S. Michael, 1377,[116] were brought forward by the prelates and the clergy of the provinces of Canterbury and York.[117] It will be remembered that the petitions of

[112] *Ibid.*, II, 244—5, nos. 57—69.
[113] The Register of Simon Islep, Archbishop of Canterbury (1349—66), preserved in the archives at Lambeth Palace, fol. 49.
[114] *Rot. Parl.*, II, 357.
[115] *Ibid.*, II, 357—8, nos. 199—208.
[116] *Rot. Parl.*, III, 25—7, nos. 112—25.
[117] *Ibid.*, III, 25: "Les Prelatz & la Clergie de la Province de Canterbirs & d'Everwyk."

the clergy that have been mentioned in former parliaments were presented by the Archbishop of Canterbury in one instance with the other bishops of his province, [118] in another instance for " tote la clergie," [119] a vague expression that is made clearer by the preceding sentence, which speaks of the petitions being made for the clergy of the land. [119] At yet another time they had been presented by the Archbishop of Canterbury and other prelates and clergy of his realm. [120] In 1376 the petitions were brought forward by the clergy of the whole province of Canterbury. [121] The petitions of 1377 are so clear-cut that they show that the clergy were quite alive to the evils of the day. The clergy begged for experienced men as the king's councillors and for a modification in his household, so as to lessen expenses. [122] They desired a ratification of their rights by letters patent. [123] They pointed out that they were badly treated by lay people because they executed the commands of their ordinaries and superiors. [124] They entered complaints because men of Holy Church had been taken by *ministri* of the marshalsea, [125] because purveyors, *ministri,* buyers had entered the benefices and places of Holy Church and carried off goods, [126] because sheriffs and others had come to abbeys and priories and caused great expense; [127] because the courts Christian were oppressed. [128] They begged that the judge of Holy Church should preside where the payment was due from one church to another. [129] They further complained that the judges of Holy Church were disturbed by prohibitions. [130] Another request was that a plea of tenths concerning

[118] *Rot. Parl.,* II, 129.
[119] *Ibid.,* II, 244.
[120] *Ibid.,* II, 151, n. 23.
[121] *Ibid.,* II, 357.
[122] *Ibid.,* III, 25—6, n. 112.
[123] *Ibid.,* III, 26, n. 113.
[124] *Ibid.,* III, 26, n. 114.

[125] *Ibid.,* III, 26, n. 115.
[126] *Ibid.,* III, 26, n. 116.
[127] *Ibid.,* III, 26, n. 117.
[128] *Ibid.,* III, 26, n. 118.
[129] *Ibid.,* III, 26, n. 119.
[130] *Ibid.,* III, 26, n. 120.

tenths due through the right and possession of a church should be held before a judge of Holy Church.[131] They also requested that in a case pending before a judge of Holy Church wherein the prohibition of the king might be put forward, and the consultation of the king made in a fixed form, that the judge should proceed freely in the cause.[132] They, moreover, prayed that the tithe of the forest called " silva cedua," due to God and to Holy Church, should be loyally paid,[133] that the immunity of the Church in certain places be guarded.[134] Their last complaint was that people of Holy Church were arrested.[135] To these petitions the king's answers were given as in the past.

In the parliament held November 5th, 1380, after long discussion apart, the Commons said that they would grant a certain sum of 100,000 pounds if the clergy would grant a third part of it, and they prayed the king and the Lords that they would beseech the clergy to be willing to hasten the time of their council, and to assemble and undertake this charge.[136] The clergy (we are not told in particular, but we infer that the Archbishop of Canterbury answered for the body) replied that their grants were never made in parliament, nor ought to be, nor could the laity dictate to them, nor could they on their part force the laity; but if they must be frank, they believed it would be as pleasing to the clergy as to the laity.[136]

At the parliament which assembled October 26th, 1383, the Commons again made their grant on the condition that a grant similar to those in the past be made by the clergy.[137] No protest was forthcoming from the clergy. The same condition was laid down by the Commons at the parliament which met at

[131] *Ibid.*, III, 27, n. 121.
[132] *Ibid.*, III, 27, n. 122.
[133] *Ibid.*, III, 27, n. 123.
[134] *Ibid.*, III, 27, n. 124.

[135] *Ibid.*, III, 27, n. 125.
[136] *Ibid.*, III, 90, n. 13.
[137] *Ibid.*, III, 151, n. 113.

Salisbury, April 29th, 1384,[138] and again no protest was made. When, however, in the parliament which assembled November 12th, 1384, the laity granted two fifteenths to the king[139] on the condition that the prelates and clergy should give two tenths,[140] Archbishop Courteney uttered a strong protest in which he declared that since Holy Mother Church from the time of the present king as well as of his forefathers had remained in full liberty, she could not by law, nor should she be forced to observe a condition of this kind.[140] He further demanded that this condition should be rejected and destroyed before he should treat with his clergy or hold a convocation concerning this subsidy.[141] The king, therefore, commanded the condition to be taken out of, or to be erased from the schedule.[141] The clergy shortly afterwards in their convocation granted one tenth, of which the first moiety was absolute, the second conditional.[142] The following year (1385) at the parliament which met October 20th, the laity made a grant of a fifteenth and a half to the king,[143] and stipulated that the clergy should give a tenth and a half.[144]

---

[138] *Rot. Parl.*, III, 168, n. 10.

[139] *Ibid.*, III, 185, n. 10.

[140] The Register of William Courteney, Archbishop of Canterbury (1381—96), preserved in the archives of Lambeth Palace, I, fol. 81v.—2. Printed in Wilkins, *op. cit.*, III, 193.

[141] Reg. Courteney, I, 82. Printed in Wilkins, *op. cit.*, III, 193. Archbishop Courteney's protest has been discussed elsewhere in this study. *Infra*, chapter V, pp. 169—73; VII, pp. 209—10.

[142] Reg. Courteney, vol. I, fol. 80. This convocation was in session December 1st—19th, 1384. *Ibid.*, I, fol. 79v.—80.

[143] *Rot. Parl.*, III, 204, n. 10.

[144] Walsingham, *Hist. Anglicana*, II, 139. Cf. *infra*, chapter V, p. 171. Walsingham states that this parliament was held near the feast of S. Martin. It is true that it was in session then, but it is known that it assembled October 20th, 1385 (*Rot. Parl.*, III, 203). It is possible that Walsingham has confused his years and is giving an account of the archbishop's protest which was made in the preceding year, December 17th, 1384. Courteney's register does not contain a protest for the year 1385. Walsingham's statement of the grants made in the parliament that was in session in November 1385 does not tally with the parliament roll for that year (*Rot. Parl.*, III, 204). There may, therefore, have been a second protest. Cf. *infra*, p. 171, note 116.

Archbishop Courteney again made a protest, asserting that this could by no means be done since the Church was free, and was not to be taxed by the laity.[144] The laity, therefore, raised vigorous opposition to the archbishop's protest and proposed the partition of the temporalities of the Church, but the king thwarted their plans by taking the side of the clergy.[145] The latter in their convocation shortly afterwards made a voluntary grant of one tenth absolute and a moiety on conditions.[146]

Archbishop Courteney in the parliament which assembled at Westminster on the morrow of the Purification, 1387(–8), made another famous protest.[147] This time he protested against the clergy's taking part in parliament in certain discussions which were to be held.[147] It is interesting to note that in his protest he included his suffragans, confrères and co-bishops, abbots and priors and other prelates, who held by barony, and therefore were held to come to parliament.[148] He enumerated their rights as those of being present in parliament, counselling, treating, determining and defining, and doing those things which were to be done at the time of parliament.[148] Not one word was said of the proctors of the clergy. If they were of any importance, we should expect them to have been mentioned by the archbishop. At the request of the archbishop and other prelates, and with the consent of the king and the temporal lords, the archbishop's protest was recorded on the parliament roll.[149] The bishops of Durham and Carlisle made similar protests and requested that their protests be recorded, too.[149]

[145] Ibid., II, 140. Cf. infra, chapter V, p. 172.
[146] Reg. Courteney, I, fol. 84. This convocation was in session from November 6th—December 7th, 1385. Ibid., I, 83v.—84. Walsingham, Hist. Ang., II, p. 140 mentions the grant of only one tenth " unanimi voluntate consensu spontaneo."
[147] Rot. Parl., III, 236—7.
[148] Ibid., III, 236.   [149] Ibid., III, 237.

After the protests, the Archbishop of Canterbury and all the other bishops and lords spiritual of the province of Canterbury, as well as of York, departed from the hall. [149]

The parliament held at Westminster on January 22nd, 1396(–7) witnessed another protest. It was from the Archbishops of Canterbury and York for themselves, and for their prelates. [150] They protested against any ordinance that should be assented to by the king or the lords temporal for power and authority of parliament touching the provisions of the court of Rome. [150]

In 1397 at the parliament at Westminster, September 17th, the Commons pointed out to the king that before now many judgments, ordinances made in the time of his forefathers, had been repealed and annulled because the estate of the clergy was not present. [151] They, therefore, prayed the king that the prelates and clergy should have a proctor with sufficient power to consent in their name to all ordinances in this present parliament. [151] Then we are told that when the said spiritual lords were severally examined, they consented to commit their full power generally to a lay person. Thomas Percy, knight, was chosen. [151] The fact that the spiritual lords were the only ones mentioned as interviewed, and that it was they who gave their full consent, shows that when a matter came up in parliament concerning the clergy, they had complete power to settle it without consulting the clergy subordinate to them. The form of the appointment of the proctor begins " Nos Thomas Cantuar' & Robertus Ebor' Archiepiscopi ac Prelati & Clerus utriusque provincie Cantuar' & Ebor'." [152] The clergy, therefore, were given a nominal place in the appointment of their proctor.

[150] *Rot. Parl.,* III, 341, n. 22.
[151] *Ibid.,* III, 348, n. 9.
[152] *Ibid.,* III, 348, n. 9.

In the same parliament the Commons showed that the Duke of Gloucester and the Earl of Arundel were continuing their evil and traitorous purposes.[153] With the consent of the lords spiritual and temporal, and of the proctors of the clergy, and at the request of the Commons, the pardon was annulled.[153] The term "proctors of the clergy" is here a difficult one to define. It is stated that Sir Thomas Percy was made a proctor of the clergy, but since he was to act *for* the spiritual lords, one would conclude that he would not be acting *with* them. The repeal of a pardon did not demand the shedding of blood. There was no reason, therefore, why the clergy should not take part in the decision. Though it cannot be said definitely, it may be suggested that this phrase "procuratours del clergie,"[153] referred to the proctors of the lower clergy.

When the Commons requested that oaths should be given by the lords spiritual and temporal for the maintenance of the statutes of this parliament, the spiritual lords took personally the oath at the shrine of S. Edward,[154] but Sir Thomas Percy took the oath in the name of the clergy.[155] Here then is found an instance of the proctor of the clergy, a layman, acting with the lords spiritual. Later, the king, the prelates and the temporal lords left the shrine, and went before the high altar and reaffirmed the keeping of all the things established in this parliament[155]—the prelates of the provinces of Canterbury and York, ordaining that all the aforesaid should be observed inviolably by their subjects.[156] This parliament later adjourned to meet at Shrewsbury in the quindene of Hilary.[157]

Soon after the parliament was again in session, the

---

[153] *Ibid.*, III, 350, n. 12. It was also in this parliament that the Commons accused and impeached Thomas of Arundel, Archbishop of Canterbury, of high treason for his actions in the tenth and eleventh years of the king's (Richard II) reign. *Ibid.*, III, 351, n. 15.

[154] *Ibid.*, III, 355, n. 37.

[155] *Ibid.*, III, 356, n. 42.

[156] *Ibid.*, III, 356, n. 43.

[157] *Ibid.*, III, 355.

lords appealed to the king that he would annul every-
thing that had been done by the parliament held on
the morrow of the feast of the Purification, the eleventh
year of his reign (February 3rd, 1388).[158] This parliament, they maintained, had been illegally forced upon
the king.[158] The Commons made a similar appeal.[159]
It is stated later that when the spiritual and temporal
lords and the proctors of the clergy (" Procureurs de la
clergie ") had been examined severally, they assented
expressly to the annulment of the statutes, judgments,
ordinances and all other things.[159] Perhaps some may
understand by " Procureurs de la clergie " the proctors
of absent bishops or abbots, but there is certainly no
evidence against regarding them as the proctors of the
lower clergy. If they are interpreted as the latter, there
were at the end of the fourteenth century representatives of the lower clergy in parliament in a consultative capacity.

The Commons again prayed that the prelates would
appoint a proctor.[160] This time the archbishops
appointed William le Scrope, Earl of Wiltshire, giving
him full power as they had previously given to Sir
Thomas Percy.[160]

Furthermore, we are told that in this parliament the
king held a deliberation with the prelates and clergy of
his realm.[161] He told them that he well understood
that he could not bind his successors by their oath, but
he would write to the Holy Father, the Pope, asking
him to give sentence on those who went against the
said judgments and ordinances.[161]

For a discussion of the libel against the king made by
the Duke of Norfolk and the Duke of Hereford a commission was formed. Among those appointed to this
commission were listed the Earl of Worcester and the

[158] *Rot. Parl.*, III, 357, n. 47.   [160] *Ibid.*, III, 359, n. 50.
[159] *Ibid.*, III, 357, n. 47.   [161] *Ibid.*, III, 359, n. 52.

Earl of Wiltshire as " procureurs del clergie." [162]   Sir
Thomas Percy, who had been recently created Earl of
Worcester, therefore, was still empowered to act for the
clergy. The question to be discussed by the commission
evidently involved the death penalty. Later, however,
the bishops and lords gave their oaths, as before, for
the maintenance of the measures passed by this parliament. [163] Among those who gave their oaths were the
Earls of Worcester and Wiltshire, but they were
grouped with the other lay lords, and were not distinguished especially as the proctors of the clergy. [164]

The evidence which has thus been found available
indicates that throughout the fourteenth century the
clergy were sending their proctors to parliament. There
is no instance of their taking any part in the assembly
other than in a consultative capacity. There is abun-
dance of evidence to show that convocation afforded to
the lower clergy a great opportunity for the discussion
of their grievances. They could depend upon their
prelates to present these grievances for them later in
parliament. As far as their money grants were concerned, it had become fully established before the
middle of the fourteenth century that grants on spiritualities were made in convocation. By constant
refusal to give a definite answer in parliament
concerning a grant, the clergy deflected their activity
more and more to their separate body—convocation,
where they knew that they could have a greater voice
and would be able to deliberate more freely. The
position of the lower clergy in parliament was nominal;
in convocation it was important. In the latter body
they could not have failed to realize the king's depen-
dence on their grants, or their own power to delay royal
procedure, as well as to make conditions for their
grants.

[162] *Ibid.*, III, 360, n. 54.
[163] *Ibid.*, III, 372, 373, nos. 89—90.   [164] *Ibid.*, III, 373, n. 89.

CHAPTER III

THE ATTITUDE OF THE CLERGY IN THE THIRTEENTH AND FOURTEENTH CENTURIES TOWARDS THE OBLIGATION OF ATTENDANCE ON CONVOCATIONS AND PARLIAMENTS

In a discussion of the attitude of the clergy towards the difficulties and obligations associated with attendance on convocations and parliaments, the mind must first be cleared of any modern conceptions in regard to attendance on ecclesiastical and political assemblies. The modern man speaks of the right to be present or to be represented in an assembly. To the man of the Middle Ages this was an entirely foreign idea.[1] Attendance for counsel and aid (" consilium et auxilium ") was to him a burden, something from which to be freed, or in the *strictly feudal* sense an irksome duty to be fulfilled as part of the feudal contract. This is quite evident from the various accounts extant of exemptions[2,3] in which the freedom from attendance on all parliaments, convocations and councils is a privilege to be guarded.

There are many reasons why the man of the Middle Ages would consider attendance on assemblies a burden. In the first place, not only were the distances great, but the roads were rough, and apt to be fre-

[1] A. F. Pollard, *The Evolution of Parliament* (1920 ed.), p. 139 : " The members came to Westminster not as sent from sovereign constituencies, but as summoned by a sovereign lord ; they attended not as delegates with imperative mandates to do what their constituents told them, but as the unfortunate and unwilling persons selected by their fellows to carry out the requirements of the crown." Quoted by Professor A. B. White in his volume *The Making of the English Constitution* (ed. 1925), p. 381, n. 1.

[2] T. Rymer, *Foedera* (1816—69 ed.), II, ii, 1158 (Pat. Roll, 15 Edw. III, Pt. 1, m. 13).

[3] P.R.O., Exch. K.R. Mem. Roll 108, " Communia Easter Term," 6 Edw. III, m. 221 : " Ita quod in conciliis archiepiscoporum seu Episcoporum aut aliis cleri conuocacionibus comparere minime teneantur."

quented by marauders ready to attack the peaceful traveller.[4] It was not until the eighth year of Henry VI in the parliament held at Westminster on September 22nd, 1429, that the clergy gained for themselves the privilege of freedom from attack on their way to and from convocation.[5] Furthermore, there was the expense of the journey to be considered and the matter of the cost of living during a prolonged session. The convents, colleges and chapters would be responsible for the procurations of their proctors as would be the dioceses for theirs. But in the latter case, it was perfectly possible for the dioceses to be slow in making their payments,[6] and in the meantime the proctors would have to bear the brunt of their travelling and living expenses. With the bishops there were other considerations. There were, first of all, arduous duties in their dioceses connected with their episcopal office, that might prevent them from desiring to take a

[4] *The Register of Thomas de Cobham, Bishop of Worcester* (1317—1327), ed. Ernest Harold Pearce (Worcester Historical Society), p. 111 (fol. 68b).
Cf. *infra*, p. 84, note 19.
[5] *Rot. Parl.*, IV, 347, n. 32: A petition was presented by the clergy in the parliament held at Westminster on September 22nd, 1429, that they and their servants and "familiares" should enjoy the same liberty and immunity in coming to and from Convocation as the Magnates and Commons enjoyed when called to parliament. The king granted their request. To confirm the grant of privilege the following statute was enrolled.
Statutes of the Realm, II, 238 (8 Henry VI, stat. 1): "In primis quia prelati et Clerus regni Anglie ad convocacionem evocati, eorumque servientes et familiares qui cum eisdem ad convocacionem hujusmodi veniunt, sepius ac frequenter arestantur molestantur et inquietantur: Volens igitur dictus dominus noster Rex pro securitate et quiete dictorum prelatorum et Cleri in hac parte perspicere gratiose ad supplicacionem eorumdem Prelatorum et Cleri et de assensu procerum Magnatum et Communitatis predictorum ordinavit et statuit quod vocandi in futurum ad Convocacionem Cleri pretextu brevis regii eorumque servientes et familiares eadem libertate sive immunitate veniendo expectando et redeundo plene gaudeant et utantur perpetuis futuris temporibus, qua gaudent et gaudere consueverunt sive gaudere debent in futurum proceres sive Magnates et Communitas regni Anglie ad parliamentum domini Regis vocati sive vocandi."
W. Prynne, *A Brief Register*, Pt. IV, 664: An allusion is made here to this statute.
[6] *The Register of Thomas de Brantyngham, Bishop of Exeter*, 1370—94, ed. F. C. Hingeston-Randolph, I, 524—5 (vol. II, fol. 120b).

long journey and to spend days in tedious sessions. In the raids was a further excuse for bishops not to absent themselves from their dioceses.[7] Lastly, many bishops were old and could not take the risk of exposure to the perils of a long journey. Many elaborate excuses on the score of health are found in the episcopal registers. One may venture to doubt if the excuse of health or of old age was always the dominant reason. Perhaps the bishop may have considered the great expense that the journey to London or some other place of meeting would entail. A bishop necessarily travelled to a certain degree in state and had to take many of his household with him for the upkeep of his establishment.[8] The sending of men who might alternate in acting as a proctor, and being responsible for their expenses, would cost a bishop very little by comparison with what it would cost him to go to a parliament or convocation personally with his suite. Hence bishops often sent proctors.

In the latter part of the thirteenth century and in the fourteenth century are found many kinds of excuses in the letters or " procuratoria " sent by the bishops to explain their absence from convocation and from parliament. Space does not allow a detailed discussion of these letters; it will suffice to examine certain of them during the period of this study. Many of the excuses seem valid enough, but one is often inclined to wonder whether the real reason at the back of some of them was not the very human unwillingness on the part of the bishops to be bothered with a long and expensive journey followed by days of tedious discussion.

In 1281(-2) the Bishop of Worcester gave as his reason for not being present at a congregation of pre-

---

[7] *Reg. Halton* (Carlisle) I, 241, 314—15 (fol. 44b, 60b).
[8] *A Roll of the Household Expenses of Richard de Swinfield, Bishop of Hereford During Part of the Years 1289 and 1290,* ed. John Webb (Camden Soc.), I, 39—42, 123, note for Sect. 12; II, cxxvii—cxxix.

lates the fact that the king was delaying in his diocese. [9]
The following year, 1282(-3), the same bishop asked to
be excused from attending the gathering at Northampton because of his lasting weakness of body. [10] In 1286
Bishop Giffard again sent men to act as his proctor in
the congregation of prelates, explaining that while he
was administering orders in his private chapel the
accustomed infirmity of his foot [11] became suddenly so
much worse that he could scarcely in consequence of
the heaviness fulfil the office. [12]

The Bishop of Hereford in 1295 gave as his excuse
for not coming to parliament the serious weakness
which seized him on his way to London. [13] Seventeen
years later the same bishop gave adverse health and
weakness of body as a reason for not attending the
legatine council at London in 1312. [14] During this same

[9] Wilkins, *op. cit.*, II, 65 (Ex reg. Giffard, Wigorn, fol. 125): "Licet
die tertia post instans festum pureficationis B.M. virginis gloriosæ apud
novum templum London una cum cæteris vestris suffraganeis pro negotio
liberationis domini Almarici de Monteforti secundum tenorem mandati
apostolici, divina favente clementia, faciendæ affectaremus plaudenti
animo coram vobis nostri præsentiam personaliter exhibere ; domino
tamen nostro regi Angliæ illustri, dum in nostra moratur dioecesi,
vacantes indies, et non nobis vestræ paternitatis sanctitatem requirimus
reverenter, quatenus absentiam nostram hac vice quoad diem et locum
prædictos, occasione præmissa habere dignemini, si libeat, excusatum."

[10] *Ibid.*, II, 92 (Ex reg. Giffard, Wigorn, fol. 148). He speaks of
"nostri corporis gravi et diuturna infirmitate."

[11] This was probably gout.

[12] Wilkins, *op. cit.*, II, 125 (Ex reg. Giffard, Wigorn, fol. 159):
"pedis nostri infirmitas solita angore multiplici subito nos gravavit,
adeo quod ipsius Dei officium hujusmodi prætextu gravedinis vix
potuimus adimplere ; et huc usque quia indies illius morbi materia
multiplicando sic anxium se prætendit, quod in camera velut in privato
carcere remanemus," Wilkins' reference is incorrect. The folio should
be 259 (or new foliation 258). Cf. *Worcester Episcopal Registers* (Reg.
Giffard), II, 294.

[13] Wilkins, *op. cit.*, II, 215 (Ex reg. Swinfield, Hereford, fol. 115):
"Ecce, cum nuper fuissemus versus London. in itinere constituti,
affectantes personaliter interesse apud Westm. die dominica prox. post
festum sancti Martini in hyeme nunc instanti, secundum formam mandati
vestri nobis directi, tam gravis infirmitas nos arripuit, quod iter inceptum
perficere non potuimus infra diem dominicam prænotatam sine evidenti
periculo vitæ nostræ ; "

[14] *Ibid.*, II, 421 (Ex reg. Swinfield, fol. 180): "adversa valetudine et
debilitate nostri corporis his temporibus impediti, . . . in synodo apud
London. . . . absque imminenti mortis periculo non poterimus personaliter comparere."

period Simon of Ghent, Bishop of Salisbury, was giving poor health as his excuse for not attending parliaments and convocations. [15]

In 1320 Bishop Cobham, of Worcester, wrote to the king about his inability to come to the parliament at Hilarytide on account of his health. [16] If it would be profitable to the discussion for him to come, he would. [16] The king replied that he did not wish him to be away and charged him to be there on the day. [17] The bishop, therefore, replied that he would be there. [18] The following year (1321) the same bishop sent an excuse to the archbishop for not coming to the council on account of the floods of the fields, the dangers of the road since the land was not cleared of evil men, the considerable distances of places, the shortness of winter days, and on account of his inability to collect the absent " familia " and to prepare the bundles, since there was scarcely ten days between the reception of the letters and the day appointed for appearance at the council. [19] He trusted that the archbishop would see fit to excuse him in consideration of his labours for peace in London and in the March of Scotland. [20]

[15] *Registrum Simonis de Gandavo Episcopi Saresbirensis,* ed. Cyril T. Flower (C. and Y. Soc.), pp. 230, 480, 484—5 (fol. 68—68d, 161, 162—162d).

   Ibid., p. 392 (fol. 132d): " Sachetz, cher seignour, qe nous sumes taunt grevetz de graunt age, feblesse et enfirmite de corps qe, a ceo qe nous meismes sentoms et qe ceaux qe conoissent nostre estat certeinement dient, nous ne le porrioums faire saunz peril de vie ; "

[16] *Reg. Cobham* (Wor. Hist. Soc.), p. 99 (fol. 63).

[17] *Ibid.,* pp. 99—100 (fol. 63—63b).

[18] *Ibid.,* p. 100 (fol. 63b).

[19] *Ibid.,* p. 111 (fol. 68b): " tum propter inundaciones agrorum, que in partibus nostris plus quam alibi et plus solito hiis diebus vndis pluuialibus intumescunt, tum quoque propter viarum discrimina, cum non sit patria malis hominibus expurgata, tum eciam quod, considerata locorum distancia, dierum iemalium breuitate, et profundidate viarum, non erat nobis possibile absentem congregasse familiam, sarcinulas preparasse, et ad diem venisse in vestris litteris assignatum cum vix essent inter diem recepcionis earum et diem comparicionis intermedii decem dies,"

[20] *Ibid.,* p. 111 (fol. 68b).

As his excuse in 1321, Bishop Adam de Orleton of Hereford said merely that he was prevented by " just and urgent necessities " from coming to the provincial council. [21]

The reason presented by Bishop Grandisson of Exeter in 1328 in his letter to the king requesting freedom from attending parliament, seems to be that of a conscientious bishop or of a skilled diplomat. [22] He declared that his predecessor was so occupied in the service of the king's father that he could not spend much time in Cornwall. He begged to be excused from this and other parliaments and assemblies of his council, adding that he could not come without peril to his soul and the souls of those subject to him. [23] He closed by saying, " E, beneit soit Dieux, trescher Seignour, vous avey si bon Counsail de noz honourables Freres Evesques et outres Grantz qe y serront, qe nostre presence tendrait petite ou nul value illoeques. Mes nous prieroms Dieu pur vous qe vous doynt issynt faire qil soit a Soun honour et a vostre, et al proffit de vostre Roialme." [24] In 1328(-9) the excuse presented by the same bishop for not coming to a provincial council was " cause urgentes legitime et necessarie . . . non voluntarie, . . . set invite." [25] Three years later Bishop Grandisson offered the late reception of the king's writ and other causes as his excuse for not going to parliament. [26] In 1341 Grandisson sent an elaborate excuse

[21] Wilkins, op. cit., II, 509 (Ex reg. Adæ de Orleton, episc. Hereford, fol. 55): " quod tamen sacro concilio vestro . . . occurrere personaliter non valemus, justis et urgentibus necessitatibus multipliciter impediti,"

[22] The Register of John de Grandisson, Bishop of Exeter, 1327—1369, ed. F. C. Hingeston-Randolph, I, 179 (vol. I, fol. 57—57b).

[23] Ibid., I, 179 (vol. I, fol. 57b): " qar loialment, trescher Seignour, nous ne pussoms mye santz nostre tresgraunt damage et deshonour, et auxi peril de nostre alme et des almes de noz suggietz unquore yssir nostre Eveschie."

[24] Ibid., I, 179 (vol. I, fol. 57b).

[25] Ibid., I, 450 (vol. II, fol. 107).

[26] Ibid., II, 680 (vol. II, fol. 158b).

G

for not appearing at the provincial council: the late appearance of the Bishop of London's letters, the difficulties of the way and the floods happening at this time of year, the distance, and his bodily sickness and infirmity.[27]

Even the Archbishop of Canterbury was known to send an excuse for not being present in parliament. In 1370(-1) Archbishop Witlesey gave the serious infirmity of body, with which he was suffering, as his reason for not coming to parliament.[28]

One could cite numerous other " procuratoria " with excuses, but they would only be similar in character to these. The " procuratoria," which have been here examined, indicate the tendency that there was among the bishops to try to free themselves from the burden of attendance on convocations and parliaments when they could produce a feasible excuse.

For those ecclesiastics who failed to attend parliament without a legitimate excuse punishment was reserved to the archbishop or to his deputy.[29] In convocation the situation was similar. The archbishop was apt to continue the convocation from day to day awaiting the absent. Then finally the preconization would take place, and those who were absent without a legitimate excuse the archbishop would pronounce contumacious, reserving the punishment to himself. The first step in the procedure towards punishment was sometimes a summons to the archbishop's court. One form of punishment for contumacy was the sequestration of the lands of the offender.

[27] *The Register of John de Grandisson, Bishop of Exeter,* II, 970—71 (vol. I, fol. 115): " tum propter tarditatem recepcionis dictarum Literarum, tum eciam propter viarum discrimina inundacionesque aquarum, hoc tempore anni subito accidencium, et loco(rum) distanciam, corporeamque gravitatem et invalitudinem,"

[28] The Register of William Witlesey, Archbishop of Canterbury (1368—74), preserved in the archives at Lambeth Palace, fol. 40v. Printed Wilkins, *op. cit.,* III, 89.

[29] Reg. S. de Gandavo (C. and Y. Soc.), p. 417 (fol. 140).

Rot. Parl., II, 146, n. 1.

Reg. Witlesey, fol. 69v.

The archbishops had to contend with the problem of the absence from their councils or convocations of those who had been expressly summoned to them. In Archbishop Pecham's register is found an order in 1281 under date of 14 kal. November (October 19th) to the Bishop of London to sequestrate in the London dioceses the lands of those unexempt churches which belonged to exempt monasteries that had refused to obey the order to come to his provincial council.[30] The severity with which the archbishop regarded those who had scorned to come to his council is evident from the irony of the words with which he lashed the offenders in speaking of their conduct to their bishop.[31] He complained, moreover, that they had not even taken care to send proctors with an excuse for their absence.[31] "The boldness of such ingrate presumption," he wished to correct, he said, in accordance with sacred law.[31] He therefore commanded the bishop to see to it that all unexempt churches, appropriated to exempt monasteries, should be kept under strict sequestration until he should receive a further mandate.[32] He stated, moreover, that he had suspended from entrance into

[30] Reg. Pecham, fol. 59. Printed in *Regist. Epist. J. Peckham,* I, 237—8.

[31] *Ibid.,* fol. 59. Printed in *Regist. Epist. J. Peckham,* I, 237—8: "Exempti vero tanquam pullos onagri liberos se putantes minime vel modice condolentes sue sancte matris angustiis, cuius viscera multi ex eis plus onerant quam honorant, quasi per effectum vel defectum verius de se dictum illud Johannis propheticum allegarent: 'Atrium quod foris est Templum eiice foras, et ne metias illud'; nec parturentum cervarum audire rugitus, nec ad ipsum consilium in anxiate matris auxilium consilium et solacium venire dignati sunt, utpote filii alieni a semitis claudicantes, quin potius ne in aliquo detumesceret distenta eorum nimis elacio nec procuratores ad sue excusacionem absencie mittere curauerunt, tam reuerendum collegium contemnentes, Agar ex parte similes, que illustrem dispexit dominam, videns, sedicionis filium concepisse. Sic agonizante olim Dei milicia et se laudabiliter periculis exponente diuisi a preliantibus Rubenite intra terminos proprios quieuerunt gregum sibilis delectati. Nos autem tam ingrate presumpcionis audaciam sacri secundum iuris regulas corrigere cupientes, scientesque iuxta saluatoris sentenciam contra nos esse qui nobiscum esse despiciunt, severitati tamen plurimum detrahentes quam possemus in contemptores huiusmodi si vellemus, canonice exercere,"

[32] *Ibid.,* fol. 59. Printed *Regist. Epist. J. Peckham,* I, 238.

church all those whose names were in the schedule enclosed, who had been contumacious in regard to attendance on his council.[32] The bishop was ordered to announce publicly the suspension of these persons.[32] It is added in the register that similar letters were sent to other bishops.[32]

About two months later Archbishop Pecham sent a letter to his official commanding the relaxation of the sequestration that had been put upon the fruits of S. Augustine's Abbey, Canterbury, for non-attendance on the provincial council.[33] His reason for the release was that he had heard that a composition had been arranged between his predecessor and the abbot and " Venerabile Collegium " of S. Augustine whereby the archbishop should not be able to execute such an order against him.[33] The release was to hold until the archbishop could inquire into the rights and privileges of the composition.[33] Here then is evidence of an exemption that had been granted to the abbot and " college " of S. Augustine, whereby they were not held to come to provincial councils.

Archbishop Winchelsey had likewise to deal with the problem of contumacy. The summons to the council of bishops which was to assemble on the ides of July (July 15th), 1295 demanded that they appear personally in virtue of obedience to their profession to him and the See of Canterbury, and under penalty of canonical distraint.[34] In his summons to the convocation which was to meet January 13th, 1296(-7) Winchelsey held out a threat to those who should be absent that was similar to the one which we have just

[33] Reg. Pecham, fol. 59. Printed in *Regist. Epist. J. Peckham*, I, 255.
[34] Reg. Winchelsey, fol. 168v. Printed in *Reg. Winchelsey* (C. and Y. Soc.), p. 31: "in virtute sancte obediencie quam nobis et ecclesie nostre Cantuariensi exhibere iuramento prestito, personaliter sunt professi et sub pena districcionis canonice suam exhibeant presenciam personalem."

noted, but more elaborately stated.[35] For the next convocation, called for March 24th, 1296(-7), Winchelsey warned them that they should remain until the final completion of the business. No one was to be excused.[36] He varied the form slightly in the mandate for the convocation on August 10th, 1297 by saying that no one could be excused "except for an evident and inevitable hindrance."[37] The mandate issued to summon a convocation on November 20th, 1297 included a warning similar to those sent in the past.[38] With only a few variations from those previously issued

[35] Reg. Winchelsey, fol. 204v. Printed in *Reg. Winchelsey* (C. and Y. Soc.), p. 145 : "in virtute sancta obediencie qua nobis et ecclesie nostre Cantuariensi iuxta sue professionis seriem iuramento personaliter prestito sunt astricti ; nec non sub pena districcionis canonice cuius rigorem exercere dante Deo, disponimus convocacionis seu citacionis edictum totaliter contempnentes aut eciam quesitis coloribus, sese frustratorie excusantes ; "
Reg. Winchelsey, fol. 205. Printed in *Reg. Winchelsey* (C. and Y. Soc.), p. 146. They were commanded to appear "sub pena excommunicacionis maioris et interdicti que merito poterunt formidare, qui in forma prenota contumaciter omiserunt seu contempserint comparere,"

[36] Reg. Winchelsey, fol. 211. Printed in *Reg. Winchelsey* (C. and Y. Soc.), p. 162 : ". . . cum diebus continuandis eidem vsque ad finalem expedicionem tractatus, omni inevitabili excusacione cessante, que si pretensa et non probata exititerit absentem nullatenus excusabit." The date given in the caption of the account of this convocation transcribed in the Canterbury and York Society's edition of Winchelsey's register is wrongly calculated. (*Reg. Winchelsey*, C. and Y. Soc., p. 162.) The date should be March 24th, not 26th, as "die dominica cantabitur officium Letare Jerusalem" (*Reg. Winchelsey,* fol. 211), the day for which the convocation was summoned, is the Fourth Sunday in Lent, which in the year 1297 (old style 1296) was March 24th.

[37] Reg. Winchelsey, fol. 218v.—219. Printed in *Reg. Winchelsey* (C. and Y. Soc.), p. 180 : "vos eciam premunimus et ceteros sic citandos premunire mandamus quod absentes in citacione predicta nisi euidens et ineuitabile impedimentum per probaciones certas superesse docuerunt, tanquam inobedientes et offensores notorios grauiter puniemus." The use of "premunimus" might lead one to think that this was a premonishment to parliament, but the contents of the mandate, as well as the marginal note in the register at the side of the mandate which reads "citacio pro convocacione episcoporum apud novum templum," establish the fact that it was a convocation.

[38] Reg. Winchelsey, fol. 226. Printed in *Reg. Winchelsey* (C. and Y. Soc.), p. 199 : "Denunciantes dictis cœpiscopis et per eos suos subditos sic vocandos faciatis idonee premuniri et vos similiter de eodem premunimus, quod absentes in citacione predicta nisi euidens et ineuitabile impedimentum sufficienter probetur, tamquam inobedientes grauiter puniemus."

a warning was inserted in the mandate for a convocation on June 25th, 1298. [39]

Archbishop Winchelsey's letter addressed to Simon of Ghent, Bishop of Salisbury, on May 29th, 1303, in regard to the absence of the Treasurer of the Church of Salisbury and the Abbots of Cerne and Milton, did not lack the fire of the letters of his predecessor. He began by saying, [40] " Those who put their peculiar business in vain affairs before the advantage (' utilitate ') of the state and the salvation of souls, not considering that they are called by a superior to common discussions for the preservation of ecclesiastical liberty, it is expedient to chastise, in order that committing to their memory the very worthy punishment (' penam condignam '), they may at other times obey the mandates of their superior. Forsooth to discuss how the danger of souls could be avoided and of the Church legislated for more deliberately, we decreed that the prelates and clergy of our province of Canterbury should be summoned to certain places, once at the feast of the Ascension of our Lord and again at the feast of S. Nicholas. And although some of them, just like sons of obedience, appeared in accordance with the summons to treat concerning business of this kind, many nevertheless whom the business concerned especially, on account of no urgent necessity, by no means took care to appear in accordance with the aforesaid form so that they have been a hurt to the common advantage and incurred culpably the mark of disobedience. Wherefore we command your brotherhood by virtue of obedience,

---

[39] Reg. Winchelsey, fol. 242v. Printed in *Reg. Winchelsey* (C. and Y. Soc.), 252 : " Et vos ipsi quo ad vos et subditos vestros hoc ipsum mandatum nostrum in singulis suis articulis similiter observetis, Denunciantes dictis Episcopis et per eos suis subditis denunciari facientes quod absentes in dicto termino cessante legittimo (sic) impedimento de quo evidenter et legitime doceri volumus graviter pro contumacia puniemus ; "

[40] Translated from the transcription in *Reg. S. de Gandavo* (C. and Y. Soc.), p. 121 (fol. 33d).

firmly enjoining you to the extent that you cause to be peremptorily cited all those who were contumacious in the said convocations, whose names are contained in the present schedule that they should appear sufficiently before us wherever we then are in our said city, diocese, and province to receive very worthy punishment for their demerits and to obey the law, announcing to the same, that whether they come then or not we shall punish as is fitting the contumacies committed." [41] The letter concluded with the command to the bishop to notify the archbishop by letters patent what he shall have done as to the execution of this mandate. [42] Beneath the archbishop's letter in the Salisbury register is found, therefore, a copy of the letter sent by Bishop Simon of Ghent to the Dean of the Church of Salisbury or the " locum tenens " and the Archdeacon of Dorset commanding them to cite the Treasurer of the Church of Salisbury and the Abbots of Cerne and Milton to appear before the archbishop. [43] The note is added that the bishop's mandate was fully executed. [44]

Letters identical with the one sent to the Bishop of Salisbury were probably sent to all the other dioceses where there were clergy who had been contumacious in regard to these councils, as in Winchelsey's register there is a copy of a letter sent to the Bishop of Lincoln [45] which is the same (" mutatis mutandis ") as that which was sent to the Bishop of Salisbury.

In Archbishop Winchelsey's mandate for the first of the convocations (that of the morrow of the Ascension, June 1st, 1302), mentioned in his letter reprimanding the contumacious in the diocese of Salisbury, a warning had been included for those who failed to obey the

[41] *Ibid.*, p. 121 (fol. 33d).
[42] *Ibid.*, p. 121 (fol. 33d).
[43] *Ibid.*, pp. 121—2 (fol. 33d).
[44] *Ibid.*, p. 122 (fol. 33d).
[45] Reg. Winchelsey, fol. 150. Printed in Wilkins, *op. cit.*, II, 273.

summons. [46]   In the mandate for the second of the two
convocations no warning against absence was inserted. [47]
The next mandate found for the assembling of a convocation [48] was issued in 1307 by the Prior of Christ
Church, Canterbury, during the suspension of
Archbishop Winchelsey, and contains an injunction
against absence which is almost identical with that
issued by Winchelsey in 1302. [49]   Archbishop Winchelsey's mandates for the next two convocations, those
summoned for November 24th, 1309, [50] and April 18th,
1312, [51] were strikingly similar to those which he had
inserted in the past. We learn, however, from a letter
of the Archbishop of Canterbury to the Bishop of
Worcester written 12 kal. May (April 20th), 1312, [52]
that when the latter of these convocations assembled,
although the Bishop of London had certified duly by
letters patent that he had executed the mandate and

[46] *Reg. S. de Gandavo* (C. and Y. Soc.), p. 95 (fol. 26d): " denunciantes dictis episcopis et per eos suis subditis denunciari expressius
facientes quod absentes in dicto termino cessante inevitabili impedimento,
de quo evidenter et legitime doceri volumus, ut jus exigit graviter pro
contumacia puniemus."

[47] *Reg. S. de Gandavo* (C. and Y. Soc.), pp. 102—3 (fols. 28d—29).

[48] Summoned for May 5th, 1307.

[49] Wilkins, *op. cit.*, II, 292 (Ex reg. Cantuar. P., fol. 52a, b): " Denunciantes dictis episcopis et per eos suis subditis denunciari expressius
facientes, quod contra absentes in dicto termino cessante inevitabili impedimento, de quo evidenter et legitime doceri volumus, prout jus exigit
graviter pro sua contumacia procedimus."

[50] Reg. Winchelsey, fol. 128v. Also in *Reg. S. de Gandavo* (C. and
Y. Soc.), pp. 376—7 (fol. 127): "Vos enim premunimus et ceteros
citandos per vos premuniri mandamus quod absentes in termino supradicto nisi propter euidentes causas et racionabiles de quibus fidem
faciant, fuerunt impediti tamquam inobedientes et contumaces iuxta
iuris exigenciam puniemus."
Again the use of "premunimus" might lead one to think this a premonishment for parliament, but the account in Winchelsey's register
shows that it was for the provincial council to consider matters
touching the Templars.

[51] *Reg. S. de Gandavo* (C. and Y. Soc.), p. 422 (fol. 141d): " . . .
denunciantes eisdem quod nullius quem inevitabilis necessitas non excusat absenciam a dicto concilio habebimus excusatam."

[52] Wilkins, *op. cit.*, II, 419—20 (Ex reg. Raynold, Wigorn., fol. 47).
Translated in the *Register of Walter Reynolds, Bishop of Worcester,
1308—1313*; ed. by Rowland Alwyn Wilson (Dugdale Society and
Worcester Historical Society), p. 38 (fol. 47—47d).

some of the suffragans had appeared and duly certified, others, among them the Bishop of Worcester, had not appeared. In that it was alleged by clerks and friends of the absent bishops that the Bishop of London's citation and mandate might not have come to their notice, it was decided to await their coming to the council until the Monday after the feast of the Ascension and not to dissolve the present council. If the abbots and priors wished to appoint proctors to act for them, they could do so, the priors of churches being excepted.[53] He added that he would provide full power for the bishop and other bishops to be excused from personal appearance, just as he had excused the religious of the province, cathedral priors excepted.[53]

Archbishop Reynolds' mandate for the convocation at S. Paul's on April 25th, 1316 contained no warning against absence.[54] From the transcript available of the record of a mandate issued for a convocation on October 11th, 1316, it is impossible to tell whether a warning was included.[55] The warning sent in the mandate for a convocation on December 1st, 1321 was slightly different in wording, but as in the past, punishment in accordance with law was threatened to those who were negligent about attending.[56] Again it is im-

---

[53] Wilkins, *op. cit.*, II, 420 (Ex reg. Raynold, Wigorn, fol. 47): " Porro, si abbates et priores vestræ civitatis et dioec. velint per se, et sui conventus per se, vel conjunctim, procuratores idoneos ad dictum concilium destinare, quibus ad tractandum super præmissis, et consentiendum hiis, quæ ordinabimus, dante Domino, et providebimus de vestro et venerabili fratrum nostrorum concilio, plenariam potestatem, ipsos a personali comparitione, sicut et religiosos alios nostræ provinciæ, cathedralium ecclesiarum prioribus duntaxat exceptis, habebimus excusatos."

[54] Wilkins, *op. cit.*, II, 456—7 (Ex reg. Henr. prior. Cantuar., fol. 168).

[55] Wilkins, *op. cit.*, II, 458 (Ex reg. epistolarum Rob. de Langele, prior. Norwic., n. 102). Wilkins has not transcribed fully the mandate for this convocation. Time did not allow me to see the manuscript.

[56] *Registrum Ade de Orleton, Episcopi Herefordensis,* transcribed and edited by A. T. Bannister (C. and Y. Soc.), pp. 207—8 (fol. 56): " . . . fratribus nostris et personis superius nominatis expresse denunciantes quod contra ipsos non comparentes, et in pacis prosecucione

possible to state whether a warning was included, for the available transcript of the record which gives evidence of a convocation summoned for June 9th, 1322 seems not to have been taken fully.[57] In a summons for convocation on October 13th, 1326 the warning was very brief and reflected those of the past.[58] Although Archbishop Reynolds, as we have seen, did not always insert in his mandates to convocation a warning against those who might be contumacious, he denounced in his summons to a convocation to be held at Leicester on November 2nd, 1327, anyone who should be absent " save for an adequate hindrance."[59]

Archbishop Simon Mepeham issued a summons to a provincial council to be held January 27th, 1328(-9), which did not contain a threat to the absent. It did, however, include an express command such as had been employed in the time of Winchelsey, that those summoned should remain until the business was completed.[60]

We have not been able to discover again a warning against absence[61] until we find one appearing in the

negligentes ad quam quibus ipsorum fratrum ex injuncto canonis sub gradus sui amissionis pena tenetur, quantum nobis a jure permittitur, puniendo procedemus, ipsosque in hiis, in quibus nostra se jurisdiccio non extendit, de tam dampnabili negligencia defermus sine mora."

[57] Wilkins, *op. cit.*, II, 515—16 (Ex libro 3. memor. Henr. Burghersh, Lincoln. Episcopi, fol. 54). Time did not allow me to see the manuscript.

[58] *Reg. Orleton* (Heref.), C. and Y. Soc., p. 369 (fol. 103): " denunciantes eisdem quod nullius quem inevitabilis necessitas non excusat absenciam dicto septimo die habebimus excusatam."

[59] *Reg. Reynolds* (Cant.), fol. 207v.: ". . . nisi impedimentum sufficienter probetur tanquam inobedientes grauiter puniemus." Cf. *Ibid.*, fol. 106 for the same wording used in the summons for July 14th, 1314. Wilkins (*op. cit.*, II, 538—9) in quoting this document omits the part which includes the warning.

[60] *Reg. Grandisson*, I, 446 (vol. II, fol. 105b): " . . . cum continuacione et proragacione dierum subsequencium usque ad finalem expedicionem agendarum nobiscum et cum Fratribus nostris. Episcopis antedictis,"

[61] In Archbishop Mepeham's mandate for a convocation on September 4th, 1332, there may have been a warning, but Wilkins (*op. cit.*, II, 561) in quoting from *Liber 2, Actorum capituli Lincoln.* has not transcribed the mandate in full.

mandate of Archbishop John de Stratford for a convocation on May 4th, 1346. [62] In this there are only
slight verbal changes. [62]

When Archbishop Simon Islep issued his first mandate for a convocation (May 2nd, 1351), [63] he seems not
to have felt it necessary to include a warning to insure
attendance. In sending a summons, however, for his
next convocation (May 16th, 1356), he took care to
touch upon absence. [64] In spite of the warning, certain
prelates, we know, were absent from this convocation,
appearing insufficiently by proctors, and were fined for
their offence. [65] In his summons to the next convocation the archbishop definitely mentioned the absence of
certain bishops and other prelates at the previous convocation and emphasized strongly the penalty that
would be inflicted for absence at the coming session. [66]

[62] Wilkins, *op. cit.*, II, 727—8 (Ex reg. Wulstan. Wigorn., fol. 174):
"Vos etiam præmunimus, et cæteros sic citandos per vos præmuniri
volumus et mandamus quod absentes in dicto concilio, nisi de evidenti
ipsorum impedimento et rationabili in ea parte coram nobis, vel nostris
commissariis tunc fecerint plenam fidem, nos illos, tanquam inobedientes
et contumaces quatenus juste poterimus, juxta juris exigentiam
puniemus." Cf. *supra* footnotes 37 and 50 for similar warnings.

[63] Reg. Islep, fol. 42v. Printed in Wilkins, *op. cit.*, III, 16—17.
N.B. Wilkins, who used March 25th as the beginning of the new year,
has placed this document under 1351 although it is dated "Vii idus
Martii" (March 9th). To be logical he should have put it under 1350.
1351 is, of course, correct new style. Printed also in *Reg. Grandisson*,
II, 1099—1100 (vol. I, fol. 167b).

[64] Reg. Islep, fol. 111. Printed in Wilkins, *op. cit.*, III, 38. Wilkins
gives incorrect foliation. (Printed also in *Reg. Grandisson*, II, 1099—
1100 (vol. I, fol. 167b):) "Intimantes eisdem quod contra absentes in
forma canonica procedemus nullius sic absentis excusacionem penitus
admissuri nisi quatenus ad hoc nos arctarunt canonici sancciones."

[65] Reg. Islep, fol. 117: "Isti vero domini per procuratores comparentes minus sufficientes comparuerunt quod nullam excusacionem per
litteras aut per procuratores eorum destinarunt aut proposuerunt contra
canonem *placuit* xviii denarii."

[66] Reg. Islep, fol. 155. Printed in *Reg. Grandisson*, II, 1206 (vol. I,
fol. 205b): "Verum quia confratrum et cœpiscoporum nostrorum predictorum et aliorum prelatorum dicte nostre prouincie aliqui se a prouinciali nostro concilio ultimo celebrato absentarunt voluntarie et absque
causa quorum presenciam fuisse non ambigitur profuturum; volumus
et mandamus quod intimetis, seu denunciari faciatis dicte nostre pro-
nuncie cœpiscopis et confratribus ac vicariis huiusmodi, decanis,
abbatibus, prioribus, et ceteris ecclesiarum prelatis supradictis, quod eos
a personali comparicione in huius modi congregacione dictis die et loco

When preparing to assemble his suffragans for a council at S. Mary's, Southwark, on May 31st, 1361, Archbishop Islep stressed the fact that none of the bishops should be excused from personal appearance, because the quality of the business demanded special industry from them and from himself.[67]

Following his predecessor, Archbishop Witlesey in 1369(-70) sent a warning not to be absent that was almost identical in form with that used by Archbishop Islep.[68] From the acts of this convocation as recounted in the archbishop's register, we know that the archbishop on the second day of the session pronounced contumacious all religious, as well as secular, who were held and compelled to appear in this convocation and who having been lawfully cited, did not appear.[69] The punishment for this kind of contumacy was reserved to him.[69] Witlesey's injunction for the convocation that was to assemble May 30th, 1373 was similar to those we have found previously with its promise of procedure

per nos, seu nostra auctoritate, deo annuente, celebrando, habere non intendimus excusatos ea vice nisi ex causa necessaria tunc ibidem alleganda et probanda; set, eorum contumacia si qui forsitans absentes fuerint, secundum iuris exigenciam canonice punietur."

[67] Reg. Islep, fol. 170. *Reg. Grandisson*, III, 1223 (vol. III, fol. 212): "Neminem, vero, dictorum fratrum excusatum habere poterimus propter dicti negocii qualitatem nobis et illis ex electa speciali industria demandati nisi graui infirmitate vel debilitate corporis excusetur quo casu aliquem de confratribus loco suo constituere teneatur."

[68] *Wykeham's Register*, ed. T. F. Kirby (Hampshire Record Society), II, 97—8 (pt. III, fol. 28b): "Volumus insuper et mandamus, quod intimetis seu denunciari faciatis dicte nostre provincie cœpiscopis et confratribus ac vicariis huiusmodi decanis, abbatibus, prioribus et ceteris ecclesiarum prelatis supra dictis quod eos a personali comperacione (sic) in huiusmodi congregacione dictis die et loco per nos seu nostra auctoritate Deo annuente, celebranda, habere non intendimus ista vice excusatos, nisi ex causa necessaria tunc ibidem alleganda eciam et probanda set eorum contumacia si qui forsitan absentes fuerint secundum juris exigenciam canonice punietur."

[69] Reg. Witlesey, fol. 17v. "Et in super omnes tam religiosos, quam seculares qui in ista conuocacione tenentur et artantur comparere licite citatos et non comparentes pronunciauit contumaces, pena eisdem pro huiusmodi contumacia iniungenda sibi reseruata."

in accordance with the sacred canons.[70]   In sending
forth the archbishop's mandate the Bishop of London
held out a threat of punishment to the absent similar to
that which had been issued in 1370.[71]

For the convocation which he was summoning for
February 3rd, 1376(-7) Archbishop Sudbury sent a
warning[72] against absence that reflects the warnings of
the past.   During the convocation that met on May
9th, 1379 Sudbury warned the proctors of the prelates
and clergy against leaving the city " before the business
of the convocation was finished, under penalty of the
loss of their procurations, and of the imposition upon
them by him of many other things."[73]

By the time that William Courteney became Archbishop of Canterbury procedure in regard to the form
and content of mandates for convocation was falling
into definite grooves.   An examination of the warnings

[70] Reg. Witlesey, fol. 69v.   Reg. Brantyngham, I, 302 (vol. I,
fol. 35): " . . . intimantes eisdem quod contra absentes debite procedemus nullius sic absentis excusacionem penitus admissuri nisi
quatenus ad hoc artati fuerimus per Canonicos Sancciones."

[71] Reg. Brantyngham, I, 318 (vol. I, fol. 42b): "Vobis, eciam,
Domino Episcopo supradicto intimamus, et per vos Decanis, Abbatibus,
Prioribus, et ceteris Ecclesiarum vestre Diocesis Prelatis, intimari volumus,
quod vos, aut eos, a personali comparicione in huiusmodi Congregacione,
dictis die et loco, prefatus Venerabilis Pater non intendit ista vice habere
excusatos, nisi ex causa necessaria, tunc ibidem alleganda eciam et probanda, set absencium contumacia, si qui fuerint, secundum juris
exigenciam Canonice punietur."

The warning may have been given directly by the archbishop, but the
editor of Bishop Brantyngham's register has not transcribed the archbishop's mandate in its entirety.

[72] The Register of Simon of Sudbury, Archbishop of Canterbury
(1375—81) preserved in the archives at Lambeth Palace, fol. 31:
" . . . Volumus insuper et mandamus quod intimetis seu denunciari
faciatis dicte nostre prouincie cœpiscopis et confratribus ac decanis
abbatibus prioribus et ceteris ecclesiarum prelatis supradictis quod eos
a personali comparicione in huiusmodi congregacione dictis die et loco
seu nostra auctoritate deo annuente facienda habere non intendimus
ista vice excusatos nisi ex causa necessaria tunc ibidem alleganda eciam
et probanda set eorum contumacia si qui forsan absentes fuerint
secundum iuris exigenciam canonice punietur."   Cf. supra, p. 96, n. 68.

[73] Reg. Sudbury, fol. 55: "Et dominus post tractatum huiusmodi
monitionem fecit ibidem publice procuratores dictorum prelatorum et
Cleri ne quis ipsorum recederet a Ciuitate London. ante dicte Con-
uocacionis negocium finitum sub pena amissionis procuracionum suarum
et alie multe eis per eum imponende."

against absence in the mandates found in Courteney's register for the convocations summoned November 18th, 1382,[74] April 17th, 1391,[75] and February 5th, 1394(-5),[75] reveal them to have been modelled along the lines of the warnings issued by preceding archbishops. An examination of the mandates for other convocations during Courteney's archiepiscopate (1381—96), available in registers not yet transcribed, would probably reveal the same usage.[76] Archbishop Arundel also inserted a warning in his mandates similar to those issued previously by his predecessors.[77]

It is interesting to find in Courteney's register a record of his official act of pronouncing contumacious those who were absent in the convocation that met on April 17th, 1391.[78] The form was as follows: " Nos

[74] Reg. Courteney, I, fol. 33v. The warning here issued is identical with that issued by Sudbury (Reg. Sudbury, fol. 31) for the convocation summoned for February 3rd, 1376—7. Cf. *supra*, p. 97, n. 72.

[75] Reg. Courteney, I, fol. 75; II, fol. 195v. With only a slight change in the order of some of the words these two warnings, which are alike, follow the form issued by Courteney for the convocation summoned for November 18th, 1382. Cf. preceding note, 74.

[76] *Reg. Brantyngham*, I, 502 (vol. I, fol. 110b). The mandate calendared here for the convocation summoned for December 2nd, 1383, is not fully transcribed. The statement is made that it was issued in " the common form." *Ibid.*, II, 675 (vol. I, 193b). The mandate calendared here for the convocation summoned for October 12th, 1388, is not transcribed even in part. The statement is made that it was issued in " the common form." Wilkins (*op. cit.*, III) has not transcribed any mandates for convocation in the period 1381—96.

[77] The register of Thomas Arundel, Archbishop of Canterbury (1396—1414), preserved in the archives at Lambeth Palace, II, fol. 178v.

The warning in the mandate for the convocation summoned for January 26th, 1400—1 is similar, except for a few slight changes of wording, to that issued by Sudbury for the convocation summoned for February 3rd, 1376—7. Cf. p. 97, n. 72.

Ibid., I, 54—54v. The warning in the mandate for the convocation summoned for October 21st, 1402, is identical with those issued by Courteney for the convocations of April 17th, 1391, and February 5th, 1394—5. Cf. *supra*, n. 75.

The mandates for the convocations summoned for February 19th, 1396, and October 6th, 1399, were issued by Thomas, Prior of Canterbury. Reg. Arundel, I, fol. 44b, 51. No warnings against absence are contained in these mandates.

Wilkins (*op. cit.*, III) has transcribed no warnings for the period which closes this study (1396—99).

[78] Reg. Courteney, I, fol. 76v. Printed in Wilkins, *op. cit.*, III, 213. *N.B.* Wilkins' foliation here is incorrect.

Willelmus, permissione diuina Cantuar. archiepiscopus
tocius Anglie primas, et apostolice sedis legatus, clerum
Exonien et Lincoln diocesum nec non archidiacona-
tuum Wigorn. Suthfolc. et Sudbur. ac omnes et singulos
abbates, priores exemptos, decanos prepositos, archi-
diacanos, et alias personas ecclesiasticas nostre prouincie
Cantuar. ad presens concilium nostrum legitime et
peremptorie citatos preconizatos et diucius expectatos,
et non comparentes, reputamus et pronunciamus contumaces. Et in penam contumaciarum suarum huiusmodi decernimus declaramus et pronunciamus omnia
et singula in presenti concilio habita atque facta, suum
debitum sortiri debere effectum ipsorum contumaciis in
aliquo non obstantibus in hac parte; penam aliam
canonicam eis et eorum singulis inflegendam a nobis seu
commisario nostro quem ad id duxerimus deputandum
nihilominus specialiter reservantes." [78]

From the various warnings against absence which
have been noted above as inserted in the archiepiscopal
mandates, one concludes that absence of the clergy
from convocation during the period of this study created
continual anxiety in the minds of the archbishops.

While they exercised severity against the absent, the
Archbishops of Canterbury were nevertheless fully
aware of the burdens that attendance on convocations
and parliaments entailed. In various mandates are
found apologies for summoning convocation. In his
mandate for the convocation to be held March 24th,
1296(-7), Archbishop Winchelsey apologized for calling
the prelates and clergy again so soon in that lately they
had been fatigued much by a similar convocation, a
fact which troubled him exceedingly. [79] When the

[79] Reg. Winchelsey, fol. 211. Printed in *Reg. Winchelsey* (C. and Y.
Soc.), p. 162: "ex magna et diligenti super hoc deliberacione premissa
concepimus ac perpendimus euidenter quod dictos prelatos et clerum
adhuc ex causis premissis conuocare celeriter, licet nuper ex alia
conuocacione consimili multum fatigati fuissent, quod nos quam plurimum angit, modis omnibus oportebit."

archbishop found that it was necessary to call yet another convocation the following autumn (November 20th, 1297), he phrased his apology in even stronger terms than in his preceding mandate.[80]   In 1298 Winchelsey was very loth to comply with the request of the king on his return from Flanders for another convocation, and showed himself in his mandate to be very sympathetic with those who had to be troubled again by another summons.[81]   The following year Winchelsey gave the adverse conditions of the time as his reason for calling the clergy together again,[82] although, as he declared, he was loth to do so.   He gave no apology in summoning a convocation for June 1st, 1302,[83] but in calling one the following winter he expressed his unwillingness in having to issue the mandate.[84]

Archbishop Simon Mepeham in summoning a convocation for March 11th, 1329(-30), spoke of being

[80] Reg. Winchelsey, fol. 225—225v.   Printed in *Reg. Winchelsey* (C. and Y. Soc.), p. 198 : " Casus repentini, cuius occasione Regni et ecclesie Anglicane magnum timetur periculum imminere, recens et inopinatus euentus nos, licet anxios et inuitos impellit extra propositum preconceptum prelatos et clerum nostre prouincie licet per similia, de quo dolemus et angimur, sepius fatigatos, pro eiusdem Regni et Ecclesie, atque Cleri periculo propulsando cum festinacione consulere, et ad id modis omnibus, prout eciam cum quibusdam nostris cœpiscopis et aliis sapientibus deliberacione habita censuimus conuocare."

[81] Reg. Winchelsey, fol. 242v.   Printed in *Reg. Winchelsey*, p. 251 : " Cuius deprecantis recenter ad Regnum suum regressi supereminens condicio autoritatisque sublimis post-regni eiusdem ingressum prima supplicacio nobis facta nos licet anxios de nimiis fatigacionibus subditorum, secundum discrimen temporis transacti compacientesque per sepius repetitas conuocaciones huiusmodi tediosis vexacionibus eorumdem extra preconceptum prepositum quodammodo inuitos compulit tantis precibus animum inclinare."

[82] Reg. Winchelsey, fol. 131v.   Printed in Wilkins, *op. cit.,* II, 253 : " Licet transacti temporis aduersa condicio hactenus cogeret nos inuitos prelatos et Clerum nostre Cant. prouincie per frequentes conuocaciones grauiter fatigare ; multipharia tamen et evidens ecclesie nostre prouincialis vtilitas, quam prosequi intendimus et tenemur ad iteratam ipsorum conuocacionem ob id mixima affectatam, nos animosius excitat et inducit."

[83] Reg. Winchelsey, fol. 147.   Printed in Wilkins, *op. cit.,* II, 272—3.

[84] Reg. Winchelsey, fol. 148v.   Printed in Wilkins, *op. cit.,* II, 273 : " Cogimur, licet inuiti, prelatos nostre prouincie, quos res tangit, protinus conuocare."

" compelled " by the urgent business of the Church and the Realm to hold a discussion. [85] The use of the word " compelled " perhaps implies that the archbishop felt it necessary to defend himself against expected complaints because of the summons.

The mandate for a convocation on September 19th, 1334, [86] reveals the unwillingness of Archbishop Stratford to burden his clergy. In calling another convocation (September 30th, 1337), he declared that inevitable danger and great necessity urged him to summon it. [87]

Not until he issued a mandate for a convocation for a fourth time did Archbishop Islep express an apology for summoning the clergy. [88] This was for the convocation on February 3rd, 1359(–60). [88] He then said that since he had been presiding over the church of Canterbury he had desired to spare the prelates and clergy from " laborious and expensive convocations and vexations," and to cherish them in peace that they might serve the Most High King of kings more freely. [88]

Although the clergy had met as recently as December 1st, 1384, [89] King Richard II issued another mandate

[85] Wilkins, *op. cit.*, II, 557. Wilkins does not quote the source from which he obtained this document : " Ex assumpta solicitudine pastoralis officii multoties cogimur pro varietate temporum et urgentibus ecclesiæ et regni negotiis cum prælatis et clero nostræ prov. communem habere tractatum : instans enim reipublicæ magna necessitas, etc. inevitabiliter nos impellunt prælatos et clerum nostræ provinciæ prædictæ juxta effectum brevis regii convocare."

[86] Wilkins, *op. cit.*, II, 575—6 (Ex reg. Linc. Burghersh): " Nos igitur super contentis in brevi suprascripto cum quibusdam de nostris fratribus et oliis multis peritis tractatu habito diligenti, nolentes, quantum in nobis est, vos, et alios prælatos, ac clerum nostræ provinciæ occasione præmissorum duplicatis expensis et laboribus fatigari, sed optantes vestris et earum discriminibus, quantum possumus, obviare, convocationem, hanc ex causis prædictis cum minori quo vestris possumus incommodo, et eorum fore censuimus faciend."

[87] Wilkins, *op. cit.*, II, 582—3 (Ex reg. Lincoln, Burgh., fol. 340b).

[88] Reg. Islep, fol. 155. Printed in Wilkins, *op. cit.*, III, 44 : " Quamuis a tempore quo Cantuar. ecclesie domino disponente prefuimus, licet immeriti et indigni, corditer optassemus prelatos et clerum dicte nostre prouincie a laboriosis et sumptuosis conuocacionibus et vexacionibus preseruare ; ipsosque inquiete fouere, vt altissimo regi regum possint liberius deseruire."

[89] Reg. Courteney, I, fols. 79v.—80.

H

to Archbishop Courteney to summon a convocation before mid-Lent Sunday (March 12th), 1384(-5).[90] The archbishop thereupon wrote a personal letter[91] in French to the king, pointing out the impossibility of fulfilling his request in that the clergy had met so recently, and adding that they would marvel if he called them now, and difficulties would ensue.   He called the king's attention to the terms of the last grant by which no one could or would make a levy upon the clergy until the appointed times of the quindene of Easter and the feast of S. John (the feast of the Nativity of S. John Baptist, June 24th) were past.[91]   The archbishop also wrote in the same vein to the chancellor and treasurer of England in regard to the king's request and urged them to assist him to dissuade the king.[92]   In the same fashion he wrote to the Bishop of Landaff, the king's confessor, asking his counsel should the matter be discussed in his presence.[93]

Just as the archbishops laid stress upon attendance at convocations, so the king in issuing summons to the prelates to appear in parliament was apt to incorporate a warning to them to attend.   In 1328 Edward III, in sending a writ for a parliament at Northampton on April 24th, warned the Archbishop of Canterbury to be present, and stated that he could not admit a proctor for any prelate[94] on account of the arduousness of the

---

[90] Reg. Courteney, I, fol. 82.   Printed in Wilkins, *op. cit.*, III, 185.

[91] *Ibid.*, I, fols. 82—82v.   Printed in Wilkins, *op. cit.*, III, 185—6. *Vide infra*, Appendix D.

[92] *Ibid.*, I, fol. 82v.   Printed in Wilkins, *op. cit.*, III, 186.

[93] *Ibid.*, fols. 82v.—83.   Printed in Wilkins, *op. cit.*, III, 186—7.   The result of the archbishop's efforts at this time will be pointed out in a later chapter.   *Infra*, chapter V, 170—1.

[94] Wilkins, *op. cit.*, II, 545 (Ex reg. Eccles. Cantuar. P., fol. 138b): " ne, quod absit per vestri absentiam expeditionem dictorum negotiorum non absque nostri et totius regni nostri dispendio contingat prorogari diutius seu deferri : scientes pro certo, quod aliquem procuratorem pro vobis seu pro aliquo prelato, vel magnate ad præsens propter arduitatem negotiorum prædictorum admittere non intendimus quoquomodo." *Rep. Dignity of a Peer*, IV, 381.

business. The writ of summons in 1331 to the
Archbishop of Canterbury to a parliament on
September 30th held this admonition, " And since
before these times the common business of our realm
has been frequently retarded to the damage of the
people of our realm on account of the absence of some
prelates and magnates who have come to convocations
and parliaments, not on the appointed days but long
afterwards, we will and enjoin you and command you
that you be before us in every way on the said morrow
at the aforesaid place . . ." [95] The same writ was sent
to the Archbishop of York, nineteen bishops, the Abbot
of S. Augustine's, twenty-six abbots and three priors.[96]
In the summons for a parliament on January 19th,
1348(-9), the king demanded the personal appearance
of the Bishop of London. He declared that he was unwilling to admit proctors for him or to excuse his
absence in any way.[97] The same was sent to sixteen
bishops, twenty-eight abbots, three priors.[98] A special
writ was sent to the Bishop of Worcester stating that he
must be present notwithstanding any concession previously made to him for immunity.[98] To the Archbishop of York was also sent a special writ granting
him permission to send proctors on account of his
weakness in body.[98] The importance of presence in
parliament on the first day was particularly stressed in

[95] *Rep. Dignity of a Peer*, IV, 403: " Et quia ante hec tempora communia regni nostri negocia propter aliquorum prelatorum et magnatum
absenciam qui ad convocaciones et parliamenta hujusmodi non ad dies
statutos set diu postmodum venerunt frequenter retardata fuerunt, ad
commune dampnum populi regni nostri, volumus et vobis injungimius et
mandamus, quod dicto crastino omni modo sitis ad nos ad locum predictum. . . ."

[96] *Ibid.*, IV, 403ff. (From Close Roll, 5 Edw. III, m. 7d.)

[97] *Ibid.*, IV, 578: " Scituri pro certo quod attenta dictorum negociorum arduitate Procuratores aliquos pro vobis seu ex parte vestra ad
diem predictum admittere seu absenciam vestram excusatam habere
nolumus ullo modo."

[98] *Ibid.*, IV, 578ff.

1357.[99] No one who was summoned was to be excused, nor was any excuse to be admitted for not being present on the first day.[99] This clause was used twice this year.[100] A slight concession was made in 1362: no one was to be excused or to be allowed to send a proctor except for a legitimate reason.[101] The same clause appeared in 1363[102] and in 1364.[103] The royal command in January 1370(-1) was somewhat similar.[104] Other instances could be quoted wherein the royal authority insisted on attendance at parliaments, but to do so would be only a repetition. The clauses in the writs which have been cited illustrate sufficiently the urgency of the royal commands.

The royal insistence on obedience to the summons to parliament naturally provokes the question as to what was the penalty meted out to those who were absent or late. The excuses sent by certain prelates for non-attendance at both convocation and parliament have been examined above. Let us see what evidence there is as to what happened to those who did not have legitimate excuses. In regard to clerical obedience to summonses to parliament Archbishop Winchelsey exercised a rigour that was similar to that which he used in regard to obedience to his mandates to convocation. On November 27th, 1311 he sent a commission to the Bishops of Salisbury and Chichester for examining the proxies of the parliament then in

[99] *Rep. Dignity of a Peer,* IV, 611: "Et quia propter arduitatem negociorum predictorum ac celeriorem expedicionem eorumdem volumus primo die parliamenti personaliter interesse, nolumus, nec intendimus vos aut aliquem alium ad dictum parliamentum summonitum, quin eodem primo die personaliter intersitis habere ullo modo excusatos nec excusacionem a vobis admittere aliqualem."

[100] *Ibid.,* IV, 611, 614.

[101] Ibid., IV, 631: "Scientes insuper, quod propter arduitatem negociorum predictorum procuratores, seu excusacionem aliquam legitimo cessante impedimento pro vobis admittere nolumus ista vice."

[102] *Ibid.,* IV, 634.

[103] *Ibid.,* IV, 636.

[104] *Ibid.,* IV, 646.

session.[105] He stated that he was canonically prevented from being present. They were to approve or
to reject the " procuratoria " and excuses presented at
the end (" termino ") of the meeting, just as it should be
done by law.[105] He committed to them full power
with canonical coercion, the penalty to be imposed for
not taking care to appear nevertheless especially reserved to him.[106] Here we find that though the
assembly was the parliament of the realm the clergy
who were summoned to it remained separate from the
laity to the extent that their punishment for absence,
etc. was meted out to them by the archbishop in
accordance with canonical law, or proper coercion was
given to them by his deputies. Whether a similar procedure was always customary it is difficult to gather for
lack of evidence.

In 1344 when parliament assembled on June 7th
many of the magnates were not present, and many of
the bishops who were summoned to the convocation
summoned for the preceding week had not appeared[107]
at the convocation, nor had they come later to the
parliament. The king marvelled at their disobedience.[107] He prayed the archbishop to do towards
clergy who had not come to convocation and had not
obeyed his (the archbishop's) command what belonged
to his right, and he (the king) would take measures
against those who had not come to his parliament, nor
obeyed his command.[107] In the meantime the parliament was to be continued until the following day.[107]

In the discussion of clerical attendance on parliament
it is interesting to note that clergy who refused to obey

[105] *Regist. Simonis de Gandavo* (C. and Y. Soc.), p. 417 (fol. 140).
[106] *Ibid.*, p. 417 (fol. 140): " vobis et alteri vestrum ad approbandum
vel reprobandum procuratorio in termino convocacionis huiusmodi
exhibenda necnon et excusaciones absencium, prout de iure fuerit
faciendum, penitencia tamen canonica comparere non curantibus im-
ponenda nobis specialiter reservata, committimus hac vice cum cohercione
canonica plenariam potestatem."
[107] *Rot. Parl.*, II, 146, n. 1.

a summons to a parliament which was held outside of
their province could not be counted contumacious, nor
be compelled to come.   Archbishop Reynolds stated
this very clearly when in his mandate for a convocation on June 9th, 1322,[108] he referred to a discussion
that had taken place at York in regard to a very necessary grant demanded of the clergy in the parliament
that had assembled there on May 2nd, 1322. He wrote
that " in the present discussions held in regard to this
it was alleged on the part of the clergy that because the
clergy of certain dioceses were at the time absent with
whom they did by no means intend to differ, they would
not give an answer for themselves, especially as those
who were absent could not in this place be imputed or
called according to law contumacious."[109]   And later
in the same mandate he alluded to the fact that a great
part of the clergy were absent who could by no means
be compelled to come outside of their province of
Canterbury.[110]   In the same fashion the clergy of the
province of York refused to come to a great council at
Lincoln on September 15th, 1327, because the council
was to be outside of their province.[111]

The difficulties created by the absence of the clergy
from parliament began to be realized more and more.
Finally at the parliament held at Westminster,

---

[108] Wilkins, *op. cit.*, II, 516 (Ex libro 3, memor. Henr. Burghersh,
Lincoln, episcopi, fol. 54).

[109] *Ibid.*, II, 516 (Ex libro 3, memor. Henr. Burghersh, Lincoln,
episcopi, fol. 54): " Cumque inter præsentes tractatus super hoc habi-
tos extitisset ex parte cleri allegatum quod cum clerus quarumdam
dioec. tunc abesset, a quo præsentes discrepare minime intendebant, circa
hoc responsum dare per se non volebant, præsertim cum iidem absentes
reputari non potuissent in loco ipso aut dici de jure contumaces."

[110] *Ibid.*, II, 516 (Ex libro 3, memor. Henr. Burghersh, Lincoln,
episcopi, fol. 54): " Verum, quia magna pars cleri a loco tractatus tunc
abfuit, ad quem venire, tanquam extra suum territorium provinciam
viz. Cantuar. compelli minime potuit. . . ."

[111] Wake, *op. cit.*, p. 278, n. 3 (from Regist. Melton Arch., Ebor.,
fol. 468): " Per quosdam Excusatores ipsius Cleri nostri extitit Responsum quod idem Clerus apud Lincoln extra Provinciam nostram non
tenebatur Comparere, etc."

September 17th, 1397, " the Commons pointed out to
the king how before this time several judgments and
ordinances made in the time of his forefathers, had
been repealed and annulled because the estate of the
clergy were not present in parliament at the making of
the said judgments and ordinances. And because of
this they prayed the king for surety to his person and
the salvation of his realm that the prelates and clergy
would appoint a proctor with sufficient power to consent in their name to all things and ordinances in this
parliament; and that on this each spiritual lord speak
fully his advice." [112]

An allusion has been made earlier in this chapter to
certain immunities granted to some ecclesiastics by
which they were freed from coming to parliament. [113]
The current attitude towards attendance at parliaments is brought out clearly in such an immunity as
that granted by letters patent in 1341 to the Abbot of
S. Augustine's, Bristol. [114] In this letter the king explained that the Abbot of S. Augustine's, Bristol, had
shown that he did not hold by barony or in any other
manner of the king " in capite," nor was there anything
from the foundation of the king's forefathers or from
the king's (foundation) by which his house should be
lawfully summoned to parliaments or councils. [114] He
likewise pointed out that the abbot or his predecessors
before the tenth year of the king's reign had not,

---

[112] *Rot. Parl.*, III, 348, n. 9 : " Item, mesme le Marsdy les Communes monstrerent au Roy, Coment devant ces heures pluseurs Juggementz, Ordenances faitz en temps des progenitours nre Sr le Roy en
Parlement, ount este repellez et adnullez pur ceo q l'Estat de Clergie ne
feust present en Parlement a la faisaunce des ditz Juggementz et
Ordenances. Et pur ceo prierent au Roi, q pur seurte a sa persone, et
salvation de son Roialme, les Prelatz et le Clergie ferroient un Pro-
curatour, avec poair sufficeant pur consenter en leur noun as toutz choses
et ordenances a justifiers en cest present Parlement ; et q sur ceo chescun
Seignr Espirituel dirroit pleinement son advis."

[113] See *supra*, p. 80, p. 103.

[114] Rymer, *Fœdera* (1816—69 ed.) II, ii, 1158 (Patent Roll, 15 Edw.
III, pt. 1, m. 13).

as was fitting, been summoned to parliaments.[114] In the said tenth year by the manipulation and at the instigation of certain of his rivals and afterwards continuously the same abbot was of his own free will ("voluntarie") summoned to the king's parliaments and councils, and even to this time on the pretext of summons to the king's parliaments and councils of this kind was duly and from day to day burdened.[114] For this cause the abbot begged the king that he would see fit to provide a remedy.[114] And since neither the abbot nor his predecessors had been summoned before the aforesaid tenth year to parliaments and councils of this kind as was evident from the inspection of the rolls of the chancery, out of consideration of the aforesaid, wishing to provide security and quiet for the abbot and his successors, the king willed and granted for himself and his heirs that the said abbot or his successors should by no means be summoned to his parliaments and councils nor on the occasion of their non-appearance at parliaments or councils should they by himself or by his heirs or his heirs' heirs be attacked (" occasionentur "), impeded, molested in any way or burdened.[114] They should nevertheless consent to the proctors sent by the clergy and should contribute to their expenses.[114]

From an appeal of Simon of Ghent, Bishop of Salisbury, to Archbishop Winchelsey in which he asked that he excuse the withdrawal of the proctors of the clergy from the parliament[115] which assembled at Westminster on November 12th, 1311,[116] it is quite easy to draw conclusions as to why the lower clergy were loth to attend parliaments, and why by degrees their activity was transferred more and more from parliament to convocation. The bishop inserted the clergy's appeal

[115] *Reg. S. de Gandavo* (C. and Y. Soc.), p. 418 (fol. 140).
[116] *Cal. C.R.* (1307—13), 5 Edw. II, p. 439. Printed in *Rep. Dignity of a Peer*, III, 210. *Reg. S. de Gandavo* (C. and Y. Soc.), p. 410 (fol. 138).

in a letter[117] to the archbishop, written to notify him of the execution of the commission which the archbishop had entrusted to him.[118]   He said[119] that after he had read aloud in the chapter house of Westminster to the prelates and clergy who, thus summoned, had come thither, the mandate and the certificate of the Bishop of London, the prelates and clergy had declared that although as it seemed to them he had no power to execute at Westminster, a place exempt, an act of such kind as had been committed to him, out of reverence nevertheless for the one commanding it, they had been prepared to obey his (the archbishop's) mandate to be present in the parliament, and to consent to the things to be ordained there.   They further added that since it then appeared that no parliament was meant for them, and since they had not been admitted to certain other discussions which certain prelates and " proceres " had there secretly during two days and afterwards at

[117] *Reg. S. de Gandavo* (C. and Y. Soc.), pp. 417—18 (fol. 140).

[118] *Ibid.*, p. 417 (fol. 140).   The Archbishop of Canterbury had issued a commission to the Bishops of Winchester and Salisbury to examine proxies for him in the parliament.   Cf. *supra*, p. 105, notes 105 and 106.

[119] This part of the letter is of such great significance that it is given here in full: " Hoc igitur mandato et litteris vicarii domini . . . . episcopi Londoniensis super convocacione pretacta certificatoriis, quas cum presentibus vobis transmittimus sigillo dicti vicarii consignatas, in capitulo Westmonasteri per nos prelatis et clero die Jovis predicta comparentibus recitatis ab hiis qui sic vocati venerant dicebatur quod, quamquam apud Westmonasterium, utputa locum exemptum actum huiusmodi nobis commissum, prout eis videbatur, potuissemus nullatenus exercere, ob reverenciam tamen mandantis in parliamento predicto, si quod tunc fuisset et permitteretur eisdem, fuerunt parati mandato vestro parere et dicto parliamento interesse ac ordinandis in eo prout iustum fuerat consencire, verum quia parliamentum aliquod tunc eis minime apparebat et ad quosdam alios tractatus quos cum ministris regiis quidam prelati et proceres ibidem per duos, et apud Sanctum Paulum postmodum per decem, et iterum apud Westmonasterium per duos dies secrete fecerunt, idem clerus nequaquam fuerat admissus, nec sibi per idem tempus super hiis que parliamentum tangere videbantur quicquam ab aliquo dicebatur, quidam ex eis pro tedio, alii vero deficientibus ut conquerebantur sumptibus, infecto pro quo venerant negocio, recesserunt humiliter supplicantes ut ipsos super hiis habere dignaretur vestra paternitas excusatos."

The word " convocacione " here used refers to the parliament (summoned for November 12th, 1311), *not* to a convocation.

S. Paul's for ten and again at Westminster for two days, and since nothing was said to them during the same time in regard to those things which seemed to touch the parliament, certain of them from tedium, others because their funds (" sumptes ") were deficient as they complained, departed, although the business for which they had come was incomplete.[119] They, therefore, humbly beseeched his paternity that he would deem them to have been excused.[119]

The above account offers an instance of the summoning of the clergy to parliament and of their having duly arrived at Westminster to find that their presence was not only unessential for the discussions but not even demanded. And all the time their expenses were accumulating from day to day, while secret discussions between certain prelates and " proceres " dragged on. It is small wonder that under such conditions the clergy wished to avoid going to parliament, and to be free from having to furnish procurations for proctors in both parliament and convocation. It is possible that the seed of discontent with a summons to Westminster was sown among the lower clergy as a result of their treatment at this parliament of 1311. This discontent was to find vigorous expression three years later in the articles[120] presented to Archbishop Reynolds in the purely clerical assembly which met at Westminster in May, 1314. Here again they protested against being summoned to Westminster, and declared that the clergy of the province of Canterbury had by no means been accustomed to being summoned thither.[121] The question presents itself as to what would have been the attitude of the clergy to being called to Westminster in 1314 and in parliaments in general had they been

---

[120] Wilkins, *op. cit.*, II, 442—3 (Ex reg. Eccl. Cantuar. H., fol. 194 seq.).

[121] *Ibid.*, II, 443 (Ex reg. Eccl. Cantuar. H., fol. 194 seq.).

allowed a more vital part in the discussions which took place at Westminster in November 1311.[122] If they had not been altogether ignored then, is there a possibility that the tendency for the clergy to withdraw more and more into convocation would have failed to develop? The question gives one pause.

In addition to their dislike to being called to Westminster, an exempt place (" locum exemptum "),[123] a further annoyance to the clergy was the use of the term " venire faciatis."[124] This was used in 1314.[125] The king the following year altered this form to " convocari faciatis " when issuing a request to the archbishop to hold a convocation.[126] This phrase or one similar to it, i.e. " convenire faciatis,"[127] was used throughout the fourteenth century when a request was sent to the archbishop for a convocation[128] or a writ that he should premonish the clergy to come to parliament.[129]

As we have pointed out elsewhere the tendency was as the fourteenth century progressed for the activity of the clergy to be transferred from parliament to convocation. The continued absence of some of the clergy from parliament, and the insistence on the part of those clergy who were present in parliament that they could not give a definite answer then and there, but would do so in a convocation to be held for that purpose,[130]

---

[122] *Reg. S. de Gandavo* (C. and Y. Soc.), pp. 417—18 (fol. 140).

[123] *Ibid.*, p. 418 (fol. 140). Wilkins, *op. cit.*, II, p. 443 (Ex reg. Eccl. Cantuar. H., fol. 194 seq.).

[124] *Ibid.*, II, p. 443 (Ex reg. Eccl. Cantuar. H., fol. 194 seq.). Cf. *supra*, chapter II, p. 85, n. 14.

[125] *Ibid.*, II, 442 (Ex rot. claus., 7 Edw. II, m. 8d, et reg. Henr. Prior Cantuar., fol. 147).

[126] *Ibid.*, II, 456 (Ex rot. claus., 9 Edw. II, m. 17d, et ex reg. Raynold, fol. 73).

[127] *Ibid.*, II, 558 (Ex rot. claus., 4 Edw. III, m. 38d).

[128] Wilkins, *op. cit.*, II, 516 (Ex rot. claus., 16 Edw. II, m. 20d). Reg. Islep, fol. 42v. Printed in Wilkins, *op. cit.*, III, 16. Reg. Witlesey, fol. 17v. Printed in Wilkins, *op. cit.*, III, 82. Wilkins, *op. cit.*, III, 219 (Ex rot. claus., 16 R. II, m. 23d).

[129] Wilkins, *op. cit.*, II, 563 (Ex rot. claus., 7 Edw. III, pt. 2, m. 8d).

[130] *Vide supra,* chap. II, 61.

forced the king to realize that to gain his end he must yield to their will.

The question of the expenses of clerical proctors for parliament and convocation is closely allied to that of attendance on these two bodies. The archbishops and bishops were aware of this problem and were anxious to spare their clergy labour and expense wherever possible. Many instances in the records reveal a sympathetic attitude on their part whereby they showed themselves the protectors of both the clergy, who were to be taxed for the expenses of the proctors, and of the proctors, who were to receive remuneration for their services.

When a mandate for the provincial council which was appointed to meet January 17th, 1326(-7) reached the Bishop of Lincoln at an inconveniently late date, the bishop, expressing frankly his desire to save his clergy, proposed that the clergy of his diocese grant free power ("potestatem liberam") to their parliamentary proctors (who had been appointed to attend parliament on January 7th, 1326(-7)) to consent to those things which should be ordained in the provincial council.[131] They would thereby be freed from the burden of electing a new set of proctors. This incident is significant not only because it shows the desire on the part of Henry Burghersh, Bishop of Lincoln, to spare his clergy the difficulties of a journey to London at short notice, but also because it reveals in this period a consciousness that there was a duplication of labour then in practice which

[131] Wilkins, *op. cit.*, II, 534 (Ex reg. Burghersh, Lincoln, fol. 152): " Unde licet tempore receptionis mandati supracripti comparitionisque in eodem præfixæ, brevitate pensata difficile quibusdam videri possit, atque tædiosum ad diem comparere assignatum ; quia tamen ex alio latere evidenter prospicimus laboribus cleri nostræ dioec. parci posse in ea parte, et expensis, si eidem mandato juxta possibile pareatur, quod satis commode fieri poterit, si dictus clerus procuratoribus suis pro parliamento jam destinatis, ad consentiendum hiis, quæ in dicto concilio provinciali per cæteros de clero ipsius provinciæ Cantuar. ordinari contigerit seu concedi potestatem liberam transmiserit, et mandatum speciali. Dat. 3 cal. Januarii, M. ccc. xxvi."

might be avoided by the consolidation of the offices of proctor in parliament and of proctor in convocation into one office. The Bishop of Lincoln's proposal is, moreover, of further importance, for it was probably the granting of requests such as his in regard to the use of the same proctors for both parliament and convocation, which led the royal authority in time to the conclusion that there was no need to insist upon the presence of the lower clergy in parliament because frequently their constituents there were the same who represented them in convocation, and that, therefore, as long as the royal needs were supplied, the clergy might just as well be humoured in their preference to make their grants on their spiritualities in convocation rather than in parliament. It is interesting that it was in the decade following this incident in regard to the Lincoln proctors that there began to be a sharp distinction between the grants made in parliament by certain of the clergy who were present there by virtue of their temporalities, and those made in convocation by the clergy on their possessions accustomed to be taxed for a clerical tenth.[132] In the allocation of the latter grants to convocation the clergy had achieved their desire and a larger measure of freedom. Although it cannot be asserted that after 1338 or thereabouts the clergy were thus relieved from the tedium of coming to parliament,[133] the small evidence obtainable bears out the conclusion that after this date the position of the proctors of the lower clergy in parliament was merely nominal in comparison with the position enjoyed by the proctors of the lower clergy in convocation.

Avoidance of further expense had been one of the motives of Bishop Burghersh in suggesting the use of the same proctors for both parliament and convocation.

[132] *Vide supra,* chapter II, 67—8.
[133] *Vide supra,* pp. 69—79.

Twenty years earlier, in 1307, his predecessor in the See of Lincoln, wished to spare the clergy of his diocese from taxation that year for the procurations of their parliamentary proctors.[134] He, therefore, wrote to his archdeacons, saying that while they were waiting for the clergy to be burdened with new contributions and gifts, they should not make an impost upon their clergy for the expenses of clerical proctors in the next parliament, but should provide for their expenses from what remained of the impost made for the clerical proctors sent to the parliament at Carlisle, of which it was reported that a large part remained.[134]

In safeguarding their clergy from burdensome taxation, the bishops, however, did not intend the proctors to suffer. Bishop Grandisson of Exeter showed full appreciation of the proctors' services when in 1334 he issued an order for a levy for the payment of them.[135] Writing to his four archdeacons, he alluded to two proctors who were appointed for the recent provincial council, to whom the rectors, vicars and others holding benefices in the city and diocese should show their gratitude for their labour and merit.[136] He therefore commanded all benefices accustomed to contribute to pay a certain amount at appointed times under penalty of ecclesiastical censures.[137] Similarly in 1384 Thomas

[134] Wake, *op. cit.*, 258, n. 7 (from Lib. Memorand., Jo. Dalderby (Linc.), fol. 192): "Vobis (Archidiaconis) quanto districtius possumus inhibemus, ut attendentes quantum Clerus nostræ Diœceseos contributionibus & præstationibus variis gravatus fuerit—impositione nova pro dictorum Procuratorum sumptibus facienda Clerum ad præsens non Gravetis, si ex residuo impositionis Ultime pro Expensis Procuratorum apud Carliol. missorum, quod penes Vos in quantitate magna Residet, ut Refertur, prospici Valeat Procuratoribus nunc mittendis."

[135] *Reg. Grandisson*, II, 766 (vol. II, fol. 185).

[136] *Ibid.*, II, 766 (vol. II, fol. 185): "Si, igitur, Ecclesiarum Rectores, Vicarii, et ceteri Beneficiati ejusdem nostre Civitatis et Diocesis gratanter advertant dictorum Procuratorum in hoc laborem et meritum non equidem erit eis molestum, quinimmo placidum atque gratum, si modis utique non onerosis set decentibus et licitis *(sic)*, dictis Procuratoribus satisfieri de procuracione debita provide Pastorali presidio jubeamus."

[137] *Ibid.*, II, 766 (vol. II, fol. 185).

Brantyngham, another Bishop of Exeter, issued a mandate to his archdeacons for the levy of procurations for the clerical proctors of the Exeter diocese in the last convocation. These proctors, who had not been fully satisfied with a recompense for their labours, had sought a remedy from the bishop. [138] The bishop, showing the utmost sympathy for those who had endured such labours and expense, declared that they should receive their due. [139] Wherefore he commanded the levy of the usual payment under penalty of excommunication.

The records mentioned in the preceding chapter, which have recently been brought to light, of the bailiff's accounts for the manor of Gamlingay in Cambridgeshire, [140] with their entries of payments by the parish of Gamlingay in the diocese of Ely for clerical proctors in parliament and convocation show that there was a continuous system of taxation (sometimes intermittent) for the expenses of clerical proctors in the period from 1294(—5) to 1373(—4). [141] It may be

---

[138] *Reg. Brantyngham*, I, 524—5 (vol. I, fol. 120b).

[139] *Ibid.*, I, 524 (vol. I, fol. 120b): "Cumque iidem Nicholaus et Thomas, Procuratores predicti, in Convocacione predicta nomine tocius Cleri nostrarum Civitatis et Diocesis predictarum et pro eo comparuissent, et in eadem ad utilitatem Ecclesie Anglicane et Regni Anglie per non modice Tempora pro viribus institissent indefesse, sub gravibus eorum laboribus, sumptibus, et expensis; fecissetque et sit ex parte eorundem nobis expositum quod ipsis pro hujusmodi laboribus, sumptibus, et expensis suis nullatenus extiterat satisfactum; super quibus de oportuno petierunt eis per nos remedio provideri; nos igitur, attendentes juri aut racioni consonum non extare quod quis dampnum senciat unde meruit premiari, aut quod debeat quis stipendii propriis militare; in recompensacionem aliqualem, licet pusillam suorum hujusmodi sumptuum et laborum, et si Clerum noverimus diversis gravaminibus plus solito nunc offici et jacturis, eorum peticioni justicia previa, duximus annuendum."

[140] Lowry, *op. cit.*, pp. 443—55, *passim*. Cf. *supra*, p. 64.

[141] *Ibid.*, p. 448. Mrs. Lowry lists an entry "in expensis Petri Clerici eundo et redeundo ad Parliamentum" for 1280(—1), but one ventures to suggest that further evidence is needed to show that this proctor was a proctor for the same purpose, for which the others were, who are mentioned in these accounts as proctors for subsequent parliaments and convocations. As has been stated previously the diocesan clergy were not called to parliament until 1295. Terminology was, however, so fluid, "parliamentum" may have been used to refer to an ecclesiastical assembly as sometimes happened. Cf. *infra*, chapter IV, 122, n. 25.

suggested that similar entries of the payment of expenses for clerical proctors for other dioceses during this period would probably be found if other records alike in character to those of the manor of Gamlingay were extant and available for investigation. What was the scope of the activity of proctors such as these of the diocese of Ely when sent to parliament in the period after the first decade of Edward III's reign it is impossible to say. Of the part played by them and their kind in convocation during the fourteenth century there is more definite information. [142]

An attempt has been made in the discussion in this chapter to point out that the problem of attendance on parliaments and convocations was one that affected all degrees of the clergy. In this period there was no idea of a " quorum " in the modern sense. The current theory was that no one was held to contribute to a grant who had not consented to it either in person or by proxy. If funds were to be raised, it was, therefore, most important to have a full attendance at the assemblies summoned to grant them. It became essential for the king and the archbishop to insist on attendance with threats of punishment. The archbishops, however, were not unconscious of the burden entailed upon the clergy by attendance nor unsympathetic in regard to it. They felt it incumbent upon them to protect their clergy against too frequent meetings of convocation. The individual diocesan bishops assumed the responsibility of seeing to it that those who gave their services as proctors for convocations or parliaments were fully recompensed by the clergy whom they represented. It is not difficult to understand the point of view of the clergy. Even when they were not burdened with personal attendance, assemblies meant to them not only payment for the

[142] *Vide infra,* chapters IV and V.

salaries of the clergy who should represent them, but new taxes that could be levied upon their spiritualities. Loth as they were to attend such gatherings for these purposes or to send proctors, it is not strange that they bent their efforts towards transferring their greater activity to convocation where at least their influence could be more weighty and where they would have a greater chance to influence the terms of a grant.

CHAPTER IV

PROCEDURE IN THE CONVOCATION OF THE PROVINCE OF CANTERBURY DURING THE THIRTEENTH AND FOURTEENTH CENTURIES

A DISCUSSION of the procedure of convocation demands first a definition of the word " convocation."[1] It is well known that terminology was still fluid during the period covered by this study. For ecclesiastical assemblies in the second half of the thirteenth century and in the fourteenth century the terms " convocacio " and " concilium provinciale " were both used. Sometimes even the word " parliamentum " was employed for a reference to what is known to have been distinctly an ecclesiastical assembly.[2] It must be acknowledged that it is difficult to draw a line between a convocation and a provincial council. It cannot be said that the former was limited to secular matters, nor that the latter was called for purely ecclesiastical affairs. Evidence in the accounts of these gatherings support this statement. In such instances as when the clergy were dealing with secular problems like the Duchy of Aquitaine,[3] and the petition of the Despensers for the repeal of their sentence,[4] the assembly was called a provincial council.

---

[1] A fuller treatment of the nomenclature of ecclesiastical assemblies is given by Dr. I. J. Churchill in her recent work, *Canterbury Administration*, I, 364—6 ; II, Appendix G, 168—70. My conclusions in regard to the interchangeability of the two terms, " convocacio " and " concilium provinciale " were formed independently before reading Dr. Churchill's discussion as to their usage.

[2] The usage referred to was probably due to a thoughtless scribe. Cf. *infra*, p. 122, n. 25.

[3] P.R.O., Ancient Correspondence, vol. XXXV, n. 99. P.R.O., Close Roll 4 Edw. II, pt. 2, m. 16.

[4] *The Register of Walter de Stapeldon*, Bishop of Exeter, 1307—1326, ed. F. C. Hingeston-Randolph, pp. 441—2 (fol. 215b). Wilkins, *op. cit.*, II, 509—10 (Ex reg. Stapeldon Exon.).

On the other hand, ecclesiastical matters were discussed in gatherings called convocations which are known to have been summoned at the king's request primarily for money-granting purposes.[5] Wake and Wilkins sometimes distinguished between convocation and a provincial council, but at other times they used the terms interchangeably.[6] In that the Archbishops of Canterbury themselves employed the two words on a par such as when Witlesey used the expressions " concilium siue conuocacio prouincialis "[7] and " in Concilio seu conuocacione prouinciali,"[8] and Courteney the terminology " Concilium prouinciale seu conuocacio,"[9] it must be admitted the two words were interchangeable in the current usage of the fourteenth century. Because of this, it is safer for us to-day not to draw a distinction between the two types of assembly. Convocation then in this study may refer in its narrowest sense to the assembly called by the archbishop at the king's request for money-granting purposes, or it may be used in a broader sense to denote an ecclesiastical or provincial council which was concerned with both the affairs of Church and State.

PART I

Procedure before and after the Meeting of Convocation

WHEN a convocation in the province of Canterbury was to be summoned the archbishop sent his mandate to the Bishop of London, who was dean of the

[5] Reg. Courteney, I, fol. 33—4v. Cal. C.R. (1381—85), 6 R. II, pp. 209—10.
[6] Wake, op. cit., 269—70, 272 et passim. Wilkins, op. cit., II, III, passim.
[7] Churchill, op. cit., II, Appendix G, 168 (from Reg. Witlesey, fol. 22b).
[8] Ibid., II, Appendix G, 168 (from Reg. Witlesey, fol. 64).
[9] Ibid., II, Appendix G, 169 (from Reg. Courteney, fol. 35).

province.[10] If the convocation was called at the archbishop's initiative alone, he mentioned in his mandate the purpose of the convocation.[10] If it was called by papal authority, that was mentioned.[11] If, however, it was called at the king's request, the archbishop might follow one of three courses. He might incorporate the king's writ into his mandate, he might give in his own words the substance of the king's writ, or he might merely allude to the king's request or writ. There are, of course, many convocations for which there are no records of mandates extant, and for the summoning of which consequently the method used cannot be known. Let us consider the use of the various methods in certain of the mandates which have survived. The incorporation of the king's writ was employed by Archbishop

[10] Wilkins, *op. cit.*, II, 30 (Ex reg. Giffard Wigorn, fol. 71). Calendared in *Wor. Epis. Registers (Reg. Giffard)*, II, 93 (71d). If the See of London was vacant, the Bishop of Winchester acted as sub-dean of the province of Canterbury. Archbishop Parker (*Antiq. Eccl. Brit.* (1729 ed.) p. 31) quotes a letter from the Bishop of Winchester in 1284 to Archbishop Pecham in which the following passages occur: " Præminentiæ vestræ litteras per harum bajulum nobis missas recepimus undecima die mensis Decembris, quæ mixturam quandam doloris & gaudii continebant: Ingerit nimirum animo nostro mœstitiam, quod hominem Deo gratum, justum, mansuetum & pium & hiis diebus malis regno Angliæ tam necessarium, bonæ memoriæ Dominum Richardum London Episcopum ab hac luce mors amara subtraxit; sed materiam gaudii & consolationis subministrat, quod excellentiam vestram ad nostra & ecclesiæ nostræ Wyntoniensis jura conservanda & augenda litterarum earundem relatu cognovimus quadam specialis delectionis prærogativa solicitam & intentam; pro quo vestræ dignitationi grates, licet exiles & tantis meritis impares, quantas pro tempore possumus, exhibemus. . . . Quod ejus vices, eo mortuo vel absente, gerere & exequi ad nos tanquam ad vestrorum Suffraganeorum Subdecanum jure consuetudinario dicitis pertinere; consultis nostris dilectis filiis Priore & Capitulo nostro Wyntoniensi, cum omini celeritate accomoda absque moræ dispendio rescribemus: firmum semper habentes propositum & promptum gerentes animum ad vestra præcepta & beneplacita exequenda."
Parker states as his source " Ex Archetypo."
B.M. MS. Add. Ch. 36449. Letters which are found here in regard to the consecration of Eustachius de Faukunberg to the bishopric of London (in 1221), mention the Bishop of London as dean of the province of Canterbury, the Bishop of Winchester as sub-dean, and the Bishop of Salisbury precentor, and next in succession in the matter of prerogative. For this reference I am indebted to Prof. J. C. Russell.

[11] Reg. Winchelsey, fol. 128v. Printed in Wilkins, *op. cit.*, II, 311—12. Reg. Islep, fols. 170—170v.

Pecham for the assembly held on Jan. 20th, 1282(–3). This, however, was not a purely ecclesiastical assembly at Northampton.[12] The same method was again used for the assembly summoned before the king's commissioners on September 21st, 1294.[13] Again, the archbishop incorporated the king's writ in his mandate for the assembly on the morrow of the Ascension, May 17th, 1314.[14] There appears to be no evidence of incorporation occurring again until the Prior of Christ Church, Canterbury, during the vacancy of the See of Canterbury, made use of it in his mandate for a convocation on January 10th, 1333(–4).[15] After this, a record of incorporation of the king's writ has not again been found until Archbishop Islep inserted the king's writ in his mandate when he called a convocation for May 2nd, 1351.[16] In the period, however, from 1359 to 1395 the practice of incorporating the king's writ seems to have been used with a certain degree of regularity.[17]

The method of quoting the substance of the king's writ was introduced for the convocation which Archbishop Reynolds summoned on July 8th, 1314.[18] It was a definite step on the part of the archbishop to avoid offending the clergy who had resented his incorporation of the king's writ in a summons for an assembly on

---

[12] Reg. Pecham, fol. 82v. Printed *Regist. Epist. J. Peckham*, II, 486—8. Wilkins, *op. cit.*, II, 91—2 (Ex reg. Giffard, Wigorn, fol. 166). Calendared in *Worc. Epis. Reg.*, II, 187 (Reg. Giffard, fol. 166d).

[13] Wilkins, *op. cit.*, II, 201 (Ex reg. Henr. prior. Cantuar., fol. 63a).

[14] Wilkins, *op. cit.*, II, 442 (Ex rot. claus 7 Edw. II, m. 8d., et reg. prior. Cantuar., fol. 147).

[15] Wilkins, *op. cit.*, II, 563 (Ex reg. Eccles. Cant. P., fol. 8, et ex rot. claus 7 Edw. III, p. 2, m. 8d).

[16] Reg. Islep, fol. 42v. Printed in Wilkins, *op. cit.*, III, 16—17.

[17] Reg. Islep, fol. 155v. Printed in Wilkins, *op. cit.*, III, 44—5. Reg. Witlesey, fol. 17v. Printed in Wilkins, *op. cit.*, III, 82. Reg. Witlesey, fol. 40v. *Ibid.*, fol. 63. Reg. Sudbury, fols. 30v., 31. *Ibid.*, fol. 58v. *Ibid.*, fol. 70v. Reg. Courteney, I, fol. 33. Reg. Courteney, II, fols. 195—195v.

[18] Reg. Reynolds, fols. 105v.—106. Printed in Wilkins, *op. cit.*, II, 444—5.

May 17th (the morrow of Ascension), 1314.[19]   A similar procedure of quoting the substance was used by Reynolds for the convocation summoned for November 4th, 1327.[20]

The third method used may be seen in the mandates for convocations on June 25th, 1298,[21] and April 26th, 1357,[22] in which there was merely an allusion to the king's writ.   In summoning a convocation for April 25th, 1316 Archbishop Reynolds did not mention a royal writ, but in giving perils of the times as a reason for the need of assembling, he also declared that he had been stirred to do so, by the prayers of the king (" preciis regiis ad id nihilominus ").[23]   It is known definitely, however, that the king had issued a writ to the archbishop requesting that he summon a convocation.[24]

When a mandate from the Archbishop of Canterbury in the form of any of those which have just been described was received by the Bishop of London, the latter incorporated it *in toto* into the letters which he thereupon issued to his fellow bishops of the province.[25] In these letters he instructed the bishops to execute the archbishop's mandate in regard to summoning the various clergy of their dioceses to convocation, and to certify the archbishop by their letters patent of their

---

[19] *Supra*, chapter II, 58—9.

[20] Reg. Reynolds, fol. 207.   Printed in Wilkins, *op. cit.*, II, 538—9.

[21] Reg. Winchelsey, fol. 242v.   Printed in *Reg. Winchelsey* (C. and Y. Soc.), p. 250 ; also Wilkins, *op. cit.*, II, 236.

[22] Reg. Islep, fol. 131.   Printed in Wilkins, III, 41.

[23] Wilkins, *op. cit.*, II, 456—7 (Ex reg. Henr. prior. Cantuar., fol. 168).

[24] Reg. Reynolds, fol. 73—73v.   Printed in Wilkins, *op. cit.*, II, 456. *Cal. C.R.* (1313—18), 9 Edw. II, p. 325.

[25] *Registrum Stephani Gravesend Episcopi Londoniensis*, ed. R. C. Fowler (C. and Y. Soc.), pp. 203—6 (fol. 42d).   Here is an illustration of the incorporation of the archiepiscopal mandate by the Bishop of London in a letter of summons to a convocation at London on April 19th, 1319.   The scribe has entitled this " convocacio ad Parliamentum." This meeting, however, was a convocation.   Parliament was summoned for a later day (May 6th, 1319), at York.   *Cal. C.R.* (1318—23), 12 Edw. II, p. 131.

execution of the same. [26]   After he had issued letters to
the bishops, the Bishop of London later had to certify
the archbishop on the day of convocation at the place
of meeting, stating the day on which he had received
his mandate, and his manner of executing the same,
and enclosing in a separate schedule a list of those
whom he had cited. [26]   After receiving the Bishop of
London's letter it was the task of each bishop to see to
it that the clergy of his diocese were summoned for the
election of their proctors for convocation.   An instance
showing the execution of the archbishop's mandate
contained in the letter which he had received from the
Bishop of London is the mandate sent by Bishop
Brantyngham of Exeter to the Dean and Chapter of
Exeter and to the archdeacons of the diocese to come to
the cathedral of Exeter on May 23rd (the Monday after
the feast of S. Dunstan), 1373 to a meeting which was
preparatory to the convocation to be held in London
on May 30th. [27]   The names of the cited and the list of
the proctors chosen as a result of the Exeter meeting
were later sent enclosed in a schedule to the Archbishop
of Canterbury. [28]

Those summoned to a full convocation of the
province of Canterbury included the archbishop of the
province, his suffragans or their vicars-general, the
bishops, confirmed and elect, the deans and priors of
cathedral churches, abbots and priors elective, exempt
and non-exempt, archdeacons—all personally, and the
chapters, convents and colleges by one proctor, the
clergy of each diocese by two proctors. [29]   By the last
quarter of the fourteenth century the list of the summoned had become uniform. [30]   During the latter part

[26] *Reg. Gravesend,* p. 205 (fol. 42d).   The letter in which the Bishop of
London reported to the Archbishop of Canterbury the execution of his
mandate was called the certificate ("certificatorium").
[27] Reg. Brantyngham, I, 302 (vol. I, fols. 35—35b).
[28] *Ibid.*, I, 304 (vol. I, fol. 36).
[29] Reg. Sudbury (Cant.), fol. 70v.   [30] Cf. chart, Appendix A.

of the thirteenth century and during the fourteenth century there were sometimes variations. [30]   Occasionally other dignitaries were summoned, such as chancellors, treasurers, precentors and " prepositi." [31]

Besides the full convocations, however, there were from time to time councils at which were present only the archbishop and bishops of his province. [32]   The last quarter of the thirteenth century held a number of this type. [33]   In the fourteenth century the councils summoned for May 4th, 1346, May 7th, 1361 and November 16th, 1378 stand alone as councils which comprised only the archbishop and his suffragans. [33]

When the convocation was over, if the business of it had been concerned with a grant to the king, the archbishop sent a letter to the king stating the amount of the grant, the terms, the dates of payments, and the conditions on which the grant was made. [34]   If the clergy had failed to make a grant, he might in his letter simply state the substance of the discussion of the convocation. [35]   After receiving the archbishop's letter telling him of a grant, the king then replied to the archbishop and wrote letters to the various bishops quoting the terms of the grant as the archbishop had stated them, and asking them to appoint collectors in their respective dioceses and to notify the Treasurer and Barons of the Exchequer of the names of the collectors by a certain date. [36]   This the archbishop and bishops [37] did after notifying the various collectors of their appointment. [38]

[31] Reg. Winchelsey, fol. 205.   Printed in *Reg. Winchelsey* (C. and Y. Soc.), p. 146.   Printed Wilkins, *op. cit.*, II, 219—20.
[32] Councils in 1279(—80), 1280, 1281, 1281(—2), 1282, 1286, 1287.
[33] Cf. chart, Appendix A.
[34] P.R.O., Ancient Correspondence, vol. XLIII, n. 27.
[35] Reg. Islep, fols. 126v.—127.   Reg. Winchelsey, fol. 222v.   Printed in *Reg. Winchelsey* (C. and Y. Soc.), pp. 189—90.
[36] P.R.O., Exchequer K.R. Ecclesiastical, Bundle 10, n. 15.   P.R.O., Subsidy Roll 3, n. 6.
[37] P.R.O., Subsidy Roll 8, n. 2a.   P.R.O., Subsidy Roll 15, n. 8c.
[38] P.R.O., Subsidy Roll 24, n. 2.

PART II

Procedure during the Convocation

Full accounts of the procedure followed in the Convocation of the Province of Canterbury do not appear with even moderate regularity in the archiepiscopal registers until the middle of the fourteenth century. Perhaps if the registers of Archbishops Simon Mepeham, John Stratford and Thomas Bradwardine were extant, accounts would be found in them entitled "Acta Convocacionis." There is material, however, concerning the procedure of three convocations of the province of Canterbury before the middle of the fourtenth century.

The first description is of a convocation that met on November 25th, 1309. Winchelsey's register holds a brief account of it,[39] but the fullest description comes from a register of the cathedral church of Canterbury[40] and gives the proceedings in great detail. The account is prefaced by the information that on the day appointed for the convocation, November 25th, the archbishop heard mass privately at Lambeth, and then set forth, going via Southwark, over the bridge, and through the city to S. Paul's, where the council was to be held.[41] All the bishops present were clad in sacred vestments and "cappa chori." The Bishop of Norwich, the archbishop being opposite him, celebrated mass and gave "solemn benediction."[41] After the mass, the archbishop, sitting on a great throne in front of the high altar, preached from a text in Acts xx., "Attendite vobis et subditis vestris." When the sermon was over, the assembly adjourned until the following day, Tuesday.[41] This day was given over to the reading of

[39] Reg. Winchelsey, fol. 125.
[40] Wilkins, *op. cit.*, II, 312-14 (Ex reg. Eccl. Cantuar. P., fol. 34 seq.).
[41] *Ibid.*, II, 312.

the apostolic letters by the authority of which the council was summoned.[41]   Then followed the reading of the certificate (" certificatorium ") of the Bishop of London, concerning the citation of suffragans, abbots, priors, chapters, colleges and clergy, and the letters of excuse of the absent.[41]   Three knights of the king's council then made certain prohibitions, reading the royal letter[42] in which the king warned the ecclesiastical council to do nothing to the prejudice of his rights.   At this point ended the business of the second day.

On the third day, Wednesday, the assembly met in the church of the brothers of Mount Carmel.[43]   The bishops and clergy of each diocese were requested to have ready in writing the grievances suffered by the Church and ecclesiastical persons.[43]   Since many were not yet prepared to do so, the meeting was adjourned until Saturday, each bishop being told to discuss with the clergy of his diocese the articles of grievance and to hand the result of the discussions in written form to the archbishop.[43]

On Saturday all the bishops by common counsel and assent handed in the articles of grievance and certain supplications to the pope, asking for a remedy of them.[43]   These were read aloud, and later the bishops presented other articles to the archbishop to be shown to the king in an appeal for redress.[43]   Since all articles were not ready, the meeting adjourned until the Monday next.[44]

On this day the archbishop was prevented by illness from attending.   The council, therefore, adjourned to assemble the next day at Lambeth.[44]   There in the " camera " of the archbishop, in the presence of the archbishop and the suffragan bishops appointed as

---

[42] Wilkins, *op. cit.*, II, 312—13.
[43] *Ibid.*, II, 313.
[44] *Ibid.*, II, 313.

inquisitors by the pope, depositions were made in
regard to the crimes attributed to the Templars.[44] A
copy of these reports was demanded for the several
bishops.[44] Whereupon the meeting adjourned.[44]

On the next day, Wednesday, still at Lambeth, it
was ordained that three bishops should be appointed
together with the inquisitors, to go to the king to ask
for permission to carry on further investigation of the
crimes of the Templars.[44] Two clerks skilled in canon
and civil law were to examine and extract all articles
of grievances of each bishop and the clergy of his
diocese, touching the king, and those to be expedited in
the provincial council.[44] Six other clerks were
appointed to write down these articles in legal form.[44]
The council adjourned to the following day, Thursday,
when they met again at S. Paul's.[45] A constitution of
Archbishop Boniface was read and later the charter of
the Blessed Thomas Martyr. To these they subscribed.
Then the bishops, priors, deans and proctors of the
clergy were requested to remain.[45] The rest were
allowed to depart after appointing a proctor in their
name to consent to all things.[45] A multitude of the
religious and others took their leave and were to await
a mandate from the archbishop for another council.[45]
The former council was adjourned to the next day,
Friday, to meet at Lambeth, where discussion centred
now upon the king's business.[45] Then the council adjourned until Sunday to meet at the same place.[45] On
this day petitions were ordained to be made to the king
in regard to the Templars and in regard to certain
grievances.[45] The following day all articles of
grievances concerning the king were recited.[45] On
Tuesday the suffragans and inquisitors approached the
king for permission to proceed farther against the
Templars.[46] The king gave this permission on condi-

[45] *Ibid.*, II, 313.　　　　[46] *Ibid.*, II, 313—14.

tion that they should do nothing against the Crown or the State of the realm.[47]   On the same day the archbishop and bishops were told by the king to come to Westminster the following day, Thursday.[47]   Thursday and Friday brought a delay in the business of the council on account of the discussions at Westminster,[47] but on Saturday the business of the provincial council was continued. A certain form was then ordained for citing to appear for examination all the Templars in the several dioceses, and likewise, the apostates.[47]

There was no business on the Monday following for the prelates were at the king's council.[47]   On Tuesday the Bishops of Winchester and Norwich presented to the king the grievances of the Church of England (" ecclesiae Anglicanæ "[47]). The next day, since the inquisitors were preparing to leave to examine certain Templars in the dioceses of York and Lincoln, the council was adjourned until the following autumn, the Tuesday after the feast of S. Matthew.[47]

The second convocation of the province of Canterbury from which may be learned something of procedure, was summoned to Lincoln on the feast of S. Hilary (January 13th), 1322(-3).[48]   In this account nothing is said of the opening ceremonies which were undoubtedly held.   It is stated, however, that the religious and clergy held a common deliberation in regard to an aid for the king which had been requested of them by the Archbishop.[49]   After their deliberation, an answer was presented to the archbishop by the abbots, priors, deans of cathedral churches, archdeacons and proctors of the chapters and clergy of the province of Canterbury.[49] They repeated the grievances of which they had complained in 1314, and concluded

---

[47] Wilkins, op. cit., II, 314.
[48] B. M. Cotton MS. Faustina A. V., fols. 2v.—3.
[49] Ibid., fols. 3v.—4. Printed in Wilkins, op. cit., II, 517—18.

by refusing to grant an aid to the king because he had already been granted two-tenths by the pope. [49]

The third convocation of the province of Canterbury before the middle of the fourteenth century, from which can be gleaned a few details concerning procedure, comes from a fourteenth century chronicle. The council here described was the first council held by Archbishop Simon Mepeham. It met on January 27th, 1328(-9), at S. Paul's. [50] At earliest dawn the Bishop of Chichester celebrated the Mass of the Holy Spirit, with prelates and abbots standing around clad in pontifical robes. [50] After mass the *Veni Creator* was sung. [50] Then the archbishop preached a long sermon to the clergy. [50] The reading of the certificate of the Bishop of London in regard to the citation of the clergy concluded the acts of the first day. [50] We are told that they assembled there each day treating concerning the statutes of the Church of England. [50] Evidently this continued for some days, for the next item mentioned by the chronicler took place on February 10th, the feast of S. Scholastica, the Mass for Peace (" Missa de pace ") was celebrated by the Bishop of Norwich, the bishops and other prelates and the whole clergy being present. [50] After the gospel the archbishop and all the bishops and other prelates, standing before the altar clad in pontifical robes and holding candles uplifted, excommunicated all those who killed the Bishop of Exeter [51] or laid violent hands on him; and similarly all those who plundered the abbot of S. Edmunds and the monks of S. Edmunds by fire and similarly the abbey of Abingdon, and all who carried off ecclesiastical goods or committed sacrilege. [52] In this council it was determined that the feast of the Conception of

[50] *Chronicles of the Reigns of Edward I and Edward II (Annales Paulini)*, I 344.

[51] Walter Stapeldon, Bishop of Exeter, 1307—1326.

[52] *Chronicles of the Reigns of Edward I and Edward II (Annales Paulini)*, I, 344—5.

the Blessed Mary should be solemnly celebrated in all churches of England, and that on the day of Parasceve (i.e. Good Friday) everyone should refrain from all manual work.[53]   As this account comes from a chronicler we should naturally not expect to find a detailed description of procedure.   It may be inferred, however, that deliberations were carried forward in the ordinary manner.

The next description of a convocation of the province of Canterbury comes from Archbishop Simon Islep's register, and recounts the convocation that took place at S. Paul's, London, on May 16th, 1356.[54]   At this assembly the archbishop himself celebrated mass at the high altar.[55]   There were present the Bishops of London, Exeter, Ely and Rochester, all clad in pontifical robes.[55]   The archbishop also preached the sermon on this occasion.[55]   Other bishops in session were those of Winchester, Lincoln and St. Asaph.[55]   Proctors are mentioned[55]—evidently those of the absent bishops. When the sermon was concluded, nothing more was done on the first day.

The following day the archbishop and bishops assembled in the chapel of the Blessed Virgin Mary, Mother of God, with the proctors of the absent bishops, who bore certificates which showed the execution of the Bishop of London's mandate which had been issued at the mandate of the archbishop.[55]   Present also were seven men, several of them titled, who appeared there on behalf of the king.[55]   Among these men were the Justiciar, the Seneschal of the King's Household, and the Keeper of the Privy Seal.[55]   When one of them had declared a prohibition, which was similar in content to the royal warning which had been given to the council in 1309, against anything being done in the council to

[53] *Chron. Edward I and Edward II, I, 345.*
[54] Reg. Islep, fols. 117—117v.
[55] *Ibid.,* fol. 117.

the prejudice of the king or the realm, another made a request that a grant of a tenth for six years be made to the king by the prelates and the clergy of the province of Canterbury, and that the whole should be paid within three years. [56]

After this request there followed the preconization openly and publicly of all those cited in the Bishop of London's certificate. [56] The archbishop and bishops then withdrew into the chapter house to hold a discussion. [56] The abbots, priors, deans and others with the proctors of the clergy remained by themselves. [57] After an interval the latter appeared in the presence of the lord bishop [58] and other bishops. [59] The council, however, was adjourned until the next day. In doing so the archbishop enjoined the religious and others of the clergy to propose their petitions the next day. [59]

The following day the entire body assembled in the chapter house. The Bishop of Hereford appeared late on this day and certified for his diocese. [59] A proposal was made that for certain petitions there should be one speaker as well as one writing. [59] An altercation took place in regard to the Bishop of Lincoln's certificate. [59] Petitions were later proposed and discussed. [59] The assembly was then adjourned by the archbishop until the following day when they again met in the chapter house. [59] Another certificate of the Bishop of Lincoln for the council was shown of like tenour with the first

[56] *Ibid.*, fol. 117.

[57] *Ibid.*, fols. 117—117v.: "Archiepiscopo vero predicto et ceteris episcopis in domium capitularem ecclesie Sancti Pauli predicte se dimittentibus et ibidem tractantibus. Abbatibus Prioribus decanis et aliis vna cum procuratoribus cleri in dicta domo capitulari remanentibus et post intervallum temporis coram prefato domino Episcopo et suis cœpiscopis predictis comparentibus."

It will be seen that the scribe has evidently made an error in his wording as the abbots, priors, etc. could not remain in the chapter house and then go to the bishops who had withdrawn to the chapter house.

[58] *Ibid.*, fol. 117v. The scribe has probably made another error here as he undoubtedly means the archbishop. Cf. preceding note for a quotation from the register.

[59] *Ibid.*, fol. 117v.

which revealed that he had called those of his diocese
to the council by his own authority rather than by the
archbishop's.[59]   A third, however, was brought forth
showing that he had duly executed the archbishop's
mandate.[59]   The lord of Lincoln promised that his cita-
tions should be obediently drawn up and ordained.[60]
After certain petitions had been read and answered,
the council adjourned until the morrow. The following
day the archbishop could not be present on account of
illness.[60]   He, therefore, commissioned the Bishop of
London to preside in his stead—an act which we have
not met hitherto.[60]   When the commission had been
read in the chapter house to the bishops and clergy, the
Bishop of London adjourned the council until the
following day.[60]

The archbishop appeared the next day with the
bishops and clergy in the chapter house.[60]   After the
reading and discussion of petitions the council was
adjourned until the Monday following.[60]   On Monday
the clergy gave their answer to the king's request.[60]   In
their reply, which we shall consider in the next chapter
of this study, they gave explicit reasons why they did
not feel it incumbent upon them to give a grant to the
king.[60]   At the pressure of the archbishop and other
bishops, the clergy were persuaded to deliberate further
that they might give a better answer to the king.[61]
The council was adjourned until the morrow. Then
the clergy gave a final answer in which they granted
one tenth—one moiety to be paid at the feast of
S. Andrew (November 30th).[62]   They stipulated that
before the second moiety should be paid, their
grievances should be reformed.[62]   When this was done
the other moiety would be paid.[62]   A further condition
was added that those in evident need should not be
taxed for the tenth.[62]

[60] Reg. Islep, fol. 117v.   [61] *Ibid.*, fol. 117v.   [62] *Ibid.*, fol. 118.

When the archbishop had pronounced all those con-tumacious who had been summoned to the council and had not attended, the council came to an end.[62] The form of punishment for the contumacious was reserved to the archbishop.[62]

In comparing this council with those of 1309, 1322(-3) and 1328(-9), certain points in common may be noted. In three instances the council began with mass and a sermon on the opening day. In one of the councils the Bishop of London's certificate was read on the first day, whereas in two it was read on the second. In three councils there was separation for discussion. In the council in November 1309, the bishops went apart to discuss respectively with the clergy of their dioceses. In the councils of 1322(-3) and 1356 the archbishop and bishops withdrew to deliberate, while the abbots, priors and proctors of the clergy formed another group. The councils of 1309 and 1356 are alike in their prolonged sessions from day to day.

The convocation held at S. Paul's, London, January 21st, 1369(-70),[63] was similar to that of 1356 in pro-cedure except that mass was celebrated in the chapel of the Blessed Virgin Mary rather than at the high altar.[63] Much more, too, was accomplished on the first day than previously. Not only was mass celebrated, followed by a sermon,[63] but the king's commissioners were received and the Bishop of London's certificate read.[64] The archbishop empowered his chancellor or the auditor of cases to receive and examine the certi-ficates and proxies (" procuratoria "). After these had been presented, the meeting was adjourned until the following day to assemble in the chapter house.[64] When the examination of the proxies had been com-pleted by the archbishop's commissaries, there was a

[63] Reg. Witlesey, fol. 22v.
[64] Ibid., fol. 23.

K

discussion concerning an aid to the king.[64]   Then the
archbishop requested the religious to withdraw to treat
by themselves in another part of the church and the
clergy also to withdraw to treat by themselves in still
another part, and to report the result of their deliberations on the following day.[64]   Here there is yet a
different grouping for deliberation from any hitherto
noted. The archbishop then pronounced contumacious
all secular and religious who were held to appear and
had not appeared in this convocation.[65]   It will be
remembered that the act of pronouncing contumacious
in the convocation of 1356 did not take place until the
end of the council.   Now in 1369(–70) it was given on
the second day. The clergy reported their grant to the
archbishop the next day in the chapel of the Blessed
Mary, though they had been asked to assemble in the
chapter house.[65]   As in 1356 they stipulated that the
grant should be paid only on the condition that certain
grievances which were to be put in writing and handed
by the archbishop to the king should be reformed.[66]
Those of impoverished benefices should be free from
making the grant.[66]   The archbishop commanded the
clergy and religious to put their grievances in writing
and to present them to him the following day in the
chapel, so that when he had deliberated in regard to
them with his confrères (brother bishops) he could
present them.[66]   Here again as in 1309 the demand
was made that the grievances to be presented to the
king should be in written form.   The clergy and
religious were to gather on Saturday in the chapel at
the first hour to hear the king's will and to receive the
royal thanks.[66]   But the archbishop was unable to be
present on the Saturday, and empowered Masters
Nicholas Chaddesden, Richard de Warmyngton, his

[65] Reg. Witlesey, fol. 23.
[66] *Ibid.*, fol. 23v.

1371 no mass is mentioned, though doubtless one was celebrated at the opening. The scribe evidently was interested only in what took place in the chapter house. After the reading of the Bishop of London's certificate,[73] which is to be noted as having come back to the more advanced position in the order of proceedings which it occupied in 1309, the king's commissioners appeared.[74] They explained the king's need in the vulgar tongue,[74] as had been done by the commissioners in 1369(–70) and by the Bishop of London in 1371. This time the sermon followed the departure of the king's commissioners.[74] Then a discussion took place and there was a further explanation " in vulgari " by the Bishop of London on the part of the archbishop in regard to the necessity of the king.[74] As in 1356, the Bishop of London was empowered by commission to act for the archbishop. A new detail is given in the announcement by certain bishops that they did not receive mandates from the Bishop of London to be present, nor to cite their clergy.[75] At length there was separation for discussion—this time the secular clergy going by themselves and the religious by themselves as in 1369(–70).[76] The clergy later returned bringing a list of excuses for not making a grant and demanding reform of certain grievances.[76] As previously, they were urged to deliberate further about the grant and to formulate their grievances.[76] The following day the clergy granted a tenth. The clergy met again the next day in the chapter house, the official of the archbishop now presiding.[76] Neither the bishops nor their proctors were present. The clergy still refused an increase in their grant.[76] The Bishop of London met them the next day in the chapter house.[76] The clergy made their grant in writing and presented in writing certain supplications for reform.[76] Written grievances had now

---

[74] *Ibid.*, fol. 64v.   [75] *Ibid.*, fols. 64v.—65.   [76] *Ibid.*, fol. 65.

become the established form. It is interesting that in the chapter house on the following day in the presence of some proctors of the clergy and other clerks, the Bishop of Hereford declared that he would not grant one penny unless the injuries to himself and to his church of Hereford were reformed.[77] His speech indicates the length to which discussion was allowed to go.

The meeting of the clergy was continued the next day in the chapter house, now under the presidency of the Dean of the Church of S. Mary of the Arches.[77] The grant and articles were still under discussion.[77] The convocation adjourned until Vespers, and then the Dean of the Arches allowed the proctors of the clergy to depart at the command, as he said, of the Archbishop of Canterbury.[77]

There are allusions to six convocations[78] under Archbishop Sudbury. We have detailed accounts of five of these convocations, four of which were held at S. Paul's, London, the other at the house of the Brothers Minor, Northampton. The dates for the five are February 3rd, 1376(-7); November 9th, 1377; May 9th, 1379; February 4th, 1379(-80), and December 1st, 1380. Three of them, those in November 1377,[79] May 1379,[80] and February 1379(-80),[81] began with mass at the high altar at S. Paul's. In all four convocations at S. Paul's the sermon was delivered in the chapel of the Blessed Mary.[82] In 1376(-7)[83] and 1379(-80)[84] they adjourned after the sermon to the chapter house. In 1376(-7) the reading of the certificate of the Bishop of London took place.[85] In November 1377[86] and May 1379[87] the certificate followed the

---

[77] Reg. Witlesey, fol. 65.
[78] Reg. Sudbury (Cantuar.), fols. 26, 33v., 44, 55, 59v., 72.
[79] *Ibid.*, fol. 44.
[80] *Ibid.*, fol. 55.
[81] *Ibid.*, fol. 59v.
[82] *Ibid.*, fols. 44, 55, 59.
[83] *Ibid.*, fol. 33.
[84] Reg. Sudbury, fol. 59v.
[85] *Ibid.*, fol. 33.
[86] *Ibid.*, fol. 44.
[87] *Ibid.*, fol. 55.

sermon in the chapel of the Blessed Mary. In three of the convocations at S. Paul's the king's ministers or commissioners appeared, once on the first day,[88] twice on the second day.[89] In lieu of the king's commissioners, in May 1379[90] and December 1380,[91] the archbishop himself explained the king's needs. Discussion generally followed the request for a grant.[92] As previously the proctors of the clergy were asked to withdraw from the chapter house for their discussion.[93] Another new form of procedure was introduced in 1377 when one clerk of each diocese was commanded by the archbishop to appear at an appointed hour for the discussion of the petitions.[94] The bishops were especially mentioned in February 1376(-7)[95] and May 1379[96] as holding secret deliberations. This seems to have been different from the ordinary discussions apart. In four of these convocations the archbishop appointed various substitutes to preside for him, similar to those appointed in the past—his chancellor or official, or the Dean of the Arches.[97] The proctors of the clergy were warned in May 1379 by the archbishop that if they left before the business was finished they would lose their procurations and have impositions put upon them.[98]

These convocations reveal some interesting matter in regard to grants which will be presented elsewhere in this study.[99]

It is of interest to note that since so great a crowd of laity had assembled for the convocation at Northampton the archbishop changed the place of meeting. His

[88] Ibid., fol. 33v.
[89] Ibid., fols. 44, 59v.
[90] Ibid., fol. 55.
[91] Ibid., fol. 72v.
[92] Ibid., fols. 33v., 44v., 55, 59v.
[93] Ibid., fols. 33v., 55, 59v.
[94] Ibid., fol. 44v.

[95] Ibid., fol. 33v.
[96] Ibid., fol. 55.
[97] Ibid., fols. 33v., 44v., 55, 72v.
[98] Ibid., fol. 55.
[99] Infra, chapter V.

method of notification was by schedules posted on the doors of the church. [100]

Four of these convocations seem to have been concerned purely with money grants. [101]   The one of which we know so little is mentioned as having been summoned at the supplication of the Bishop of Norwich. [102] In the convocation held on May 9th, 1379 the archbishop announced distinctly that the cause of summoning was twofold—to reform attempts against the jurisdiction and liberty of the Church, and to aid the king and the realm for the defence of the same realm. [103]   The account of the convocation is concerned purely with the second cause.   Once there is mention made of their going apart to discuss matters of the convocation, [103] but of the formulation of any constitutions to protect the jurisdiction and liberty of the Church nothing is said.

Under Archbishop Courteney there are recorded fifteen [104] convocations one of which may have been a court.   Accounts exist of twelve [105] of these convocations.   Of the others, information is gleaned through references to grants. [104] Of the twelve convocations of which we learn from the two parts of Courteney's register, one was held at S. Frideswides, Oxford and continued at S. Paul's, London, [106] another at S. Mary's, Salisbury, [107] and all the rest at S. Paul's, London. [108] The procedure by now had become definite.   The Mass

---

[100] Reg. Sudbury (Cantuar.), fol. 72.
[101] The Convocations of February 3rd, 1376(—7); November 9th, 1377; February 4th, 1379(—80); December 1st, 1380.
[102] Reg. Sudbury (Cantuar.), fol. 26.
[103] Ibid., fol. 55.
[104] Vide chart, Appendix A.
[105] Reg. Courteney, I, fols. 33—34v.; 35v.; 73; 73v.—74v.; 75—76v.; 78—78v.; 79; 79v.—80; 83; 83v.—84; 84v.—85; II, fols. 195; 195v.—196v.   Reg. Wykeham, pt. III, fol. 258v.   Printed Wykeham's Register, II, 437; 600.
[106] Reg. Courteney, I, fols. 33, 35.
[107] Ibid., I, fol. 79.
[108] Ibid., I, fols. 73, 74, 75, 78, 79v., 83v., 84v.   Reg. Courteney, II, fol. 195v.

of the Holy Spirit in each case was celebrated at the high altar.[109] Then the entire assemblage adjourned to the chapel of the Blessed Mary where a sermon was preached, and later the certificate of the Bishop of London was read publicly.[109] Though there are one or two exceptions when they adjourned immediately to the chapter house,[110] the procedure of the first day generally closed at this point. On the second day they met in the chapter house for discussion of the business of the convocation.[111] Of the ten convocations described there is only one instance of a minister of the king being present to explain the king's demands.[112] Several times it is distinctly stated that the archbishop explained the business.[113] It may be inferred that he did so on the other occasions. As in the past, there are instances of the archbishop's absence.[114] It had become a set practice that prelates and clergy should deliberate apart.[115] At the final convocation of Courtney's time we are told the exact spot to which the lower clergy withdrew. Of these ten convocations nine were concerned with grants to the king.[116] One of these nine also dealt with a papal grant.[117] In the other remaining convocation, that of April 1391, the sole grant was to the pope.[118] In every instance except the convocation of November 18th, 1382 and its continuation at S. Paul's, the clergy presented their response in

[109] *Ibid.*, I, fols. 73, 74, 75, 78, 79, 79v., 83v., 84v. Reg. Courteney, II, fol. 195v.

[110] Reg. Courteney, I, fols. 33, 83v., 84v.

[111] *Ibid.*, I, fols. 73, 74, 75, 78, 79, 80. Reg. Courteney, II, fol. 196.

[112] Reg. Courteney, I, fol. 33.

[113] *Ibid.*, I, fols. 33, 74, 78, 79.

[114] *Ibid.*, I, fols. 34, 83v., 84v.

[115] *Ibid.*, I, fols. 33, 73, 78, 79. Reg. Courteney, II, fol. 196.

[116] Reg. Courteney, I, fols. 33, 73, 74, 78, 79, 80, 83v., 84v. Reg. Courteney, II, fol. 196v.

[117] Reg. Courteney, I, fol. 78.

[118] *Ibid.*, I, fol. 76.

writing. [119]   Five times it was addressed to the
" Reverend Fathers." [120]   Three times it was addressed
to the archbishop. [121]   In the case of the papal grant
the conditions were put in writing, but addressed to
neither archbishop or bishops. [122]

The convocation at S. Frideswides, Oxford is
particularly noteworthy as in it we have an instance of
ecclesiastical business being treated in addition to the
grant. [123] The question of heresy was brought up. [124] A
commission was appointed to investigate certain
heresies. [124] Several men abjured their heresies before
the assembled body. [125] Following this, a constitution
was formulated in regard to heresy. [126]

At the convocation on December 2nd, 1383, the
apostolic letters were read by the papal collector and
the dean of Chichester. [127] The business of the convocation in April 1391 was the Church and pope [128];
that of the convocation of February 1394(–5) embraced other matters besides a grant to the king. [129]

From the various accounts of the convocations under
Courteney we conclude, therefore, that the procedure
of convocation had fallen into quite definite grooves.
Uniformity had been established almost entirely for the
sequence of ceremony and business. Separation in the
body for the purposes of discussion had become clear-
cut when the proctors of the lower clergy went to a
definite place for their deliberations. A written
response with the grant and conditions clearly formulated had become the custom.

In the period from 1396 to 1400 allusions have been

---

[119] Reg. Courteney, I, fols. 73, 74, 76, 78, 79, 80, 84, 84v.   Reg.
Courteney, II, fol. 196v.
[120] Reg. Courteney, I, fols. 78, 79, 80, 84, 84v.
[121] Ibid., I, fols. 73, 74.   Reg. Courteney, II, 196v.
[122] Reg. Courteney, I, fol. 76.
[123] Ibid., I, fols. 33—5.
[124] Ibid., I, fol. 33.   [127] Ibid., I, fol. 78.
[125] Ibid., I, fol. 34v.   [128] Ibid., I, fol. 76.
[126] Ibid., I, fol. 35.   [129] Reg. Courteney, II, fol. 196v.

found to six convocations[130] of the province of Canterbury, one of which probably never met. Of these five
there are full accounts of two.[131] When each of these
convocations assembled on the appointed day, each was
prorogued by the person whom the archbishop had
commissioned to do so.[131] To the first of these convocations (that which had been prorogued to February
26th, 1396, and which was the first convocation since
Archbishop Arundel had received the pallium) the
archbishop came from Lambeth in his small boat to the
conventual church of the Friars Preachers, and thence
approached S. Paul's.[132] The Bishop of London clad
in pontifical robes met him, the bells of the cathedral
and of other churches ringing throughout the day, and
led him to the east end of the cathedral in a solemn
procession.[132] With the singing of canticles and to the
sounds of the organs, the archbishop was led to the high
altar, where a speech was made by the Bishop of
London. The Mass of the Holy Spirit was celebrated
at the high altar.[132] Afterwards, as in the past, they
adjourned to the chapel of the Blessed Mary for the
sermon and later the reading of the Bishop of London's
certificate.[133]

The convocation summoned for October 6th, 1399
and prorogued until October 11th followed the usual
form of opening, and was similar to the convocation
just described except for the special ceremonies before
the mass.[134] In both convocations the business was
carried on in the chapter house.[135] In February 1396
they assembled there the afternoon of the opening. In
October 1399 the business did not follow until the day

---

[130] *Vide* chart, Appendix A.
[131] Reg. Arundel, I, fol. 44. The convocation was summoned for
February 19th, 1396(—7) and prorogued February 26th. Reg. Arundel,
I, fol. 51. The convocation was summoned for October 6th, 1399 and
prorogued to October 11th.
[132] Reg. Arundel, I, fol. 44.   [134] *Ibid.*, I, fol. 51.
[133] *Ibid.*, I, fols. 44—44v.   [135] *Ibid.*, I, fols. 52, 74.

after the opening ceremonies.[136]   The latter gathering reflects the convocations of the earlier period in that representatives of the king were present.[137]   They came this time, however, not to seek a grant, but to thank the clergy for their prayers and to give the king's promise not to ask for aid save in the case of evident necessity.[137] In both of these convocations, as had generally happened in the time of Courteney, the archbishop explained the cause of the convocation.[138]   These two assemblies are of particular interest as they give a clear picture of what a convocation was like when the matters treated were purely ecclesiastical.

At the convocation held in February 1396 there were present many doctors of canon and civil law of the University of Oxford.[139]   There was also present a proctor of the university and the faculty of bachelors and scholars, with a " procuratorium " with certain grievances presented by the chancellor to the doctors for the purpose of seeking a remedy.[140]   The archbishop took counsel with the bishops, prelates and clergy and doctors and promised to provide a remedy when the provincial council was over, and after a mature deliberation had been held.[141]   A verbal renunciation of a certain privilege of exemption claimed by the bachelors was made by Master Michael Cergeaux, doctor of both laws, and proctor of the bachelors and scholars of the university.[142]   This infuriated the chancellor and he left the council in wrath.[142]   The archbishop, however, commanded that he be summoned to appear the next day to treat concerning the articles.[142]

After the university business there followed a report concerning a certain theologian, master and bachelor in

---

[136] Reg. Arundel, I, fol. 45v.
[137] *Ibid.*, I, fol. 52.
[138] *Ibid.*, I, fols. 45v., 52.
[139] *Ibid.*, I, fol. 47.
[140] *Ibid.*, I, fols. 45v.—46.
[141] *Ibid.*, I, fols. 46v.—47.
[142] *Ibid.*, I, fol. 47.

arts, who had written many opinions, heresies and errors in certain books. [142] This was Master John Wyclif. The articles were then given in detail. [142] The doctors, bachelors and scholars of canon and civil law gathered there supplicated that an opportune garrison of defence be secured for the Christian faith. [143] The archbishop, therefore, held a discussion with his suffragans in regard to the conclusions and opinions, and later adjourned the convocation until the morrow. [144] Of the subsequent events of this convocation Arundel's register contains no account.

On the second day of the convocation held in October 1399, when the archbishop had explained the cause of the convocation, he and the bishops went apart. [145] The other prelates and clergy assembled by themselves. [145] We are told that the archbishop thought it would be difficult to congregate all the prelates and proctors of the clergy to compose articles on the part of the clergy in regard to the burdens put upon them and the Church. [145] He therefore appointed five men to compose the articles. [145] The archbishop then adjourned the convocation until the following day. [145] When they reassembled the archbishop and his suffragans withdrew to the chapel of the Blessed Mary, leaving the other prelates and proctors in the chapter house. [145] The articles of grievances to be reformed by the apostolic see were read through by Master John Prophet, Dean of Hereford. They then sent for the papal collector that they might consult him concerning the articles. [145] He said it would be seemly and expedient (" satis honestum et expediens ") to write to the

---

[143] *Ibid.*, I, fol. 47v.: " Super quibus opinionibus iidem doctores Bacallarii et Scolares iuris Canonici et Civilis in multitudine copiosa inibi congregati per provinciale consilium in sustentacionem fidei Catholice certam declaracionem fieri petiuerunt et supplicarunt humiliter de oportuno christiane fidei defensionis presidio subveniri."

For the transcription of this passage I am indebted to Dr. I. J. Churchill.

[144] Reg. Arundel, I, fol. 47v.   [145] *Ibid.*, I, fol. 52.

pope for the reform of the same and promised to work for the reform. [146]   The archbishop then sent for the other prelates and proctors of the clergy in the chapter house to come to the chapel of the Blessed Mary to report any grievance. [146]   When the proctors had come thither, one rose in the name of the clergy of the province of Canterbury and read aloud certain articles, beseeching an opportune remedy. [147]   Since the archbishop did not consider the articles to be of their full burden, he proposed that there should be further deliberation. [147]   He therefore adjourned the convocation to another day when the speaker who had spoken previously for the clergy explained publicly many more articles. [147]   The account ends with the articles given in full detail. [148]

This convocation shows a definite advance in procedure in that there was one person who seems to have been delegated to read the articles presented by the lower clergy who belonged to what might arbitrarily be called the lower house of convocation.   The commission for formulating the articles was similar to what had been done in the past, but the spokesman at this time was the forerunner of the one who was later in the fifteenth century called the " Prelocutor." [149]

The convocation of 1396 shows progress over the convocation in Courteney's time which dealt with heresies in that the articles of heresy were presented in full.   Otherwise these two convocations serve only as other illustrations to show that the framework for procedure in convocation—the definite order of ceremony and business, the separate deliberations of higher and lower bodies, and the precise formulation of grievances and reforms—had by the end of the fourteenth century become fixed.

[146] Reg. Arundel, I, fol. 52.   [147] Ibid., I, fol. 52v.   [148] Ibid., I, fols. 52v.—53v.
[149] For a discussion of the growth of the office of " Prelocutor " see Churchill, op. cit., I, 368—9, 378—9, note B.

CHAPTER V

GRANTS AND GRIEVANCES IN THE PROVINCE OF CANTERBURY DURING THE THIRTEENTH AND FOURTEENTH CENTURIES

THE kings of England claimed as part of their prerogative the right to impose taxes upon their subjects,[1] but by the thirteenth century the practice had become established that previous consent to taxation was necessary in the national council or parliament.[2] Sometimes those who were not represented in the council, laity and ecclesiastics, were assembled locally by the king's commissioners, but as parliament grew in the extent of its representation and in the frequency of its meetings, the unwieldy method of local discussion was abandoned.

The taxation of the laity took the form of a tenth or a fifteenth. Among the clergy a tenth or a fifteenth or a half-tenth was used. The assessment according to the clerical tenth went through various stages.[3] First there was the *valde antiqua taxatio,* later the *antiqua taxatio,* followed in turn by the taxation of Walter Bishop of Norwich in 1254, of Master Raymond de Nogeriis in 1274, and finally by the taxation of Pope Nicholas IV. in 1291.[3] From 1292 to 1335 the clerical grants in parliament and convocation were based on the assessment of 1291, with the exception that in 1318 a new valuation was made for the northern province because of the devastations by the Scots.[4] The assessment of

[1] Felix Makower, *The Constitutional History and Constitution of the Church of England* (translated from the German), p. 33.
[2] Cf. *supra*, chapter I, pt. I, *passim.*
[3] R. Graham, *English Ecclesiastical Studies,* pp. 271—301, *passim.* Raymond de Nogeriis was appointed collector in 1274.
[4] Stubbs, *Const. Hist.,* II (4th ed.), 580. Graham, *Eng. Eccles. Studies,* p. 271. W. E. Lunt, "Clerical Tenths levied in England by Papal Authority during the Reign of Edward II." *Anniversary Essays by Students of Charles Homer Haskins,* pp. 172—3.

1291 included spiritualities and temporalities.[5]   Any lands acquired by the clergy after that date were taxed with those of the laity, the temporalities before that date being spoken of as " annexed to their spiritualities."[6]   A clerical tenth then from 1292, with the exception mentioned above in regard to the northern province, was a tenth according to the assessment of 1291.

Taxation for every particular grant in the thirteenth and fourteenth centuries was treated separately and as an individual matter.   The principle was stressed that the grant was being made with the consent of those conceding it, and emphasis was sometimes put upon the fact that it was being made voluntarily (" sua voluntate spontanea ").   Even to-day the phrase used for the royal assent to a money bill in Great Britain reflects the relationship which existed in medieval England between the king and his subjects: " Le roy remercie ses bons sujets, accepte leur benevolence et ainsi le veult."[7]

A grant from the clergy might be requested by the king or the pope. Sometimes the pope imposed a tenth for the king's uses.[8]   It was within the power of the archbishop to impose a tax on the province for church expenses.   In the course of this chapter illustrations will be given of the various demands made upon the clergy—royal, papal and archiepiscopal and the reception they received.

The word used most frequently for a grant was " subsidium," generally accompanied by the adjective " competens."[9]   Sometimes " auxilium " was used also

[5] Stubbs, *Const. Hist.*, II, 580.
[6] *Ibid.*, II, 416, 443, 580.
[7] J. Redlich, *The Procedure of the House of Commons*, translated from the German by A. Ernest Stenethal, III, 109.
[8] Lunt, " Clerical Tenths levied in England by Papal Authority during the Reign of Edward II," pp. 157—82.
[9] *Rep. Dignity of a Peer*, IV, 590, *et passim*.

modified by " competens." [10] The use of " donum " [11]
and " subvencio " [12] also occurred. A grant, however,
might be described in the terms of its amount—a single
tenth, a tenth for two years or a tenth for three years.

We have seen that in the thirteenth century there
was considerable resistance on the part of the clergy of
the province of Canterbury to making grants. Excuses
of various kinds were given. In the thirteenth century
too they were becoming conscious of their grievances,
and as the century advanced they established a link
between grants and grievances. At the council held
January 13th, 1226, the clergy made the illness of the
king and the absence of the archbishops and certain
bishops their excuse for not giving a reply to the
demand made by Pope Honorius III in a bull issued
the previous year. [13] In this bull the pope had asked
that a prebend be reserved for papal uses in each
cathedral and conventual church, and that " equivalent
revenue be provided from the estates of bishops and
monasteries." [14] In the council which assembled on
November 19th, 1237 [15] in the presence of the papal
legate, Otho, the archbishops, bishops and clergy had
formulated grievances, and petitioned the legate to
warn and induce the king to redress the grievances there
listed that were being caused in the realm of England
by him and his bailiffs to the prejudice of the liberty of
the Church. [16] Three years later at the council of
May 1240 at Reading, the bishops gave the need of
prolonged counsel as a reason for not giving an
immediate answer to the papal legate, Otho, in regard
to the demand of Pope Gregory IX for a fifth part of

---

[10] *Ibid.*, IV, 427, "super aliquo auxilio competenti."
[11] Wilkins, *op. cit.*, II, 221 (Ex reg. Winchelsey, fol. 207b).
[12] *Rep. Dignity of a Peer*, IV, 485.
[13] Wendover, *op. cit.*, IV, 114—16. Churchill, *op. cit.*, I, 361.
[14] *Vet. Regist. Sar.*, I, 366—9. Churchill, *op. cit.*, I, 361—2.
[15] *Ann. Monast. (Theokesberia)*, I, 105.
[16] *Ibid. (Burton)*, I, 253—7.

L

their goods for the war with the emperor.[17] This council was adjourned until late June, when it met at London.[18] The clergy again opposed the grant and gave their reasons against it in detail,[19] but finally at the persuasion of the bishops they yielded.[20] The council at Merton in 1258 was entirely concerned with drawing up a long list of grievances against the king.[21] At the council of October 1269, the clergy again formulated their grievances to the bishops in which they refused to grant a subsidy to the king on the score that the pope had not been consulted, and made an appeal to the apostolic see[22] and to the See of Canterbury against being committed to such grants by their bishops.[23] The year 1283 brought further opposition

---

[17] Mat. Paris, *Chron. Maj.*, IV, 10—11.

[18] *Ann. Monast. (Theokesberia)*, I, 115—16.

[19] *Ibid.*, I, 116. Mat. Paris, *Chron. Maj.*, IV, 37—8. Among the reasons given against the grant were these : That they should not make a contribution against him who was united with (" contraxit ") their prince, nor should they make one for the shedding of blood ; that they had given other tenths to the pope in order that a similar exaction should not be made ; because of this two acts would render it customary ; that if they contributed for war against the emperor they would fear capture in going through his lands on business to the Roman Court ; that money was needed for wars against the king's enemies ; that this grant would be to the prejudice of the patrons of churches since their consent was not certain ; that since the general state of the Church was imperilled, a general contribution was needed ; that if it had been necessary, a general contribution would have been made ; that there was a report that a council would be summoned where such things would be determined.

[20] *Cal. MSS. of the Dean and Chapter of Wells*, I, 403. A letter of Otho mentions the council in June. Lunt, *Consent*, pp. 130—1.

[21] *Ann. Monast. (Theokesberia)*, I, 163. *Ann. Monast. (Burton)*, 412—25. Among the many grievances formulated were the following : That bishops and prelates were summoned to a secular court to answer for what concerned ecclesiastical affairs ; that laymen were instituted to parishes and prebends ; that excommunicated persons were set free by the secular power ; that clerks were imprisoned unjustly ; that royal prohibitions were procured to escape ecclesiastical judges.

[22] The papal see was vacant from 1268—71. E. A. Fry, *Almanacks for Students of English History*, p. 133.

[23] Wilkins, *op. cit.*, II, 19—20 (Ex MS. C.C. Christi, Oxon., n. 154). They first listed the burdens of the Church of England in the past— various grants from the clergy to the king for war, the depredations made in time of war, the grants requested by the legate, and the triennial tenth recently granted the king. Other grievances included taxation of their temporalities by laymen " contra formam juris

to grants when the proctors of the clergy again opposed a contribution which was sought from them by the king.[24]   They gave their articles against the grant of a tenth for three years in very specific terms.[24]   First they complained that they could not give because of the diminution of fruits, the exchange now made of English money ("monetæ Anglicanæ jam factum excambium"), the destruction of animals, the payments to the king, the subsidy for the Holy Land, and also because their provisions sufficed only for the daily stipends of servants.[25]   Secondly, they held that as there was still another payment to be made on the fifteenth granted to the king,[26] it was not fitting that his royal majesty should demand another, especially since a large sum of money was procured separately from all the prelates a very few days before.[27]   Thirdly, they gave as their reason against the grant the fact that the remedy promised by the king for certain grievances was not yet effected, especially in regard to royal prohibitions.[27]   Fourthly, they maintained that the cause for which an aid ("auxilium") was sought was one of savagery or vengefulness on the blood of Christians which was

canonici," the extortionate methods of the exactors of the tenth granted to the king by the pope, the exaction of procurations.   They finally refused to grant the subsidy sought from them by the king, since the pope had not been consulted.   They declared that to grant it without his being consulted would incur the sentence of excommunication in accordance with the proclamation made in the Lateran Council.   Lunt, *Consent*, p.160: "This invocation of the canon of the fourth council of the Lateran as a protection against royal taxation is the first made by the English clergy of which I have found record."

[24] *Ann. Monast. (Dunstaplia)*, III, 295—6.

[25] *Ibid. (Dunstaplia)*, III, 295.

[26] A fifteenth for three years had been granted to Edward I by the clergy of the province of Canterbury in 1280.   The clergy of the province of York granted a fifteenth for two years.   *Ann. Monast. (Oseneia)*, IV, 286.   Florence of W. (Continuation), II, 224.   Bart. Cotton, *op. cit.*, p. 160.   Stubbs, *Const. Hist.*, II, (4th ed.), 118, n. 1.   Stubbs states that Edward applied for a grant on November 15th, 1279.   The Osney annalist gives the year of application as 1280.

[27] *Ann. Monast. (Dunstaplia)*, III, 295.

more expressly forbidden to clerics.[28] Finally, they declared that the pope hoped to place the yoke of a new gift or contribution (" novæ præstationis seu contributionis jugum ") on the Church of England, since never within the time of memory had the Church of Rome been exposed to so many perils and oppressions as it was now.[29] On account of this they did not dare to put themselves under an obligation or to promise anything for making a new concession of tribute (" novam tributi concessionem ") to the king unless the pope had previously been consulted in regard to it.[30] They ended by saying that in case of evident necessity they would extend their hands liberally in assistance to the king.[31] This practice of the clergy's making a partial concession at the end even though they had listed valid reasons for not making a grant, we shall see appearing again.

At the parliament of November-December 1295, the clergy of the realm held fast to granting only a single tenth though the king urged more.[32] This is one instance when they were able to maintain their stand. They promised, however, to assist the king a year hence if a

---

[28] *Ann. Monast. (Dunstaplia)*, III, 295 : " Quia causa propter quam hujusmodi petititur auxilium, est sævitia seu vindicta sanguinis Christianorum, quod clericis est expressius interdictum ; præsertim propter irregularitatis maculam quam inducit."

This is interesting as an illustration of the influence which the clergy might have exercised and also of the constitutional position as they viewed it in regard to their being concerned with any acts which involved the shedding of blood.

[29] *Ibid.*, 295—6.

[30] *Ibid.*, 296.

[31] *Ibid.*, 296 : " Verumtamen, si causus emerserit in quo clericis de bonis ecclesiasticis conferre seu contribuere liceret ; ut puta, si princeps esset obsessus, incarceratus, seu aliter ab hostibus detentus, quod absit ; vel ubi archiepiscopus vel clerus tantam inpresserint necessitatem vel utilitatem, quod ad relevandam necessitatem communes fecultates non sufficerent, vel alia ubi sine periculo et scrupulo conscientiæ subsidia providerint ab ecclesiis conferenda, manus domino nostro regi porrigeremus liberaliter adjutrices ; de consilio tamen summi Pontificis, cujus interest communibus utilitatibus providere."

[32] *Flores Historiarum* (Rolls Series), III, 95. *Ann. Monast. (Wigornia)*, IV, 524.

peace had not yet been concluded. [33] The following February, Pope Boniface VIII issued the bull *Clericis laicos* [34] forbidding the clergy to pay contributions or taxes. In accordance with this at their convocation at Hilarytide, 1296(−7), the clergy refused to grant an aid to the king. [35] They put their reasons in writing and sent them by solemn messengers to the king. [36] Another convocation was held on March 24th, 1297, but in it no definite step was taken other than that the archbishop dismissed the gathering to act individually according to their consciences. [37] The following August the clergy again assembled and again gave their answer that they could not make a grant without leave from the pope. [38] They asked permission to send messengers to the pope. [39] They also declared that the king must not be offended if they excommunicated those who seized ecclesiastical goods. [40] The king replied that if they could not give, he would take. He refused to give them permission to apply to the pope, and he forbade excommunication for seizure. [41] When the clergy met

[33] *Flor. Hist.*, III, 95.

[34] Wilkins, *op. cit.*, II, 221 (Ex reg. Winchelsey, fol. 207b): " . . . quod quicumque prælati, ecclesiasticæ personæ, religiosæ, vel seculares quorumcumque ordinum, conditionis, seu statuum, collectas vel tallias, decimam, vicesimam, seu centesimam suorum et ecclesiarum proventuum, vel bonorum laicis solverint vel promiserint, vel se soluturos consenserint, aut quamvis aliam quantitatem, portionem, aut quotam ipsorum proventuum, vel bonorum æstimationis, vel valoris ipsorum sub adjutorii, mutui, subventionis, subsidii, vel doni nomine, aut quovis alio titulo, modo, vel quæsito colore, absque auctoritate sedis apostolicæ; necnon imperatores, reges, . . . et quivis alius . . . qui talia imposuerint, exegerint, vel receperint . . . eo ipso sententiam excommunicationis incurrant. Universitates quoque, quæ in his culpabiles fuerint, idem papa ecclesiastico interdicto supponit; . . ." Archbishop Winchelsey is here quoting the words of the bull.

[35] *Ann. Monast. (Dunstaplia)*, III, 405.

[36] Reg. Winchelsey, fol. 207. Printed in *Reg. Winchelsey* (C. and Y. Soc.), p. 153. *Ann. Monast. (Dunstaplia)*, III, 405.

[37] *Ibid. (Wigornia)*, IV, 531.

[38] Reg. Winchelsey, fol. 222v. Printed in *Reg. Winchelsey* (C. and Y. Soc.), pp. 189—90. Bart. Cotton, *op. cit.*, p. 327.

[39] Reg. Winchelsey, fol. 222v. Printed in *Reg. Winchelsey* (C. and Y. Soc.), p. 190. Bart. Cotton, *op. cit.*, p. 335.

[40] *Ibid.*, p. 328.

[41] *Ibid.*, p. 335.

again in a new convocation on November 20th, 1297, they anticipated the king's request and granted a tenth. [42]   In this way they avoided a violation in the letter of the papal bull. [43] At the convocation, however, held the following June (1298) they again refused to grant more than the remaining part of the tenth due until they had the pope's permission. [44]

The clergy took the opportunity of the council held at S. Paul's on November 25th, 1309, to draw up certain petitions to be presented to the king in regard to grievances of the Church of England. [45] Appealing to the laws of William I, by which he had separated the ecclesiastical and secular jurisdictions, they petitioned against being summoned to secular courts. [45] They brought forward Magna Charta as a promise of freedom for the Church in all things. [46] They listed in detail the matters for which they could not be summoned to a secular court, and they threatened excommunication to all those who harmed the clergy in any respect as to summoning them to courts, or to assuming power in spiritual matters within the spiritual jurisdiction. [47] They referred to the grievances that the clergy

---

[42] Reg. Winchelsey, fols. 230v.—231. Printed in *Reg. Winchelsey* (C. and Y. Soc.), pp. 211, 230. Stubbs, *Const. Hist.*, II (4th ed.), 147.

[43] *Ibid.*, II (4th ed.), 147.

[44] Reg. Winchelsey, fol. 245. Printed in *Reg. Winchelsey* (C. and Y. Soc.), p. 261.

[45] Reg. Winchelsey, fol. 1. Printed in Wilkins, *op. cit.*, II, 314—15. They actually quoted the words of William I's decree. For the substance of this decree *vide supra*, chapter I, 24—5.

[46] Wilkins, *op. cit.*, II, 314 (Ex reg. Winchelsey, fol. 1a): " . . . prout hæc et alia in charta prædicti Willelmi regis plenius inscribuntur, continenturque in Magna Charta de libertatibus concessa per celebris memoriæ Henricum regem Angliæ; quod idem rex pro se et hæredibus suis in perpetuum concessit et charta sua confirmavit archiepiscopis, episcopis abbatibus, et prioribus hujus regni, quod Anglicana ecclesia libera sit, et habeat omnia jura sua integra, et libertates suas illæsas, . . ."

[47] *Ibid.*, II, 315 (Ex reg. Winchelsey, fol. 1a): " . . . cum statuentes contra liberatem eandem et statuta servantes, consuetudines introducentes, et introductas servantes, scribentes statuta hujusmodi, consilarii, et executores, necnon et qui secundum ea præsumpserint judicare scienter, incurrant majoris excommunicationis sententiam, innovatam pluries, et per sedem apostolicam confirmatam, damnabiliter ipso facto."

had presented in the parliaments at London in 1280 and at Lincoln in 1300, and declared that these grievances had not yet been effectually withdrawn ("nec fuissent hucusque effectualiter revocata").[48] Finally they made a strong plea to the king that he would give a competent and benign response to their petitions, and furthermore, would consider those things which would be "opportune for the state of the Church just as canonical sanctions demand."[48]

We have noted in a preceding chapter the clergy's grounds of complaint to the archbishop against the form of summons to convocation in 1314, and how their complaint was effective in bringing about the summons of another convocation for the purpose of making the grant which they had refused to make at the former.[49] The clergy were beginning at least to see that there was value in standing for certain principles even if they were not always successful in securing their desires.

In 1319 when an aid was sought from the clergy by the king, they took the position that they had assumed in 1297 and refused to make a grant until they had received the pope's permission.[50]

In 1329 the response of the clergy was very down-right.[51] They flatly refused to make a grant, declaring that they could barely support the pope's burdens.[51] Furthermore, they claimed that the subsidy ("subsidium") voted recently by the laity was sufficient for the king's needs.[51] In addition, they referred to the subsidy ("subsidium") which they had conceded the king at Leicester.[51] The conditions, moreover, of the past grant, they declared, had not been fulfilled.[51]

[48] *Ibid., op. cit.,* 315 (Ex reg. Winchelsey, fol. 1a).
[49] *Supra,* chapter II, 58—9.
[50] *Chronicles of the Reigns of Edward I and Edward II (Ann. Paulinus),* I, 286. Adam de Murimuth, *Continuatio Chronicarum,* ed. E. M. Thompson (Rolls Series), p. 30. Adam de Murimuth was sent as a messenger to the pope at the king's expense. Pope John XXII granted the king permission for a tenth for one year.
[51] *Chronicles of the Reigns of Edward I and Edward II (Ann. Paulinus),* I, 348.

By the middle of the century the idea that a grant should be made conditional on the reform of grievances was developing more and more. In 1351 the clergy promised the king a tenth payable at Midsummer (June 24th) and at the feast of S. Andrew (November 30th).[52] They stipulated that this tenth should not be levied from benefices which were insufficient or unable to support the burdens of their benefices.[53] Neither the king nor his servants (" ministri ") were to make inquiries concerning the insufficiency and impotency of these benefices, but were to accept the testimony from certificates of the ordinaries of the places.[54] The bishops could be trusted, they said, by virtue of their obedience to the See of Canterbury and their allegiance to him not to commit any frauds in their concessions as reported in their certificates.[54] They asked at the same time, if before the last term of payment, he would not have leisure to hear their grievances, and entreated that he or those having power would duly reform them, and give them his letters patent in confirmation of the reform.[55] If all this should be done, they held out to him the promise (without the necessity of another summons of the clergy) of another tenth payable the year following on the feast of the Purification and at

[52] Reg. Islep, fol. 49.

[53] *Ibid.*, fol. 49 : " Sub infrascriptis modo forma et condicionibus vnamiter concesserunt videlicet de beneficiis insufficientibus seu non valentibus beneficiorum suorum onera supportare, nichil omnino ad solucionem decime huiusmodi exigatur nec ipsa beneficia quecumque fuerint et cuiuscumque spei eciam si dignitates fuerint sub eadem concessione minime concludantur. . . ."

[54] *Ibid.*, fol. 49.

[55] *Ibid.*, fol. 49 : " . . . humiliter rogavit clerus dominum nostrum Regem quatenus si sibi de presenti non vacaret peticiones cleri alias et tunc proponitas audire discutere et gravamina in eis contenta rationaliter reformare quod maiestati sue regie citra vltimum terminum solucionis predicte per se vel suos habentes ad hoc potestatem placeret propter reverenciam dei et sancte ecclesie debite reformare et in eventu quo sic fieri fecerit litteras suas patentes inde testimoniales faciens vt est moris idem clerus absque nova vocacione vnam aliam decimam . . . dummodo alia decima ex concessione pape vel aliter non concurrat de beneficiis vt premittitur ad hoc cum aliis oneribus sufficientibus et non de aliis concessit liberalite et pure."

Midsummer, provided it was not concurrent with a
tenth for the pope or other burdens, and that it was not
collected from the aforementioned, who were impoverished.[55]   But this grant was made entirely conditional on the reform of their grievances.[56]   They
stated this fact in no uncertain terms: " Si vero quod
absit, contingeret dictum dominum Regem huiusmodi
grauamina que rationabiliter reparanda fuerint citra
dictum terminum minime reparare noluit tunc idem
clerus concessionem huiusmodi secundi anni optinere
robur aliquod firmitatis sed viribus et effectu omnino
carere nec eorum ordinarii possint aut debeant eos ad
hoc compellere uel execucionem huiusmodi super ea
facere quouis modo." [56]   And again at the end they
asked for royal letters patent in confirmation.[56]

Here we see on the part of the clergy in a number of
points a growing precision.   First of all the right was
asserted to declare who should pay and who should not.
Secondly, there was to be no royal interference; the
bishops' testimonies should stand as evidence of the
inability to pay of those who had insufficient benefices.
Thirdly, grievances were requested to be reformed
before the last term of payment for the year. Fourthly,
what the king had done was to be put in black and
white—that is, confirmed by his letters patent. Fifthly,
we note a desire on the clergy's part to avoid a summons in the following year. Whatever grant, however,
they promised for the future was to be safeguarded. It
was contingent only on the reform of the grievances
presented with the first grant.

In the next parliament (January 13th to February
11th, 1351(–2)) that was held after this convocation, the
archbishop prayed the king that he would command
the clergy's petitions of grievances and wrongs ("tortes")
done to them to be heard and tried, and that he would

[56] *Ibid.,* fol. 49.

give a good and suitable answer and remedy to them.[57]
These petitions, of course, embraced the grievances
formulated in the last convocation. That the conditions for the grant of the second year (i.e. the redress of
their grievances) were sought in this parliament may
also be learned from a letter of the king to Archbishop
Islep enrolled on the Close Roll under date of October
20th, 1352.[58] This letter was an order to the archbishop to appoint the collectors for the levy of the
second year of the tenth for two years as " the conditions upon the grant for the second year sought in the
last parliament have now been completed and accepted
by the clergy."[58] An earlier letter under date of June
26th, 1352, from Archbishop Islep to Ralph (Stratford),
Bishop of London, enclosed the king's letters patent
containing the answers of the king with the consent of
parliament in regard to grievances which they had
prayed the king to redress.[59] These petitions were concerned with ecclesiastical jurisdiction, the arrest and
hanging of clerks, and with presentation to benefices.[60]

On the second day of the convocation which
assembled at S. Paul's on May 16th, 1356, the king's
commissioners sought for him from the clergy a tenth
for six years.[61] On May 23rd, after long discussions
apart, the clergy presented their answer in writing to
the archbishop and his suffragans.[62] Their first complaint was that in the last convocation a remedy had
been sought for certain grievances to the clergy under
certain modes and conditions which had not been fulfilled. They prayed, therefore, that a reform of the
same grievances should be made in the next parlia-

---

[57] *Rot. Parl.*, II, 244, n. 57. The petitions and the king's answers
follow the archbishop's request. *Ibid.*, 244—5, nos. 57—69.

[58] *Cal. C.R.* (1349—54), 26 Edw. III, p. 449.

[59] Reg. Islep, fol. 58v. Printed in Wilkins, *op. cit.*, III, 23—5.

[60] *Ibid.*, fol. 58v. Printed in Wilkins, III, 23—5. *Rot. Parl.*, II,
244—5, nos. 57—69.

[61] *Ibid.*, fol. 117.   [62] *Ibid.*, fol. 117v.

ment.[63] They declared further that the clergy had also granted two tenths to the king, but that meanwhile in the aforesaid and other parliaments which were held from that time, though the tenth was paid, absolutely, no remedy had been ordained.[64] As other reasons against a grant they pointed out that the clergy would undoubtedly be called upon to make a procuration for the two cardinals sent as legates of the apostolic see to France and England, and also for Simon Sudbury,[65] messenger of the said see.[66] They claimed, furthermore, that the ecclesiastical benefices of their province scarcely afforded half of the income they were accustomed to be worth.[66] They, likewise, alleged that since the custom of wool granted to the king by the commonalty of the laity (" communitas laicorum ") in the last parliament tended in fact, though it should not by right, to the grave burden of the clergy (who were not absent from the said parliament through contumacy), as well as of the laity to whom it had been conceded that no fifteenth should be sought or collected in the said six years.[66] They concluded with the following request to the bishops: " May it please your benignity kindly to have the clergy who have always stood devoted to the king and have aided him as much as possible, excused from a further burden being placed upon the Church, lest they be in an inferior position to

[63] *Ibid.*, fol. 117v.: " Et inter cetera quod in proximo parliamento reformacio fieret eorundem."

[64] *Ibid.*, fol. 117v. It is difficult to understand this complaint as we know that the petitions presented in parliament in 1352 had been answered. (Cf. notes 58 and 59 *supra*.) It is possible that another convocation had been held, though there is no record of the actual meeting. There is a request for a summons for November 16th, 1355 (*C.C.R.* (1354—60), 29 Edw. III, p. 233), but Archbishop Islep's register is silent. If a tenth for two years had been granted then, there would have been no need so far as the king was concerned to summon convocation on May 16th, 1356.

[65] Simon Sudbury was consecrated to the See of London on March 20th, 1362. He became Archbishop of Canterbury in 1375. Stubbs, *Registrum sacrum Anglicanum,* p. 78.

[66] Reg. Islep, fol. 117v.

the commonalty of the laity, and to admit the aforesaid for a full and final answer of the clergy and to
assist the said clergy and to excuse them in this behalf
to our Lord the King." [67]

The archbishop and bishops, however, persuaded the
clergy to deliberate until the morrow. [68] Their speech
on the next day [69] opened as follows:

" Although the replies of the aforesaid clergy here
given are true, and very reasonable and just, nevertheless out of reverence for our Lord the King and
sincere devotion which they have just as they have
always had hitherto, that they may procure his
benevolence, grace and favour and the request of the
prelates present in the present sacred council, the
said clergy concede to the said our Lord the King
under the form which follows a single tenth, to wit,
that under the hope of an effectual reform of the
grievances written below a moiety of the said tenth
shall be paid at the feast of S. Andrew next. And
that before the other moiety be exacted in any way
or paid the said our Lord the King likewise by his
wise and prudent advice shall command and cause
the grievances of the prelates and clergy in the said
sacred council from which and by which ecclesiastical
censures and the keys of the church are despised in
such a way the catholic faith is imperilled and the
greatest danger to souls is incurred, to be reformed
effectually and that because the liberties and rights

[67] Reg. Islep, fol. 117v.: " . . . placeat benignitati vestre absque vlteriori
onere hac vice ecclesie inponendo ipsum clerum qui dicto domino Regi
semper deuotus extitit et ipsum iuuit quantum potuit ne deterioris con-
dicionis existat quam communitas laicorum habere si libeat excusatum
et premissa pro plena et finale responsione cleri admittere ipsique clero
assistere et ipsum ergo dominum nostrum Regem in hac parte
excusare."

[68] Ibid., fol. 117.

[69] Ibid., fol. 118. Printed in Wilkins, op. cit., III, 39: " Licet
responsiones cleri predicti date sint vere et valide (sic) rationabiles atque
iuste nichilominus ab reuerenciam domini nostri Regi et sincere deuo-
cionis affectum quem habent prout semper hactenus habuerint ad

and jurisdictions of Holy Mother Church in accordance with the custom of the Christian princes of the
realm of England, his ancestors, whereby new
grievances were removed and withdrawn. If this is
done and fulfilled effectually another moiety of the
said tenth will be paid at the feast of the nativity of
Saint John Baptist (June 24th) following the aforesaid feast of S. Andrew. Nevertheless the said clergy
do not intend nor are willing that the impoverished
who on account of evident need are not able to pay
the said tenth be liable in any way for paying the
same; and that in regard to their poverty credence
should be given to a bare statement or certificate of
the several bishops in their dioceses without any
further proof whatsoever." [69]

This answer presented by the clergy illustrates very
well the position which we shall see often repeated in
the future. They made a strong attempt to be free
from a grant and presented what seemed to be valid
reasons for not making one, but in the end they were
forced to relinquish their stand. Their final position
was not one of complete surrender as they again used

captandum ipsius beneuolenciam graciam et fauorem requisicionemque
prelatorum in presenti sacro concilio presencium Idem clerus concedit
dicto domino nostro Regi sub forma que sequitur decimam tantum unam
videlicet quod sub spe reformacionis infrascriptorum grauaminum
efficacis medietas eiusdem decime soluatur ad festum sancti Andree
proxime iam futurum. Et quod antequam alia medietas exigatur quomodolibet uel soluatur dictus dominus noster Rex eciam per suum sanum
et prudens consilium grauamina ecclesie prelatorum et cleri in dicto
sacro concilio exposita ex quibus et per que censure ecclesiastice et
claues ecclesie contempnuntur quinimmo fides periclitatur catholica et
maximum incurritur periculum animarum mandet et faciat effectualiter
reformari ac libertates et iura et iurisdicciones sancte matris ecclesie
more christianorum principium antecessorum suorum regni Anglie sub-
ductis et reuocatis nouis grauaminibus in statu suo antiquo et debito
conseruari. Quo facto efficaciter et inpleto alia medietas dicte decime
ad festum natiuitatis sancti Johannis Baptiste proximum post festum
sancti Andree predictum et non aliter persoluetur. Non intendit tamen
dictus clerus nec vult quod pauperes quam dictam decimam propter
euidentem inopiam soluere non valebant ad prestandum eandem aliqualiter teneantur; super qua inopia nude relacioni seu certificacioni
episcoporum singulorum in suis diocesibus singulorum absque probacione
quacumque alia fides detur." " Claues " might be rendered " principia
festivitatum." Du Cange.

the method of promising to pay only one tenth outright, making the other conditional. But they were not
able to maintain their stand, for in the next year during
the convocation that assembled on April 26th, 1357,
they relaxed all the conditions which they had made
the previous year except the one concerning those in
need. [70]

A convocation assembled on February 3rd, 1359(–60),
and granted a tenth. [71] This time a very long list of
conditions was appended stated in precise terms. [71] The
tenth was to be paid " sub condicionibus infrascriptis et
non aliter, nec alio modo." The conditions were as
follows : Neither secular nor religious clergy were to be
burdened or taxed with any other imposition nor were
their possessions, manors, animals, vehicles to be seized
by the king's or queen's servants. [71]

Ecclesiastical jurisdiction was to be exercised freely,
nor were inquisitions to be made, nor indictments to be
received for the practice of jurisdiction, nor other
limitations to be imposed. [71]

There was to be no further vexation for poor benefices, for which the diocesan letters should serve as
adequate testimony in the Chancery and the
Exchequer. [71]

The clergy of the diocese of Canterbury were not to
be taxed for the first part of the moiety within certain
boundaries on account of the damages they had
received from the royal army. [71]

The clergy stated that the grant was made " of their
good and spontaneous will " in the hope that the royal
clemency would the sooner be moved to redress the
grievances of the clergy and Holy Church in accordance
with their repeated supplications. [72] If the aforesaid

[70] Reg. Islep, fol. 132v.
[71] Ibid., fol. 158v. Printed Wilkins, III, 46—7. N.B. Wilkins gives
the wrong foliation.
[72] Ibid., fol. 158v. Printed in Wilkins, III, 46—7. N.B. Wilkins has
the wrong foliation.

conditions were not kept the grant would lose force and could not be levied. The clergy asked the archbishop to send letters to the prelates who were absent as well as those who were present, prohibiting them from going against the concession under penalty of excommunication. [72]

The convocation held on January 21st, 1369(–70), witnessed greatly prolonged discussions on the part of the clergy. [73] A tenth for three years was requested of them. [74] At first they replied that they would grant a tenth for two years on the condition that the king would reform the injuries to ecclesiastics attempted by the king's servants (" ministris "); that small impoverished benefices would not be liable to the tax, and that letters of the ordinaries of their dioceses (in regard to their poverty) were to be believed without further proof. [75]

But the archbishop explained to the proctors of the clergy and the religious that a tenth for two years would not suffice for the king's burdens. He thought that the clergy and religious would have granted a tenth for three years to the king for the most powerful reason, that of natural law, just as the prelates moved by natural law granted him a tenth for three years. The archbishop, therefore, informed the proctors of the clergy and the religious to withdraw to other parts in the church and to come to an agreement about the tenth for three years. [76] When they appeared again and reported once more that they granted a tenth for two years, one simply, the other on conditions, they excused themselves altogether from paying a tenth for the third year on account of the various burdens to ecclesiastics and the pestilence which was rife in parts of England, offering that if necessity urged when the two years had elapsed, to be prepared to grant a third

[73] Reg. Witlesey, fols. 23v.—24. Partially printed in Wilkins, *op. cit.*, III, 82—4.
[74] *Ibid.*, fol. 23.   [75] *Ibid.*, fols. 23—23v.   [76] *Ibid.*, fol. 23v.

tenth, should they be called together in the accustomed manner for granting it as a subsidy to the king and to his land (" in subsidium regium et terræ sue predicte ").[77]

But the report of this grant did not meet the wish of the king.[78] He sent his commissioners to persuade the clergy.[78] Finally they yielded, excusing themselves from their former protest in regard to granting a tenth for three years, saying that they had not known of the grant made by the prelates, and begged that their grievances be reformed.[78]

That the lower clergy could be coerced to change the amount of their grant and raise it to the proportions of the one which the prelates had made separately was a decided check to the force of their deliberations. If the royal authority succeeded in binding the prelates first it was a canny method, but it will be remembered that this method was not always successful. Instances have been stated when the prelates refused to come to a decision separately.[79]

At the convocation which was in session from April 24th to May 3rd, 1371, the clergy of the province of Canterbury when they agreed to pay their share of a grant of £50,000 which the king had demanded of the clergy, gained within the session of the convocation the king's acceptance of their conditions that ecclesiastical persons, exempt and non-exempt, privileged and non-privileged, and likewise clerks of the royal free chapels and those having benefices not ordinarily taxed,[80] and

[77] Reg. Witlesey, fols. 23v.—24.
[78] Ibid., fol. 24.
[79] Vide supra, chapter I, 53.
[80] Mention is not made as to whether " benefices not ordinarily taxed " included the impoverished benefices which were to be released from taxation by the certificates. Cf. Adam Murimuth (Continuation), ed. T. Hog (English Historical Society), p. 210. The allusion to the grant in convocation is as follows: ". . . ad quam quidem summam persolvendam sacerdotes stipendarii, secundem valorem quem perceperunt, erant taxati ; minuta etiam beneficia, quæ nunquam prius erant taxata, ad complementum illius similiter erant taxata." Cf. Stubbs, Const. Hist., II (4th ed.), 444.

also that the clergy of the province of York should contribute to the sum granted.[81]   This was an advance for
the clergy—to have their conditions accepted before
the convocation had adjourned.

The first reply of the clergy at the convocation held
December 1st, 1373 was that they must excuse themselves from making a grant on account of the burdens
which encumbered both the prelates and the clergy, to
wit, the eight thousand marks which the province of
York ought to have paid of the last subsidy granted to
the king, and on account of the moiety of one tenth due
on the feast of Saint Andrew last past, which had to be
paid by the clergy, and on account of the sum sought
by the lord pope from the prelates and clergy of the
province of Canterbury, the request for which stood
rejected because of the impotency of the clergy.[82]   The
clergy, after giving their answer, were requested by the
Bishop of London, who was presiding, and the other
bishops to deliberate further and to formulate in writing
their petitions for the reform of injuries.[83]   The
following day in the presence of the bishops, the
proctors of the clergy granted one tenth to be paid at
the feast of the Nativity of S. John Baptist and at the
feast of the Purification following under certain
terms.[83]   The convocation adjourned until the Monday
following.[83]   At that time the proctors of the clergy,
assembled before the archbishop's deputies—the Dean
of the Church of S. Mary of the Arches, the Chancellor
and Auditor of Causes of the Court of Canterbury,—
declared expressly that on account of the impotency of
the clergy, they were unwilling to give anything further
than what they had previously yielded.[83]   The convocation again adjourned until the morrow when it reassembled.[83]   The clergy then granted only the tenth

[81] Reg. Witlesey, fols. 41v.—43.
[82] Ibid., fols. 64—5.
[83] Ibid., fol. 65.

M

above mentioned, and presented to the Bishop of London their grant in writing together with certain supplications for reform. [83]   On the following day in the chapter house the Bishop of Hereford protested publicly and expressly " quod nisi iniurie sibi et ecclesie sue Herefordensi vt dixit multipliciter iniuste illate per Regem et eius consilium essent et sint reformate quod dictus dominus Rex de eo aut clero sue dioc. racione dicte concessionis nullum haberet denarium sed dicte concessioni expresse contradixit." [84]

In the convocation held February 3rd, 1376(-7) certain articles (" articuli ") were proposed and read publicly by the Bishop of London in regard to the reform of certain grievances inflicted upon him and on his church and upon the Bishop of Winchester and the church of Winchester. [85]   The clergy instantly and universally sought that the articles proposed should be reformed on his behalf by the king and his council. [85]   A debate and discussion were held in regard to the articles.   Later a grant was made, proportionate to the various degrees of status in the ecclesiastical hierarchy, but no conditions seem to have been attached to the grant. [86]

The convocation which lasted from November 9th to December 5th, 1377, also made a grant to the king. [87] They gave two tenths for the king's wars—one to be paid on March 25th on condition that the temporal lords and the commons made a grant of a fifteenth, and another tenth for the same uses, payable at Midsummer and the feast of the Purification following, and not otherwise. [88]   In the meantime they were not to be held liable to pay other impositions. [88]   They stipulated that the money granted should be kept and expended only in the defence of the realm of England and the wars of

[84] Reg. Witlesey, fol. 65.
[85] Reg. Sudbury, fol. 33v.
[86] Ibid., fol. 34.
[87] Ibid., fols. 44—44v.
[88] Ibid., fol. 44v.

the king.[88]   The prelates, however, were not content with the dates of these payments.[89]   After deliberations, it was decided that the payment of the two tenths should be made on March 1st following.[89]   A further advance is to be noted here in the clergy's making their grant contingent on a certain grant from the laity.

When at the convocation on May 9th, 1379 the clergy conceded a grant that was apportioned according to status, they expressed their wish that the subsidy be levied in accordance with the present estimate and value of the benefices.[90]   As in 1371 they wished the privileged and non-privileged, exempt and non-exempt, the royal free chapels and their benefices, and other royal privileged clerks to contribute to the subsidy.[91] At this convocation their conditions do not seem to be asserted in as strong terms as had been done sometimes in the past.

Again at the convocation held February 4th, 1379(–80) in return for the grant of 16d. in the mark on all benefices assessed and 16d. in the mark on two thirds of the estimated value of benefices exceeding £10, not assessed, they asked the king to cause the grievances and injuries to the Church to be redressed.[92] When later the archbishop reported that this grant did not suffice for the royal burdens and those of the Church,[93] they made a further stipulation that to the list of those already appointed to be taxed should be added the chaplains of the royal free chapels, and other

[89] *Ibid.*, fol. 45.

[90] *Ibid.*, fols. 55—55v. The clerical tenth as has been stated previously was based on the taxation of Nicholas IV, 1291. A new assessment had been made in 1318 for the northern province because of the depredations. Here in 1371 we find the clergy making an appeal for a new assessment. No new assessment was made. Cf. *supra*, pp. 147—8.

[91] *Ibid.*, fol. 55v.

[92] *Ibid.*, fols. 59v.—60.

[93] No explanation is given of the conjunction of the royal burdens and those of the Church. It was customary to consider money expended in defence of the land as expended also in defence of the Church.

free chapels[94] and alien priories.[95] They stated, moreover, that the priests who were not beneficed, and advocates, registrars, proctors and notaries who were not beneficed, should be taxed two shillings.[96]

The only condition that the clergy made when conceding a subsidy for all states, conditions and sexes at the convocation which assembled December 1st, 1380, was that such a grant could not be used as an argument or evidence in future times against the clergy[97]—that is, they did not wish a precedent to be set for this kind of grant.

The next grant made was conceded at the convocation which began at S. Frideswides, Oxford, on November 18th, 1382, and was later prorogued until the following January.[98] At the first session the clergy voted a moiety of a tenth of the value of ecclesiastical benefices to be paid at the feast of the Annunciation (March 25th), and at the following session they granted a similar moiety to be paid at the feast of the Nativity of S. John Baptist (June 24th).[99] The grant of the second moiety was made conditional. It could be paid only if it should come to pass that the king after deliberate counsel should go in his proper person to foreign parts for the more necessary defence of the realm or, if on account of this, another adequate army (" armatura ") should be needed.[99] If, however, he did not need to go in person or another adequate army (" armatura ") did not have to be furnished, it was neither their wish nor intention to grant more than the moiety of a tenth yielded at Oxford.[99]

The grant yielded by the convocation held December

---

[94] Reg. Sudbury, fol. 60.
[95] The clerks of the royal free chapels had been included among those to be taxed in 1371. Cf. *supra*, p. 164.
[96] Reg. Sudbury (Cantuar.), fol. 60.
[97] *Ibid.*, fols. 72—72v.
[98] Reg. Courteney, I, fols. 33—5.
[99] *Ibid.*, I, fol. 35v.

2nd, 1383, reflects the grant which we have just mentioned.[100]   Two   half-tenths   were   granted—one
absolute, the other on conditions.[101]   The half-tenth
was granted provided that a truce between the realms
of England and France were not arranged before the
feast of Holy Trinity next.[101]   If, however, a truce
should be arranged in the meanwhile, it was not " their
intention nor wish to grant, nor did they grant the
second half-tenth nor any part of the same."[102] Of this
agreement they received a confirmation under the
privy seal.[103]

Convocation met the following year at Salisbury on
May 20th, 1384.[104]   In it the clergy presented articles
seeking a remedy and granted the half-tenth which they
had granted on conditions in the previous convocation,
but instead of holding to the date of payment appointed
in the conditional grant, they postponed the payment
to the feast of All Saints (November 1st) alleging the
poverty of the clergy.[104]

It was on December 17th, 1384,[105] in a parliament
part of the sessions of which were contemporaneous
with those of the convocation which assembled at
S. Paul's   on   December   1st,[106]   that   Archbishop
Courteney made a famous protest, quoted in full elsewhere in this study.[107]   This protest was made when
the laity answered that they would give two fifteenths
to the king if the clergy would give two tenths.[108]   The
archbishop thereupon declared that the Church was

[100] *Ibid.*, I, fols. 78—78v.
[101] *Ibid.*, I, fol. 78.
[102] *Ibid.*, I, fol. 78: " Non est intencionis seu voluntatis eorum dictam
secundam medietatem decime vel aliquam partem eiusdem aliquo modo
concedere nec condedunt."
[103] *Ibid.*, I, fol. 78.
[104] *Ibid.*, I, fol. 79.
[104] Reg. Courteney, I, fols. 81v.—82. Printed Wilkins, *op. cit.*, III,
19.
[106] *Ibid.*, I, fol. 79v.
[107] Cf. *infra*, chapter VII, 209, n. 58.
[108] Reg. Courteney, I, fol. 81v.

free and not to be taxed by the laity.[109]   He further
stated that he could not discuss the matter with his
clergy in convocation until the request of the laity was
erased from the roll.[109]   This the king caused to be
done.[109]

It will be remembered that the clergy in 1377 made
their grant on the condition that the laity would
make a certain grant[110]; yet no protest was forthcoming at that time from the latter.

When the matter of a grant was discussed in convocation shortly after the bishop's protest, the clergy
yielded two half-tenths, one absolute, the other conditional on the king's going personally to foreign parts.[111]
If the king sent others with the army or treated for
peace through others, then only the first half-tenth was
to be paid.[111]   They added that this concession seemed
to them burdensome when the half-tenth yielded at
Salisbury was remembered, which was not as yet fully
paid.[111]   They further declared that it was likewise the
intention of the clergy that they should in the meanwhile be relieved from any other burden and imposition.[111]   They supplicated, moreover, that the reverend
fathers would beseech the king effectually with affec-
tionate prayers that he would be pleased to restore the
temporalities to the Bishop of Norwich.[111]

Not long afterwards, on February 3rd, 1384(-5),
Archbishop Courteney received a letter from the king,
Richard II, asking him to call a convocation between
then and mid-Lent Sunday (March 12th).[112]   The
archbishop demurred as we have explained more fully
elsewhere,[113] but finally the king had his will, and a
convocation was summoned.[114]   It will be noted,

---

[109] Reg. Courteney, I, fol. 82.   [111] Reg. Courteney, I, fol. 80.
[110] Cf. *supra*, p. 166.   [112] *Ibid.*, I, fols. 82v.—83.
[113] *Ibid.*, I, fols. 82—82v.   Cf. *supra*, chapter III, 102.
[114] *Wykeham's Register* (Hamp. Rec. Soc.), II, 365 (pt. III,
fol. 213b).

however, that the date for the assembling of the convocation was not until May 4th [114]—the time of the year
at which it had become customary for one of the two
convocations of the province of Canterbury to assemble.
When this convocation did assemble, the archbishop
himself was not there.[115] He had commissioned the
Bishop of London to act for him.[115] Courteney's
register does not hold an account of the proceedings of
this convocation, but it does contain the archbishop's
order for the dissolution of the convocation. From this
order for dissolution we learn that the proctors had
replied in the convocation that for sufficient and
reasonable causes they could not aid the king with any
subsidy.[115]

If the chronicler, Walsingham, has not confounded
the events of the years 1384 and 1385, the laity in 1385
again made an attempt to dictate the amount of the
clergy's grant when they stated that they would make
a grant of a fifteenth and of half a fifteenth to the king
provided the clergy should grant a tenth and a half-
tenth.[116] Whereupon Archbishop Courteney protested,
saying that this could by no means be done, especially
since the Church ought to be free and should not be
taxed by the laity.[117] In a case such as this, he continued, the Holy Church of England should sooner take

[115] Reg. Courteney, I, fol. 83.
[116] Walsingham, *Historia Anglicana*, II, 139. Cf. *supra*, p. 74, n. 144.
Stubbs thinks that Walsingham may have confounded the events of
the two years. *Const. Hist.*, II (4th ed.), 491, n. 1. If Walsingham has
confounded the events of the two years, then the events cited here from
his chronicle for the year 1385 belong to the year 1384 when Archbishop Courteney made a protest on December 17th.
Walsingham (*op. cit.*, II, 139) gives the conditional grant of the laity
as "unam quintam decimam et demidiam." The parliament roll for
the parliament in the Michaelmas term, 1385, records the grant of the
laity as "unam Decimam & unam Quintam-decimam ac Medietatem
unius Decime & unius Quinte-decime." *Rot. Parl.*, III, 204, n. 10.
[117] Walsingham, *Historia Anglicana*, II, 139: " . . . cui conditioni
obnixe restitit Archiepiscopus Cantuariensis, Dominus Willelmus de
Courtenay, dicens hoc minime fore faciendum, praesertim cum Ecclesia
debeat esse libera, et per laicos nullo modo taxanda."

the lead than be made a slave. [118]   The archbishop's response met with a storm among the laity, who declared that the temporalities should be taken from the ecclesiastics, whose pride needed to be humbled. [119] The laity even began to contemplate what religious houses they should choose to appropriate for themselves. [120] The king, however, put an end to their high hopes by declaring that he would preserve the Church of England in the same status which she enjoyed when he took the realm, [121] and even in a better one. [122] The clergy on account of this felt that the king was worthy of a great gift. [123] The archbishop, therefore, after communicating with his clergy, who had already

---

[118] Walsingham, *Historia Anglicana*, II, 139—40: " . . . immo, citius caput exponeret pro hac causa, quam in tantum Sanctam Ecclesiam Anglicanam permitteret ancillari."

[119] *Ibid.*, II, 140: "Quæ responsio tantum commovit turbam communium, ut milites Comitatuum, cum quibusdam ex proceribus regni, cum summa furia deprecarentur auferre temporalia ab ecclesiasticis, dicentes clerum ad tantam excrevisse superbiam, quod opus esset pietatis et eleimosynæ, per ablationem temporalium quæ ecclesiasticos extollebant, eos compellere ad humilius sapiendum."

[120] *Ibid.*, II, 140.

[121] Richard II succeeded to the throne June 22nd, 1377.

[122] Walsingham, *Historia Anglicana*, II, 140: " . . . dicens se Ecclesiam Anglicanam in ejusdem status qualitate suis temporibus servaturum, qua ipsam cognoverat extitisse, cum regnum suscepisset, aut potius meliori." For the coronation oath taken by English kings during the period of this study see J. Wickam Legg, *Three Coronation Orders*. An Anglo-French version of the English Coronation Order is given in this volume, pp. 40—9. Mr. Wickham Legg states that the version was made earlier than 1325, but not before 1272. The following section found on p. 40 was probably the form or somewhat similar to the form of the oath taken by Richard II at his coronation:

"Et puis apres prechera le erceuesque et quant il auera preche si demaundera de celui que est a coroner si voudra granter & garder et par sermant & confermer a seint eglise & a son pœple les leys & les custumus que grante furunt des aunciens roys & que a deu furent deuout & nomement les leys coustimus & les franchises que furent granteez a la clergie & al pœple par seint edward'—

"Et il vodra promettre & se assente a tut ceque lerceuesque lui ad demande

"Donks lui dirre l'erceuesque sur que le chose il iurra.

"Garderet uous a seint eglise la clergie & al pœple la pes entierement & lamur en deu solompk† nostre pœr.

"E li roy respoundera. Ie les garderoy."

[123] Walsingham, *Historia Anglicana*, II, 140: " . . . quo facto et apud ecclesiasticos magna muneratione dignus censebatur."

assembled in convocation on November 6th,[124] announced to the king that they would grant him a tenth.[125] From the archbishop's register we know that in this convocation on the same day they granted a half-tenth, made conditional on the king's going personally with his army abroad before the feast of S. Michael.[126]

At the convocation in November 1386,[127] when the clergy gave their reply to the archbishop and bishops, they named the uses for which the king alleged that he desired the grant.[127] Later in the course of their reply they declared bluntly that experience had taught them that subsidies of this kind were often converted to uses wholly different.[128] They complained, too, that subsidies such as this which used to occur rarely in the time of the king's ancestors when war was more violent and terrible, now occurred annually.[129] They also alleged that among all their other burdens resulting from epidemics among men and diseases among animals, other and adverse misfortunes and heavy expenses in the purchase of horses and a different kind of arms and other munitions for repelling the hostile attacks, the clergy had come to such a state of want that very many were unable to support themselves without the reproach of mendicancy and the grave injury of their creditors.[129] Since, however, the bishops asserted that the necessity for defence was so great, they had nevertheless, in faith that the king would be the protector of the clergy in the future, granted a half-tenth to be paid at Easter.[129] They granted, moreover,

---

[124] Reg. Courteney, I, fol. 83v.
[125] Walsingham, *Hist. Ang.*, II, 140.
[126] Reg. Courteney, I, fol. 84.
[127] *Ibid.*, I, fol. 84v.
[128] *Ibid.*, I, fol. 85. Printed in Wilkins, op. cit., III, 200: " . . . sed non immerito ipse clerus in concessione petiti subsidii difficilem se pretendit, eo quod subsidia ob causam huiusmodi preconcessa in vsus prorsus alios vt experiencia docuit, sunt conuersa."
[129] *Ibid.*, I, fol. 85. Printed in Wilkins, *op. cit.*, III, 200.

another half-tenth to be paid at All Saints (November 1st) provided that the king preserved the clergy and the Church of England in their liberties as his forefathers had done, and that the spiritual and temporal lords elected and appointed to the King's Council for the governance of the realm should continue in office throughout the time the limits of which had been set.[130] If these lords should consider the second half-tenth necessary for the defence of the realm and the Church of England, it would be given.[130] Otherwise it was not to be levied.[131]

In the next convocation which was held at S. Paul's, February 26th, 1387(–8),[132] the clergy granted the half-tenth which they had yielded previously under conditions, under new conditions—namely, that for one whole year beginning from the day of granting, the king should preserve the clergy from other imposts whatsoever imposed or to be imposed, and in all their liberties as his forefathers had done.[132] A further condition was that the clergy of the province of York should contribute for the year past as well as for the present.[132] If the clergy of the province of York did not contribute grants for both years, they stipulated that they (the clergy of the province of Canterbury) should be released from the grant which they had just made.[132] Otherwise, they asserted, it might become a grievance to the clergy of the province of Canterbury if the clergy of the province of York were released while they were not.[132]

---

[130] Reg. Courteney, I, fol. 85.   Printed in Wilkins, *op. cit.*, III, 200.

[131] *Ibid.*, I, fol. 85.   The text of the clergy's reply at this point reads : " Alioquin concessio *vtriusque* medietatis decime nulla sit, et pro nulla penitus habeatur."   But the text of the archbishop's certificate of the grant to the king reads, " Alioquin concessio ipsius *vltime* medietatis decime nulla sit."   Regist. Courteney, pt. I, fol. 85.   Since it was customary for the second half-tenth to become null if the conditions were not fulfilled, one ventures to conclude that the archbishop's text is correct.

[132] Reg. Courteney, I, fol. 73.

At the convocation held the following autumn (October 12th, 1388),[133] in spite of their poverty the clergy of the province of Canterbury granted a tenth to the king provided that he set out for foreign parts before the feast of S. Michael next (September 29th).[133]   One half was to be paid on the quindene of Easter (May 2nd), the other on the feast of the translation of S. Thomas, Martyr (July 7th).[133]   In return for this they were to be preserved a year from all other imposts.[133]   If the king did not go abroad, the first half-tenth was to be kept entirely for the ease of the common burdens of the clergy to be imposed at the next parliament.[133]   The last half was not to be exacted or levied.[133]   Here we perceive an advance on the part of the clergy for their protection.   Limitations now were being put on the first half of the tenth.   In the conditions made by the clergy for this grant we also note that they were assuming that burdens would be the result of each succeeding parliament.   The conception of some sort of taxing system was beginning to be apparent.

On October 10th, 1389 Richard II issued a writ to Archbishop Courteney in which he reprimanded him severely for the impost which he had laid upon the clergy of the realm with the consent of his suffragans for the benefit of the pope.[134]   The king declared that the archbishop had issued his mandate for the levying of the said subsidy of pence without the common counsel and assent of the realm.[134]   He, therefore, commanded the archbishop to desist from all such impositions, to recall his mandates, and to restore all pence that had been exacted or levied.[134]   Like writs *(mutatis*

---

[133] *Ibid.*, I, fol. 74.

[134] P.R.O., Close Roll, 13 Richard II, pt. I, m. 17.   Printed in *Rot. Parl.*, III, 405.   The action taken against the archbishop was due primarily to the anti-papal feeling of the time.   Archbishops had been allowed to issue mandates for the levy of small sums in the past.   Cf. *Reg. Reynolds* (Worcester), p. 44 (fol. 52).

mutandis) were issued to the Archbishop of York, seventeen bishops, the custodians of the spiritualities of two sees, the Abbot of Battle and the Prior of Rochester. [134]

The decision for the levy of this impost for the pope must have been made privately by the archbishop and his suffragans, as there appears to be no record of a council or convocation in 1388 or 1389 when a subsidy such as this for the pope was considered.

On April 17th, 1391, a convocation met at S. Paul's to deliberate concerning a grant to Pope Boniface IX. [135] The request for the grant here sought came probably as a direct result of the failure of Archbishop Courteney through the king's prohibition to levy the subsidy of pence for the pope in 1389.

It is interesting to compare the conditions laid down by the clergy in making this grant to the pope with those which it was customary for them to make in agreeing to a grant for the king. In the first place they stipulated that the order for the levy of the subsidy should not be written, nor should the subsidy be collected until the consent and good pleasure of the king and the lords of the council were known. [136] Secondly, even though the royal consent should be given, the subsidy should not be levied by compulsion before the following Christmas. [136] Thirdly, they declared that the subsidy should be levied from benefices accustomed to pay the tax. [136] Fourthly, they asserted that the subsidy should not be exacted from nuns (" moniales ") and from others who were beneficed, who were known to be poor. [136] The bishops' letters in regard to their poverty should be accepted in full faith. [136] Finally, the subsidy could be devoted only to uses of defence for the pontiff. [136] Provided that all the conditions were faithfully observed the clergy granted four pence in the

---

[133] Reg. Courteney, I, fol. 75.   [136] *Ibid.*, I, fol. 76.

pound of the value of ecclesiastical benefices, portions and pensions.[136] If any of the conditions were not fulfilled, the clergy were not to be held to their grant.[137]

It is noteworthy that we have here a reversal of the situation which we found at the last part of the thirteenth century. At the same time it is a parallel in analogous circumstances. The clergy then refused to make a grant before asking the pope's permission. Now in 1391 they said that they must consult the king and the lords of the council before making a grant to the pope. As in the grants to the king, the clergy in giving this subsidy to the pope, safeguarded themselves against a precipitate levy of the money or against extra burdens for poor ecclesiastics. Another similarity between the procedure for both types of grants was that in both the money was stated distinctly as being given for a special purpose. If it was not used for that purpose the grant became null.

We do not know the conditions of the half-tenth granted by the clergy in the convocation which met December 9th, 1391.[138]

No full record of the acts of the convocation that met at S. Paul's, May 13th—21st, 1394,[139] has been recovered in the research for this study. Only the king's writ to the archbishop for the appointment of collectors restating the terms of the grant gives us the bare details.[140] A half-tenth was granted, payable at the feast of S. Andrew (November 30th).[140] The one condition stated was that nothing was to be exacted from any of the poor nuns (" moniales ") whatsoever.[140]

At the next convocation (February 5th, 1394(-5)),[141] we again have a record of the clergy's reply put in writing.[142] This time the clergy of the province of

---

[137] *Ibid.*, I, fols. 76—76v.
[138] *Wykeham's Register*, II, 600 (pt. IV, fol. 26b).
[139] P.R.O., Ancient Correspondence, vol. XLIII, n. 17.
[140] Reg. Courteney, II, fol. 195.
[141] *Ibid.*, II, fol. 195v.   [142] *Ibid.*, II, fol. 196v.

Canterbury " pura spontanea et libera voluntate ob
sinceram affectionem," [142] granted the king a tenth of
all benefices beyond the sum of six marks, payable July
7th and November 30th. [142] This they did because he
was " their gracious lord and protector " [142] especially
against the Lollards. [142] The grant was made on the
condition that no royal writs for the levy of the first
moiety should emanate before the feast of Pentecost
(May 30th, 1395), nor for the second before the feast of
S. Michael (September 29th). The clergy, furthermore,
desired that the poor nuns (" moniales ") and religious
women of whatever order, exempt and non-exempt,
should not be included in the concession, and that the
diocesans in their letters in regard to the appointment
of collectors should be bound to make mention concerning the poor, and that according to these letters faith
should be shown in the king's exchequer for the exoneration of the aforesaid paupers. [142] At the same time
the clergy made a special supplication [143] to the Archbishop of Canterbury and the Archbishop of York, the
Chancellor of England who was present, that for the
support of the Catholic Faith and the rooting out of
heretical depravity in the realm of England caused by
the sect of Lollards, they inform the king in order that
he could extend his arm effectually lest through silence
because he was away, the Lollards should grow strong
and the multitude of them increase. [144]

By the end of the fourteenth century [145] the clergy had

[143] Reg. Courteney, II, fol. 196v. : " Ac simul cum huiusmodi concessione quandam supplicacionem ex parte dicti cleri conceptam prefato
domino Archiepiscopo et Archiepiscopo Eboracen. pronunc Cancellario
Anglie ibidem eciam presenti tradidit."
    The presence of the Archbishop of York in his capacity of Chancellor
of England at a meeting of the convocation of the province of Canterbury as here recounted is worthy of remark.

[144] Ibid., II, fol. 196v.

[145] In the remaining convocations of Richard II's reign there is nothing
of note regarding the conditions of grants or grievances. At the convocation at London, February 19th, 1396(-7), Oxford University presented grievances (Reg. Arundel, I, 44—47v.).

established certain principles in regard to grants levied on their spiritualities. Their grant was to be made in convocation—not in parliament. The amount of it was not to be dictated to them by the laity. They were to be able freely to decide upon it. The grant was not to be without conditions. Part of it might be granted free; the other part generally had conditions attached to it which would protect the clergy from having the money that they had granted expended for any purpose which suited the king's fancy. There was to be protection for those who were too poor to contribute to the grant. The exoneration of persons from payment was not to be determined by royal officials, but was to rest with the bishops or ordinaries of the diocese concerned.

Closely linked to the subject of grants was, as we have seen, that of grievances. In return for their grants the clergy expected the reform of their grievances. The clergy never in the fourteenth century reached a position strong enough to make every grant absolutely dependent on the redress of grievances. They petitioned for reform, they expressed the hope of reform, and in a few cases gave as a reason for not making a grant the fact that the reform of their grievances had not taken place.[146] In one case we find them making their future grant entirely dependent on reform.[147] The stand thus taken on the part of the clergy though not always forceful or effectual, did mean a gain for constitutional principles. The fact that the clergy recognized that there was some connection between the grant and the redress of grievances, cleared the way simultaneously with the like attitude of the laity in the fourteenth century, for the time when the people could demand reform from the supreme authority or retaliate if it were withheld.

---

[146] *Ann. Monast. (Dunstaplia)*, III, 295. Reg. Islep, fol. 117v.
[147] *Ibid.*, fol. 49.

CHAPTER VI

THE CONVOCATIONS OF CANTERBURY AND YORK: A COMPARISON OF ACTIVITIES AND PROCEDURE IN THE THIRTEENTH AND FOURTEENTH CENTURIES

WHEN a comparison is made of the Convocations of Canterbury and York during the thirteenth and fourteenth centuries, certain salient differences between the two are apparent. In the first place there was, of course, the difference in the number of dioceses which each province comprised. Whereas the province of Canterbury during the period of this study contained many dioceses, the province of York numbered only a few dioceses. It will be remembered that the original plan of Pope Gregory the Great was that there should be two provinces in England with twelve dioceses each.[1] The fulfilment of this plan, however, proved impossible. The founding of the dioceses became a gradual process.[2] By the middle of the twelfth century the province of Canterbury which included Wales,

[1] *Venerabilis Bædæ Opera Historica,* I, 63—4.
[2] Stubbs, *Registrum Sacrum Anglicanum,* 210—47, *passim.* The dates of the founding of the sees (sometimes known only approximately through signatures) in the province of Canterbury were as follows: Canterbury 597, London 604, Rochester 604, Dunwich 630, Winchester 634, Lichfield, Chester and Coventry 656, Hereford 669, Elmham 673, Lindsey 678, Leicester and Dorchester 680, Worcester 680, Sherborne 705, Selsey 709, Ramsbury 909, Wells 909, Crediton 909, Cornwall 931, Thetford and Norwich 1070, Chichester 1070, Exeter 1072, Salisbury 1078, Bath and Wells 1088, Ely 1092, Bangor 1092, Lincoln 1094, Llandaff 1107, St. David's 1115, St. Asaph 1143. There are traditions concerning the early history of the Welsh sees before the dates given here when they were joined to the province of Canterbury.
The dates of the founding of the sees in the province of York were as follows: York 625, Lindisfarne 635, Chester-le-Street 883, Hexham 678, Whithern in Galloway 730, Durham 990, Carlisle 1133. No bishops are recorded as being consecrated for Hexham after 821, for Lindisfarne after 899, for Chester-le-Street after 990, or for Whithern in Galloway between 791 and 1133. In 1133 a bishop was consecrated to the See of Whithern.

embraced eighteen dioceses[3]; the province of York contained four dioceses.[4] Naturally, therefore, the number of those summoned to a convocation of the province of York was much smaller than that in the southern province. Unlike the Archbishop of Canterbury, the Archbishop of York had no dean for his province, but issued his mandates direct to his suffragans.[5] The classes of persons summoned is identical with those summoned in the province of Canterbury with one exception. Instead of always summoning the clergy of each diocese by two proctors, the Archbishop of York frequently (not invariably) summoned the clergy of each archdeaconry of his suffragan's city and diocese by two proctors.[6]

[3] Stubbs, *Registrum Sacrum Anglicanum,* pp. 220—41, *passim.* By the middle of the twelfth century the province of Canterbury contained the following dioceses which remained or had been consolidated or transferred from the earlier foundations: Canterbury, London, Rochester, Winchester, Coventry and Lichfield, Hereford, Worcester, Chichester, Bath and Wells, Norwich, Exeter, Salisbury, Lincoln, Ely, Bangor, Llandaff, St. David's, St. Asaph. The province of Canterbury still contained only these sees at the end of the fourteenth century.

[4] Stubbs, *Registrum Sacrum Anglicanum,* pp. 242—7, *passim.* By the middle of the twelfth century the province of York contained the following dioceses: York, Durham, Carlisle and Whithern. Stubbs does not record the consecration of a bishop of Whithern after 1358. At the end of the fourteenth century the province of York contained only the Sees of York, Durham and Carlisle.

[5] *The Register of John le Romeyn, Lord Archbishop of York* (1286—1296), (Surtees Soc.), II, 93—4 (fol. 133).

[6] Of the representation in the province of York Stubbs writes (*Const. Hist.,* II. (4th ed.), 207), "that of the province of York is somewhat differently constituted, containing two proctors from each archdeaconry, an arrangement which dates at least as early as 1279." He gives as his reference Wilkins, *Conc.,* II, 41. Wilkins quotes from Reg. Wickwane Ebor., fol. ii. (now also available in the *Register of William Wickwane, Lord Archbishop of York,* 1279—1285 (Surtees Soc.), p. 53 (113d). *N.B.* Wilkins has wrong foliation). This mandate was sent to the Archdeacon of Cleveland in the first year of Wickwane's consecration (1279). It contains the following words: " . . . ita quod die Veneris proxima ante festum Sancte Scolastice Virginis quilibet archidiaconus cum duobus digne eminencie viris et unico ipsius archidiaconatus decano, nobis apud Pontefractum, ubi personaliter erimus Deo dante, responsum pro communitate tocius archidiaconatus faciat."

Since, however, the mandate is addressed to an archdeacon of the diocese of York, it is impossible to tell whether the summons was for a provincial or diocesan convocation. If it were the latter, this mandate of 1279 cannot be taken as typical of a provincial summons.

The form of procedure in the Convocation of York
in the fourteenth century is suggestive of that in the
Convocation of Canterbury. The acts of the Council
of May 20th, 1310, may be cited as an example of York
procedure.[7] On the opening day the Mass of the Holy
Spirit was celebrated at S. Peter's, York, the archbishop and his suffragans being in pontifical vestments,[8]
the other high dignitaries such as abbots, priors, arch-
priests and archdeacons, and the proctors of the clergy
being present.[9] After the mass the archbishop preached
a sermon.[9] Then he explained to the clergy the
" articles " to be treated in the council.[9] After this
certain apostolic letters were read in regard to inquisitions to be made against the Templars, and these were
followed by the reading of the letters of citation, and

The mandate quoted below from Newark's register shows that a
different practice was sometimes observed. Wilkins, *op. cit.*, II, 235—6
(Ex reg. Henr. de Newark, Ebor., fol. 2). In this mandate from Henry
Newark, Archbishop of York, to John Halton, Bishop of Carlisle, for a
convocation on November 29th, 1297, the following words occur:
" . . . vobis mandamus, quatenus totum clerum vestræ civitatis et
diœces., et tam abbates, quam priores exemptos et non exemptos ad
certos diem et locum in eadem diocesi coram vobis faciatis celeriter
convocari; duoque de clero procuratores constituantur idonei pro eodem,
qui eum plena et sufficiente potestate die Veneris in vigilia beati Andreæ
apostoli (M. CC. XCVII) coram nobis vel officiali nostro, seu aliis commissariis nostris, quos duxerimus deputand. in nostra Ebor. ecclesia
compareant. . . ."
The mandate for a convocation at York a month after Easter 1316 did
not specify that the proctors of each archdeaconry should be sent:
" Abbates . . . Priores . . . Decani archidiaconi et propositi personaliter,
conventus vero et capitula ac collegia singula per procuratores singulos,
clerusque vestrarum civitatis et diocesis per duos procuratores ydoneos
et sufficienter instructos ac plenam sufficientem potestatem ab ipsis con-
ventibus capitulis collegiis ac clero habentes." *Reg. Halton*, II, 119.
In Archbishop Melton's mandate to the Bishop of Durham (Lewis de
Beaumont) for a convocation at York on January 20th, 1319, he summoned the clergy of each archdeaconry by two proctors: " . . . Abbates,
Priores, Decani, Archidiaconi et Præpositi personaliter, conventus et
capitula ac Collegia singula per procuratores singulos, clerusque
cujuslibet Archidiaconatus vestrarum civitatis et Dioceseos per duos procuratores ydoneos. . . ." *The Records of the Northern Convocation*
(Surtees Soc.), p. 69 (Reg. W. Melton Archiep. Ebor., f. 459 seq.).
[7] Wilkins, *op. cit.*, II, 393—4 (Ex reg. Will. Grenefeld archiepiscopi
Eborum, fol. 179, pt. 1).
[8] It is probable that some of the abbots were in pontifical vestments
too.
[9] Wilkins, *op. cit.*, II, 394 (Ex reg. Will. Grenefeld, fol. 179, pt. 1).

the certificates of the Bishops of Carlisle and Whithern and those of the Official of York and the Chapter of York. [9, 10] Thereupon those who had been cited were preconized. [11] Excuses were presented by certain men for some who were absent, and when these excuses were considered legitimate, they were admitted. [11] The procedure against those who had not appeared nor had sent legitimate excuses was postponed until the morrow for deliberation. [11] The archbishop then charged the clergy to appear on the morrow in the chapter house to give and to show " articles " and " chapters " in writing touching the state and correction of churches and ecclesiastical persons, and other things that should and could be reformed. [12] On the following day in the chapter house when the clergy came before the archbishop, certain " articles " were explained to the clergy in regard to several persons, the order of the Templars, and the state of the dioceses and province. [13] Because of the magnitude of the business the clergy felt that they could not at present complete it. [13] It was proposed, therefore, to hold another council. [13] Before the adjournment all those who had not appeared were pronounced contumacious, their punishment being reserved to the archbishop. [13] This was similar to the practice in the province of Canterbury. [14] In comparing the procedure of this council with that of the council held at York in the following year we note a

[10] Here may be noted a difference from the procedure in the Convocation of Canterbury where one certificate was read by the Bishop of London.

[11] Wilkins, *op. cit.*, II, 394.

[12] *Ibid.*, II, 394 (Ex reg. Will. Grenefeld, fol. 179, pt. 1): " . . . ad proponendum, dandum, et exhibendum in scriptis articulos et capitula, contingentia statum et correctionem ecclesiarum et ecclesiasticarum personarum, et alia, quæ in hoc concilio nostro debebunt, et poterunt reformari."

[13] *Ibid.*, II, 394 (Ex reg. Will. Grenefeld, fol. 179, pt. 1).

[14] Cf. *supra*, p. 133.

close similarity as to the fundamental details, [15] and when we compare the two with the procedure found in the province of Canterbury, we find them very much the same. Though nothing is said about the lower clergy withdrawing for discussion as was so often the case in the convocations of the province of Canterbury, the archbishop in 1310 commanded them to report the following day the substance of their deliberation. [16] One may, therefore, venture to suggest that they did withdraw to hold a discussion.

As in the province of Canterbury, the archbishop after the final adjournment of convocation, reported to the king the grant that had been made, with the conditions appended or the substance of their discussion if a refusal had been made. [17]

From the records available, the convocation of the southern province appears to have been much more active in the last forty years of the thirteenth century than that of the northern province. In the period from 1260 to 1299 in the province of Canterbury there are allusions to five legatine councils, [18] sixteen councils of bishops or bishops and other prelates, [19] of which it is known definitely that seven assembled, [20] and seventeen councils or convocations, of which it is known definitely that eleven assembled, and to which came or were summoned other members of the clergy besides pre-

[15] Wilkins, op. cit., II, 394—401 (Ex reg. Grenefeld, pt. 2, fol. 180). This council assembled at York May 24th, 1311. It was in session until May 27th and was then adjourned. It reassembled at York July 1st—10th, was prorogued until July 28th and continued in session until July 30th, 1311.

[16] Ibid., II, 394 (Ex reg. Will. Grenefeld, fol. 179, pt. 1).

[17] Reg. Romeyn (Surtees Soc.), II, 86—7 (fol. 130d).

[18] 1265, 1266, 1267, 1267, 1268. These all assembled. Cf. chart Appendix B.

[19] 1264, 1270, 1272, 1273, 1279, 1280, 1280, 1281, 1282, 1286, 1287, 1287, 1289, 1290, 1295, 1299. Cf. chart, Appendix B.

[20] 1264, 1270, 1272, 1273, 1279, 1282, 1286. Cf. chart, Appendix B.

lates.[21]   In the same period in the province of York
there are records of four councils[22] or convocations and
of another council,[23] which seems to have been
diocesan, but which may have been provincial.[24] Apart
from these there was an assembly of both provinces
called by the king for September 21st, 1294, at Westminster.[25]

In the period from 1314 to 1399 when the royal request for convocations was an established practice,
there are forty instances when the writs (or the statement of the issue of writs) requesting a convocation of
the province of Canterbury and one of the province of
York were enrolled together on the Close Roll.[26] There
are two years, 1334 and 1342, when the writs for the
two provinces were enrolled in different positions on the
Close Roll under dates six weeks or less apart.[27] In
1385 the writs were enrolled together, but under
different dates.[28] In 1339 two writs were issued for
York apart from the one that was issued for both
provinces.[29] On November 10th, 1373, extra writs
were issued for York to the dean and chapter of York

[21] 1261, 1263, 1269, 1270, 1270, 1273, 1278, 1281, 1282, 1283, 1283,
1290, 1297, 1297, 1297, 1297, 1298. Of these we know definitely that
the following assembled: 1261, 1263, 1269, 1270, 1281, 1282, 1283,
1297, 1297, 1297, 1298. Cf. chart, Appendix B.
[22] 1261, 1286, 1290, 1297. We know definitely that all these
assemblies met.
[23] 1280.
[24] Stubbs seems to regard this council as provincial as he uses it as an
example in his generalization about the representation by proctors in
the province of York. Stubbs, *Const. Hist.*, II (4th ed.), p. 207. Cf.
supra, p. 181, n. 6.
[25] Wilkins, II, 201 (Ex reg. Henr. prior., Cantuar., fol. 63a). *Flores
Historiarum*, III, 90.
[26] *Calendar of Close Rolls, passim.* Although the writs (or the statements of the issue of writs) were enrolled together, it does not necessarily
mean that they were issued on the same day. In the *Calendar of Close
Rolls (1343—46)*, 18 Edw. III, pt. 1, m. 14d, p. 368, we find the writ
to Canterbury and the statement of like issue to York calendared under
the same date. On the Close Roll itself 18 Edw. III, pt. 1 (P.R.O.,
C 54/174) we find the date of issue to Canterbury was April 22nd, that
of York May 15th. For references cf. charts, Appendix A, Appendix B.
[27] *Cal. C.R.* (1333—37), 8 Edw. III, pp. 316, 320.
[28] *Ibid.* (1385—89), 9 Richard II, p. 86.
[29] *Ibid.* (1339—41), 13 Edw. III, pp. 105, 270, 332.

and to the guardian of the spirituality of the archbishopric of York[30] but this was probably because the
archbishop of York had died before holding the convocation which the king had already requested.
Similarly another writ was issued in 1388,[31] possibly
because the see had been vacant when the other writ
was sent, and the king now wished to make sure that the
new archbishop would hold the convocation. Besides
these there were other writs issued for York alone.[32]

In the period from 1314 to 1399 (if we count the
year from January to January) there were twenty-two
years when it is certain that both provinces held convocations.[33] Of these years there were three[34] in which
the province of Canterbury held two convocations in
the same year while that of York held only one, and
two[35] years in which the province of York held two
convocations while that of Canterbury held only one.
One year they both had two convocations.[36] In sixteen
instances during this period the convocations of the two
provinces were never more than a month apart[37]; in
several of these they assembled within a fortnight of
each other or less.[38] If among the remaining years
when the two provinces both held convocations, the
gap was very wide between the two meetings, it was
probably due to the fact that one of the provinces had
held a convocation late in the preceding year when the

---

[30] *Cal. C.R.* (1369—74), 47 Edw. III, p. 595.

[31] *Ibid.* (1385—89), 12 Richard II, p. 594.

[32] *Ibid.* (1381—85), 6 Richard II, p. 196. Date of issue January 28th,
1383. *Ibid.* (1385—89), 12 Richard II, p. 594. Date of issue December
18th, 1388. *Ibid.* (1396—99), 20 Richard II, p. 118. Date of issue
April 12th, 1397. *Ibid.* (1396—99), 22 Richard II, pp. 390—1. Date of
issue August 1st, 1398. *Ibid.* (1396—99), 22 Richard II, p. 440. Date
of issue January 27th, 1399.

[33] 1314, 1316, 1319, 1323, 1327, 1334, 1336, 1337, 1340, 1344, 1347,
1351, 1356, 1360, 1370, 1371, 1377, 1378, 1379, 1380, 1391, 1395.

[34] 1377, 1380, 1391.

[35] 1319, 1340.

[36] 1336.

[37] 1316, 1319, 1323, 1327, 1334, 1336, 1340, 1344, 1351, 1356, 1360,
1370, 1377, 1379, 1391, 1395.

[38] 1323, 1340, 1360, 1370, 1379, 1391, 1395.

other had not assembled.[39]   In four[40] instances the
York Convocation sat before that of Canterbury.   In
two other instances,[41] though the York meeting seems
to be preceding that of Canterbury in point of time as
to the year, the position was not really so since the
province of Canterbury had held a convocation in each
case at the latter end of the preceding year when the
province of York had held no convocation. There were
eighteen years in the period from 1314 to 1399 when
the province of Canterbury held convocations and that
of York held none.[42]   In seven[43] of these eighteen years
the Canterbury Convocation met twice during the year
and in one[44] of the years it met three times.   The
province of York held convocations in four years[45]
during which there was no corresponding convocation
in the southern province.

From this comparison it will be seen that the Convocation of Canterbury met much more frequently than
that of York and that with only a few exceptions its
meetings antedated those of the northern province. It
must, however, be emphasized that many other convocations may have assembled for which there are
records extant to-day only of a royal request for a
summons, or of a summons, or of " procuratoria " in
which the date of summons is mentioned.

The York convocations like those of Canterbury
were practically all concerned with making grants to
the king. Apart from the records of the Council of
Beverley (1261) where new statutes were provided, and
the councils of 1310 and 1311 dealing with the question
of the Templars, it has proved impossible in the course

[39] 1347, 1378.

[40] 1327, 1379, 1391, 1395.

[41] 1347, 1378.

[42] 1321, 1329, 1332, 1338, 1341, 1346, 1357, 1363, 1373, 1376, 1384,
1385, 1386, 1388, 1389, 1394, 1397, 1399.

[43] 1329, 1377, 1380, 1383, 1384, 1385, 1388.

[44] 1395.

[45] 1342, 1381, 1382, 1393.

of the research for this study to find any record of other
matters treated by the York Convocation save grants to
the king and to the pope.[46]   The constitutions published at Ripon by Archbishop Greenfield in 1306[47]
were doubtless given out at a council since this was the
customary method of procedure, but no allusion has
been found to a council at that time.   In contrast to
this, incidents have been cited in a previous chapter
wherein the Convocation of Canterbury was requested
by the king to discuss specific matters such as at one
time (1321) the pardon of the Despensers,[48] and at
another the king's relations with the French king.[49]
There is evidence too, though not abundant, to show
various ecclesiastical matters that were on the *agenda*
of a convocation of the province of Canterbury.[50]

It has sometimes been said that the province of York
followed blindly in the wake of Canterbury in the
matter of grants.   This is not true.   It must be admitted that in requesting an aid of York, the king frequently, to promote the generosity of the clergy of the
York province, cited what the province of Canterbury
had done for him.   Sometimes the Archbishop of York
himself quoted what the clergy of the other province
had done.   But this does not establish the conclusion
that the York province acted accordingly.

It must be borne in mind that the province of York
had difficulties to face with which the province of
Canterbury did not have to cope.   The province was
frequently subject to ravages by the Scots,[51] so much so

---

[46] See chart, Appendix B.
[47] Wilkins, *op. cit.*, II, 285 (Ex MS. Cott. Vitell., D. 5, fol. 142).
[48] *Cal. C.R.* (1318—23), 15 Edw. II, 543.
[49] *Ibid.* (1341—43), 16 Edw. III, p. 639.
[50] 1280, *Ann. Monast. (Oseneia)*, IV, 285—6.   1309, Wilkins, *op. cit.*,
II, 312—14 (Ex reg. Eccl. Cantuar. P., fol. 34 seq.).   1319 *Reg.
Cobham* (Wor. Hist. Soc.), p. 40 (fol. 39b).   1328—29 Murimuth,
Continuatio Chronicarum (Rolls Series, p. 59).   1344 *Ibid.*, p. 156.
1378 Reg. Sudbury (Cantuar.), fols. 51—51v.   1382 Reg. Courteney, I,
fols. 33—34v.   1397 Reg. Arundel, I, fols. 44—47v.
[51] *Reg. Halton* (C. and Y. Soc.), I, 130—1 (fol. 23b).

that a new assessment had to be made in 1318 of the
Church property in the northern province to allow for
the losses.[52]   The bishops of northern dioceses were
often kept from attending parliament because they
were needed in their dioceses during the perils of border
attacks.[53]

The province of Canterbury, moreover, did not include any diocese that held the unique position that was
held by the diocese of Durham, whose bishop claimed
palatinate jurisdiction.[54]   The Bishops of Durham
always received the mandate of the Archbishop of York
with a protest.[55]   In convocation this protest was
always read.[55]   Together with this episcopal protest it
was customary for the prior and capitular proctor, the
archdeacons for themselves, and the proctors of the
archdeaconries to read their protests.[56]   In their protests they declared that they would adhere to and abide
by the privileges, immunities, exemptions and liberties
granted to the Church of Durham by the apostolic
see.[57]   There were probably many times when an issue
was made difficult for the Archbishop of York by the
insistence of the Bishop of Durham on independent
action for his diocese.

[52] *Supra*, p. 147.
[53] *Reg. Halton* (C. and Y. Soc.), I, 241 (fol. 44b), 314—15 (fol. 60b).
[54] For records of the Palatinate of Durham *vide Registrum Palatinum
Dunelmense,* ed. T. D. Hardy (Rolls Series), 4 vols., *passim.*
[55] *The Records of the Northern Convocation* (Surtees Soc.), p. 101.
[56] *Ibid.,* p. 99.
[57] An example of a protest by Thomas Hatfield, of Durham (1345—81),
is given in the *Records of the Northern Convocation,* p. 100 (Reg.
Hatfield Dunelm., fol. 39b (94): "In Dei nomine, Amen.   Cum nos,
Thomas permissione divina Dunolmensis episcopus ex privilegio sedis
Apostolicæ nobis indulto sumus ab obedientia et sujectione omnimodis
domini Archiepiscopi Ebor. et successorum suorum ac ecclesiæ
Eboracenses exempti et totaliter absoluti, protestamur palam et publice
quod non intendimus per comparationem nostram præsentam, nec per
aliqua per nos seu nostro nomine dicenda proponenda seu quovis modo
exercenda, privilegio et exemptioni nostris prædictis quomodolibet præ-
judicare, sed si qua per nos aut nostro nomine dici fieri aut aliqualiter
proponi contigerit, quæ in lesionem privilegii et exemptionis prædictorum
tendere poterunt, volumus quod pro non dictis non factis et non pro-
positis habeantur omnino."

It is very difficult to make a comprehensive comparison of the grants of the two provinces. Frequently, as has been said above, there has survived only the summons for a convocation. Consequently there is no way of telling whether it met. Often, however, when it is known definitely that a convocation did assemble, it may not be possible to know what was the decision of the convocation in regard to a grant. In comparing the grants of the two provinces, therefore, we can only arrive at a few general conclusions. It is possible to state that in the period from 1280 to 1399 the grants of the provinces of Canterbury and York were of the same percentage sixteen times.[58] Sometimes when it is known that both provinces made a grant, only the record of the percentage of the grant in one province[59] may be extant. We know definitely, however, certain years in which the grants of the two provinces were of differing percentage.[60] There are, moreover, years wherein the records available show that Canterbury alone made grants,[61] while there are still other years wherein they show that the grants came only from the province of York.[62] These results indicate that the action of the two provinces tended to be similar, but that it was by no means compulsory that they should be so. The road was equally open for independent action. Each province was able to name the terms of its grant and might refuse point blank to make a grant even if its sister province had complied with the king's

[58] In the years 1294, 1316, 1336 (two grants this year), 1337, 1340, 1344, 1351, 1356, 1360, 1370, 1377, 1379, 1384, 1391, 1397 the grants of the two provinces were of the same percentage. Cf. charts, Appendix A, Appendix B.

[59] 1327, 1334, 1380.

[60] 1297, 1395.

[61] 1310, 1312, 1338, 1346, 1383, 1385, 1386, 1388, 1394, 1398.

[62] 1280, 1286, 1290, 1307, 1314, 1342, 1378, 1381, 1382. It is possible that the province of Canterbury may have granted a tenth for three years in 1280.

request.[63] Yet York realized sometimes that like action
was often necessary to protect the clergy from royal en-
croachment or lay interference. As early as 1252 the
Archbishop of York and the Bishops of Durham and
Carlisle are found refusing to give an answer to the
king's demands, and declaring that in such matters it
was customary to have discussions between the clergy
of Canterbury and York.[64] This would indicate that
there was a realization of the importance to the clergy
of presenting a solid front to the royal authority.

In 1322(–3) we find both provinces asking to be excused from making a grant to the king.[65, 66] The
province of Canterbury, which was meeting on the
morrow of Hilary, begged to be excused on the ground
that the tenth for two years granted by the pope was
still running and that they had granted an aid.[65] The
province of York meeting twelve days afterwards, in
declaring their poverty, asked to be excused.[66] They
tried to propitiate the king by promising to offer masses
and prayers for him.[66]

In 1342 when York made a grant to the king, detailed
conditions were appended in writing.[67]

In 1356 when the province of Canterbury made their
grant to the king on the condition that their grievances
should be redressed,[68] the province of York made theirs

---

[63] *Records of the Northern Convocation* (Surtees Soc.), pp. 61—2 (Reg.
Archiep. Grenefeld, I, 190b). The clergy of York in 1311 refused to
make a grant. For putting the date of this document in 1311 I am
indebted to Mr. C. R. Cheney, who pointed out to me that internal
evidence and the knowledge that Archbishop Greenfield was abroad in
1312 would establish that it was issued in 1311. The date therefore
assigned in the *Records of the Northern Convocation* (p. 61) is incorrect.

[64] P.R.O., Anc. Cor., vol. III, n. 159. Printed in *Royal and other
Historical Letters*, ed. W. W. Shirley (Rolls Series), II, 94—5.

[65] Wake, *op. cit.*, Appendix, p. 48 (Regist. Eccl. Christ. Cant. H.,
fol. 252a). Printed also in Wilkins, *op. cit.*, II, 517.

[66] Wilkins, *op. cit.*, II, 519 (Ex registro Will. Melton, archiep. Ebor.,
fol. 462).

[67] Wilkins, *op. cit.*, II, 711 (Ex arch. regiis et reg. Zouch Ebor.,
fol. 281).

[68] Reg. Islip (Cant.), fol. 118a. Printed in Wilkins, *op. cit.*, III, 39.
Wilkins gives here incorrect foliation.

" sub spe emendacionis et reformacionis grava-minum." [69]

It is quite true that the king was apt to use the response of the province of Canterbury, if it had been favourable, as a lever to bring pressure to bear on the clergy of the province of York when he found them recalcitrant. In 1316,[70] 1328[71] and 1339[72] the king used this means. If a province persisted in postponing the holding of a convocation, the king continued to issue writs commanding the clergy to assemble. This was what the king did in 1339.[72] To urge the clergy of the province of York to make a similar grant to that made by the clergy of the province of Canterbury, it was even decided in the Michaelmas parliament of 1339 that sealed letters should be sent to the Archbishop and clergy of York.[73]

The king was evidently anxious in 1377 for some action on the part of the clergy of the province of York.[74] A year later the Archbishop of York recounted to the king how long discussions had taken place in the convocation of his province, and how after alleging their poverty through the raids of the Scots, they at last when the archbishop appeared personally and described what Canterbury had granted, were persuaded to concede a tenth for two years.[75]

When in 1386 the province of Canterbury granted two half-tenths, York did not grant a similar supply. King Richard II sent at this time several requests for convocations to be held in the province of York.[76]

[69] P.R.O., Anc. Cor., vol. LVI, n. 4.

[70] *Cal. C.R.* (1313—18), 9 Edw. II, p. 271.

[71] *Records of the Northern Convocation* (Surtees Soc.), pp. 73—4 (Reg. Joh. de Kirkby, Ep. Carl., fol. 327). The date is given incorrectly here.

[72] *Cal. C.R.* (1339—41), 13 Edw. III, pp. 105, 270. The Latin text is printed in *Records of the Northern Convocation*, pp. 78—80.

[73] *Rot. Parl.*, II, 105, n. 16.

[74] *Cal. C.R.*, (1377—81), 1 Richard II, p. 92.

[75] Wilkins, *op. cit.*, III, 125—6 (Ex registro Alex. Nevile archiep. Ebor., fol. 2).

[76] *Cal. C.R.* (1385—89), 10 Richard II, p. 258. *Cal. C.R.* (1385—89), 11 Richard II, p. 462.

Finally the Commons petitioned in the parliament of February-March 1387(-8), that the two half-tenths in arrears due from the clergy of the province of York be paid with haste, and that if they did not pay them, it should be pleasing to the king to command a proclamation to be made that none of their lieges should do them service as a punishment to them for being put out of the protection of the king.[77] At length at the end of December 1388, the Official of the Archbishop of York (Thomas Arundel), in the absence of his lord, issued a mandate for a convocation in which he mentioned the fact that the Archbishop of York had already intimated to them by his letters that after the parliament at Cambridge, the province of Canterbury had freely granted a tenth, and that in regard to the concession of a tenth in his province he was disturbed by daily clamours.[78] The Official further pointed out how the clergy of Canterbury also exceeded the province of York in the payment of the moiety of one tenth—a like grant having in no wise been granted by the York clergy.[78] In order, therefore, that the boldness of delay in yielding a tenth of this kind should not redound to the blame or injury of the archbishop in the future, he now as the archbishop had ordained him to do, called the prelates and clergy together for the purpose of making a grant " in æquipollentia gratitudinis provincial. et præcipue in dicti venerabilis patris primordiis ipsi domino nostro regi plenarie recompensari censeatur."[78] It was then rather pride for their archbishop and their province which led the clergy of the province of York to want to make a grant proportionate to the one made by the southern province and not any hard and fast principle that the two provinces should always grant alike.

[77] *Rot. Parl.*, III, 247, n. 27.
[78] Wilkins, *op. cit.*, III, 205 (Ex reg. Arundel Ebor., fol. 8, et reg. Dunelm. in ann.).

A comparison of the two provinces undoubtedly shows that the province of Canterbury generally occupied the place of leader in the decisions. The very size of the southern province, with its eighteen dioceses in the more highly-populated region of the kingdom and with its freedom from the border raids of the Scots, naturally gave it a superior position financially, and made it consequently of very great importance to the king. The ascendancy of the province of Canterbury came, therefore, not from a principle consciously assumed nor forcibly maintained, but rather as a natural outcome from circumstances of size and geographical position. In all other respects the two provinces were very similar. The king's requests to the Archbishop of York for convocations of his province cannot be read without a realization that the meetings of the clergy of the province of York and their grants were of prime importance to the royal authority.

CHAPTER VII

CONVOCATION AS A CONTRIBUTORY FORCE TO THE DEVELOPMENT OF THE ENGLISH CONSTITUTION

THE influence of lay bodies on the growth of representative institutions has received for several generations full attention by historians. Occasionally the possible influence of the clergy upon these institutions has been traced,[1] but generally the part played by the clergy in this sphere has received but slight notice. Little account has been taken of the inevitable interaction that there must have been of ecclesiastical and lay institutions during the Middle Ages. As principles evolved and methods of procedure in representation grew up to fit a particular occasion, it would be at least not unnatural to expect both unconscious and conscious imitation in the ecclesiastical and secular spheres. In the present study an attempt has been made to trace the growth of representative assemblies in the Church of England and their relationship to the government of the land. As one works through the various vicissitudes of these ecclesiastical assemblies and the problems that beset those directing them or the constituents of them, one is moved to suggest that it is highly probable that the clergy in their machinery of government, in their attitude towards certain principles of taxation, in their stand for the maintenance of their own peculiar rights, directly or indirectly influenced the course of the representative idea. They presented indeed an equal thrust with that presented by the laity in the king-post that the two united to form for the support of the roof

---

[1] E. Barker, *The Dominican Order and Convocation*. Lunt, "The Consent of the English Lower Clergy to Taxation during the Reign of Henry III."

of popular rights against the attacks of a monarchy that was ready to satisfy at the expense of its subjects its rapacious demands for carrying on the wars in France.

While emphasizing the contribution of the clergy in convocation and the imitation that they may have inspired in the laity as regards institutions, and the laity in the clergy, one must remember as a previous writer has pointed out, that there was a distinct individuality in the assemblies of each of these groups—the ecclesiastical and the secular.[2] Whereas the secular power had a national parliament, the Church had two distinct bodies for carrying on its business—the Convocations of the provinces of Canterbury and York. Occasionally there were national ecclesiastical councils, but for administrative purposes the provincial system proved less unwieldy and became the general rule. As the same historian has suggested, the course of English history might have been entirely different had the national government adapted to its uses the ecclesiastical idea of two bodies, and sanctioned a parliament of the south and a parliament of the north.[3]

It is well known that since Saxon times the high ecclesiastics in England held many of the major offices in the realm. It would, therefore, have been only natural that procedure used for ecclesiastical matters should be employed also for the secular or *vice versa*. This was probably the inevitable practical result of churchmen being active in the two spheres. The man of the medieval period did not theorize before acting. Theory came in the succeeding generations after the principle which, later recognized as good or bad, had been adapted to the need of the moment.

It has been suggested by a previous writer that the system of representation in provincial assemblies came

[2] A. F. Pollard, *The Evolution of Parliament* (1st ed.), pp. 137, 196—9.
[3] *Ibid., op. cit.,* p. 137.

to England through the Dominican Order.[4]   Such a
thesis seems hardly tenable, resting as it does on the
slender premises—first of the close touch in France of
Simon de Montfort, the elder, with the Dominican
Order, and thereby the probable influence of the same
Order on his son, the so-called Founder of the House
of Commons,[5] and secondly on the various contacts of
Stephen Langton, the champion of popular liberties
against the tyranny of King John, with members of the
Dominican Order in England.[6]   On the contrary, it
seems impossible to attribute the representative idea in
England to any one source—either secular or ecclesiastical.   The practice of representation was being experimented with in various parts of Europe.   It had
been employed in England in pre-Conquest time in
the hundred court where the priest and the reeve were
present, representing the ecclesiastical and lay powers,
and in the shire court where sat the bishop and the
ealdorman or the steward of the latter.   A fuller use of
representation came in the thirteenth century in both
Church and State.   It is, however, possible to suggest
various ways in which the conciliar activity of the
Church in England in the thirteenth and fourteenth
centuries tended to promote and strengthen the idea of
representation for all time.   For her influence in this
respect the Church has not received her due.   She has
been assailed frequently for her oppressive rule, for the
laxity and the greed of certain of her number, both
individually and corporately.   Too little, however, has
been said of the utterances that those of her representatives made in defence of certain principles (even
though it must be admitted it was often to their own
interest to do so), which must have made their
impress on the minds of those who heard them,
both secular and ecclesiastical, and thus did service to

[4] Barker, *op. cit., passim.*   [5] *Ibid.,* pp. 27—8.   [6] *Ibid.,* p. 43.

the moulding of public thought in regard to those principles which have since become the requisites of English constitutional government.

Though it is known that King John issued a writ in 1213, summoning the barons and four discreet knights of each county to meet him at Oxford,[7] there is no proof that this writ was executed. A year later (1214) King John, in a letter to the Prior of Glastonbury, ordered him to bring five or six of the more discreet men of his chapter to a council at Reading.[8] The fact that many years previous to this, in the twelfth century, men of the manorial or communal court had been appointed to bring up the record (an oral record) from their locality gives a suggestion as scholars have pointed out,[9] of the beginning of the representative idea. It is not, however, until 1254 when there was an actual summons of two knights from each shire to come to Westminster to grant an aid,[10] that there is actual proof of the working of the representative procedure in full force in the secular government. Furthermore, it has been recently demonstrated that the representative idea was also in this period in actual effect for the clergy in relation to the national government.[11] Evidence has been produced which leaves little doubt that the clergy who were summoned to Westminster in

[7] W. Stubbs, *Select Charters* (9th ed.), revised by H. W. C. Davis, p. 282: "Rex Vicecomiti Oxon. salutem. Precipimus tibi quod omnes milites ballivæ tuæ, qui summoniti fuerunt esse apud Oxoniam ad nos a die Omnium Sanctorum in quindecim dies venire facias cum armis suis; corpora vero baronum sine armis similiter; et quatuor discretos milites de comitatu tuo illuc venire facias ad nos ad eundem terminum ad loquendum nobiscum de negociis regni nostri. Teste me ipso apud Wytten, VII die Novembris.

Eodem modo scribitur omnibus vicecomitibus." (Taken from *Report on the Dignity of a Peer*, App. 1, p. 2.) Cf. D. Pasquet, *An Essay on the Origins of the House of Commons*, translated by R. G. D. Laffan, p. 44, n. 1.

[8] *Rot. Lit. Claus.*, I, 176. Cf. *supra*, pp. 40—1.

[9] C. H. McIlwain, *Cambridge Medieval History*, VII, 668—9.

[10] Stubbs, *Select Charters* (9th ed.), pp. 365—6.

[11] Lunt, *Consent*, pp. 142—3. Professor Lunt bases his conclusions on the evidence revealed in a memorandum made at the priory of Durham (B.M. Stowe MS. 930, fols. 57v., 58).

1254 came with powers to decide then and there and not as has been hitherto held, merely to certify at Westminster as to what had been decided locally in their respective dioceses before they set out for Westminster.[11] Previous to 1254, however, a graded scale of representation seems to have had its beginnings in ecclesiastical assemblies.[12] A letter sent by King John on May 26th, 1207, forbidding the members of an ecclesiastical assembly sitting at S. Paul's for the consideration of a subsidy imposed on the clergy of England by the pope (Innocent III), to continue in session, was addressed to the archbishops, bishops, abbots, archdeacons and all the clergy.[13] As has been stated in a previous chapter the phrase " omni clero " leads one to wonder whether representatives of the lower clergy were called to this ecclesiastical assembly.[13]

Furthermore, the idea of representation and the stipulation of powers for the representatives and the limitation of their powers was taking shape in the southern province as early as 1226, as is apparent from the *Vetus Registrum Sarisberiense alias dictum Registrum S. Osmundi Episcopi* to which allusion has been made by previous writers[14] in their discussion of convocation, and to which a reference has been made elsewhere in this study.[15] The Salisbury record is of utmost importance in illustrating the point to which procedure had developed in the Church and the necessity felt at the time for gaining strength through corporate action. Archbishop Stephen Langton sent a letter to the Bishop of Salisbury in which he included a bull from Pope Honorius III under date of February 3rd, 1225(–6), exhorting the clergy to make

---

[12] *Supra,* pp. 34—41, *passim.*
[13] *Rot. Lit. Pat.,* I, 72. Cf. *supra,* p. 40.
[14] J. Armitage Robinson, *The Convocation of Canterbury, its Early History,* pp. 86—9. Lunt, *Consent,* 120—3. Churchill, *op. cit.,* I, 361—3.
[15] *Supra,* pp. 43—4.

a grant to the king.[16] It was the archbishop's purpose to levy the grant when the amount of it had been settled upon locally.[17] He suggested a twelfth or a fourteenth.[17] The king (Henry III) also sent a letter to the clergy of the various dioceses under date of May 27th, 1226, in which he urged them to comply with the papal bull.[18] The Bishop of Salisbury evidently executed the archbishop's mandate, for it is stated that the Salisbury Chapter received the papal mandate.[19] All the canons were summoned to a " convocatio " to be held on the feast of the Assumption (August 15th), 1226.[20, 21] Procedure in ecclesiastical affairs as illustrated by this meeting of the Dean and Chapter had advanced to the point that those who could not come to the assembly sent excuses.[22] The canons must have realized the seriousness of the problem before them. It is true that before this time there had been no royal requests for funds from the spiritualities of the clergy. There had been the Saladin tithe[23] and taxes in the king's council on temporalities of the clergy.[24] The consensus of those gathered together in the assembly at Salisbury was that a request should be sent to their bishop, beseeching him to ask the archbishop to call together the clerics of the several churches into his presence so that by a uniform provision and counsel a uniform response might be given.[25]

[16] *Vet. Reg. Sar.*, II, 57—8.
[17] *Ibid.*, II, 58—9.
[18] *Ibid.*, II, 55—6.
[19] *Ibid.*, II, 59.
[20] *Ibid.*, II, 59: " Videns capitulum suum hoc negotium omnes fratres suos tangere, noluit absque eis super hoc aliquid respondere, quod in aliquo posset fratribus suis prejudicium generare."
[21] *Ibid.*, II, 59—60.
[22] *Ibid.*, II, 61: " Isti autem sunt qui litteras suas excusatorias miserunt ratihabitionem continentes."
[23] Stubbs, *Select Charters* (9th ed.), p. 189.
[24] For example in 1225. Cf. *supra*, p. 42.
[25] *Vet. Reg. Sar.*, II, 61—2: " . . . paternitatis vestræ genibus provoluti devotissime supplicamus, quatinus inducatis dominum archiepiscopum ut ipse convocet coram eo, de singulis ecclesiis ubi clerici con-

When the Bishop of Salisbury (Richard Poore) complied with their request, the archbishop accepted their suggestion. A council was called for October 14th, 1226,[26] to which were summoned prelates, deans of cathedral churches or their proctors, archdeacons or their proctors,[27] men of religion or their proctors. It has been concluded by a previous writer from the fact that it was recorded in the Salisbury register that the Bishop of Durham died on the way to the council, that the council must have been a national one.[28] What is particularly interesting as contributory to representative government is the procedure in the Salisbury chapter. In the course of the research for this study it has proved impossible to find anything in secular records earlier than or contemporary with this Salisbury incident, which is indicative of a similar procedure in the secular government of the period. First of all the Salisbury chapter felt compelled to come together to discuss this question of the grant.[29] This was, of course, not unique. A corporate gift from the chapter demanded a corporate discussion by the chapter. But we are fortunate in knowing that they outlined clearly their *agenda* under four points[30]:

> "*Primo,* utrum domino regi in hac parte, decernerent esse subveniendum?

versantur, ad certam diem et locum, singulos procuratores, ut de uniformi eorum provisione et consilio, tam certa et tam uniformis procedat responsio, ut domini P.P., si viderint expedire, obtemperetur mandato et ad honorem totius ecclesiæ Anglicanæ, et ad cleri protectionem, de cetero, devotius assurgat gratitudo. Propterea, sancte pater, necesse habemus una cum tota ecclesia Anglicana ut diligenter inquiratur a domino archiepiscopo, forma securitatis domino regi facienda si procuratores in præfatum auxilium consenserint, ne hoc factum in dampnosam in posterum, trahatur consequentiam. Et quia ex hoc generale potest procedere periculum; necesse est ut majoris muniminis et roboris habeat fulcimentum."

[26] *Ibid.,* II, 62—3.
[27] *Ibid.,* II, 66.
[28] Armitage Robinson, *op. cit.,* p. 87.
[29] Cf. *supra,* p. 200, n. 20.
[30] *Vet. Reg. Sar.,* II, 61.

"*Secundo,* qualiter esse posset ut una et eadem forma in diversis ecclesiis servaretur.

"*Tertio,* utrum expediret dare *duodecimam* vel *quartamdecimam,* secundum formam mandati Cantuaro[31] vel non.

"*Quarto,* qualiter posset ecclesiis commode provideri? ne istud postea trahetur ad consequentiam."

Furthermore, we are told not only the *agenda* of this meeting, but later the powers with which the chapter vested their proctors[32] for the assembly of representatives of the several dioceses. This was, of course, done after their suggestion had been taken to the archbishop by their bishop, and the former had agreed and commanded the several bishops that they signify to their chapters to appoint proctors for such a meeting.[33] In prescribing within strict limits the powers of their proctors they were so precise and so forward looking that it seems worth while to give their directions[34] in full here:

1. "Inprimis,—utrum capitulum Sarum honestum esset et decens ut domino regi subveniatur:—si sic procuratoribus capituli, et aliorum capitulorum placuerit.

2. "Item, credit expedire quod *quintadecima* non præstetur vel aliqua summa inferior.

3. "Item, si autem fieri potest et aliis placuerit stetur in *vicesima* sicut in subventione 'Terræ Sanctæ' factum fuit, nec excedat aliquo modo sextam portionem.

4. "Item, fiat hæc præstatio de prebendis et redditibus, et hoc secundum estimationem quæ facta fuit ad subventionem 'Terræ Sanctæ' et nullo modo de mobilibus.

---

[31] "Cantuaro" is given in the transcription (*Vet. Reg. Sar.*, II, 61). It should probably be "Cantuariensis."
[32] *Ibid.*, II, 64—5.   [33] *Ibid.*, II, 62—3.   [34] *Ibid.*, II, 64—5.

5. " Item, colligatur hæc pecunia ad aliquibus fide-
dignis ad hoc assignatis per capitulum, et non per
officiales episcopi, vel ejus archidiaconos.

6. " Item, collecta pecunia tradatur domino episcopo
vel cui ipse decrevit, domino regi solvenda.

7. " Item, nullo modo consentiant procuratores ut
propter hoc, aliquid [35] juramentum a canonicis
præstetur, vel quod sententia excommunicationis super hoc generaliter proferatur.

8. " Item, inquiratur ab aliis quid faciendum sit si
aliqui canonicorum singulariter contradixerint
his quæ a majore parte capituli provisa fuerint.

9. " Item, laborent procuratores capitulorum ad hoc
ut de præbendis quæ in aliis episcopatibus con-
sistunt, fiat a singulis collecta.

10. " Item, quærant procuratores securitatem a
domino Cantuar. et domino rege et episcopis
quod, propter hanc præstationem non generaliter de cetero aliquid [36] prejudicium ecclesiæ
Anglicanæ.

11. " Item, nitantur procuratores ad perquirendum
prolixos terminos ad solvendum hoc tallagium."

The Salisbury register states that a sixteenth was
granted. [37] In order, moreover, that their grant might
not create a precedent, they requested and received the
king's letters patent to that effect. [38] Further details in
the register as to the procedure employed for the col-
lecting and payment of the grant throw light on the
ecclesiastical machinery of the day. It has been
pointed out in a recent work that though the chapter
received the king's letters establishing that their act
could not work to their detriment in the future, the

---

[35] This form is probably again an error in transcription or an error of
the scribe. It should be " aliquod."

[36] Again an error in transcription or a scribal error. It should be
" aliquod."

[37] *Ibid.*, II, 66—7.

[38] *Ibid.*, II, 67—8.

demands of the king and the pope through papal legates in the succeeding years became so frequent that the clergy perforce were assembled often during the next twenty-five years.[39] It may be further suggested that the procedure necessary for these meetings of the clergy from time to time for money-granting purposes made its impress upon the machinery that was being formulated contemporaneously by the laity for the fulfilment of their business. Certainly by 1260, as has been shown in a previous chapter, the clergy had worked out a system of representation for their assemblies to the extent that archdeacons were requested to bring with them letters of proxy[40] from the clergy under them to treaties where the affairs of the Church were to be discussed. It has been pointed out also that even so early as 1229 rectors of churches ("ecclesiarum rectores") were present in a great council at Westminster when " the pope's business " was discussed.[41] While it has been acknowledged that they possibly had little influence on the outcome, it has nevertheless been suggested that through the fact of their being " assembled with the council when it discussed a project for their taxation their interest in the matter received a significant recognition."[42] If, furthermore, the speech of the bishops recorded in Matthew Paris[43] as having been delivered at the Council of Northampton in 1240 is not accurate for that particular occasion, at least it is noteworthy as revealing current opinion in the author's time.[44] The spirit of this reply was reiterated from time to time.[45] Whether the

---

[39] Churchill, *op. cit.*, I, 363.
[40] *Supra,* p. 49.
[41] Lunt, *Consent*, p. 124. Cf. *supra,* pp. 44—5.
[42] *Ibid.,* pp. 125—6.
[43] Mat. Paris, *Chron. Maj.*, IV, 37: " Habemus archidiaconos nobis subjectos, qui norunt beneficiatorum sibi subjectorum facultates, nos autem ignoramus. Omnes tangit hoc negotium, omnes igitur sunt conveniendi, sine ipsis nec decet nec expedit respondere."
[44] Lunt, *Consent*, pp. 129—30.   [45] *Ibid.,* p. 133.

bishops delayed to give themselves time to consider their grant or whether they had really a very settled belief in the principle that those of every status contributing to a subsidy should be consulted, certainly they frequently had resort to the plea that they could give no answer because other prelates or the lower clergy were not present. The same complaint came in Pecham's time at the council in January 1282(-3), [46] and it appeared often in the following century as a means of deflecting ultimate decisions where the clergy were concerned, from parliament to convocation. [47]

If the lowest order of the clergy was essential to the discussion of a grant from their spiritualities, is it not likely that the same idea—namely, that those contributing to a grant should have some part in deciding its amount—was also in the minds of those in secular circles and may have impelled the summoning of the knights in 1254? In this case, however, it must, of course, be admitted that the summoning of the knights in 1254 was by no means a magnanimous gesture of the royal authority for representative government, but rather a canny move on the part of the deputy rulers for obtaining the best results in amassing necessary funds. [48]

The second half of the thirteenth century, as we have seen, was a period of experimentation among the archbishops with their councils. The various steps can be traced in Kilwardby's and Pecham's councils. It is

[46] *Supra,* p. 53.
[47] *Supra,* pp. 60—1.
[48] A letter (P.R.O., Anc. Cor., vol. X, n. 48) written by Eleanor, Lady of England (one of the deputy rulers), to John de Kirkeby in regard to the business of an aid (" super negotii subsidii ") from the clergy is of interest. She mentions that she has written to the Archdeacons of Wylcestr', Chester and Northampton. She trusts his promotion of the aid. The letter is dated January 8th. It was doubtless written in 1254 as Queen Eleanor remained in England as deputy ruler only from August 6th, 1253 to May 20th, 1254, when she departed for Bordeaux despite the king's prohibition (*Dictionary of National Biography*, XVII, 179).

interesting to see that when Edward I experimented with two assemblies in 1283—one at Northampton and one at York—he used the form of representation among the clergy which Pecham had used two years before (1281),[49] and that when he called the clergy to Westminster on September 21st, 1294, in a purely clerical body he again summoned the same degrees who had been called to Archbishop Pecham's council in 1283.[50] Furthermore, when the king summoned all five " communities " that made up the body of the realm to parliament in November 1295 (representatives of the diocesan or parochial clergy being then called for the first time, together with the spiritual and temporal lords, the knights, burgesses and regular clergy), he embodied in his writ of summons to the archbishops and bishops the so-called " premunientes " clause, by which he commanded them to premonish to come to Westminster the same degrees of the clergy, it appears, as Pecham had called in 1283, and as he himself had called when he summoned the clergy alone to Westminster in 1294.[51] Although the " premunientes " clause was not always incorporated in the writs of summons to parliament issued to bishops in the period up to 1333, as has been shown above, beginning with the parliament summoned for February 21st, 1333(-4),[52] it became invariable to include it, and even to this day it is embodied in the writs of summons to the spiritual lords of parliament. The actual execution, however, of the " premunientes " clause was allowed by degrees to be considered fulfilled if the archbishops summoned the clergy of their respective provinces to their own presence in convocations.[53] In the repre-

[49] Supra, p. 53.
[50] Supra, pp. 54—7.
[51] Supra, pp. 54—7.
[52] Cf. chart, Appendix C, passim.
[53] Cf. supra, pp. 60, 63. This was true for the parliaments at Lincoln, January 26th, 1315(-16), Winchester, March 11th, 1329(-30). This was

sentation, therefore, in parliament or convocation that took place among the clergy may be seen a permanent contribution to the government of England. The special significance of the contribution brought to the general government in the medieval period by representation among the clergy was the development and strengthening of convocation, which in its role at the time of a money-granting body, was most necessary to the king, and remained an indispensable part of the financial element of the constitution, apart from its own special ecclesiastical interests, until it had its rights of separate taxation set aside in the middle of the seventeenth century. [54]

An allusion has been made above, as well as in preceding chapters, to the insistence of the clergy on the principle that those contributing to grants should play

also the case for the parliament summoned to London, March 11th, 1335(-6). The Register of Adam de Orlton, Bishop of Winchester (1333—45), preserved in the archives of the Diocesan Registry at Winchester, I, fol. 33v.

In each case in executing the "premunientes" clause the archbishop summoned the clergy before himself in the cathedral of the city in which the parliament was to meet. This was by no means a provincial council, but it seems to illustrate the transition point. Very soon after this the greater activity of the clergy was definitely in a convocation for which there was a special summons. The "premunientes" clause continued in the summons to the bishops to parliament, but the really important meeting for taxation of the spiritualities was in convocation in the summons for which the archbishop generally embodied the king's writ requesting it, but not always. In a previous chapter of this study the impossibility of trying to distinguish between a convocation and a provincial council has been discussed. *Supra*, pp. 118—19.

[54] W. Stubbs, *Report of the Commissioners appointed to inquire into the constitution and working of the ecclesiastical courts* (1883), vol. I, Historical Appendix V, pp. 142—3: ". . . the Submission of the clergy in 1532 and the Statute of Submission of 1534 materially altered the relations in which the Convocations stood to the Crown, and so incidentally their relations to Parliament also. . . .

"Under Charles I no attempt was made to secure joint working: the King was seldom on good terms with the Parliament; the Convocation, by granting a subsidy without the confirmation of Parliament and by passing Canons with the royal licence in 1640 drew down upon itself the condemnation of both Lords and Commons.

"After the Restoration the Convocations recovered their constitutional power of granting subsidies which required Parliamentary confirmation and exercised that power until, in 1665, it was tacitly surrendered."

a definite part in the making of them and in taking a stand against oppressive taxation. One ventures to suggest that the custom of adherence by the clergy to this principle, granted it may have been for their own selfish protection, welded itself into the fundamental structure of English political ideals and criteria.   It became ingrained in the nation. It must be acknowledged that it was not a new contribution in the Middle Ages, for the same spirit appeared in ancient times in the city state of Athens, which became later the purest democracy that has ever existed. The same spirit, moreover, was to crop up again in England in the Stuart period, when the question of ship money was the issue of the day, and was still later to burst forth in the eighteenth century as if it were a new discovery, when it came in eloquent and far-reaching tones from the lips of a young Virginian against the high-handed methods of the mother government in their policy towards the colonies in America. The substance of Patrick Henry's declaration, " Taxation without representation is tyranny," had found expression long before this among those in whose veins coursed English blood. Let us trace those assertions of the English medieval clergy in the cause of their own liberty, which may have done much to help to embody this fundamental principle in the English Constitution. A few instances have already been cited in the thirteenth century in the time of Henry III, such as the questionable speech of the bishops at Northampton in 1240,[55] and the stand of the clergy under Pecham in the succeeding reign when they refused to come to a decision because the lower clergy were not present.[56] Several times we have seen in the fourteenth century—in the reigns of Edward II and Edward III—the question of taxation in parliament deflected to convocation[57] on the ground that the

[55] *Supra*, p. 204, n. 43.   [56] *Supra*, p. 53.   [57] *Supra*, pp. 60—1, 106.

clergy were not in full attendance in parliament either from disregard of their bishops' premonishment, or because there was no law in existence which could enforce their attendance outside their province.

A notable protest came from Archbishop Courteney in full parliament at Westminster in the late fourteenth century (December 17th, 1384), when he discovered that the knights of the shires, the citizens and burgesses of the realm of England had made a grant of two fifteenths to the king to be levied from the people of the realm on the condition that the clergy should grant two tenths from their benefices, and at the same time learned that they (the laity) had already presented the terms of the formulated conditions in a schedule to the king.[58] In opposition to this high-handed measure the

[58] Reg. Courteney, I, fols. 81v.—82. Printed in Wilkins, *op. cit.*, III, p. 193: "Protestacio facta per dominum archiepiscopum Cant. in pleno parliamento pro ecclesia in sua libertate conservanda. Memorand. quod decimo septimo die mensis Decembris anno Domino M. CCC. LXXXIV et regni regis Richardi secundi post conquestum octavo. In pleno parliamento eiusdem domini Regis die et anno supradictis tent. apud Westm. audito per reuerendissimum in Christo patrem dominum Willelmum, dei gracia Cant. Archiepiscopum, tocius Anglie primatem et apostolice sedis legatum quod milites comitatuum, Cives ciuitatum et burgenses Regni Anglie, tunc ibidem pro dicto parliamento conuocati, dicto domino nostro regi quoddam Subsidium in supportacionem oneris eidem domino nostro Regi, et Regno suo incumbentis, duas quintas decimas, a populo regni sui leuandas, sub certa condicione eidem domino nostro Regi soluendas concesserunt; videlicet quod Prelati et Clerus dicti regni prefato domino nostro Regi duas decimas de beneficiis suis ecclesiasticis ad decimam soluere consuetis simili modo concederent prout in quadam cedula indentata concessionem et condicionem huiusmodi continent. per eos porrecta, plenius apparebat. Et statim prefatus dominus Cant. archiepiscopus, assistentibus sibi aliis confratribus et suffraganeis suis tunc presentibus coram dicto domino Rege, Episcopis, et aliis Prelatis comitibus, Baronibus, et populo in pleno parliamento inibi congregatis dixit expresse et publice protestabatur: 'Quod cum sancta mater ecclesia tam toto tempore dicti domini Regis, quam progenitorum suorum in plena sua libertate perstiterit; non potuit, de iure nec debuit, ad condicionem huiusmodi obseruandum arctari; dixit insuper publice idem archiepiscopus, quod nunquam de cetero cum clero suo super aliquo subsidio regi concedendo tractaret, nec conuocacionem faceret hac de causa, donec dicta condicio rejecta fuerit et deleta.' Qua protestacione facta, prefatus dominus noster Rex, volens, ut asseruit, ecclesiam sua pristina libertate gaudere, huiusmodi condicionem de cedula memorata extrahi, siue abradi omnino precepit, et fecit publice tunc ibidem."

An allusion has been made to this protest in a previous chapter. Cf. *supra*, pp. 169—70.

archbishop declared in clear-cut terms that since Holy
Mother Church from all time, both during that of the
king as well as of his forefathers, had stood in full
liberty, neither could she, nor should she by law be
forced to observe a condition of this kind.[58]   He said,
moreover publicly, that never otherwise should he treat
with his clergy in regard to granting a subsidy to the
king, nor would he hold a convocation until the said
condition should have been rejected and deleted.[58]
After this protest, the king, wishing as he said, the
Church to enjoy her pristine liberty, commanded the
aforementioned condition to be extracted and abraded
publicly from the schedule, and he did it then.[58]   It
will be remembered with what fury the earls and
" proceres " opposed a similar protest made by
Courteney the following year (1385),[59] how the king
thwarted the nobles' greed, and how the clergy later in
their convocation acquiesced with the wishes of the
king by granting him spontaneously a tenth.[60]   Whereupon the king declared that he preferred this free gift
(" donationem liberam ") to one of quadruple value
that had been forced.[60]   Money was the king's main
object; as long as he obtained it he was willing to protect the Church in their way of granting it.   Richard II
cannot be credited with magnanimity for the way he
acted on this occasion, but at least he supported the
clergy in their stand for the freedom of the grantor.

Another decided contribution made by the clergy (it
cannot be maintained that it originated with them, yet
they did their part in perpetuating the process so that
it became custom) was their habit of making a simple
and direct statement of their reasons when they refused
to make a grant, or of their conditions as a means of
protection to themselves when they yielded a grant.   In

[59] It is possible that Walsingham's account refers to the protest in
1384. Cf. *supra*, p. 171, n. 116.
[60] Walsingham, *Historia Anglicana*, II, 140.

an age where there was much disorder, and when an autocratic king could ride roughshod over his people, orderliness of thought and clarity of terms were precedents to promote. An orderliness of thought was noted in the Salisbury chapter in regard to the arrangement of their *agenda,* as well as in the stipulation of the powers with which they vested their proctors, and the limitations which they put upon their proctors' future actions.[61] In 1237,[62] 1257,[63] 1258[64] and 1269[65] the clergy presented articles of grievances for reform. In 1283, in Pecham's time, the clergy's reasons against making a grant at the Council of London were drawn up in orderly fashion.[66] Again in Winchelsey's archiepiscopate at the council which assembled January 13th, 1296(−7), the clergy sent their replies in written form.[67] The bishops during the council of 1309 were admonished to meet the representatives of the clergy of their respective dioceses who were present, have them draw up their grievances, and later present these grievances in writing that they might ultimately be incorporated in a joint set of articles to be transmitted to the king or to the pope.[68] Articles of grievance were again drawn up by the clergy in 1314 against the form of summons to Westminster.[69] The orderliness of clerical procedure is again illustrated in the period of Archbishop Stratford, who in issuing his mandate for a provincial council to be held at S. Paul's, London, on the first law day after the feast of S. Luke (October 19th), 1341, commanded that the bishops summon before themselves locally the clergy of their cities and dioceses, confer with them on matters needing reform, and draw up in writing proposals for reform to

[61] *Supra,* pp. 201—3.
[62] *Supra,* p. 149.
[63] *Supra,* pp. 148—9.
[64] *Supra,* p. 150.
[65] *Supra,* p. 150.
[66] *Supra,* pp. 150—2.
[67] *Supra,* p. 153.
[68] *Supra,* p. 126.
[69] *Supra,* pp. 58—9.

be submitted at the council in London.[70] The archbishop pointed out that he ordered this that judgment
might be more mature and time saved at the general
meeting.[70] Is it going too far to say that orderliness of
procedure as has been instanced here among the clergy,
may have influenced the growth of orderliness of
thought in lay circles? Certainly the rolls of parliament and other lay records of the fourteenth century
offer abundant evidence of the growth of orderliness of
thought in the secular government. It may be replied
that there was orderliness of thought and arrangement
among the laity in 1215 in Magna Carta, in 1258 in the
Provisions of Oxford, and in the Statutes of Edward I.
That is admittedly true. But has not Stephen Langton,
Archbishop of Canterbury, a churchman who was
active for reform within the Church as evidenced by
the canons of the Council of Oxford (1222),[71] been
called the moving spirit of Magna Carta? And were
not some of the most eminent officers of state during
the reign of Edward I bishops of the Church? Were
not, moreover, the first clerks of the rolls themselves
clerics, Church trained? The Church was undoubtedly
the school of orderliness of the age. The dignity and
ritual, and the insistence on form, as revealed in the
canonical legislation of the time, show that deliberateness of movement was an outstanding quality of the
medieval church. It is easy to conjecture that this
same deliberateness may have permeated the acts of
churchmen in lay matters. The very coronation cere-

[70] Winchester Chartulary preserved in the Library of the Dean and
Chapter of Winchester Cathedral, fol. 127 (nos. 524 and 528).
Calendared in *Chartulary of Winchester Cathedral,* ed. A. W. Goodman,
p. 222: " . . . vobis inungimus et per vos dictis episcopis et confratribus electi vicariis et Offic. predicto inungi volumus et mandamus
vt vos et ipsi cum Religiosis et clero vestre suarumque dioc. super
reformandis in concilio supradicto deliberatis et deliberent et circum-
scripte ac in scriptis redigatis et redigent reformanda vt super illis dictis
(sic) et loco plenior et maturior informacio valeat optinere et quod expedit conuenientibus ordinari. . . ."

[71] Wilkins, *op. cit.,* I, 585—97 (Ex MS. Cotton. Otho A., XV).

mony, itself a sacred service, was the act in the Middle Ages that gave final validity to a king's exercise of his prerogative. In this rite there was the union of the sacerdotal and the secular to form the keystone of medieval monarchy and a significant illustration of their interdependence in the period of this study.

The records of conditional grants which were made by the province of Canterbury and which are incorporated in the archiepiscopal registers of the second half of the fourteenth century, reveal the tenacity of the clergy to the principle that a grant must be accompanied by redress of grievances or that money must be used for the express purposes for which it was conceded.[72] It is true that the grievances were not always redressed (we have found the clergy complaining to this effect), but at least the clergy took a stand that they *should be*, and in so doing, did much to make customary the principle of this kind of bargaining between monarch and people. At the same time they made their contribution to precision of government. They stated in precise terms their grievances, and when the opportunity came for them to be heard, the triers and hearers of petitions in parliament had a definite set of problems with which to deal. It may be argued that the same custom of stating grievances was growing up among the laity—both in the case of individuals and of the commonalty of the realm, and that thus it was not original with the clergy. It is granted that this is true, but the point may nevertheless be stressed that because the formulation of grievances was resorted to *constantly* and *consistently* among the clergy—one of the commonalties of the realm—strength was thereby given to make this principle endure for all time as a requisite of constitutional government.

In conclusion, we should say that the contributions

[72] *Supra,* chapter V, *passim.*

P

of the clergy in convocation towards the English Constitution in the Middle Ages, which was then in the process of formation, are distinguished not so much for their originality as for the strength which they gave through the consistent and regular usage of them by the clergy, to the definite establishment of certain practices, which appeared almost simultaneously in both clerical and lay circles. In addition to this, it must be acknowledged that whatever learning there was in the period had its beginnings to a certain degree through Church influence. Keeping in mind these two statements, one ventures to say that the contributions of the clergy more specifically were their adherence to the principle that in assemblies or congregations which concerned the whole body of the clergy, there should be representatives from every degree of clerical status; their insistence that those who were to give money for a grant should take part in the deciding of the amount thereof and the terms on which it should be yielded; their maintenance of the practice that the conditions of a grant and the grievances to be redressed should be presented in writing with clarity and precision of statement; and finally their constant emphasis on the principle that redress of grievances should be the inevitable recompense for a grant.

APPENDIX A

CHART OF ECCLESIASTICAL ASSEMBLIES IN THE PROVINCE
OF CANTERBURY DURING THE THIRTEENTH & FOURTEENTH
CENTURIES (1222—1399)

NOTE

THE archiepiscopal registers at Lambeth Palace were indispensable for the preparation of this chart of the ecclesiastical assemblies of the province of Canterbury. The publications of the Canterbury and York Society have also been of infinite help. It is hoped at some future date that it will be possible to examine the manuscripts in the various episcopal and chapter archives to which allusion has been made, but of which time did not permit an examination.

Sources.	Date.	Place of Meeting.	Composition.	Matters Treated.	Results.	Form of Mandate.
(A) (PROVINCIAL COUNCIL.) Mat. Paris, *Chron. Maj.* III, 73–74. *Chron. Ang. Petriburg,* p. 124. Wilkins, *Conc. Mag. Br.* I, 585–97. (Ex. MS. Cotton. Otho. A. XV.)	April 17 (15 Kal. Maii) 1222	Oxford.		Decrees.	Promulgation of decrees. A deacon burned.	
(A) (LEGATINE COUNCIL.) Wendover, IV, 114–115 *Ann. Monast. (Dunst.)* III, 99. *Vet. Reg. Sar,* II, 45–46. Wilkins, I, 602–3. (Ex.Reg. Poore Sarum Fol. 109, 138 seq.)	January 13. (F. of S. Hilary) Date also given as January 7, (Morrow of Eph.) 1225(–6).	London	Otho, papal legate Bishops. Abbots. Priors. Deans of Cathedral Churches. Archdeacons.	Reading of Apostolic letters.	Bishops and prelates discuss apart. Refuse to reply on account of illness of king and absence of Archbishops & Bishops.	
(A) (NATIONAL COUNCIL.) *Vet. Reg. Sar,* I, 370–71, II, 46–7, 51, 54.	May 3, 1226.	London	Papal Nuncio. Archbp. (Cant.) Bishops. Abbots, non-exempt. Priors. Deans of Cathedral & prebend. Churches. Archdeacons. Proctors of Cath. and prebendal Churches. Monasteries, religious houses.	Request made by the Papal Nuncio for the Pope.	Request refused as had been done at a council at Bourges.	

Sources.	Date.	Place of Meeting.	Composition.	Matters Treated.	Results.	Form of Mandate.
(A) (NATIONAL COUNCIL) Vet. Reg. Sar., II, 55ff., 66–76. Royal Letters, I, 299. Ann. Mon. (Wykes, Oseneia), IV, 67, 68.	October 14, 1226.	London.	Bishops. Prelates. Deans of Cathedral Churches. Archdeacons. Religious. Proctors of Chapters and monasteries.	Grant.	Grant of one sixteenth.	
(S) (COUNCIL) Cal. Pat. Rolls (1232–47), 18H. III, p. 33.	November 26 (Saturday the Morrow of S. Catherine) 1233.	Gloucester.	Bishops.	Royal prohibition issued to the council not to touch anything belonging to the king's crown or estate.		
("GENERAL COUNCIL") (A) (LEGATINE) Ann. Monast. (Theokesberia), I, 105. (Burton), I, 253–6. M. Paris, Chron. Maj., III, 416–42.	November 19 (Morrow of the Octave of S. Martin) 1237.	S. Paul's, London.	Otho, legate. Abps. of Cant. & York. Bps. Abbots. Priors. Deans. Archdeacons or their proctors.	Grievances of the clergy.	Grievances of the clergy presented afterwards.	
(A) (LEGATINE COUNCIL) Mat. Paris, Chron. Maj., III, 484.	May 17 (16 Kal. June) 1238.	London.	Otho, legate. Abp. of York. All bps. of England. Clergy.	The state of the Church and the clergy.		

Sources.	Date.	Place of Meeting.	Composition.	Matters Treated.	Results.	Form of Mandate.
(A) (NATIONAL COUNCIL) (LEGATINE) Mat. Paris, *Chron. Maj.*, III, 567 Wilkins, I, 663–4. (Ex Pryn., vol. II, Record, fol. 505.)	March 6 (Day when is sung "Lætare," Jerusalem.) 4th Sun. in Lent. 1238(–9).	London.	Otho, legate. All bishops of England.	Business of the Church. Demands of the legate. Certain statutes given to the Black Monks.	Bishops say that they will not tolerate further demands.	
(A) (LEGATINE COUNCIL) (NATIONAL) Mat. Paris. *Chron. Maj.*, IV, 10–11. *Hist. MSS. Com. Cal. MSS. of the Dean and Chapter of Wells*, I, 403. Lunt, *Consent*, 127–32.	May 1240. Adjourned until summer.	Reading.	Otho, legate. Abps. Bps. Major Abbots. Deans. Chapters. Archdeacons. Certain magnates.	Reading of the Papal Mandate.	Decision postponed. Bishops refuse to take upon themselves such a burden without prolonged counsel.	
(A) (LEGATINE COUNCIL) *Ann. Monast.*, I, 115. (*Theokesberia*.) Lunt, *Consent*, 127–32.	July 1240. ["About the feast of S. John Bap., June 24."]	London.	Otho, legate. Clergy.	Mandate of the Pope.	All and singular clergy spoke against consenting to a contribution at the mandate of the Lord Pope.	
(A) (LEGATINE COUNCIL) *Ann. Monast.* (*Theokesberia*) I, 116. (*Burton*), I, 366. (*Dunstaplia*), III, 154.	November 8 (Octave of All Saints), 1240.	London.	Otho, legate. Clergy.			

Sources.	Date.	Place of Meeting.	Composition.	Matters Treated.	Results.	Form of Mandate.
(A) (COUNCIL) Cal. P.R. (1232–47), 26 H. III, p. 267. M. Paris, Chron. Maj., IV, 173. Wilkins, I, 682. (Ex Pryn. Record, vol. II, p. 577.)	1241. (After November 29.)	Oxford.	Abp. of York. Bps. of Lincoln, Norwich, Carlisle. Discreet ecclesiastical persons. The king's deputy.	The desolation of the Church.		
(A) (COUNCIL) Mat. Paris, Chron. Maj., IV, 581–5.	December 1, 1246.	S. Paul's, London.				
(A) (COUNCIL) Cal. P.R. (1247–58), 37 H. III, p. 77. Wilkins, I, 697 (Ex Rot. Par., 34 H. III, in dors., n. 1).	April 1250	Oxford.	Prelates.			
(A) (COUNCIL) Mat. Paris, Chron. Maj., V, 225. Lunt, Valuation of Norwich, p. 47.	February 24, 1250(-1).	Dunstable.	Bishops.	Opposition to the archbishop's right of visitation.		
(A) (COUNCIL) Chronicle of the Monastery of Abingdon, p. 7.	March 12 (2nd Sunday in Lent), 1250(-1).	Reading.	Bishops.			
(A) (COUNCIL) MSS. Dean & Chapter of Wells, II, 563.	November 6, 1251.	Winchcombe.				

Sources.	Date.	Place of Meeting.	Composition.	Matters Treated.	Results.	Form of Mandate.
(A) (COUNCIL) Mat. Paris, Chron. Maj., V, 359–60. *Ann. Monast. (Burton)*, I, 305ff. *Chronicle of John of Oxenedes*, p. 194. *Cal. P.R.* (1247–58), 37 H. III, p. 171.	January 13 (Octaves of Epiphany), 1252(–3).	London.	Abp. All bps. of the Province of Canterbury. Two proctors of the king.	Articles.	King's reply favourable to demands of the clergy.	
(A) (COUNCIL) Mat. Paris, Chron. Maj., V, 524–37. *Ann. Monast. (Burton)*, I, 360–3. Wake, *State of the Church*, p. 202.	October 13, 1255.	London.	Rostand, papal nuncio. Prelates. Archdeacons.	Demand for money.		
(A) (COUNCIL) Mat. Paris, Chron. Maj., V, 524–7; 539–44; VI, 314.	January 13, 1255(–6).	New Temple, London.	Bps. Abbots. Priors with proctors. Deans. Archdeacons with proctors. 3 or 4 discreet men of archdeaconries.	A reply to the Pope.	Grievances of the diocese of Coventry and Lichfield presented. Clergy later refuses to make a grant.	
(A) (COUNCIL) *Ann. Monast. (Burton)*, I, 388.	March 25 (Passion Sunday), 1257.	London.	Prelates. Deans. Regular clergy. Archdeacons.			
(A) (COUNCIL) Mat. Paris, Chron. Maj., V, 632, 637, 638; VI, 353–65. *Ann. Monast. (Burton)*, I, 389. Lunt, *Consent*, 148.	April 22, 1257.	London.	Prelates. Deans. Regular clergy. Archdeacons.	State of the Church. Grievances.	Grievances formulated. King promises to remedy them.	

Sources.	Date.	Place of Meeting.	Composition.	Matters Treated.	Results.	Form of Mandate.
(A) (" CONVOCATION ") Ann. Monast. (Burton), I, 401. (Wintonia), II, 96.	August 22, 1257.	London.	Abp. Bps. Abbots and Priors with letters of proxy. Deans. Priors. Archdeacons with letters of proxy.	Whether to send to the king. A number of matters touching the state of the Church.	Large sums of money granted.	
(A) (COUNCIL) Ann. Monast. (Theokesberia) I, 163. (Burton), I, 412–22. Cheney, Legislation, pt. II, pp. 402–3.	June 6 (Thursday before the Feast of S. Barnabas), 1258.	Merton (and possibly Westminster).	Abp. Bps. Deans of Cathedral Churches. Abbots. Priors. Archdeacons with letters of proxy from those under them.	State of the Church. Articles presented.	Articles of grievances.	
(A) (COUNCIL) Mat. Paris, Chron. Maj., V, 707. Cheney, Legislation, pt. II, p. 403.	1258.	Oxford.	Four bishops. Exempt Abbots (or their proctors).	Articles of Merton (or Westminster.)	Four bishops present articles. Business unfinished.	
(A) (COUNCIL) Flores Historiarum, II, 465, 468. Cheney, Legislation, pt. II, 403.	Summoned for May 8. In session May 16, 1261.	London.	Papal Legate. Both provinces.	The papal mandate.		
(A) (COUNCIL) B.M. MS. Cotton Otho A, XVI, 29. Wilkins, I, 746. (Ex MSS. Cotton, Otho A XVI et Vitell. A ii collat. cum MS. Lambeth, n. 17; et MS. Elien, n. 235.)	May 13, 1261.	Lambeth.	Bishops.		Constitutions published.	

Sources.	Date.	Place of Meeting.	Composition.	Matters Treated.	Results.	Form of Mandate.
(A) (COUNCIL) *Flores Historiarum*, II, 468–9. Cheney, *Legislation*, pt. II, p. 403.	May 16, 1261.	London.	Papal nuncio. Abps. Bps. Abbots. Priors of Churches. Archdeacons. "Other ordinaries."	The papal mandate.	Provincial canons promulgated. King's clerks appeal against canons.	
(A) (COUNCIL) *Flores Historiarum*, II, 478–9.	After the Feast of Trinity (May 27), 1263.	Westminster.	Papal nuncios, "Pontiffs." Clergy.	Grant for the Emperor of Constantinople.		
(A) (NATIONAL COUNCIL) *Chron. of Mon. of Abingdon*, pp. 12–13.	June 3, 1264.	Merton.				
(A) (COUNCIL) *Ann. Monast. (Wigornia)*, IV, 453.	1264.	Reading.	Bishops.			
(A) (LEGATINE COUNCIL) Wilkins, I, 762. (Ex MS. Cotton. Titus A. XIII, et Chron. Hemingford in ann.) [*N.B.* Hefele–Le Clercq, VI, pt. I, 121, says the first council was at Westminster – then a council at Northampton in Oct., 1266.]	November 1, 1265.	Northampton.	Othobon, legate.	Simon de Montfort and his adherents.		

Sources.	Date.	Place of Meeting.	Composition.	Matters Treated.	Results.	Form of Mandate.
(A) (LEGATINE COUNCIL) Wilkins, I, 762–3. (Chronicon Prioratus Dunstaplensis in MS. Cotton. Tiberius A.X.)	Lent, 1266.	London.	Othobon, legate. Bishops.	Statutes of Othobon. The publication of a tenth for 6 years granted to the King by the Pope.		
(A) (LEGATINE COUNCIL) Florence of Worcester (Continuation), II, 199. *Letters of Cardinal Otto-boni*, ed. R. Graham, Eng. Hist. Rev., XV (1900), 102.	February 22, 1266(–7).	Bury St. Edmunds.	Othobon, legate. Prelates. Clergy.	Aid sought by the King.		
(A) (LEGATINE COUNCIL) Lunt, *Consent*, 158–9. *Letters of Card. Otto-boni*, 110 (gives July 1 for date).	June–July, 1267.	London.	Othobon, legate. Bishops. Prelates. Chapters by the Dean or one of Archdeacons.			
(A) (LEGATINE COUNCIL) Wilkins, II, 1. *Ann. Monast.* (*Wykes*), IV, 215.	April 22, 1268. (Quindene of Easter.)	S. Paul's, London.	Othobon. All the prelates of the realm (major and minor).	Constitutions.		
(A) (CONVOCATION) Wilkins, II, 19–20. (Ex. MS. C. C. Christi, Oxon., 1 n., 154.) Lunt, *Consent*, p. 160.	October 14, 1269.	New Temple, London.	Bishops. Abbots. Priors. Proctors of Rectors and Vicars.	Grievances drawn up by Abbots, Priors, Proctors of Rectors and Vicars and presented to Abp. with reasons against a grant.		

Sources.	Date.	Place of Meeting.	Composition.		Matters Treated.	Results.	Form of Mandate.
(COUNCIL) Royal Letters, II, 336.	April 27, 1270.	London.	Bishops. Priors.	Abbots.	Grant.	Grant of a twentieth of personal property, demesnes and villeins.	
(CONVOCATION?) Cal. P. R. (1266–72), pp. 508–9, 536.	1270.		Clergy.		Grant.	Grant by the commonalty of the clergy of the diocese of Canterbury.	
(COUNCIL) Ann. Monast. (Wigornia), IV, 460.	Lent (2nd feria of Lent), 1271(–2).	Reading.	Bishops.		Jurisdiction of the Church of Canterbury.		
(A) (COUNCIL) Wilkins, II, 24. (Ex reg. Giffard Wigorn, fols. 36, 37). Cal. in Wor. Epis. Reg. (Reg. Giffard), I, 51, II, 53.	January 19, 1272(–3). (and before).	London.	Abp. of Cant. 11 bps.		Request made by Pope Gregory X for an aid for crusading expenses of Princes Edward and Edmund.	Compliance with papal request. Grant of tenth for two years according to Taxation of Norwich.	
(S) (COUNCIL) Wilkins, II, 26. (Ex reg. Giffard Wigorn, fol. 41.) Cal. in Wor. Epis. Reg. (Reg. Giffard), II, 58.	Summoned for October 11 (Wednesday after the beginning of the Feast of S. Dionysius), 1273.	New Temple, London.	Abp. of Cant. Bps. 3 or 4 persons of "the greater, more discreet and prudent men of dioceses and churches.		State of the Church and ecclesiastical liberty.		Called independently by the Archbishop.

Sources.	Date.	Place of Meeting.	Composition.	Matters Treated.	Results.	Form of Mandate.
(S) (CONVOCATION) Wilkins, II, 30. (Ex reg. Giffard Wigorn, fol. 71.) Cal. in Wor. Epis. Reg. (Reg. Giffard), II, 93.	January 14 (Morrow of S. Hilary), 1277(-8).	London.	Abp. of Cant. Major persons of Chapters. Archdeacons. Proctors of the clergy of each diocese.	Business touching the honour & welfare of the Church.		Called independently by the Archbishop.
(A) (COUNCIL) Reg. Pecham, fol. 10. Printed Wilkins, II, 32–6. Ann. Monast., II, 391; IV, 281. Chron. Mon. Abingdon, p. 26.	July 29 or 30 (4 or 3 Kal. Augusti), 1279.	Reading.	Abp. of Cant. Bps.			Called independently by the Abp.
(CONGREGATION) Reg. Pecham, fol. 165. B. Cotton, p. 160. Florence of W. (Continuation), II, 224. Ann. Monast. (Oseneia), IV, 286.	January 20 (Octaves of Hilary), 1279(-80).	London.	Abp. of Cant. Bps. King's deputies.	An aid to the King.	A grant of a fifteenth for three years may have been made at this council. (Cf. Reg. Pecham, fol. 25. Printed in Regist. Epis. J. Peckham, I, 145.)	Called independently by the Abp.
("CONVENTUS") Wilkins, II, 49. (Procuratorium of the Bishop of Exeter.)	May 12, 1280.	London.	Abp. of Cant. Bps.			
(COUNCIL) Reg. Pecham, fol. 99. Wilkins, II, 49–50.	May 4, 1281.	London.	Abp. of Cant. Bps.	Grant.		At the instance of the King's letter.

Sources.	Date.	Place of Meeting.	Composition.	Matters Treated.	Results.	Form of Mandate.
(A) (CONVOCATION) Reg. Pecham, fol. 101v. *Ibid.*, fols. 175v.–76. Printed in Wilkins, II, 50–1. *Chron. Mon. Abingdon* (gives year as 1280). *Ann. Monast.* (*Waverleia*), II, 396. (*Dunstaplia*), III, 288. (*Wigornia*), IV, 481, gives year as 1282. (*Wykes, Oseneia*), IV, 285, give year as 1280. Walsingham, *Hist. Ang.*, I, 20. Johnstone, "Archbishop Pecham and the Council of Lambeth of 1281," *passim.*	October 7–10, 1281.	Lambeth.	Abp. of Cant. Bishops. Abbots & Priors, elective, exempt & non-exempt. Archdeacons. Proctors of Chapters. Three deputies of the king.	Royal prohibition issued to the Council. Constitutions of Otho and Othobon ordered to be kept. Certain statutes added.	In spite of the royal prohibition, the Abp. was able to regain some of his lost ground.	Called independently by the Abp.
(A) (CONVOCATION) Reg. Pecham, fols. 14–14v, fol. 64v. Printed *Regist. Epis. Peckham*, I, 256–7, 293–7. *Reg. Swinfield*, p. 32 (fol. 106).	February 5, 1281(–2).	New Temple, London.	Abp. of Cant. Bishops. Proctors of absent Bishops.	Fulfilling papal mandate about the liberation of Almaricus de Monteforte.	Request of the liberation of Almaricus de Monteforte.	

Sources.	Date.	Place of Meeting.	Composition.	Matters Treated.	Results.	Form of Mandate.
(A) ("CONGREGATION") Reg. Pecham, fol. 99. Printed *Regist. Epist. Peckham,* I, 323. *Wor. Epis. Reg.,* II, 146–7. (*Reg. Giffard,* fol. 133.)	April 19 (3 weeks after Easter), 1282. (Given also as April 18, Saturday before the Sunday on which "Jubilate" is sung [Easter III].)	Lambeth and London.	Abp. of Cant. Bishops.	Articles.	Articles ordained.	
(A) (ASSEMBLY) Reg. Pecham, fols. 82v., 83v., 101v. *Regist. Epist. Peckham,* II, 508. Wilkins, II, 92–3. (*Reg. Giffard,* fol. 166d.) *Cal. Wor. Epis. Reg.,* II [*Reg. Giffard*], 187. Wilkins' foliation incorrect.	January 20 (Octaves of Hilary, 1282(–3).	Northampton.	Abp. of Cant. Suffragan Bps. Abbots. Priors. "Prefecti" of religious houses. Deans & Chapters of Cathed. and Colleg. Churches & their Proctors.	Grant of a tenth for three years.	No answer given because the greater part of the clergy absent — "not duly called." It was agreed that the whole clergy of the province of Cant. should be assembled at another time.	King's writ incorporated in the Abp. of Canterbury's mandate to the Bp. of London.
(A) (CONVOCATION) Reg. Pecham, fols. 83v., 84v., 86v. *Ann. Monast.* (*Dunstaplia*), III, 295–6. Wilkins, II, 94. (*Rot. Walliæ* XI EI., m. 2, apud Pryn. to 3 eccl. jurisd., p. 303.)	May 9 (3 weeks after Easter), 1283.	New Temple, London. Adjourned to Lambeth.	Abp. of Cant. Prelates. Bishops. Archdeacons or by Proctors. Clergy of Cathed. & Coll. Churches by *one* Proctor. Clergy of each diocese by *two* Proctors. Commissioners of the King.	Grant.	Proctors of the clergy oppose a contribution. Articles *versus* a contribution.	Called independently by the Archbishop.

Sources.	Date.	Place of Meeting.	Composition.	Matters Treated.	Results.	Form of Mandate.
(S) (CONVOCATION) Reg. Winchelsey, fols. 168v.–69. Printed *Reg. Winchelsey* (C. and Y. Soc.), pp. 30–1.	July 15, 1295.	New Temple, London.	Abp. of Cant. Bishops.	The state of the Church and all ecclesiastical persons.		Summoned independently by the Abp.
(A) (CONVOCATION OF THE CLERGY OF *both* PROVINCES) Reg. Winchelsey, fols. 204v., 205–205v., 207. Printed C. and Y. Soc., pp. 144–7. *Ann. Monast.* (*Dunstaplia*), III, 404–5. *Flores Hist.*, III, 291.	January 13 (Feast of S. Hilary), 1296(–7). (Treated 8 days.)	S. Paul's, London.	Abps. of Cant. & York. Bishops. Vicars-general or Proctors of the absent. Bps.-elect. Chancellors. Precentors. Treasurers. Abbots. Priors. "Prepositi." Archdeacons. "Magistri et alii in dignitate." Chapters by *one* Proctor. Clergy by *two* Proctors.	Dangers to the Church. The king's demand. Division into 4 classes for discussion: (1) Bishops and their Proctors. (2) Deans of Cathed. and Archdeacons. (3) Abbots. Priors. (4) Proctors of the commonalty of the clergy.	Reply sent in writing to the king.	Called independently by the Abp.
(A) (CONVOCATION) Reg. Winchelsey, fols. 210v.–11. Printed C. and Y. Soc., pp. 162–3. *Flores Historiarum*, III, 294.	March 24 (Sunday when is sung "letare Jerusalem"), 1297.	S. Paul's, London.	Abp. of Cant. Bps. Abbots (non-exempt). Deans and Priors of Cathed. Churches. Priors of Convents & Monasteries.	State of the Church.	Abp. dismissed them to act according to their consciences.	Called independently by the Abp.

Sources.	Date.	Place of Meeting.	Composition.	Matters Treated.	Results.	Form of Mandate.
Wake, *State of the Church*, Appendix, p. 25. [Ex Chron. Anonym MS. Laud, Bibl. Bod. Oxon. 1284.] *Ann. Monast.* (*Wigornia*), IV, 531.			Chapters. Convents by *one* Proctor. Clergy of each dioc. by *two* Proctors. Exempt to be urged to come.			
(A) (CONVOCATION) Reg. Winchelsey, fols. 218v.-19, 220v., 222v. Printed C. and Y. Soc., pp. 179–80. Wilkins, II, 226. P.R.O. Anc. Cor., vol. XXX., no. 98. (*Ann. Monast.* (*Wigornia*), IV, 532–3.	August 10, (Feast of S. Laurence), 1297.	New Temple, London.	Abp. of Cant. Bps. "Presidents" of Cathedral Churches. Deans & Priors (secular and religious). Priors of Convents of each dioc. Chapters by *one* Proctor. Clergy by *two* Proctors. Exempt are requested to come.	Grant to the King.	Abp., Bps., and clergy send letter to the King, saying they cannot make a grant without leave from the Pope. Ask leave to send a message to the Pope for permission.	Called independently by the Abp.
(A) (CONVOCATION) Reg. Winchelsey, fols. 225-6, 230v., 231. Printed C. and Y. Soc., pp. 198–200, 212. Wilkins, II, 228. Wake, *State*, Appendix, pp. 26-7. (Reg. Giffard.)	November 20 (Feast of S. Edmund the King), 1297.	New Temple, London.	Abp. of Cant. Bps. Deans and Priors of Cathedral Churches. Abbots and Priors. Chapters by *one* Proctor. Clergy of Wales by *one* Proctor. Clergy of England by *two* Proctors.	Grant of a tenth for repelling the invasion of the Scots.	Grant of a tenth of the value of ecclesiastical goods in accordance with the last valuation (Taxation of Pope Nicholas IV). Terms: S. Hilary and the middle of Lent, by equal portions.	

Sources.	Date.	Place of Meeting.	Composition.	Matters Treated.	Results.	Form of Mandate.
Cal. *Wor. Epis. Reg.* (*Reg. Giffard*), II, 491. Bart. Cotton, p. 339. Graham, *Eccles. Studies*, p. 318.			Exempt urged to come.		*N.B.* Parochial Clergy to pay according to Taxation of Norwich.	
(CONVOCATION) Reg. Winchelsey, fols. 242v., 245–245v. Printed C. and Y. Soc., pp. 250, 260. Wilkins, II, 236.	June 25, 1298.	New Temple, London.	Abp. of Cant. Bps. Precentors. Chancellors. Treasurers. Priors of Cathedral Churches. Abbots (non-exempt). Priors (perpetual and elective). "Prepositi", "Magistri", and custodians of Cathedral Churches. All others "constituted in dignity." Convents, Colleges & Chapters by *one* Proctor. Clergy by *two* Proctors. Two Proctors for the King.	A reply to the four requests of the King. (Each degree of the Clergy discussed the matter by themselves.)	Reply: (1) Cannot grant aid without leave from the Pope. (2) The second half of the grant made for use against the Scots they wished used for the defence of the land and Holy Church. (3) Assure the King of their prayers. (4) Excommunicate all disturbers of the peace of the realm.	No royal writ incorporated, but the King's request for summoning is mentioned in the Abp.'s mandate.

Sources.	Date.	Place of Meeting.	Composition.	Matters Treated.	Results.	Form of Mandate.
(A) (CONVOCATION) Reg. Winchelsey, fol. 131v. Printed in Wilkins, II, 253. *Ann. Monast.* (*Wigornia*), IV, 543.	November 4 (Second court day after All Saints.) (*Ann. de Wigornia* say morrow of All Souls), 1299.	New Temple, London.	Abp. of Cant. Prelates. Proctors of Prelates.	(Secrecy as to the discussions.)		Called independently by the Abp.
(A) (COUNCIL) Wilkins, II, 257. [Ex Lib. Memorand. Jo. de Dalderby (Linc.), fol. 9.]	June 13 (Ides of June), 1300.	Chapter House of the Cathedral, Canterbury.	Abp. of Cant. Bps. of Salisbury, Lincoln, Rochester. Proctors of other bishops.	The publication anew of the statutes published the preceding Lent concerning the preaching of the friars, preachers minor and their hearing confessions. (Three bishops consecrated before the Council.)		
(A) (CONVOCATION) Reg. Winchelsey, fols. 147-147v., 150, 285v.-86. Printed C. and Y. Soc., pp. 433-5. Wilkins, II, 272.	June 1 (Morrow of the Ascension), 1302.	New Temple, London.	Abp. of Cant. Bps. Precentors. Chancellors. Treasurers. Abbots, non-exempt. Priors, perpetual & elective. "Prepositi." Custodians of Cathed. & Colleg. Churches. "Others in dignity." Chapters, Convents, Colleges by *one* Proctor. Clergy of England by *two* Proctors. (Wales by *one* Proctor.)	Dangers of the time. State of the Church.		Called independently by the Abp.

Sources.	Date.	Place of Meeting.	Composition.	Matters Treated	Results.	Form of Mandate.
(A) (CONVOCATION) Reg. Winchelsey, fols. 148v., 150. Wilkins, II, 273.	December 10 (Monday after the Feast of S. Nicholas). 1302.	S. Paul's, London.	Abp. of Cant. Bps. Abbots and Priors, non-exempt. Other ecclesiastical persons, secular and religious from whom a fifteenth is exacted. Colleges, Chapters, Convents by themselves or by one Proctor. Exempt persons whom the matters to be discussed concerned.	The grant forced upon the Abp. in the last parliament.		Called independently by the Abp.
(COUNCIL) Wilkins, II, 278. (Ex MS. Cotton. Otho A. 15. collat. cum MS. Lambeth 17 et MS. Elien, 235.) N.B. No record of a summons.	1305.	Merton.		Constitutions published.		
(S) (COUNCIL) Wilkins, II, 292. (Reg. Cantuar. P., fols. 522a, b.)	May 5 (Morrow of Ascension), 1307.	New Temple, London.	Bishops. Deans. Precentors. Chancellors. Treasurers. Priors. Cathed. Churches. Abbots not exempt. Priors perpetual. All others in dignity. Archdeacons. Chapters, Convents, Colleges by one. Clergy by two.	State of the Church.		Called independently by the Prior of Christ Church, Canterbury, during the suspension of Abp. Winchelsey.

Sources.	Date.	Place of Meeting.	Composition.	Matters Treated.	Results.	Form of Mandate.
(A) (PROVINCIAL COUNCIL) Reg. Winchelsey, fol. 125. Printed Wilkins, II, 304. *Reg. S. de Gandavo*, C. & Y. Soc., pp. 375–6 (fols. 127–127d). Wilkins, II, 312–14. (Ex reg. Eccl. Cantuar. P., fol. 34 seq.) Wake, *State*, p. 259. (Ex Regist. Memorand. Jo. Dalderby, Linc., fol. 141.) Spelman, II, 466.	November 24 (Monday after Feast of S. Edmund), 1309, to December 17, 1309. Adjourned until the autumn. [Tuesday after Feast of S. Matthew, Sept. 22, 1310.]	S. Paul's, London. Adjourned to Church of Carmelite Friars on November 26; to Lambeth on December 2; to S. Paul's on December 4th; to Lambeth on December 5. (Bps. at Westminster, Dec. 11 and 12.)	Abp. of Cant. Bishops. Prelates. Provosts. Archdeacons. Archpriests. Proctors of Chapters and Colleges. Proctors of Clergy of each diocese. Inquisitors appointed by the Pope in regard to the Templars.	Affairs of the Templars. Reading of the King's letter by three knights. Grievances. Supplications to the Pope. Depositions to be published.	Ordained that 3 bishops, together with the inquisitors should be sent to the King to supplicate that the "ordinaries of places" and inquisitors should proceed to inquire the truth about the Templars.	Called at the mandate of the Pope.
(A) (PROVINCIAL COUNCIL) *Reg. Simon de Gandavo*, C. & Y. Soc., p. 389 (fol. 131d). Wilkins, II, 401. (Ex Reg. R. de Langele, Prior of Norwich, no. 9). Wake, *State*, p. 260. (Ex Reg. Memorand. Jo. Dalderby, Linc., fol. 170.)	September 23 (Wednesday after Feast of S. Matthew), 1310. Still in session November 9.	S. Paul's, London.	Abp. Bps. Chapters of Cathed. Churches by *fitting* Proctors.	The Templars.		

Sources.	Date.	Place of Meeting.	Composition.	Matters Treated.	Results.	Form of Mandate.
(A) (CONVOCATION) Reg. Stapledon (Exeter), pp. 119–21 (fol. 58a, fol. 58b). Wake, *State*, pp. 259–60. (Ex Memorand. Jo. Dalderby, fol. 170). (Reg. Greenfield, pt. I, fol. 81)	December 9, 1310.	S. Paul's, London.	(Abp. of Cant. unable to preside.) Bps. Chapters. Clergy by *two* Proctors.	Anticipation of the tenth for 3 years granted to the King by the Pope.	The first and the last term of the second year to be paid by Christmas, 1310.	
(A) (CONVOCATION) ("Provincial Council") *Cal. P.R.* (1307–13), 4 E. II, pp. 338, 341. P.R.O., Anc. Cor., vol. XXXVIII, no. 171. Wilkins, II, 407. (Ex reg. Hen. Prioris Cant., fol. 117.) Wake, *State*, p. 263. (Ex Mem. Jo. Dalderby, Linc., fol. 179b.) Adam Murimuth, pp. 14–15 (R.S.).	April 24 (6th Feria after the Octaves of Easter), 1311. (Reg. S. de Gandavo, p. 400. Ed. says 6th Feria is April 23). Lasted until June.	S. Paul's, London. (Wake says Bp. of London's Hall.)	Abp. of Cant. Bishops. Prelates. Priors. Chapters. Clergy by *one* or more Proctors. Every bp. to send three weeks before a doctor of canon and civil law. King's deputies: Masters Thomas de Cobeham, Walter de Thorp, Gilbert de Middleton.	Templars. Certain rolls in regard to the Duchy of Aquitaine sent by the King for them to discuss. Advice asked by King.		Called independently by the Archbishop.
(MEETING) *Reg. S. de Gandavo*, pp. 418–19 (fol. 139d).	March 13, 1311(–12).	S. Paul's, London.	Bishops. "Proceres."			

Sources.	Date.	Place of Meeting.	Composition.	Matters Treated.	Results.	Form of Mandate.
(PROVINCIAL COUNCIL.) Reg. Winchelsey, fol. 60v. *Reg. S. de Gandavo*, C. & Y. Soc., pp. 421–2 (fol. 141d.) Reg. Reynolds, Wigorn (Wor. Hist. Soc.), pp. 38, 44 (fols. 47a & b, 52a & b). Wake, *State*, p. 263. (Reg. Henr. Prior. Cant., fol. 119b). *Cal. C.R.* (1307–1313), 6 E. II, p. 537. *Reg. Palat. Dunelm* (R. S.), I., 415–16. Wilkins, II, 420. (Reg. Mag. Wigorn., fol. 53).	April 18, 1312. New mandate for May 8 (Monday next after Ascension.) Still in session May 24 (9 Kal. June), 1312.	S. Paul's, London.	Abp. of Cant. Bps. Deans and Priors. Abbots exempt and not exempt. Chapters and Convents by Deans or Abbots or by their Proctors. Archdeacons, Clergy of each diocese by *one* or *two* Proctors.	Letters sent to the Pope on behalf of the University of Oxford.	Grant of 4d. in the mark of the value of all ecclesiastical goods & benefices (according to the "New Taxation"). Money to be kept until further notice. Terms: Moiety at F. of S. Margaret (July 20). Moiety at F. of S. Matthew (Sept. 21). Arrears of procurations for the Lords, the Abbot of Latignac and Sicard de Vauro.	Called independently by Abp.
(PAPAL ENVOYS' COUNCIL.) Wilkins, II, 421. (Ex Reg. Swinfield, fol. 180). *Reg. S. de Gandavo*, C. & Y. Soc., p. 435. (fol. 147), pp. 437–8, (fol. 148). (*N.B.* Wake, p. 269 gives wrong date.)	September 28 prorogued to October 9, 1312.	London.	The Cardinal of S. Prisca. Abp. of Cant. Bishop of Poitiers. Bishops of Province of Canterbury. Certain Abbots & Priors.	The state of the realm of England.		Abp.'s mandate encloses request of the papal envoys to meet them in London.

Sources.	Date.	Place of Meeting.	Composition.	Matters Treated.	Results.	Form of Mandate.
(A) ("PROVINCIAL COUNCIL") *Reg. Reynolds* (Wigorn), translated p. 59 (fol. 77a). Latin text in Wake, *State*, Appendix, pp. 35–6. Wake also quotes Lib. Mem. Jo. Dalderby, Linc, fol. 238b. Wake, *State*, Appendix, p. 36. (Ex Reg. Swinfield, fol. 186.) Calendared *Reg. Swinfield*, C. & Y. Soc., but date is given incorrectly, Assumption being read for Ascension. Cf. Wake, Ap., p. 36. *Reg. S. de Gandavo*, C. & Y. Soc., pp. 444–5 (fol. 150d). *Cal. C.R.* (1307–1313), 6 E. II, p. 537. *Reg. Palat. Dunelm* (R. S.), I, 415–16. Wilkins, II, 426. (Ex Reg. Eccl. Cant. P., fol. 82b.) Possible allusions in P.R.O., Anc. Cor., vol. XXXIV, nos. 84, 199.	March 27 (Tuesday after Mid-Lent Sunday), 1312(–13). Lasted until at least May 25 (Friday after Ascension.)	S. Paul's, London.	Bp. of Landaff, vice-gerent. Bps., Deans and Priors of Cathed. Churches to be assembled if they petitioned. (Abp. Winchelsey died May 11, 1313. *Reg. Sac. Ang.*)	Grant of a subsidy?	It may be possible that the prelates *in this Council* allocated to the King the 4d. in the mark voted the preceding year.	

Sources.	Date.	Place of Meeting.	Composition.	Matters Treated.	Results.	Form of Mandate.
(A) (ASSEMBLY) Reg. Reynolds (Cant.), fols. 36v., 105v.–106. Wilkins, II, 442–3, 444–5. (Ex Reg. Henr. Prior, Cant., fols. 194 seq., 195.) *Cal. C.R.* (1313–1318), 7 E. II, p. 96.	May 17 (Day after Ascension), 1314. Adjourned on May 22.	Westminster.	Abp. of Cant. Bishops. Abbots. Deans & Priors of Cathedral Churches. Archdeacons. Chapters by *one* Proctor. Clergy of each diocese by *two* Proctors.	Competent subsidy. Clergy presented their grievances on May 20 against the method of summoning.	Articles drawn up by Clergy against form of summons.	Called both by diocesan and provincial writs. Abp. incorporates King's writ which commanded that the clergy come into the presence of his deputies.
(S) (CONVOCATION) Reg. Reynolds (Cant.), fols. 105v.–106. Printed Wilkins, II, 444.	July 8 (Morrow of the Translation of S. Thomas, Martyr), 1314.	S. Paul's, London.	Abp. of Cant. Bishops. Deans and Priors of Cathed. Churches. Abbots. Archdeacons. Chapters of Cathedral Churches by *one* Proctor. Clergy of diocese by *two* Proctors.	Subsidy. State of the Church.	(Grant mentioned in *Reg. Gandavo,* pp. 519–21 (fol. 173) may have been made at this convocation—tenth payable May 3 (Exalt. of Cross), Sept. 14 (Inv. of Cross).)	Abp. gives the substance of the King's writ in his mandate.
(A) (ASSEMBLY OF THE CLERGY FOR PARLIAMENT) Wake, *State,* Appendix, pp. 41–2. (Reg. Woodlock Winton, fol. 197, collat. with Reg. Henr. Prior, Cant., fol. 168b.) Wilkins, II, 456. (Ex Reg. H. Prior, fol. 168b.) *Cal. C.R.* (1313–1318), 9 E. II, pp. 314, 325.	January 26 (Morrow after Feast of S. Paul), 1315(–16).	Cathedral, Lincoln.	Bishops. Deans and Priors of Cathed. Churches. Archdeacons. Chapters by *one* Proctor. Clergy of each diocese by *two* Proctors.	The dangers of the realm.	No grant because of absence of Abp. of Cant. & many clergy.	King's writ *not* incorporated, but Abp. mentions the King's request. "Premunitione Regia."

Sources.	Date.	Place of Meeting.	Composition.	Matters Treated.	Results.	Form of Mandate.
(S) (" CONVOCATION ") Reg. Reynolds (Cant.), fols. 73–73v. Wake, Appendix, pp. 42–3; also Wilkins, II, 456. (Ex reg. Henr. Prior, Cant.), fol. 168. *Cal. C.R.* (1313–1318), 9 E. II, p. 325.	April 26 (Wednesday after the Quinzaine of Easter), 1316.	S. Paul's, London.	Prelates. Religious. Clergy.	Subsidy.		Royal writ not incorporated, but King's request is mentioned in the Archbishop's mandate.
(PROVINCIAL COUNCIL) Reg. Reynolds (Cant.), fol. 75. Wilkins, II, 458. (Reg. Epist. Rob. des Langele, Prior. Norwich), n. 102. *Cal. C.R.* (1313–1318), 10 E. II, pp. 380, 433.	October 10 (Sunday after the Octaves of Michaelmas), 1316. [Reg. Ep. Langele says Monday after Feast of S. Faith (October 6)—October 10.]	S. Paul's, London. (*Cal. C.R.* (1313–1318), 10 E. II, p. 436 says *Lambeth.*)	Abp. Bishops. Clergy.	A moiety or a third part of the ecclesiastical possessions to the King. Aid for Scottish War.	Bps. in favour. Clergy against. Proctors of the Clergy grant a tenth to the King. Payments: Purif., B.V.M., 1316(–17). (Feb. 2). Purif., B.V.M., 1317(–18).	Without the King's writ, but at the instigation of the King's writ.
(S) (CONVOCATION) Wake, *State*, p. 270. Cal. P.R. (1317–1321), 11 E. II, p. 104. (ROYAL REQUEST FOR CONVOCATION) *Cal. C.R.* (1318–1323), 12 E. II, p. 30. *N.B.* Not known whether this was summoned. Wake, *State*, p. 271.	February 23 (Morrow of S. Peter in Cathedra), 1317(–18). February 3 (Morrow of Purif., B.V.M.), 1318(–19).	London.	Prelates. Clergy.	Subsidy.		

Sources.	Date.	Place of Meeting.	Composition.	Matters Treated.	Results.	Form of Mandate.
(A) (CONVOCATION) Reg. Cobham, Wigorn, Wor. Hist. Soc., p. 40 (fol. 39b). Wake, State, 271. (Mem. Dalderby, Linc., fol. 393). Reg. Stephen Gravesend, Lond., C. & Y. Soc., pp. 203–4 (fols. 42v., 43v., 46). A. de Murimuth, p. 30, R.S. Chron. E. I & E. II (R.S.). (Ann. Paulinus), I, 286.	April 20 (Friday after the Octaves of Easter), 1319. (Ann. Paulinus say Quindene of Easter— April 22.)	S. Paul's, London.	Prelates. Clergy.	Subsidy. Chancellors and Masters of Oxford explain the condition of the poor clerks.	Prelates refused to grant anything without the Pope's leave. Adam de Murimuth sent to the Pope. Unanimous agreement that in the next subsidy a halfpenny in the mark be given to the University.	
(A) (PROVINCIAL COUNCIL) Wake, State, Appendix. [Ex Reg. Orleton, pp. 45–6, Heref. (fol. 55).] Wake, State, 272 (Ex Reg. Hen. Prior Cant. (fol. 125).) Reg. Cobham, Wor. Hist. Soc., p. 111 (fol. 68b), p. 117 (fol. 73). A. de Murimuth (R.S.), p. 35. Wilkins, II, 509–10, pp. 441–2. Reg. Stapledon, (fol. 215b). Cal. C.R. (1318–1323), pp. 410, 506, 543. Chron. E. I & E. II, II, 71.	December 1, 1321. (Murimuth says December 10.)	S. Paul's, London.	Abp. of Cant. Prelates. Clergy. Messengers from the King (Earls of Richmond and Arundel and Archdeacon of Middlesex.)	The petition of the Despensers. [Ordered by the King to make no ordinance to the prejudice of the Crown.] Cal. P.R. (1321–1324), 15 E. II, p. 37.	Bishops & Prelates declared the Act of the preceding Parliaments against the Despensers null and void because it was done without their consent. Counselled the repeal of the exile.	Called independently by the Abp.

Sources.	Date.	Place of Meeting.	Composition.	Matters Treated.	Results.	Form of Mandate.
(CONVOCATION) Wake, State, Appendix, p. 47. (Ex Reg. Henr. Burghersh, Linc., fol. 54; also Wilkins, II, 515–16.) P.R.O. K.R. Mem. Roll, 108. "Communia Easter Term, 6 E. III."	June 9 (Wednesday after Trinity), 1322.	S. Paul's, London.	Abp. of Cant. Prelates. Clergy.	Confirmation of a grant made in Parliament at York three weeks after Easter, five pence in the mark from spiritualities.	Grant of 5d. in the mark yielded by Clergy in 15 E. II. K.R. Mem. Roll. (It is to be inferred therefore that this Convocation which was summoned, met.)	Abp. does not incorporate King's writ.
(A) (CONVOCATION) Reg. Reynolds (Cant.), fol. 306. B.M. MS. Cotton, Faustina A.V., fols. 2v.—3v. Wilkins, II, 517–18. Prints, fols. 3v.–5. Wake, State, Appendix, pp. 48–9. (Ex reg. Eccl. Christi Cantuar. H., fol. 252); also in Wilkins, II, 517. Cal. C.R. (1318–1323), 16 E. II, p. 686.	January 14 (Morrow of Hilary), 1322(–3).	Cathedral, Lincoln.	Abp. of Cant. Bps. Deans and Priors of Cathed. Churches. Archdeacons. Other Abbots Priors. exempt and non-exempt. Religious. Clergy.	"Aid and counsel" for the King.	Petitions presented in writing by Abbots, Priors, Deans of Cathed. Churches, Archdeacons, Proctors of Chapters and Clergy. Desired to be excused as the tenth for two years granted by the Pope was still running and they had granted an aid.	No writ incorporated but Abp. mentions the requests from the King.
(S) (CONVOCATION) N.B. Did not meet. Summons superseded. Reg. Reynolds (Cant.), fol. 308.	Summoned for January 20 (Octaves of Hilary), 1323(–4).	S. Paul's, London.	Prelates. Clergy.		This order was superseded.	

Sources.	Date.	Place of Meeting.	Composition.	Matters Treated.	Results.	Form of Mandate.
Wilkins, II, 518-19. (Ex Lib. Mem. H. Burghersh, Linc., fol. 116.) *Cal. C.R.* (1323-1327), 17 E. II, pp. 145, 153.						
(S) (CONVOCATION) *N.B.* Doubtful if this met. (Wake, p. 277.) *Reg. Reynolds* (Cant.), fols. 312v.-13. Printed Wilkins, II, 532. *Reg. Orleton* (Heref.), C. & Y. Soc., pp. 368-9 (fol. 103). *Cal. C.R.* (1323-1327), 20 E. II, p. 647.	Summoned for October 13 (Quindene of Michaelmas), 1326. Prorogued to November 3, 1326.	S. Paul's, London.				In proroguing, Abp. quotes the King's writ.
(S) (CONVOCATION) Printed Wake, *State*, Appendix, pp. 54-5. Wilkins, II, 534. (Reg. Memorand. H. Burghersh, Linc., fol. 152.)	January 17 (Friday after Hilary), 1326(-7).	S. Paul's, London.	Abp. Bps. Vicar's general. Deans. Archdeacons. Abbots & Priors. exempt & non-exempt. "Prepositi." Archpriests. Master Priors. Locum-tenentes. Preceptors. Chapters & Convents by their Deans, Abbots or Priors or fitting Proctors. Clergy of each diocese by *one* or *two* Proctors.	Business touching the whole Church.		Called independently by Abp. at the advice of the Apostolic Nuncios and at the advice of the bishops.

Sources.	Date.	Place of Meeting.	Composition.	Matters Treated.	Results.	Form of Mandate.
(A) ("CONVOCATION") Reg. Reynolds (Cant.), fols. 207, 208. Wilkins, II, 538–9. (Ex Reg. Reynolds, fol. 207.) Wake, *State*, Appendix, pp. 55–6 (Ex Reg. Reynolds, fol. 207.) P.R.O. K.R. Mem. Roll 106, m. 30 (Michaelmas Term, 4 E. III). P.R.O. K.R. Mem. Roll 108, m. 125 (Easter Term, 6 E. III). *Cal. C.R.* (1327–1330), 1 E. III, p. 187.	November 4 (Wednesday after All Souls), 1327. Still in session November 28, 1327.	Chapter House, S. Mary's Abbey, Leicester.	Abp. Bps. Deans and Priors of Cathed. Churches. Abbots exempt. Archdeacons. Other Abbots & Priors by their Proctors. Chapters by *one* Proctor. Clergy by *two* Proctors.	Counsel and aid.	Grant of a tenth of the value of ecclesiastical goods to the King. Terms:—Moiety: Ascension, 1328 (May 15). Moiety: All Saints, 1328 (November 1).	King's writ summarized in Abp.'s mandate.
(A) (PROVINCIAL COUNCIL) Wake, *State*, p. 279. (Ex Mem. H. de Burghersh, Linc., fol. 190b.) *Reg. Grandisson, Exeter*, I, 446–7; also Wilkins, II, 548–9. A. de Murimuth (R.S.), p. 59. *Chron. of E. I & E. II* (*Ann. Paulinus*), I, 344.	January 27 (Friday after the Conversion of S. Paul), 1328(–9).	S. Paul's, London.	Abp. Clergy.	Ecclesiastical Constitutions (Spelman, II., 49). Grievances of the Exeter diocese. Grievances.	Excommunication of the murderers of the Bp. of Exeter. On days of Good Friday, All Souls all to cease from servile work. Feast of Conception of the B.V.M. to be solemnly celebrated.	Called by Abp. (Excited by warning of Pope John XXII.)

R

Sources.	Date.	Place of Meeting.	Composition.	Matters Treated.	Results.	Form of Mandate.
(A) (CONVOCATION) Chron. of E. I & E. II (Ann. Paulinus), I, 348.	After September 3, 1329.	Lambeth.	Abp. of Cant. Clergy. Two spokesmen of the King.	A grant.	Response: Refusal. Reasons: Could barely support the Pope's burdens. Subsidy voted recently by the laity sufficient for King's needs. Conditions of past grant not fulfilled.	
(S) (ASSEMBLY OF THE CLERGY FOR PARLIAMENT) Wake, State, p. 279. (Ex Reg. H. Burghersh, Linc.), fol. 169. Wilkins, II, 557–8. (Does not give source.)	March 11, (Sunday before the Feast of S. Gregory), 1329(–30).	Cathedral, Winchester.	Abp. of Cant. Prelates. Clergy.	Urgent affairs of the Church and the realm.		Abp. quotes King's writ for Parliament but calls them into his presence at Cathedral.
(S) (CONVOCATION) Wake, State, p. 280. (Ex Reg. H. Burghersh, Linc.), 214. Reg. Grandisson, I, 563 (fol. 135). Cal. C.R. (1330–1333). 4 E. III, p.130. Printed Wilkins, II, 558–9. N.B. Under wrong year.	April 16 (Monday after the Feasts of SS. Tyburtius & Valerianus), 1330.	Lambeth.	Abp. of Cant. Prelates. Men of religion. All clergy.	The dangers of the French War. Grant of a supply.		At the instance of the King's writ.

Sources.	Date.	Place of Meeting.	Composition.	Matters Treated.	Results.	Form of Mandate.
(A) (CONVOCATION) Wilkins, II, 561. (Ex Lib. Act. Capit. Linc.) *Chron. E. I & E. II (Ann. Paul.)*, I, 356-7. A. de Murimuth (R.S.), p. 66.	September 4 [*Cal. C.R.* (1330-1333), 6 E. III, p. 595 says Friday after S. Barthol. (Aug. 28), 1332.] Murimuth says September 8), 1332.	S. Paul's, London.	Abp. of Cant. Bishops. Provosts. Archpriests. Archdeacons. Deputies for the King.	[To do nothing to the King's prejudice.]	Terminated ineffectually because of discord between the Abp. and his suffragans.	Called independently by Abp.
(S) (CONVOCATION) *Cal. C.R.* (1333-1337), 7 E. III, p.184. Wilkins, II, 563. (Ex Reg. Eccl. Cantuar. P., fol. 8.) (S)	January 10 (Monday after Epiphany), 1333(-4).	Northampton.	Prelates. Clergy.	An aid for the expenses of the late Scottish War.		Prior of Christ Church, Canterbury, incorporates the King's writ.
(ASSEMBLY OF CLERGY FOR PARLIAMENT) Reg. Orleton (Winton), pt. I, fols. 7-7v., 13v.	September 19 (Monday after Exalt. of Cross), 1334.	S. Paul's, London.	Abp. of Cant. Bishops. Deans. Priors. Archdeacons. Chapters by one Proctor. Clergy each dioc. by *two* Proctors.	Business of Parliament.		*Significant:* Abp. incorporates in his mandate to the Bp. of London the King's writ for Parliament and the King's writ of privy seal for Convocation.
(A) (CONVOCATION) *Reg. Grandisson* (Exeter), II, 766. Wake, *State*, p. 283. (Ex. Reg. Burghersh, Linc., fol. 275.) Reg. Montacute Wigorn, fol. 38. *Cal. C.R.* (1333-1337), 8 E. III, pp. 269-70, 314. (Murimuth (R.S.), p. 72 gives under 1333.)	September 26 (Monday after Feast of S. Matthew), 1334.	S. Paul's, London.	Same group summoned as above.	Such things as mentioned in the King's last writ.	Grant of a tenth. Terms: Moiety-Purificat. B.V.M. (Feb. 2), 1334(-5). Moiety-Midsummer (June 24), 1335.	

Sources.	Date.	Place of Meeting.	Composition.	Matters Treated.	Results.	Form of Mandate.
(A) (ASSEMBLY OF THE CLERGY FOR PARLIAMENT) Reg. Orleton (Winton), pt. I, fols. 33–33v. Wake, *State*, p. 284. (Ex Reg. H. Burghersh, fol. 316.) Wilkins, II, 581. (Ex Reg. Eccl. Cant., fol. 31.) *Cal. C.R.* (1333–1337), 10 E. III, p. 661; 11 E. III, p. 80.	March 11 (Monday after Mid-Lent Sunday), 1335(–6).	S. Paul's, London.	Abp. of Cant. Bishops. Abbots. Priors. Deans. Archdeacons. Chapters by *one* Proctor. Clergy by *two* Proctors.	Grant. Business of Church and realm.	Grant of a tenth.	*Significant:* In execution of the "premunientes" clause the Abp. cited the clergy to appear before himself to treat in regard to business of Parliament.
(CONVOCATION) ("CONGREGATION") Reg. Orleton (Winton), pt. II, fols. 43v–44. P.R.O., Close Roll, 10 E. III, m. 16. P.R.O., Close Roll, 11 E. III, pt. I, m. 8. P.R.O., K.R. Mem. Roll 113. "Communia Trinity Term," 11 E. III, m. 176. Wake, *State*, p. 285. (Ex Reg. H. Burghersh, fol. 357.) Wilkins, II, 582–3. (Ex Reg. Burghersh, fol. 340b.)	September 30 (Monday after the Feast of S. Michael), 1336.	Conventual Church of the Blessed Mary, Leicester.	Abp. Bps. Deans. Abbots. Priors. Archdeacons. Chapters of Cathed. by *one* Proctor. Clergy by *two* Proctors.	Grant.	Grant of tenth.	Abp. incorporates King's writ.

Sources.	Date.	Place of Meeting.	Composition.	Matters Treated.	Results.	Form of Mandate.
(A) (Convocation) ("Congregation") P.R.O., Close Roll, 12 E. III, pt. III, m. 2. Reg. Hamo Roff, C. & Y. Soc., p. 327 (fol. 108). Wilkins, II, 622. (Ex. Reg. Hemenhale Wigorn), fol. 39. Wilkins, II, 623. Wake, *State*, Appendix, 63. (Ex Reg. Montacute, Ely, fol. 38.) P.R.O., K.R. Mem. Roll 114, 12 E. III, m. 174. "Communia Trinity Term." A. Murimuth (R.S.), p. 80.	September 30 (Morrow of the Feast of S. Michael), 1337.	S. Paul's, London, thence to S. Bridget's (or S. Bride's), Fleet Bridge, London.	Abp. of Cant. Bishops. Prelates. Archdeacons. Clergy. Deans. Priors. Abbots exempt and non-exempt. Chapters by *one* Proctor. Clergy of each diocese by *two* Proctors.	Grant.	Grant of a tenth for three years on spiritualities. Terms: Moiety: Purif. B.V.M. (Feb. 2). Moiety: Nat. S. John Bap. (June 24) for three years.	Abp. incorporates the King's writ in his mandate.
(A) (Convocation) P.R.O., K.R. Mem. Roll 115, 13 E. III, m. 13. "Brevia directa Baron." P.R.O., Anc. Cor., vol. XXXIX, no. 72. *Cal. C.R.* (1337–1339), 12 E. III, p. 607. P.R.O., Close Roll, 13 E. III, pt. I, m. 35d. A. de Murimuth (R.S.), p. 85. Wake, *State*, p. 287. (Ex Reg. H. Burghersh, fol. 332b.)	October 1 (Morrow of S. Jerome) (September 30), 1338.	S. Bride's, London.	Bishops. (Abp. of Cant. abroad.) Deans. Priors. Abbots exempt & non-exempt. Archdeacons. Chapters by *one* Proctor. Clergy of each diocese by *two* Proctors.	Grant.	Shorter Terms of paying tenth. Terms of payment: Feast of S. Andrew moiety (Nov. 30). Ann. B.V.M. moiety (Mar. 25). Another tenth to be paid after lapse of the tenth for three years. Terms: By equal portions, Feb. 2—Purif. B.V.M.; June 24—Nat. S. John Bap.	

Sources.	Date.	Place of Meeting.	Composition.	Matters Treated.	Results.	Form of Mandate.
(S) (COUNCIL) Reg. Orleton (Winton), pt. II., fol. 20v.	January 31 1338(–9).	London.	Bishops.			Called by Cdnls. Peter & Bertrand.
(A) (CONVOCATION) Cal. C.R. (1339–1341), 13 E. III, p. 332. Wake, State, p. 288. (Reg. H. Burghersh, fol. 367b.) Reg. Wulstani (Braunsford), Worcester, fol. 153. Reg. H. de Lexington, Linc. (fol. 212).	January 27 (Thursday after the Conversion of S. Paul), 1339(–40).	S. Paul's, London.	Abp. of Cant. Bishops. Deans and Priors of Cathedral Churches. Archdeacons. Religious exempt and non-exempt. Chapters by one Proctor. Clergy of each diocese by two Proctors.	Matters not terminated in the last Parliament.	Grant of a tenth on February 17 (Murimuth (R.S.), p. 104), together with those previously conceded.	
(A) ("PROVINCIAL COUNCIL") Chartulary of Winchester Cathedral, fol. 127 (nos. 524 & 528). Cal. in Chartulary of W. Cathed., ed. Goodman (nos. 524 & 528). Cal. C.R. (1339–41), 13 E. III, p. 382. Wilkins, II, 680. (Ex. Reg. Montacute, Ely, fol. 64); also in Wake, Appendix, pp. 65, 66. Cal. C.R. (1341–1343), 15 E. III, p. 335. A. Murimuth (R.S.), p. 122.	October 19 (First Court Day after Feast of S. Luke), 1341.	S. Paul's, London.	Abp. of Cant. Bps., personally. Deans & Priors of Cathedral Churches. Abbots. Priors. Archdeacons if it seems expedient. Chapters by one Proctor. Clergy by two Proctors if they have business in this Council.	[Not to do anything derogatory to the King.] Preservation of Ecclesiastical Liberty. Reform of customs.	Business not completed.	Called independently by the Abp.

Sources.	Date.	Place of Meeting.	Composition.	Matters Treated.	Results.	Form of Mandate.
(S) (CONVOCATION) Wilkins, II, 697, note (Lib. Memorand. T. Beck, Linc., fol. 2); also Wake, State, 290. Cal. C.R. (1341–1343), 16 E. III, 639. Reg. Orleton (Wint.), pt. I, fols. 113–113v. Cheney, Legislation, pt. II, p. 416.	October 9 (King called it for October 5, Cal. C.R.), 1342.	S. Paul's, London.	Abp. of Cant. Bishops.	Counsel and advice to the King's deputies. The King had offered to treat with his adversary for peace. Publication of Constitutions.		At the instance of the King's writ.
(S) (PROVINCIAL COUNCIL) Reg. Orleton (Wint.), pt. I, fols. 114–114v. Wake, Appendix, p. 66. (Ex Lib. Mem. Beck, Linc., fol. 1.) Reg. Grandisson, Exeter, II, 968 (vol. I, fol. 114.)	October 14 (Monday after the Translation of S. Edward), 1342.	S. Paul's, London.	Abp. of Cant. Bishops or Vicars personally. Deans and Priors of Cathed. Churches. Other Priors and Abbots if they think it useful. Chapters by one Proctor. Clergy by two Proctors.			Called independently by the Abp.

Sources.	Date.	Place of Meeting.	Composition.	Matters Treated.	Results.	Form of Mandate.
(A) (CONVOCATION) P.R.O., K.R. Mem. Roll 121, 19 E. III, Hilary Term, m. 4. Wake, *State*, p. 291. (Reg. Wulstan, Wigorn, fol. 170; *Jura Cleri*, p. 62.) *Rot. Parl.*, II, 146, 148. A. Murimuth (R.S.), p. 156, Appendix, p. 247. *Cal. C.R.* (1343–1346), 18 E. III, 305, 368.	May 31 (Morrow of Trinity), 1344.	S. Paul's, London.	Abp. of Cant. Bishops. Clergy.	Grant. Many things concerning the dignity of clerks that are rarely observed.	Grant of a tenth for three years to the King. Terms: Moiety–Purif. B.V.M., February 2. Moiety–Feast of S. Barnabas, June 11.	
(S) (CONVOCATION) *Reg. Trelleck* (Heref.). C. & Y. Soc., pp. 15, 271, 275. Reg. Edyndon (Winton), pt. I, fol. 9. Wake, *State*, Appendix, p. 68. (Ex. Reg. Wulstan (Braunsford) Wigorn., fol. 95b.)	May 4 (Next Court Day after Feast of Invention of the Cross), 1346.	S. Paul's, London.	Abp. of Cant. (for Commissaries). Bishops.	Urgent business of the Church.		Called independently by Abp.
(A) (CONVOCATION) Reg. Edyndon (Winton), pt. II, fols. 4v.–5, 69. Wake, *State*, p. 294. (Reg. Trelleck, Heref., fol. 138.) *Cal. C.R.* (1346–1349), 20 E. III, p. 154.	October 16 (Monday after the Translation of S. Edward), 1346.	S. Paul's, London.	Abp. of Cant. Bishops. Deans. Priors of Cathed. Chapters, Archdeacons. Abbots. Priors. Convents, Colleges by *one* Proctor. Clergy of each diocese by *two* Proctors.	State of England. Defence of the realm. War with France.	Grant of tenth for two years. Terms of payment: August 15 (Feast of Assump. B.V.M.). November 11 (F. of S. Martin).	King's writ incorporated in the Abp.'s mandate.

Sources.	Date.	Place of Meeting.	Composition.	Matters Treated.	Results.	Form of Mandate.
(S) (PROVINCIAL COUNCIL) Reg. Edyndon (Winton), pt. II, fols. 11v.–12. Wake, State, p. 295. (Ex. Reg. Instit. Jo. Gynewell, Linc., fol. 28.)	October 1 (First Court Day after the Feast of S. Jerome), 1347.	S. Paul's, London.	Abp. of Cant. Bishops. Deans and Priors of Cathedral Churches. Abbots and Priors. Archdeacons. Chapters. Convents. Clergy by Proctors. [invited]	For correcting excesses. Reforms.		Called independently by the Abp.
(A) (CONVOCATION) Reg. Islep, fols. 42v., 49. Partially printed in Wilkins, III, 16–17. Cal. C.R. (1349–1354). 24 E. III., p. 322. Reg. Grandisson (Ex.), II, pp. 1099–1100.	May 2 (Monday next after the Quindene of Easter), 1351.	S. Paul's, London.	Abp. of Cant. Bishops. Deans and Priors of Cathedral Churches. Abbots. Priors and other "electi." Archdeacons. Chapters. Convents. Colleges by one Proctor. Clergy of each diocese by two Proctors.	Grant to the King.	Grant of a tenth for two years. One absolute, one on condition that grievances should be redressed by the King's authority. Four terms of payment: 1st year— S. Andrew (November 30); Midsummer (June 24). 2nd year— Purif. B.V.M. (February 2); Midsummer (June 24). If grievances were not reformed, they were not held for second year.	King's writ incorporated in the Abp.'s mandate.

Sources.	Date.	Place of Meeting.	Composition.	Matters Treated.	Results.	Form of Mandate.
(CONVOCATION) N.B. It is not known whether this met. Cal. C.R. (1354–1360), 29 E. III, P. 233. Wake (State, p. 299) thinks this did not meet.	King's request for summons on November 16 (Monday after Feast of S. Martin), 1355.	S. Paul's, London.	Abp. of Cant. Bishops. Abbots. Deans and Priors of Cathed. and Colleg. Churches. Abbots & Priors exempt & non-exempt. Archdeacons. Chapters, Colleges, Convents by *one* Proctor. Clergy by *two* Proctors.			
(A) (CONVOCATION) Reg. Islep, fols. 111, 117–18. Wilkins, III, 38 (gives incorrect foliation).	May 16, 1356.	S. Paul's, London.	Abp. of Cant. Bishops. Abbots. Deans and Priors of Cathed. Churches. Abbots & Priors elective. "Prepositi." Archdeacons. Convents, Colleges, Chapters by *one* Proctor. Clergy by *two* Proctors.	Grant of a tenth. Petitions exhibited. Complaint that grievances had not been redressed.	Grant of a tenth. Terms: 1st, S. Andrew's (November 30). 2nd, Nat. S. John Bap. (June 24). Second payment conditional on reform of grievances.	No writ incorporated but called at the instance of the king's writ.

Sources.	Date.	Place of Meeting.	Composition.	Matters Treated.	Results.	Form of Mandate.
(A) (CONVOCATION) Reg. Islep, fols. 131, 132–132v. P.R.O., Anc. Cor., vol. XXXVIII, nos. 80, 82. *Cal. C.R.* (1354–1360), 31 E. III, p. 398.	April 26 (Wednesday next after the Sunday on which is sung " Misericordia Domine "), 1357.	S. Bride's, London.	Abp. of Cant. Bps. Bps.-elect. Vicars-general. Deans & Priors of Cathed. Churches. Abbots & other Priors. Arch-deacons. Chapters, Colleges, Convents by *one* Proctor. Clergy by *two* Proctors.	Safety of the Church and the realm.	Conditions stipulated in previous grant relaxed except for those in need.	Mention of king's writ in mandate—not incorporated.
(A) (CONVOCATION) Reg. Islep, fol. 155. Wilkins, III, 45–6. Reg. Islep, fol. 158v.	February 3 (Monday after the Purification), 1359(–60).	S. Paul's, London.	Abp. Bps. Bps.-elect. Vicars-general. Deans & Priors of Cathed. Churches. Abbots & Priors & other Prelates of Churches exempt & non-exempt. Chapters by *one* Proctor. Clergy by *two* Proctors.	Grant.	Grant of tenth on February 3. Payments: Moiety: Nat. of S. John Bap. June 24. Moiety: Purif. B.V.M. (February 2), by equal portions. Conditions.	

Sources.	Date.	Place of Meeting.	Composition.	Matters Treated.	Results.	Form of Mandate.
(S) (PROVINCIAL COUNCIL.) (A) Reg. Islep, fols. 170—170v., 184, 194v.	May 7 (Morrow of Ascension), 1361.	S. Mary's, Southwark.	Abp. of Cant. Bishops.	Grant to the Pope.	Secret deliberation. Grant of one tenth to the Pope. Probably made at this Council for urgent business of Holy Church. Terms: Feast of S. John Baptist (June 24), 1362. Purif. B.V.M. (February 2), 1362–1363; by equal portions.	Abp. alludes to the Pope's letter in his mandate.
(S) (PROVINCIAL COUNCIL.) Reg. Islep, fols. 170—170v.	May 31 Morrow of the Octaves of Trinity), 1361.	S. Mary's, Southwark.	Abp. of Cant. Bps. Clergy. Secular and religious by *one*, *two* or *three* Proctors.	Grant to the Pope.		Abp. alludes to the Pope's letter in his mandate
(A) (CONVOCATION) Wake, *State*, p. 300. (Ex. Act. Capit. Lichfield, fol. 150.)	December 2, 1363.					

Sources.	Date.	Place of Meeting.	Composition.	Matters Treated.	Results.	Form of Mandate.
(A) (CONVOCATION) Reg. Witlesey, fols. 17v., 22v.–24. P.R.O. Subsidy Roll 67/11. *Cal. C.R.* (1369–1374), 43 E. III, p. 111. Reg. Wykeham (Winton), vol. II, pt. III, fols. 34v., 37, 43v.–44. Printed *Wykeham's Register*, vol. II, pp. 110–13, 123–4. Reg. Wykeham, vol. II, pt. III, fol. 3v. Printed *Wykeham's Register*, vol. II, 372.	January 21 (Monday after SS. Fabian and Sebastian), 1369(–70).	S. Paul's, London.	Abp. Bps. Vicars-general. Deans & Priors of Cathed. Churches. Archdeacons. Abbots, Priors, & other Prelates (exempt & non-exempt). Chapters by *one* Proctor. Clergy by *two* Proctors.	Grant.	Grant of a tenth for three years. Request reform of grievances.	Abp. incorporates the King's writ.
(A) (CONVOCATION) Reg. Wykeham (Winton), vol. II, pt. III, fols. 46–46v. Reg. Witlesey, fols. 40v.–43. *Cal. C.R.* (1369–1374), 45 E. III, p. 286. Walsingham, *Hist. Ang.*, II, 312–13.	April 12, (Thursday after S. George), 1371, to Saturday, May 3, 1371.	S. Paul's, London.	(Abp. of Cant. absent.) Bps. Prelates. Clergy. Secular and religious.	The business set forth in the last Parliament. Grant.	Grant of £50,000 (the whole to be paid by clergy & laity). To be paid during two years. Terms: Feast of S. Michael (September 29). Purif. B.V.M. (February 2). Exempt to pay. Also those of Prov. of York. Also King's chaplains of royal free chapels.	Abp. incorporates King's writ in his mandate.

Sources.	Date.	Place of Meeting.	Composition.	Matters Treated.	Results.	Form of Mandate.
(A) (CONVOCATION) Reg. Witlesey, fol. 59v. Wilkins, III, 93. Reg. Wykeham, pt. I, fols. 93v.–94. ("Procuratorium" dated 26 May, 1373.) Wake, *State*, 303. (Ex. Reg. Wykeham, Winton, pt. III, fol. 91.)	May 30, 1373.	S. Paul's, London.	Abp. of Cant. Bps. Vicars-general. Deans and Priors of Cathed. Churches. Archdeacons. Abbots, Priors, other Prelates (exempt and non-exempt). Chapters Clergy.			Called independently by Abp.
(S) (CONVOCATION) Reg. Witlesey, fol. 62v.	October 6 (Octaves of S. Michael), 1373.	S. Paul's, London.	Abp. of Cant. Bps.	To discuss the arrears of grant to King & other matters in writing.		Called independently by Abp., but he mentions King's letters.
(A) (CONVOCATION) Reg. Witlesey, fol. 63–65. *Cal. C.R.* (1369–1374), 47 E. III, p. 587.	December 1, 1373. until December 7, 1373.	S. Paul's, London.	Abp. of Cant. Bps. Abbots, Priors & Prelates (exempt & non-exempt). Deans. "Prepositi" of Cathed. and Colleg. Churches. Archdeacons. Colleges. Clergy.	Grant of a tenth. Grievances.	Grant of one tenth. Moiety: June 24 (Feast of S. John Bap.). Moiety: February 2 (Feast of Purf. B.V.M.).	Abp. incorporates the King's writ in mandate.

Sources.	Date.	Place of Meeting.	Composition.	Matters Treated.	Results.	Form of Mandate.
(A) (CONVOCATION) Reg. Sudbury (Cant.), fol. 26, margin. *Cal. C.R.* (1374–1377), 50 E. III, p. 347. *Wykeham's Register* vol. II, p. 252 (pt. III, fol. 138b).	June 23 (9 kal. July), 1376. [Summoned for June 9 (Morrow of Trinity), but prorogued to the later date.]	S. Paul's, London.	Abp. Bps. Deans and Priors. Archdeacons. Chapters, Convents, Colleges by *one* Proctor. Clergy by *two* Proctors.	Grant.		At instance of the King's writ.
(A) (CONVOCATION) Reg. Sudbury (Cant.), fols. 30v.–31, 33v.–34. *Cal. C.R.* (1374–1377), 50 E. III, p. 469. *Wykeham's Register*, vol. II, p. 265 (pt. III, fol. 148b).	February 3, 1376(–7).	S. Paul's, London.	Abp. of Cant. Bps. confirmed & elect. Deans & Priors of Cathed. Churches. Archdeacons Abbots, Priors & others exempt and non-exempt. Chapters by *one* Proctor. Clergy by *two* Proctors.	Subsidy.	Subsidy proportionate to wealth in ecclesiastical hierarchy. To be paid within Feast of S. John Bap., June 24, 1377.	Abp. incorporates King's writ in mandate.

Sources.	Date.	Place of Meeting.	Composition.	Matters Treated.	Results.	Form of Mandate.
(A) (Convocation) Reg. Sudbury (Cant.), fols. 41, 44–44v., 45. *Cal. C.R.* (1377–1381), I R. II, p. 92. P.R.O., Anc. Cor., vol. XL., no. 27. *Wykeham's Register,* vol. II, pp. 275–6 (pt. III, fol. 157b).	November 9, (5 Ides November) to December 5, 1377.	S. Paul's, London.	Abp. of Cant. Bps. Bps. confirmed & elect. Vicars-general. Deans & Priors of Cathed. Churches. Archdeacons. Chapters, Colleges, Convents by *one* Proctor. Clergy by *two* Proctors. Abbots, Priors and other elective. Exempt and non-exempt.	Grant to King.	Grant of tenth of value of ecclesiastical benefices. Terms: March 1 to be levied "gratiose." To be expended for stipulated uses & no others.	King's writ incorporated in Abp.'s mandate.
(A) (Provincial Council) Reg. Sudbury (Cant.), fols. 51–51v. Wake, *State,* p. 315.	November 16, 1378.	Monastery of S. Peter and S. Paul, Gloucester.	Abp. Bps.	Order concerning the salaries of priests.	Punishment decreed to those who should not obey statute.	

Sources.	Date.	Place of Meeting.	Composition.	Matters Treated.	Results.	Form of Mandate.
(A) (CONVOCATION) Reg. Sudbury (Cant.), fols. 53, 55–55v. P.R.O., Excheq. K.R. Ecclesiastical Bundle 10/13. P.R.O., Anc. Cor, vol. XLIII, nos. 28, 29. Reg. Wykeham (Winton), pt. III, fols. 175v.–176. *Cal. C.R.* (1377–1378), 2 R. II, p. 234. Wake, *State*, p. 311. (Ex. Lib. Memorand. J. Bokingham, Linc., fol. 184.)	May 9, 1379.	S. Paul's, London.	Abp. of Cant. Bps. Deans and Priors of Cathed. Churches. Archdeacons. Abbots & Priors & other "elective." Chapters, Convents. Colleges. All clergy.	Grant.	Grant to the King. Various gradations of payment according to rank.	Abp. incorporates the King's writ.
(A) (CONVOCATION) Reg. Sudbury (Cant.), fols. 58v., 59v.–60. P.R.O., Subsidy Rolls, 11/7, 8/2a, 279/51, 67/15. *Cal. C.R.* (1377–1381), 3 R. II, p. 342. Reg. Wykeham (Winton), pt. III, fols. 182, 184v. Printed *Wykeham's Register*, vol. II, pp. 309, 314.	February 4 (Saturday after the Purif. B.V.M.), 1379(–80). Still in session on February 29	S. Paul's, London.	Abp. of Cant. Bps. confirmed & elect. Deans & Priors of Cathed. Churches. Abbots and Priors and other "elective." Exempt & non-exempt. Archdeacons. Chapters, Convents, Colleges by *one* Proctor. Clergy by *two* Proctors.	Grant.	Grant made on February 28. Terms: Ascension— May 3. Nat. of S. John Bap.–June 24. Equal portions. 16d. in mark on all benefices assessed, royal free chapels included. 16d. in mark on ⅔ of estimated value of benefices not assessed. 2s. in mark from certain persons listed.	Abp. incorporates King's writ in mandate.

Sources.	Date.	Place of Meeting.	Composition.	Matters Treated.	Results.	Form of Mandate.
(A) (CONVOCATION) Reg. Sudbury (Cant.), fols. 70v., 72–72v. P.R.O., Excheq. K.R. Eccles. Bundle 10, no. 15. P.R.O., Anc. Cor., vol. XLIII, no. 30. P.R.O., Subsidy Rolls 11/8, 15/7. Cal. C.R. (1377–1381), 4 R. II, p. 477.	December 1, 1380.	All Saints' Church, Northampton.	Abp. of Cant. Bps. confirmed and elect. Vicars-general. Deans and Priors of Cathed. Churches. Abbots, Priors & other "elective." Archdeacons. Chapters. Clergy.	Grant.	Grant according to status. Grant made on December 5. Terms: Feast of S. Peter in Cathedra, February 22. Feast of Nat. S. John Bap., June 24. Amounts of payments stated.	Abp. incorporates King's writ.
(A) (A "COURT" though the sessions are called "CONVOCATIONS") Spelman, II, 629–31. (Ex. MS. Cotton, Cleopatra, F. II, fol. 149 seq.; also Wake, Appendix, pp. 76–8.)	May 17–21 to July 1, 1382.	House of the Friars Preachers, London.	Abp. Bps. Doctors of Theology. Bachelors of Theology. Bachelors of Law.	Process against heretics.		
(A) (CONVOCATION) Reg. Courteney (Cant.), I, fols. 33–34v., 36. Cal. C.R. (1381–1385), 6 R. II, 209–10. Wake, State, p. 315 (Ex Jo. Malvern MS., p. 135).	November 18, 1382. Prorogued to	Church of S. Frideswide, Oxford.	Abp. of Cant. Bps. Vicars-general. Deans & Priors of Cathed. Churches. Archdeacons. Abbots, Priors & other Prelates exempt and non-exempt. The King's Treasurer.	Heresies. The grant requested. Grant made on November 26 of a moiety of a tenth payable March 25 (Annunciation B.V.M.), 1383.	Constitution published against heretical conclusions.	

Sources.	Date.	Place of Meeting.	Composition.	Matters Treated.	Results.	Form of Mandate.
(A) Reg. Courteney, I, fol. 35v. Wake, *State*, p. 315 (Ex Lib. Jo. Bokingham, Linc., fol. 248). *Cal. C.R.* (1381–1385), 7 R. II, p. 348; 6 R. II, p. 196.	January 13 (Octaves of Epiphany), 1382(–3). (Really met January 12, Courteney, I, fol. 35.)	House of the Friars Preachers, London.		Grant made January 21 of another moiety of a tenth payable on June 24, 1383 (Feast of Nat. S. John Bap.) Conditions attached.		
(CONVOCATION) Reg. Courteney, I, fols. 78–78v. *Reg. Brantyngham* (Exeter), I, 524 (fol. 120b). *Wykeham's Register*, vol. II, 351 (pt. III, fol. 203b).	December 2, 1383.	S. Paul's, London.	Abp. of Cant. Bps. Clergy by Proctors.	Grant demanded by the Pope. Grant to the King.	Grant made December 19 to the King, two moieties. Terms of payment: Moiety absolute March 1, 1383(–4). Moiety on conditions July 1, 1384.	Called independently by Abp.
(A) (CONVOCATION) Reg. Courteney (Cant.), I, fol. 79. *Cal. C.R.* (1381–1385), 7 R. II, p. 434. (King's request for May 6.)	May 20 (Morrow of Ascension), 1384.	S. Mary's, Cathedral, Salisbury.	Abp. of Cant. Bps. Deans and Priors of Cathed. Churches. Abbots, Priors & other "elective." Archdeacons. Chapters, Convents, Colleges by one Proctor. Clergy by two.	Grant.	Grant of a moiety. (The one granted previously on conditions.) Terms of payment: November 1 (All Saints), 1384.	

Sources.	Date.	Place of Meeting.	Composition.	Matters Treated.	Results.	Form of Mandate.
(A) (CONVOCATION) Reg. Courtenay (Cant.), I, fols. 79v.–80. P.R.O. Anc. Cor. vol. XLIII., no. 16. Reg. Wykeham (Winton), vol. II, pt. III, fols. 204v.–205, 217. Printed *Wykeham's Register*, vol. II, p. 352. *Cal. C.R.* (1381–1385), 8 R. II, p. 578. (King's request for November 17.)	December 1 to December 19, 1384.	S. Paul's, London.	Abp. of Cant. Bps. Deans and Priors of Cathed. Churches. Abbots, Priors & other "elective." Archdeacons. Chapters, Convents, Colleges by *one* Proctor. Clergy by *two*.	The defence of the realm and the Church. Grant.	Grant on Dec. 19 of one tenth. One moiety absolute, one moiety conditional. Payable: Quindene of Easter (April 16), 1385. Feast of S. John Bap. (June 24), 1385. Conditional on King's going to foreign parts. Beseech that temporalities be restored to Bp. of Norwich.	King's writ incorporated in Abp.'s mandate.
(A) (CONVOCATION) Reg. Courtenay (Cant.), I, fols. 82–83. Wilkins, III, 187, prints Courteney, I, fol. 83 under wrong year. *Cal. C.R.* (1381–1385), 8 R. II, p. 605. Reg. Wykeham (Winton), pt. III, fols. 213v.–214. Printed *Wykeham's Register*, vol. II, 365. Wake, *State*, p. 317. (Ex. Reg. Wakefield, Wigorn, fol. 110. Continuat. Polychron MS.)	May 4 (Morrow of the Invention of the Holy Cross), 1385. In session until June 5 (Monday after Corpus Christi), 1385.	S. Paul's, London.	(Abp. *not* present.) Bps. of London & Winchester commissioned to preside. Composition as in 1384.	Urgent business of Church and State. Grant.	Nothing granted.	King's writ incorporated (Reg. Wykeham, pt. III, fols. 213v. –214) in Abp.'s mandate.

Sources.	Date.	Place of Meeting.	Composition.	Matters Treated.	Results.	Form of Mandate.
(A) (CONVOCATION) Reg. Courteney (Cant.), I, fol. 83–84. *Cal. C.R.* (1385–1389), 9 R. II, p. 86. (Request for summons on October 27.) *Wykeham's Register*, II, 376 (pt. III, 220a).	November 6 to December 7, 1385.	S. Paul's, London.	Abp. of Cant. Composition as in 1384.	Grant.	Grant of a tenth absolute. Moiety on conditions. Terms: Moiety March 25 (Annunciation, B.V.M.) Moiety, June 24 (Octaves of Trinity). Moiety on conditions, Sept. 29 (F. of S. Michael).	King's writ incorporated in Abp.'s mandate.
(A) (CONVOCATION) Reg. Courteney (Cant.), I, fols. 84v.–85. *Cal. C.R.* (1385–1389), 10 R. II, p. 258. (Request for summons on October 13.)	November 5. Prorogued to November 8. Prorogued to November 10. Prorogued to December 3, 1386.	S. Paul's, London.	Abp. of Cant. Composition as in 1384.	Grant.	Grant of a tenth. Moiety, May 6, 1387 (Quindene of Easter). Moiety, Nov. 1 F. of All Saints), 1387.	

Sources.	Date.	Place of Meeting.	Composition.	Matters Treated.	Results.	Form of Mandate.
(A) (CONVOCATION) Reg. Courteney (Cant.), fols. 73, 85v. Reg. Wykeham (Winton), pt. III, fols. 235–36. *Wykeham's Register*, II, 411.	February 26, 1387(–8), to March 14, 1387(–8).	S. Paul's, London.	Abp. Composition as in 1384.	Grant.	Grant of moiety of a tenth (granted in last Convocation on conditions) provided the clergy of province of York should contribute for the year past as well as for the present. Payable May 1, 1388. Clergy to be free from all other imposts for a year.	Abp. incorporates King's writ in mandate.
(A) (CONVOCATION) Reg. Courteney (Cant.), I, fol. 73v.–74v. Reg. Wykeham (Winton), pt. III, fol. 237; pt. IV, fol. 24v. *Wykeham's Register*, II, 413, 599. *Cal. C.R.* (1385–1389), p. 594. (King requests Convocation for September 9 at S. Mary's, Cambridge.) Wake, *State*, p. 320. (Ex Reg. Dunham, Sarum, fol. 27; Reg. Prior and Capit. Wigorn, fol. 340.)	October 12, 1388. Prorogued to October 20, 1388.	S. Paul's, London.	Abp. of Cant. Composition as in 1384.	Grant.	Grant of tenth on October 22. Terms: Moiety–May 2, 1389. Moiety–July 7, 1389. Conditions.	Abp. incorporates King's writ in his mandate.

Sources.	Date.	Place of Meeting.	Composition.	Matters Treated.	Results.	Form of Mandate.
(A) (CONVOCATION) Reg. Courteney (Cant.), I, fols. 75–76v. Spelman, II, 640.	April 17, 1391.	S. Paul's, London.	Abp. of Cant. Composition as in 1384.	Subsidy for the Pope.	Subsidy granted to the Pope. Constitutions renewed (with consent of the Convocation) against stipendiary priests.	Called independently by the Abp.
(A) (CONVOCATION) Wake, State, p. 322. (Ex Reg. Braybrook, London, fol. 24b.) Wykeham's Register, II, 600. Cal. C.R. (1389–1392), 15 R. II, p. 495. (King requests Convocation for Nov. 13.)	December 9, 1391.	S. Paul's, London.		Grant.	Grant of moiety.	King's writ incorporated (inferred from Wake, State, p. 322).
(S) (CONVOCATION) Reg. Wykeham (Winton), pt. III, fol. 258v. Wykeham's Register, II, 437. Cal. C.R. (1392–1396), 16 R. II, p. 106. Wake, State, p. 323. (Reg. Mag. Wigorn, fol. 365.)	Summoned for February 24, 1392(–3). Possibly postponed until March 3, 1392(–3).	S. Paul's, London.		Grant.		

Sources.	Date.	Place of Meeting.	Composition.	Matters Treated.	Results.	Form of Mandate.
(A) (CONVOCATION) Reg. Courteney (Cant.), II, fol. 195. P.R.O., Subsidy Roll 15/11. P.R.O., Anc. Cor., vol. XLIII, no. 17. *Cal. C.R.* (1392–1396), 17 R. II, p. 251. (Request for Feb. 16.) *Wykeham's Register*, II, 602. Wake, *State*, p. 323. (Ex Reg. Braybrook, London, fol. 245.)	May 13–21, 1394.	S. Paul's, London.	Abp. of Cant. Bps. Prelates. Clergy.	Grant to King. Defence of the liberties of the Church and the realm.	Grant of moiety of a tenth. Payable Nov. 30 (F. of S. Andrew). Conditions about those in poverty.	King's writ incorporated in Abp.'s mandate.
(A) (CONVOCATION) Reg. Courteney (Cant.), II, fols. 195v.–196v. P.R.O., Subsidy Roll 24/7. *Cal. C.R.* (1392–1396), 18 R. II, p. 393. *Wykeham's Register*, II, 458 (pt. III, fol. 281a).	February 5 to February 18, 1394(–5).	S. Paul's, London.	Abp. of Cant. Composition as in 1384.	Grant to King. Procurations for a papal messenger.	Grant of one tenth to the King. Terms: July 7 (F. of Translation of S. Thomas, M.). November 30 (F. of S. Andrew). Conditions.	King's writ incorporated in Abp.'s mandate.
(A) (CONVOCATION) Reg. Arundel (Cant.), I, fols. 44–47v. *Cal. C.R.* (1396–1399), 20 R. II, p. 7. Wake, *State*, p. 324. (Ex Reg. Eccles. xxi, Cant. E.)	February 19, 1396(–7). Prorogued to February 26, 1396(–7).	S. Paul's, London.	Abp. not present on 19th—comes on the 26th. Composition as in 1384.	Grievances presented by Oxford University.		Mandate issued by Thomas, Prior of Cant. (Abp. had not yet received the pallium.)

Sources.	Date.	Place of Meeting.	Composition.	Matters Treated.	Results.	Form of Mandate.
(A) (CONVOCATION) Reg. Wykeham (Winton), pt. III, fol. 293–293v. *Wykeham's Register*, II, 471. *Cal. C.R.* (1396–1399), 21 R. II, p. 184.	April 6, 1397.	London.	Abp. of Cant. Prelates. Clergy.	Conclusion of Wyclif tendered. Sense of synod desired.	Grant of a tenth. Terms: June 24, 1397 (Nat. S. John Bap.). Nov. 1 (All Saints), 1397. (*N.B.* Close Rolls says one moiety only granted.)	Abp. incorporates King's writ in mandate.
(CONVOCATION) Reg. Wykeham (Winton), fols. 294v., 297v. *Wykeham's Register*, II, 471–2, 476. *Cal. C.R.* (1396–1399), 21 R. II, p. 213 (request for October 1). *Wykeham's Register*, II, 479 (fol. 300b). Wake, p. 325. (Reg. Braybrook, fol. 250).	October 8, 1397.	S. Paul's, London.		Grant.	Grant of two moieties.	
(A) (CONVOCATION) Reg. Wykeham, pt. IV, fol. 34. *Wykeham's Register*, II, 607. *Cal. C.R.* (1396–1399), 22 R. II, p. 440. *Reg. Stafford, Exeter*, p. 67 (vol. I, fol. 15).	March 2, 1396(–7).	S. Paul's, London.		Grant.	Grant of a tenth and a moiety of a tenth. Terms: Nov. 11, 1398. June 24, 1399. Nov. 11, 1399.	

Sources.	Date.	Place of Meeting.	Composition.	Matters Treated.	Results.	Form of Mandate.
(PROVINCIAL COUNCIL) Wake, *State*, Appendix, p. 80. (Ex Bibl. Cotton Cleopatra, E. II, fol. 224.)	January 27 (Monday after the Conversion of S. Paul), 1397(–8).	Oxford.	Bishops. Abbots. Deans & others.	The state of the Church.		
(CONVOCATION) Wilkins, III, 236 (Reg. Exon. Stafford. A. fol. 18).	May 9 (Morrow of Ascension), 1399.	London.				
(A) (CONVOCATION) Reg. Arundel. (Cant.), I, fols. 52–53v. Reg. Arundel (Cant.), II, fols. 5–6v. *Wykeham's Register*, II, 450 (pt. III, fol. 315a).	October 6 to October 11 Prorogued to October 15, 1399.	S. Paul's, London.	Abp. of Cant. B p s. Prelates. Clergy.	Protection of the laws and liberties of the Church & the business of the realm. Certain enemies in Parliament. Certain privileges listed & expended to the King. Articles for the Pope. Grievances drawn up by a committee.		Mandate issued by Thomas, Prior of C a n t e r b u r y, during the Abp.'s suspension.

APPENDIX B

CHART OF THE PRINCIPAL ECCLESIASTICAL ASSEMBLIES IN THE PROVINCE OF YORK DURING THE THIRTEENTH AND FOURTEENTH CENTURIES (1261—1399)

NOTE

THIS Table of ecclesiastical assemblies in the province of York does not pretend to be complete. It has been arranged for the purposes of this study for use in comparison with the ecclesiastical assemblies in the province of Canterbury. There are many gaps which must be left vacant until the archiepiscopal archives of the province of York can be examined.

Sources.	Date.	Place of Meeting.	Composition.	Matters Treated.	Results.	Form of Mandate.
(A) (COUNCIL) Wilkins, I, 755–56. *Flores Historiarum*, II, 468.	May 23 (Monday following the Feast of S. Dunstan), 1261.	Beverley.	Abp. of York. Bps. Abbots exempt & non-exempt. Priors. Archdeacons. Other ordinaries of churches.	The papal mandate. New statutes.	Certain new statutes published.	
(A) (COUNCIL) *Reg. Wickwane*, Surtees Soc., pp. 53, 243 (fols. 113d, 124d). Printed Wilkins, II, pp. 41–2. (*N.B.* Wilkins gives different foliation.) Wake, Appendix, p. 14. This may have been a diocesan council. Stubbs, *Const. Hist.*, II (4th ed.), 207 regards it as provincial.	February 9 (Friday before the Feast of S. Scholastica), 1279(–80).	Pontefract.	Abp. of York. Archdeacons. Two worthy men of eminence from each archdeacony. One Dean from each archdeaconry.	Grant.	Grant of a tenth. [Grant made on February 9, 1279(–80)] according to Taxation of Norwich. Terms of payment: Nativity of our Lord (Dec. 25), 1280; Nativity S. John Baptist, June 24, 1281. To be collected by the ordinaries or their deputies. Major as well as minor ecclesiastics who have paid the fifteenth with the laity, pay tenth on spiritualities only.	

Sources.	Date.	Place of Meeting.	Composition.	Matters Treated.	Results.	Form of Mandate.
(ASSEMBLY) Stubbs, *Select Charters* (9th ed.), p. 459. (F r o m *Parliamentary Writs*, I, 10.)	January 20 (Octaves of Hilary), 1282(–3).	York.	Abp. of York. Bps. Abbots. Priors. Prefects of r e l i g i o u s houses. Proctors of Deans and C h a p t e r s of Collegiate Churches.	Grant.		At the instance of the King's writ.
(A) (CONVOCATION) *Reg. Romeyn*, Surtees Soc., pt. II, pp. 82–83 (fol. 130), 85–87; pt. I, p. 22 (fol. 8d). Wilkins, II, 126–27 (different foliation).	November 13 (Wednesday after F. of S. Martin), 1286.	S. Peter's, York.	Abp. of York. Bps. Proctors of the clergy.	Grant.	Grant by t h e clergy of York & Carlisle of a thirtieth of income for three years. Terms: June 24 (Nat. S. John Bap.). Dec. 25 (Nat. of our Lord). To be collected by the Ordinaries. Bp. of Durham to explain what his clergy had granted.	
(A) (CONVOCATION) *Reg. Romeyn* (Sur. Soc.), pt. I, 33–34 (fol. 19–19d). Wilkins, II, 174. *Reg. Romeyn* (Sur. Soc.), II, 93–95 (fol. 133).	December 7 (Morrow of F. of S. Nicholas), 1290.	S. Peter's, York.	Abp. of York. Bp. of Carlisle. Clergy of York and Carlisle by Proctors. (Durham Bp. and clergy refuse to come.)	Grant.	Grant of tenth. Norwich taxation. Terms: Pentecost— June 10, 1291. F. of S. Martin— Nov. 11, 1291. To be collected by the Ordinaries.	

Sources.	Date.	Place of Meeting.	Composition.	Matters Treated.	Results.	Form of Mandate.
(A) (CONVOCATION) Reg. H. Newark (Sur. Soc.), vol. CXXVIII, p. 248. Printed Wilkins, II, 235–36. Wake, Appendix, p. 26. W. Rishanger, Chronica, p. 182.	November 29 (Vigil of F. of S. Andrew), 1297.	S. Peter's, York.	Abp. of York. Bps. Abbots and Priors exempt & non-exempt. Clergy of each diocese by *two* Proctors.	Grant.	Grant of a fifth.	
(A) (COUNCIL) Spelman, II, 438–45. Wilkins, II, 285–86. (Ex MS. Cott. Vitell. D. 5, fol. 142.)	September 30 (2 kal. Oct.), 1306.	Ripon.		Constitutions of Abp. Greenfield.	Publication of the Constitutions.	
(A) (CONVOCATION) Wilkins, II, p. 292. (Ex Reg. Grenefield, Ebor., fol. 68b.)	1307.				Grant of one fifteenth.	
(A) (PROVINCIAL COUNCIL) Wilkins, II, 393–94. (Ex Reg. Grenefield, pt. I, fol. 179; pt. II, fol. 180.) Reg. Halton, C. & Y. Soc., II, 15–16 (fol. 66b). Wake, State, pp. 31, 32. (Reg. Halton, fol. 132.)	May 20–21, 1310.	York.	Abp. of York. Bps. Abbots, Priors, Deans, Archdeacons, "Prepositi," Chapters by Proctors. Abbots & Priors exempt & non-exempt.	Certain articles against the Templars. Other matters touching the Province of York.	Another Council to be called.	

Sources.	Date.	Place of Meeting.	Composition.	Matters Treated.	Results.	Form of Mandate.
(A) (PROVINCIAL COUNCIL) Wilkins, II, 394–401. (Reg. Grenfield, Ebor., pt. II, fol. 180.) Wake, State, p. 262 (fol. 188b, Reg. Grenefield). Reg. Halton, II, 35–6 (fols. 70b–71a). Printed also in Wilkins, II, 409.	May 24–27, 1311. Adjourned to July 1, 1311.	York. Adjourned to Blyth, then to York.	Abp. Doctors of Divinity. Professors of Canon Law. Bps. Priors, Deans, Archdeacons, "Prepositi," Chapters by Proctors.	Reading of the Apostolic Bulls. Attestations against Templars.		
(A) (CONVOCATION) Reg. Palat. Dunelm (Reg. Kellawe), R.S., I, 6–7. Reg. Greenfield, Ebor., Sur. Soc., I, 137–38 (II, fol. 28). Wilkins, II, 394, 401. (Reg. Grenefield, Ebor., pt. II, fol. 180.)	May 24–27, 1311.	York.	Diocesan clergy.	Grant of a subsidy of 12d. in the mark.	After three days discussion the proctors of the clergy refused to make a grant as the tenth for three years granted for the Holy Land had not yet expired.	
(A) Wilkins, II, 409. (Reg. Halton, fol. 70b). Reg. Pal. Dunelm (Reg. Kellawe), I, 35–39. Wake, Appendix, p. 33 (Reg. Halton, fol. 140). Records of Northern Convocation, Sur. Soc. (Ex Reg. Greenfield, I, 190b).	Continuation of Provincial Council. July 1–10, 1311, prorogued to July 28. In session until July 30.	Summoned to Blyth, changed later to York.	Abp. of York. Bps. Abbots, Priors, Deans, Archdeacons, "Prepositi," Chapters by Proctors.	The Templars.	Templars assigned to various monasteries to do penance. Dissolution of the Order. Constitutions of Abp. of York may have been published here. (Spelman, II, 467. [Ex MS. Cotton, Vitell, D., fol. 162.])	Called independently by the Abp.

Sources.	Date.	Place of Meeting.	Composition.	Matters Treated.	Results.	Form of Mandate.
(S) (CONVOCATION) Wilkins, II, 436. Wake, *State*, p. 264. (Ex Reg. Grenefield, Ebor., pt. II, fols. 207, 208.) *Reg. Pal. Dunelm*, I, 415–16.	September 3, 1313.	York.	Abp. of York. Bps. Abbots, Priors, Chapters, Colleges by *one* Proctor. Clergy of each city and diocese by *two* Proctors.	Grant of 4d. in the mark.		King's writ incorporated in Abp.'s mandate.
(ASSEMBLY) *Cal. C.R.* (1313–1318), 7 E. II, p. 96. (Does not give correct day for York.) *Reg. Palat. Dunelm* (*Reg. Kellawe*), I, 574–77. *Rec. Nor. Convoc.*, pp. 62–64. Wake, *State*, p. 266. (Ex Rot. Claus, 7 E. II, m. 8d.)	June 10 (Morrow of Trinity), 1314.	York.			A proper convocation to be called.	
(A) (CONVOCATION) Wake, *State*, 266. (Regist. Secundum Dec. and Capit. Dunelm, fols. 26, 27. Comp. Regist. Grenefield, Ebor., II, fols. 210, 212.) *Ibid.*, II, 79b. *Cal. Pat. Rolls* (1313–1317), 7 E. II, 119. *Reg. Pal. Dunelm*, I, 577–78, 636.	June 26 (Wednesday after the Nat. of S. John Bap.), 1314.	York.	Abp. of York. Bps. Abbots, Priors, Deans, Archdeacons, "Prepositi," Convents, Chapters, Colleges by *one* Proctor. Clergy of each diocese by *two* Proctors.	Grant of a subsidy.	Grant of a subsidy of 12d. in the mark or 6d. in the £. Northumberland 8d. in the mark.	

T

Sources.	Date.	Place of Meeting.	Composition.	Matters Treated.	Results.	Form of Mandate.
(CONVOCATION) Wake, *State*, p. 269. (Regist. Decan. & Capit. Custod. Ebor. Sede Vacante, fol. 135.) *Cal. C.R.* (1313–1318), 9 E. II, 325.	About May 11 (Month after Easter), 1316.	S. Peter's, York.				
(CONVOCATION) Wake, *State*, p. 269. (Regist. Decan. & Capit. Custod. Ebor. Sede Vacante, fol. 135.) Wilkins, II, 462, also makes an allusion.	June 14 (Morrow of Trinity), 1316.	S. Peter's, York.				
(A) (CONVOCATION) Wilkins, II, 462. (Ex *Reg. Halton*, fol. 189.) Wake, *State*, 269. (Reg. Halton, fol. 189; Reg. Dec. & Capit. Ebor. Sede Vac., fols. 136, 137, 86.) Wake, Appendix, pp. 43–44. (Reg. Halton, fol. 189.)	Request for summons, October 26 (Morrow of the Translation of S. John), Beverley, 1316. May have assembled at a later date.	York.	Clergy.	Grant.	Grant of a tenth on November 23 (Feast of S. Clement).	

Sources.	Date.	Place of Meeting.	Composition.	Matters Treated.	Results.	Form of Mandate.
(S) (CONVOCATION) Wilkins, II, 485. (Reg. W. Melton, Ebor., fol. 459 seq.) Wake, Appendix, p. 44. (Reg. Halton, fol. 213.) Wake, *State*, p. 271. *Cal. C.R.* (1318–1323), 12 E. II, p. 30.	January 20 (Octaves of Hilary), 1318(–19).	York.	Abp. of York. Bps. Abbots, Priors. Deans, Archdeacons, Chapters, Convents, Colleges by *one* Proctor. Clergy of each archdeaconry by *two* Proctors.	A competent subsidy.	Nothing resolved upon.	Abp. mentions the King's request in his mandate.
(S) (CONVOCATION) Wake, *State*, p. 271. (Reg. Melton, fol. 460.) Wake, *State*, p. 273. (Regist. H. Prior, Cant., fol. 210.)	March 19 (Monday after Sunday in Mid-Lent), 1318(–19).	York.	Clergy.	Grant.	A tenth granted either here or in the Parliament after Easter.	
(S) (CONVOCATION) Wake, *State*, p. 274. (Reg. Melton, Ebor., fol. 461.) Wilkins, II, 519. (In reference gives Reg. Melton, fol. 462.) *Records of No. Convoc.*, p. 70.	May 10 (Monday after the Feast of S. John, ante Port. Lat.), 1322.	York.				
(CONVOCATION) Wake, *State*, p. 275. (Reg. Melton, fol. 462.) Wilkins, II, 519. *Cal. C.R.* (1318–1323), 16 E. II, p. 686.	January 26, 1322(–3).	York.		Grant.	They begged to be excused.	

Sources.	Date.	Place of Meeting.	Composition.	Matters Treated.	Results.	Form of Mandate.
(CONVOCATION) Cal. C.R. (1323–1327), 17 E. II, p. 145. (King's request for Jan. 20, 1323–1324.) Cal. C.R. (1323–1327), 17 E. II, p. 153. Wilkins, II, 520. (Ex Reg. Melton, Ebor., fol. 464.)	February 7 (Tuesday after the Purification B.V.M.), 1323(–4). King orders that the summons be superseded.	York.				
(A) (CONVOCATION) Wilkins, II, 546–47. (Ex Reg. Melton, Ebor., fol. 468.) An evident reference to this convocation in P.R.O., Anc. Cor., vol. XXXVIII, no. 103.	October 12, 1327.	York.		Grant.	Grant of a tenth to the King under certain conditions.	
(CONVOCATION) Cal. C.R. (1330–1333), 4 E. III, p. 130. (N.B. Wake, State, p. 280 gives York date incorrectly.)	April 25 (Wednesday after the Feast of S. George), 1330.			Dangers of the French War.		

Sources.	Date.	Place of Meeting.	Composition.	Matters Treated.	Results.	Form of Mandate.
(CONVOCATION) *Cal. C.R.* (1333–1337), 7 E. III, p. 173. *Cal. C.R.* (1333–1337), 7 E. III, p. 184. Wake, *State*, p. 282. (Reg. Jo. de Kirkby Carliol, fol. 284.)	First request of King for November 22 (Monday after Octaves of Martinmas), 1333. Altered second request for January 17 (Monday after the Octaves of Epiphany), 1333(–4).	York. York.	Prelates. Clergy. Prelates. Clergy.	Grant of aid to the King for his expenses in the late war.		
(CONVOCATION) *Cal. C.R.* (1333–1337), 8 E. III, p. 316. Wake, *State*, p. 283. (Reg. Melton, Ebor., fol. 476.) Reference to this also in Wilkins, II, 578.	October 24 (Wednesday next after the Feast of S. Luke, Evangelist), 1334.	York.		Grant.		
(A) (CONVOCATION) P.R.O., Close Roll, 10 E. III, m. 36d. P.R.O., Close Roll, 11 E. III, pt. I, m. 8. Wilkins, II, 584 (Reg. Kirkby Carliol., fol. 327).	May 6 (Monday), 1336.	S. Peter's, York.	Abp. of York. Prelates. Deans and Priors of Cathedral Churches. Archdeacons. Men of religion.	Grant.	Grant of a tenth. (*N.B.* Wilkins, II, 584 says two tenths, Ex Reg. Kirkby Carliol, fol. 327.)	

Sources.	Date.	Place of Meeting.	Composition.	Matters Treated.	Results.	Form of Mandate.
(A) (CONVOCATION) Cal. C.R. (1337–1339), 11 E. III, pt. I, pp. 51, 81. (N.B. Wake does not give this convocation.)	October 21 (Monday after the Feast of S. Luke), 1336.	S. Peter's, York.		Grant.	Grant of a tenth.	
(A) (CONVOCATION) Wake, State, p. 287. (Reg. Jo. de Kirkby Carliol, fol. 365.) Wilkins, II, 624. (Reg. Melton, Ebor.) Cal. C.R. (1337–1339), 11 E. III, p. 242. King requests summons for Octaves of Michaelmas (Oct. 9), 1337.	November 12 (Next court day day after the F. of S. Martin), 1337.	S. Peter's, York.		Grant.	Grant of a tenth for three years. (Wilkins, II, 624 says tenth for two years.)	
(S) (CONVOCATION) Cal. C.R. (1337–1339), 12 E. III, p. 527. King summons for Sept. 22, 1338. Date not given in Cal. C.R. vide P.R.O., Close Roll, 12 E. III, m. 17d. Wilkins, II, 629. (Reg. Jo. de Kirkby Carliol, fol. 376.)	October 1 (Thursday after S. Michael), 1338.	S. Peter's, York.		Grant.	Evidently refused as the King sent another writ. Cal. C.R. (1339–1344), 13 E. III, p. 105. (Printed Wilkins, II, 653.)	

Sources.	Date.	Place of Meeting.	Composition.	Matters Treated.	Results.	Form of Mandate.
(CONVOCATION) *Cal. C.R.* (1339-1340), 13 E. III, p. 105.	Request by King to summon as soon as possible (some time after February 8, 1338(-9)—date of writ), 1338(-9).	S. Peter's, York.				
(DIOCESAN COUNCIL) *Cal. C.R.* (1339-1341), 13 E. III, p. 270. Printed Rymer.	Request by King to summon on a certain day fixed by the Abp. (after Oct. 10, 1339—date of writ).	S. Peter's, York.				
(A) (CONVOCATION) *Cal. C.R.* (1341-1343), 16 E. III, p. 169. *Cal. C.R.* (1339-1341), 13 E. III, p. 332. Wake, *State*, p. 288. (Reg. Dec. and Capit., Ebor., fol. 47; Reg. Kirkby, fol. 408.) Wilkins, II, 653. (Reg. Kirkby Carliol., fol. 408.)	February 9. (Octaves of the Purification, B.V.M.), 1339(-40).	S. Peter's, York.		Grant.	Grant of a tenth. Wake, p. 288 says a two years tenth. (Reg. Dec. and Capit. Ebor. Sed. Vacant, fol. 47.)	
(CONVOCATION) Wake, *State*, p. 289. (Reg. Dec. and Cap. Ebor. Sed. Vac., fol. 79.)	Monday, December 11, 1340.	York.				

Sources.	Date.	Place of Meeting.	Composition.	Matters Treated.	Results.	Form of Mandate.
(A) (CONVOCATION) Wilkins, II, 712. (Reg. Wm. Zouch, Ebor.), fol. 281. Reg. Pal. Dunelm, III, 509-12. Cal. C.R. (1341-1343), 16 E. III, p. 677.	December 9 (Morrow of the Conception of B.V.M.), 1342.	S. Peter's, York.	Abp. of York. Bps. Abbots, Priors, Archdeacons, Chapters & Colleges by one Proctor. Clergy of dioceses by two Proctors.	Counsel to the King.	Grant of a tenth of the value of ecclesiastical goods and benefices by equal portions according to new taxation. Conditions.	
(A) (CONVOCATION) P.R.O., Close Roll, 18 E. III, pt. I, m. 14d. Rot. Parl., II, nos. 23, 24.	June 16 (Wednesday after the Feast of S. Barnabas), 1344.	S. Peter's, York.	Abp. Prelates. Clergy.	Grant.	Grant of a tenth for three years. Terms: Feast of S. Lucy (December 13). Feast of S. John Bap. (June 24).	
(A) (CONVOCATION) Cal. C.R. (1346-1349), 20 E. III, p. 154. [King requested summons for Monday after Feast of S. Lucy, December 18, 1346.] Wilkins, II, 735 refers to Reg. Zouch, Ebor., fols. 245, 258. P.R.O., Anc. Cor., vol. XLII, no. 140. Cal. C.R. (1346-1349), 22 E. III, p. 508.	January 29 (Monday after the Conversion of S. Paul), 1346(-7). In session until Tuesday, January 30, 1346(-7).	S. Peter's, York.	Abp. Prelates. Clergy. Deputies of the King.	Grant.	Grant of a tenth for two years. Terms: Feast of Conversion of S. Paul, January 25, 1347-1348. Feast of S. Mark, April 25, 1348.	

Sources.	Date.	Place of Meeting.	Composition.	Matters Treated.	Results.	Form of Mandate.
(CONVOCATION) *Cal. C.R.* (1346–1349), 22 E. III, p. 508. Wake, *State*, p. 295. (Reg. Zouch, Ebor., fol. 247.) Wilkins, II, 746 gives same reference.	June 13 (Friday in Whitsun week), 1348.					
(S) (CONVOCATION) *Cal. C.R.* (1349–1354), 25 E. III, p. 356. Wake, *State* (Reg. Zouch Ebor., fol. 250.)	May 18 (Wednesday before Feast of S. Dunstan), 1351.	York.		Grant.	Grant of a tenth for two years. (Wake, *State*, p. 296).	
(CONVOCATION) *Cal. C.R.* (1354–1360), 29 E. III, p. 233.	King's request for summons on December 7 (Morrow of S. Nicholas), 1355.	S. Peter's, York.			Grant of a tenth. "Sub spe emendacionis et reformacionis gravaminum." Payable Feb. 2 (Purif. B.V.M.), Aug. 1 (S. Peter's Chains).	
(A) (CONVOCATION) P.R.O., Anc. Cor., vol. LVI, no. 4. Wilkins, III, 39. (Reg. Thoresby.)	June 3 (Morrow of Ascension), 1356.			Grant.		
(S) (CONVOCATION) Wilkins, III, 41. (Ex Reg. Thoresby, Ebor., fol. antepenult. Ex Reg. Weston Carliol., fol. 32.)	May 19 (Friday after Ascension), 1357.	S. Peter's, York.			First moiety granted freely. Second on conditions. Ordinaries to collect the tenth. Exoneration for those in evident need.	

Sources.	Date.	Place of Meeting.	Composition.	Matters Treated.	Results.	Form of Mandate.
(A) (CONVOCATION) Wilkins, III, 46. (Reg. Thoresby, Ebor., fol. penult.; Reg. Weston Carliol., fol. 63.) Rec. Nor. Convoc., pp. 91–94. (Reg. Hatfield Dunelm, fols. 394, 39b.) Ibid., 100–101.	February 12, 1359(-60).	S. Peter's, York.	Abp. of York. Bps. Abbots, Priors, Deans, "Prepositi," Archdeacons, Chapters, Colleges, Convents by one Proctor. All clergy of dioceses by two Proctors.	Grant.	Grant of a tenth. Payments: June 24 (Nat. of S. John Bap.). February 2 (Purif. B.V.M.), by equal portions.	
(A) (CONVOCATION) P.R.O., Exchequer Subsidy, Roll 67/11. Wilkins, III, 85. (Reg. Hatfield Dunelm, fol. 48; Reg. Appleby Carliol., fol. 205.) Cal. C.R. (1369–1374), 43 E. III, p. 111.	February 4 (Monday after the Purification B.V.M.), 1369(-70).	S. Peter's, York.	Abp. of York. Bps. Clergy.	Grant.	Grant of a tenth for three years.	
(A) (CONVOCATION) Wilkins, III, 91. (Reg. Appleby Carliol., fol. 240; Reg. Thoresby Ebor., fol. 105.) Reg. Witlesey, fol. 43. Cal. C.R. (1369–1374), 45 E. III, p. 287.	Thursday, July 10, 1371.			Grant to the King jointly with the Province of Canterbury.	Grant to the King. Province of York to give £5,000.	

Sources.	Date.	Place of Meeting.	Composition.	Matters Treated.	Results.	Form of Mandate.
(S) (CONVOCATION) Wilkins, III, 96–97. Reg. Appleby Carliol. *Cal. C.R.* (1369–1374). 47 E. III, p. 595.	February 6 (Monday after the Purification B.V.M.), 1373(–4).	S. Peter's, York.	B p s. suffragan. Deans and Priors of Cathed. Churches, Abbots and Priors and other "elective," Archdeacons, Chapters, Colleges, Convents by *one* Proctor. Clergy of each diocese by *two* Proctors.	Grant.		
(CONVOCATION) Wilkins, III, 114–15. Reg. Hatfield Dunelm, fol. 88. *N.B.* Wilkins gives wrong year. Wake, *State*, p. 304. (Reg. Dec. and Capit. Ebor. ab anno 1352, fols. 125b, 126b.)	July 28 (Monday after the Feast of S. James), 1376.					
(S) (CONVOCATION) Wilkins, III, 125. (Ex Reg. Tho. de Appleby Carliol, fol. 293.) *Rec. Nor. Convoc.*, p. 103. It is said here that this convocation did not meet.	April 15, 1377.	S. Peter's, York.		Grant.		

Sources.	Date.	Place of Meeting.	Composition.	Matters Treated.	Results.	Form of Mandate.
(A) (CONVOCATION) *Cal. C.R.* (1377–1381), I R. II, p. 92. Wilkins, III, 125–26. (Ex Reg. Alex. Nevill Ebor., fol. 2; Reg. Appleby Carliol, fol. 293; MS. Cotton. Cleopatra, D3. fol. 187.)	December 1, 1377, to January 4, 1377(–8).	S. Peter's, York.	Abp. Bps. Deans, Priors, Archdeacons, Proctors of Chapters, Colleges, Convents, Proctors of clergy.	Grant.	Clergy first allege their hard times. Later grant two tenths. Terms: Before Mar. 1, 1377(–8). F. of Invention of the Cross (May 3, 1378). F. of S. Andrew (Nov. 30, 1378). Annunciation B.V.M., March 25, 1379, by equal portions according to the new taxation.	
(CONVOCATION) Wake, Appendix, pp. 74–76. (Reg. Alex. Nevill Ebor., fol. 2.) Also Wilkins, III, 125–26. *N.B.* Wake's marginal reference is obviously a printer's error. *Rec. Nor. Convoc.* pp. 105–8. (Reg. Appleby Carliol.)	Monday, March 22, 1377(–8).		Prelates. Clergy.	Clergy are exhorted to conform to the concession made by the clergy of the Province of Canterbury.	New terms of payment of the tenth for two years: Feast of SS. Philip & James (May 1), 1378; Feast of S. Margaret (July 20), 1378. According to the New Taxation.	

Sources.	Date.	Place of Meeting.	Composition.	Matters Treated.	Results.	Form of Mandate.
(A) (CONVOCATION) Wilkins, III, 145. (Ex Reg. Nevill Ebor., fol. 7b; Reg. Appleby Carliol, fols. 307, 308.) Cal. C.R. (1379–1381), 2 R. II, p. 234.	April 29, 1379, probably in session until June 20, 1379.			Grant.	Grant. Abp. of York—10 marks. Bps., mitred Abbots, Abbots & Priors of Cathedrals—6 marks. Others—according to the value of their benefices.	
(A) (CONVOCATION) Cal. C.R. (1377–1381), 3 R. II, p. 342. Wilkins, III, 150. (Reg. Hatfield Dunelm, fols. 171b, 172a.) Rec. Nor. Convoc., pp. 109–12.	April 4, 1380.	S. Peter's, York.	Abp. of York. Bps., etc. as in 1373(–4). Advocates. Public Notaries.	Grant.	Grant to the King.	
(A) (CONVOCATION) Wake, State, 312. (Reg. Alex. Nevill Ebor., fol. 10.) Cal. C.R. (1377–1381), 4 R. II, p. 473.	January 10 (Thursday after the Feast of Epiphany), 1380(–1).			Grant.	Grant of a moiety of a tenth (Wake, State, p. 315).	
(A) (CONVOCATION) Wilkins, III, 176. (Ex Reg. Alex. Nevill Ebor., fol. 12.) Cal. C.R. (1381–1385), 6 R. II, p. 210.	December 15, 1382.			Grant.	Grant of a moiety of a tenth.	

Sources.	Date.	Place of Meeting.	Composition.	Matters Treated.	Results.	Form of Mandate.
(CONVOCATION) Cal. C.R. (1381–1385), 6 R. II, p. 196.	King's request for summons at Easter or another early date. (King's writ dated January 28, sixth year [1382–3]).	S. Peter's, York.				
(A) (CONVOCATION) P.R.O., Excheq. K.R. Ecclesiastical Bundle 10, no. 8.	January 23, 1383(–4).	S. Peter's, York.		Grant.	Grant of a moiety of a tenth–New Taxation. Payment: Easter, 1385 (April 2).	
(A) (CONVOCATION) Cal. C.R. (1381–1385), 7 R. II, p. 434.	King's request for summons July 8 (Morrow of the Translation of S. Thomas, Martyr), 1384.	S. Peter's, York.		Grant.	Grant of a moiety of a tenth (Wake, State, p. 317, no reference).	
(A) (CONVOCATION) Cal. C.R. (1381–1385), 8 R. II, 579. P.R.O., Anc. Cor., vol. LVI, no. 108. (N.B., Wake does not list.)	King's request for summons January 2, 1384(–5). Abp. summoned for Wednesday after Epiphany, January 12, 1384(–5). King's request for January 11, 1384(–5).	S. Peter's, York. S. Peter's, York.	Prelates. Clergy.	Grant.	Long discussion. Grant of tenth. Terms of payment: Pentecost, (May 26, 1385.) S. Peter's Chains, (August 1, 1385.)	

Sources.	Date.	Place of Meeting.	Composition.	Matters Treated.	Results.	Form of Mandate.
(CONVOCATION) Cal. C.R. (1381–1385), 8 R. II, p. 609. [N.B. Wilkins, III, 202 gives the wrong year.] Printed Rymer, Foedera, vol. VII (1709 ed.), p. 464.	April 17 (Monday before the Feast of S. George), 1385.	S. Peter's, York.				
(CONVOCATION) Cal. C.R. (1385–1389), 9 R. II, p. 86. Wilkins, III, 195. Wake, State, p. 318. (Ex Regist. Dec. et Capit. Ebor., pt. II, fol. 60a.)	King's request for summons on the Eve of S. Simon and S. Jude, 1385. Summoned morrow of Hilary, January 14, 1385(–6).	S. Peter's, York.		Grant.		
(CONVOCATION) Cal. C.R. (1385–1389), 10 R. II, 258.	King's request for summons on December 1, 1386.	S. Peter's, York.				
(CONVOCATION) Cal. C.R. (1385–1389), 11 R. II, p. 462. N.B. Wake, State, 319 (does not think that this met).	King's request for summons on February 10, 1387(–8).	S. Peter's, York.				

Sources.	Date.	Place of Meeting.	Composition.	Matters Treated.	Results.	Form of Mandate.
(S) (CONVOCATION) Wilkins, III, 205. (Ex Reg. Arundel Ebor., fol. 8, et reg. Dunelm. in ann.) Cal. C.R. (1385–1389), 12 R. II, 594.	King's first request for Monday after Nativity B.V.M.—Sept. 14, 1388. January 24, 1388(–9).	S. Peter's, York.				Called by the Abp.'s Official.
(A) (CONVOCATION) Cal. C.R. (1389–1392), 15 R. II, p. 495. Wilkins, III, 218. Wake, State, p. 322. (Reg. Arundel Ebor., fol. 33; Reg. Dec. & Capit. Dunelm, pt. II, fol. 125.)	Summoned November 27 meets December 4, 1391. (King's request was for [Monday after S. Clement, Pope] November 27, 1391.)	S. Peter's, York.		Grant.	Grant of a moiety of one tenth in accordance with the New Taxation – monasteries excepted.	
(A) (CONVOCATION) Wake, State, p. 323. (Reg. Dec. and Capit. Dunelm, pt. II, fol. 122.) Wilkins, III, 219. Reg. Arundel Ebor., fol. 37. Cal. C.R. (1392–1396), 16 R. II, p. 106. [N.B. Date is wrongly given as S. Peter's Chains in Cal. C.R.]	King's request for summons February 18 (Monday before S. Peter in Cathedra). Abp. calls it for March 17 (Monday after F. of S. Gregory), 1392(–3).	S. Peter's, York.		Grant.	Grant of one tenth and one moiety of a tenth. One moiety simply, two moieties on conditions: (1) If King went personally to Scotland or Ireland with the army. (2) If the King went to France. If he did not go, moieties not to be levied.	

Sources.	Date.	Place of Meeting.	Composition.	Matters Treated.	Results.	Form of Mandate.
(CONVOCATION) *Cal. C.R.* (1392–1396), 17 R. II, 251.	King's request for summons March 1, 1393(–4).	S. Peter's, York.				
(CONVOCATION) Wake, *State*, p. 324. (Reg. Dec. and Cap. Dunelm, pt. II, fol. 125a.)	June 1, 1394.	York.				
(CONVOCATION) Wake, *State*, p. 324. (Reg. Dec. and Cap. Dunelm, pt. II, fol. 125.)	July 20, 1394.	York.				
(CONVOCATION) Wake, *State*, p. 324. (Reg. Dec. and Cap. Dunelm, pt. II, fol. 125.) *Rec. Nor. Convoc.*, p. 118 give the year for these as 1395.	October 1, 1394.	York.				

Sources.	Date.	Place of Meeting.	Composition.	Matters Treated.	Results.	Form of Mandate.
(A) (CONVOCATION) Wake, *State*, p. 323. (Reg. Arundel Ebor., fol. 49.) *Cal. C.R.* (1392–1396), 18 R. II, p. 393. Wilkins, III, p. 224.	February 4 (Thursday after the Purification B.V.M.), 1394(–5). [Abp. anticipated the King's request for a summons on Feb. 25, 1394(–5). morrow of S. Matthias.]			Grant.	Grant of moiety of a tenth to be paid Dec. 9, 1395.	
(S) (CONVOCATION) *Cal. C.R.* (1396–1399), 20 R. II, p. 77. *Rec. Nor. Convoc.*, p. 119. (Treasury Dec. et Capit. Dunelm, *loc.*, 20 I.)	King's request for summons on February 26 (Monday after S. Matthias). March 15 (Thursday after the Feast of S. Gregory), 1396(–7).	S. Peter's, York.				
(CONVOCATION) *Cal. C.R.* (1396–1399), 20 R. II, p. 118.	King's request for summons May 11 (Friday after S. John ante Portam Latinum), 1397.	S. Peter's, York.				

Sources.	Date.	Place of Meeting.	Composition.	Matters Treated.	Results.	Form of Mandate.
(A) (CONVOCATION) Wake, *State*, p. 325. (Reg. Dec. and Capit. Dunelm, pt. II, fol. 127b. Reg. Scroop Ebor., fol. 149.)	[On October 5 a provincial council may have been held, Wake, p. 325.] October 10, 1397.		Grant.	Grant.	Grant of a half-tenth.	
(CONVOCATION) Wake, *State*, p. 327. (Reg. Scroop Ebor., fol. 149.) Wake, Appendix, p. 79. (Reg. Dec. and Cap. Dunelm, fol. 139a.)	June 20, 1398.	S. Peter's, York.	Prelates.	Business of the Church and the realm.		
CONVOCATION *Cal. C.R.* (1396–1399), 22 R. II, p. 390. Wake, *State*, p. 327. (Reg. Scroop Ebor., fol. 149.) *N.B.* Probably not held.	King requests a summons September 1, 1398.					
(S) (CONVOCATION) Wake, *State*, p. 327. *Cal. C.R.* (1396–1399), 22 R. II, p. 440. Wilkins, III, 238.	March 11, 1398(–9). (King's request for Monday, March 3, 1398(–9).)	Beverley.				

APPENDIX C

NOTE

THE list of parliaments from 1258 to 1399 is copied
from the list published in 1932 in the *Interim Report of
the Committee on House of Commons Personnel and
Politics*. As is stated in the Report, Appendix I (p. 59)
" the list of Parliaments from 1258 to 1377 has been
taken from various publications of Mr. H. G.
Richardson and Mr. G. O. Sayles, which have
appeared in the *Bulletin of the Institute of Historical
Research* (February and November 1928, November
1930) and the *Royal Historical Society Transactions*
(1928). Mr. Richardson has also provided the Committee with a list of Richard II's Parliaments." The
dates of parliament which have been taken from the
Interim Report are the dates for which they were
summoned. The use of brackets indicates that the
parliament was summoned but that it did not meet.

The data which I have added is not as full as might
be wished. This chart has been used like those in
Appendix A and Appendix B as a tool for sifting the
materials for this study.

Sources.	Parliaments. Place and Date.	Councils and Great Councils. Place and Date.	Clerical Composition or use of "Premunientes" Clause.	Matters Treated concerning the Clergy.	Results.
Ann. Monast. (Theokesberia), I, 66; II (Waverleia), 296. Wendover, IV, 200—201.		February 22, 1225.		The Pope's business. Exaction of the tenths for war with the Emperor. Laity refused Bishops, Abbots, Priors & other Prelates after three or four days assented to the grant.	
		April 29 (Second Sunday after Easter), 1229.	Papal Nuncio, Abps., Bps., Abbots, Friars, Templars, Hospitallers, Rectors of Churches.		
Close Roll (1227—1231), 15 H. III, pp. 590, 594—5. Wilkins, I, 629.		Oxford. July 13 (Three weeks after the Sunday next before the Nat. of S. John Bap.), 1231.	All Bps. of the Province of Canterbury.	The spoliation of the churches of the land by Lewelyn and his accomplices. Punishment by ecclesiastical censure.	
Cartularium Mon. de Rameseia, I, 207. Lunt, Consent, p. 132. Lunt, Valuation of Norwich, p. 31, n. 8.		After Feast of S. Martin (November 11), 1244.	Martin. Papal Collectors. Prelates.	An aid.	
Mat. Paris, Chron. Maj., IV, 362. Ann. Monast. (Dunstaplia), III, 67.		February 23, 1245.	Martin. Prelates.	An aid. The Prelates refused as several Bps. & Prelates were absent.	Refusal.

Sources.	Parliaments. Place and Date.	Councils and Great Councils. Date.	Clerical Composition or use of "Premunientes."	Matters Treated concerning the Clergy.	Results.
Mat. Paris, Chron. Maj., IV, 375-6.		Lent, 1244-1245.	Martin. Prelates.	List of objections.	
Mat. Paris, Chron. Maj., IV, 375, 376, 441. Hody, History of Convocations, p. 328.	February 3, 1246.		Archdeacons.	Complaint. Letters to be sent to the Pope and Cardinals on the part of the commonalty of the whole clergy–in name of "universi cleri et populi."	
Ann. Monast. (Burton), I, 279. Mat. Paris, Chron. Maj., IV, 526-37.	March, 1245-1246.			Grievances.	
Mat. Paris, Chron. Maj., IV, 594.	London. February 3, 1247.		Archdeacons. Part of the clergy.		
Mat. Paris, Chron. Maj., IV, 622-3.	Oxford. April 7, 1247.		Bps. specially summoned.		
Mat. Paris, Chron. Maj., V, 324-33.	London. October 13, 1252.		Prelates.	Aid demanded.	Grant of tenth by clergy for three years.

Sources.	Parliaments. Place and Date.	Councils and Great Councils.	Clerical Composition or use of "Premunientes."	Matters Treated concerning the Clergy.	Results.
Mat. Paris, Chron. Maj., V, 373. Mat. Paris, Historia Ang., III, 136. Lunt, Consent, pp. 142–4. Cal. P.R. (1248–1257), 38 H. III, p. 370.	London. May 4, 1253.		Abp. of Cant. Bps.		
		Westminster. April 26, 1254.	Representatives of dioceses to certify concerning amount of subsidy.	Demand of Henry III for a subsidy. Representatives of the lower clergy exercised representative functions.	
Ann. Monast. (Burton), I, 360–63. Lunt, Consent, pp. 145–6.	London. October 13, 1255.		B p s. Abbots. Priors.	Taxation of lay fees.	
Ann. Monast. (Burton), I, 384, 386–9. (Oseneia), IV, 114. Mat. Paris, Chron. Maj., V, 621–3. Lunt, Consent, p. 148.	London. March 16, 1257.		Abp. of Cant. Abbots.	Peace between the Bishop of Lincoln and the Masters of Oxford. The King seeks a tenth for five years from the clergy according to the New Taxation.	Either in parliament or convocation the clergy suggested a composition of £52,000 to the King if he would remedy their grievances.
Ann. Monast. (Burton), I, 392.	London. April 22 (Quindene of Easter), 1257.				

Sources.	Parliaments. Place and Date.	Great Councils.	Clerical Composition or use of "Premunientes."	Matters Treated concerning the Clergy.	Results.
Interim Report of the Committee on House of Commons Personnel and Politics, 1264–1832, London, 1932, pp. 60–1.	Westminster. April 10, 1258.				
Ibid., pp. 60–1.	Oxford. June 11, 1258.				
Ibid., pp. 60–1.	Westminster. October 6, 1258.				
Ibid., pp. 60–1.	Westminster. February 9, 1259.				
Ibid., pp. 60–1.	Westminster. Michaelmas Term, 1259.				
Ibid., pp. 60–1.	London. Candlemas Term, 1260.				
Ibid., pp. 60–1.	Westminster. Easter Term, 1260.				
Ibid., pp. 60–1.	London. Midsummer Term, July 8, 1260.				
Ibid., pp. 60–1.	London. October 13, Michaelmas Term, 1260.				

Sources.	Parliaments. Place and Date.	Great Councils.	Clerical Composition. or use of "Premunientes."	Matters Treated concerning the Clergy.	Results.
Interim Report, pp. 60—1.	London. Candlemas, 1261.				
Ibid., pp. 60—1.	Windsor. September 21, 1261. (No evidence that this met.)				
Ibid., pp. 60—1.	London. Candlemas, 1262.				
Ibid., pp. 60—1.	London. September 8, 1263.				
Ibid., pp. 60—1.	London. October 20, 1263.		Abp. of York. Bps. of Durham & Carlisle. Ten Abbots & Priors of Northern Province. 55 Abbots. 26 Priors. Heads of military orders in Southern Province. Two clerical Proctors for each Chapter.		
Ibid., pp. 60—1.	Oxford. March 30, 1264. (Dubious if a Parliament.)				
Ibid., pp. 60—1. *Ann. Monast. (Dunstaplia)*, III, 235. Stubbs, *Const. Hist.*, II (4th ed.), 96. *Report on Dignity of a Peer*, III, 32—6.	London. June 24, 1264.				

Sources.	Parliaments. Place and Date.	Great Councils.	Clerical Composition or use of "Premunientes."	Matters Treated concerning the Clergy.	Results.
Interim Report, pp. 60–1.	Westminster. January 20, 1265.				
Ibid., pp. 60–1.	Westminster. September 8, 1265.				
Ibid., pp. 60–1.	Northampton. Kenilworth. April, 1266.				
Ibid., pp. 60–1.	Bury St. Edmunds. February, 1267.				
Ibid., pp. 62–3.	Shrewsbury. September 6, 1267. (Not certain that this was a Parliament.)				
Ibid., pp. 62–3. Ibid., p. 108.	Marlborough. November 18, 1267.	Westminster. April 22, 1268.			
Ibid., pp. 62–3.	Northampton. June, 1268.				
Ibid., pp. 62–3.	London. Michaelmas Term, 1268.				
Ibid., pp. 62–3.	London. Hilary, 1269.				
Ibid., pp. 62–3.	London. April 7, 1269.				

Sources.	Parliaments. Place and Date.	Great Councils.	Clerical Composition or use of "Premunientes."	Matters Treated concerning the Clergy.	Results.
Interim Report, pp. 62–3.	London. Midsummer, 1269.				
Ibid., pp. 62–3, 108.	Westminster. Michaelmas, 1269.	Westminster. October 13, 1269.			
	(Doubtful if a Parliament.) Westminster. April 27, 1270.				
Ibid., pp. 62–3.	Winchester. July 1, 1270.				
Ibid., pp. 62–3.	Westminster. Michaelmas, 1271.				
Ibid., pp. 62–3. Ibid., p. 108.	Westminster. Hilary, 1272. Westminster. Easter, Feb. 16, 1275, prorogued to April 22, 1275.	York and Northampton. January 13, 1273.			
Ibid., pp. 62–3.	Westminster. October 13, 1275.				
Ibid., pp. 62–3.	Westminster. Easter, 1277.				
Ibid., pp. 62–3.	(Michaelmas), 1277.				

Sources.	Parliaments. Place and Date.	Great Councils.	Clerical Composition or use of "Premunientes."	Matters Treated concerning the Clergy.	Results.
Interim Report, pp. 62–3.	Westminster. Easter Term, 1278.				
Ibid., pp. 62–3.	Westminster. Michaelmas Term, 1278.				
Ibid., pp. 62–3.	Westminster. Easter Term, 1279.				
Ibid., pp. 64–5.	Westminster. Michaelmas Term, 1279.				
Ibid., pp. 64–5.	Westminster. Easter Term, 1280.				
Ibid., pp. 64–5. Reg. Wickwane (Surtees Soc.); E. B. Graves, "Circumspecte Agatis," E. H. R., XLIII (1928), p. 13, note 3. Chronicle of Abingdon, p. 27.	Westminster. Michaelmas Term, 1280.			Grievances of the clergy. York grants either a tenth [or fifteenth] for two years.	
Interim Report, pp. 64–5. Chron. Abingdon, p. 27.	Westminster. Easter Term, 1281.			Province of Canterbury grants a tenth or fifteenth for three years.	
Interim Report, pp. 64–5.	Michaelmas Term, 1281.				
Ibid., pp. 64–5.	Easter, 1282.				

Sources.	Parliaments. Place and Date.	Assemblies and Great Councils.	Clerical Composition or use of "Premunientes."	Matters Treated concerning the Clergy.	Results.
Interim Report, p. 108. Stubbs, Select Charters (9th ed.), p. 459. Reg. Pecham, fols. 82v., 83v., 101v. Regist. Epis. J. Peckham, II, 508. [N.B. These assemblies have been listed also with the Convocations of Canterbury and York.] Interim Report, pp. 64–5.		York and Northampton. January 20, 1283.	Clergy of York Province to York. Abp. of York. Bps., Abbots, Priors, "Prefecti," Deans & Chapters by their Proctors. Clergy of Prov. of Canterbury to Northampton. Abp. of Cant. and same degrees of clergy as for York Province.	Grant. Grant.	Clergy of Province of Canterbury refused to give an answer as greater part of the clergy not duly called.
Ibid., pp. 64–5.	Shrewsbury. Michaelmas, 1283.				
Ibid., pp. 64–5.	(Easter), 1284.				
Ibid., pp. 64–5.	Michaelmas, 1284.				
Ibid., pp. 64–5.	Westminster. March 25, 1285.				
Ibid., pp. 64–5.	Winchester. October 8, 1285.				
Ibid., pp. 64–5.	Westminster. Easter, 1286.				
Ibid., pp. 64–5.	Westminster. Easter, 1289.				

Sources.	Parliaments. Place and Date.	Assemblies and Great Councils.	Clerical Composition or use of "Premunientes."	Matters Treated concerning the Clergy.	Results.
Interim Report, pp. 64–5.	Westminster. Hilary, 1290.				
Ibid., pp. 64–5.	Westminster. January 30, 1290.				
Ibid., pp. 64–5.	Westminster. April 22, 1290. July 15, 1290. Chepstow. October 26, 1290. Ashridge.				
Ibid., pp. 64–5.	January 7, 1291. Westminster.				
Ibid., pp. 64–5.	January 7, 1292. Westminster.				
Ibid., pp. 64–5.	Easter, 1292. London.				
Ibid., pp. 64–5.	Easter, 1293. Westminster.				
Ibid., pp. 64–5.	Sept. 30, 1293. Westminster.				
Ibid., pp. 64–5.	Easter, 1294. Westminster.				
Ibid., pp. 64–5. Ibid., p. 108.	Sept. 21, 1294.	Westminster. November 12, 1294.	First use of "Premunientes" Clause. Abp. of Cant. Abp. of York. Bps. "Ad tractandum ordinandum et faciendum."		
Ibid., pp. 66–7.	Westminster. August 1, 1295.				
Ibid., pp. 66–7.	Westminster. Nov. 13, 1295. (Clergy summoned.)				

Sources.	Parliaments. Place and Date.	Assemblies and Great Councils.	Clerical Composition or use of "Premunientes."	Matters Treated concerning the Clergy.	Results.
Stubbs, Select Charters, pp. 480–1. Rep. Dignity of a Peer, III, 66–7, 69.	Nov. 27, 1295.				
Ann. Monast. (Wigornia), IV, 524. Flores Historiarum (R.S.), III, 95. Cal. C.R. (1288–1296), 23 E. I, 459.	Nov. 29, 1295. (Clergy summoned.)				
Interim Report, pp. 66–7. Rep. on the Dignity of a Peer, III, 75.	Bury St. Edmunds. Nov. 3, 1296.		"Premunientes" Clause. "Ad ordinandum."		
Int. Rep., pp. 66–7.	Salisbury. Feb. 24, 1297.		No		
Rep. Dig., III, 77.	Westminster. Trinity Term, 1297.		"Premunientes."		
Int. Rep., pp. 66–7.	London. October 6, 1297.		No		
Int. Rep., pp. 66–7. Rep. Dig., III, 87.	London. April 6, 1298.		"Premunientes."		
Int. Rep., pp. 66–7. Rep. Dig., III, 94. Int. Rep., p. 108.		York. May 25, 1298.	No		
Ibid., pp. 66–7. Rep. Dig., III, 102–3.	Westminster. March 8, 1299.		"Premunientes."		
Int. Rep., pp. 66–7. Rep. Dig., III, 105.	Westminster. May 3, 1299.		No		
Int. Rep., pp. 66–7. Rep. Dig., III, 9.	London. October 18, 1299.		No "Premunientes."		

x

Sources.	Parliaments. Place and Date.	Assemblies and Great Councils.	Clerical Composition or use of "Premunientes."	Matters Treated concerning the Clergy.	Results.
Int. Rep., pp. 66–7. Rep. Dig., III, 115. Int. Rep., p. 108.	Westminster. March 6, 1300.		"Premunientes." "Ad faciend. et consenciend."		
		York. May 20, 1300.	No "Premunientes."	Grievances of clergy proposed.	
Int. Rep., pp. 66–7. Rep. Dig., III, 121. Wilkins, II, 315. Int. Report, pp. 66–7. Rep. Dig., III, 143. Int. Rep., pp. 66–7. Rep. Dig., III, 149. Int. Rep., p. 108.	Lincoln. January 20, 1301. Westminster. July 1, 1302. Westminster. Sept. 29, 1302. Oct. 14, 1302.		No "Premunientes." No "Premunientes." No "Premunientes."		
		June 25, 1303. York.	"Premunientes." "Ad faciend. et consenciend."		
Rep. Dig., III, 157–8. Int. Rep., pp. 66–7.	Westminster. (Feb. 16, 1305.) Feb. 28, 1305.		"Premunientes."		
Rep. Dig., III, 164–5. Int. Rep., pp. 68–9.	Westminster. (July 15, 1305.) Aug. 15, 1305. Sept. 15, 1305.		No "Premunientes."		
Int. Rep., pp. 68–9. Rep. Dig., III, 165. Ibid., pp. 68–9. Rep. Dig., III, 169.	Westminster. May 30, 1306. Carlisle. Jan. 20, 1307.		"Premunientes." "Premunientes." "Ad faciend. et consenciend."		
Rot. Parl., I, 189. Flores Hist., III, 457. Wake, State, 258. (Ex Lib. Mem. Jo. Dalderby Linc., fol. 192.)			Proctors of clergy of 11 dioceses present and from 5 archdeaconries.		

Sources.	Parliaments. Place and Date.	Assemblies and Great Councils.	Clerical Composition or use of "Premunientes."	Matters Treated concerning the Clergy.	Results.
Int. Rep., pp. 68–9. Rep. Dig., III, 172. Wake, State, p. 258. (Ex Lib. Mem. J. Dalderby Linc., fol. 192.) Reg. Pal. Dunelm., I, 122. Reg. Reynolds (Wor. His. Soc.), p. 160 (fol. 99d).	Northampton. Oct. 13, 1307.		"Premunientes." "Ad faciend. et consenciend." Lincoln dioc. sent Proctors.	Grant from the clergy.	Clergy grant one-fifteenth.
Int. Rep., pp. 68–9. Rep. Dig., III, 177.	Westminster. March 3, 1303.		No "Premunientes."		
Int. Rep., pp. 68–9. Rep. Dig., III, 179.	Westminster. April 28, 1308.		No "Premunientes."		
Int. Rep., pp. 68–9. Rep. Dig., 184.	Westminster. Oct. 20, 1308.		"Premunientes."		
Int. Rep., pp. 68–9. Rep. Dig., III, 187.	Westminster. April 27, 1309.		"Premunientes." "Ad faciend. et consenciend."		
Int. Rep., pp. 68–9. Rep. Dig., III, p. 190.	Stamford. July 27, 1309. Summons only.		No "Premunientes."		
Int. Rep., pp. 68–9. Rep. Dig., III, 199. Int. Rep., pp. 68–9. Rep. Dig., III, 205.	York. Feb. 8, 1310. London. Aug. 8, 1311.		No "Premunientes." "Premunientes." "Ad faciend. et consenciend."		
Int. Rep., pp. 68–9. Rep. Dig., III, 208.	Westminster. Nov. 12, 1311.		"Quod premunientes."		

Sources.	Parliaments. Place and Date.	Assemblies and Great Councils.	Clerical Composition or use of "Premunientes".	Matters Treated concerning the Clergy.	Results.
Reg. S. de Gandavo, C. & Y. Soc., pp. 417–18 (fol. 140).	Deans, Priors, Abbots, Archdeacons, Proctors of the clergy to come on Octaves of Martinmas, Nov. 18, 1311.		"Potestatem ab eisdem capitulis et clero hiis qua in parliamento predicto ordinari contigerit consenciendi habentes."		Proctors of the clergy asked leave to withdraw since they did not seem to be needed.
Int. Rep., pp. 68–9. Rep. Dig., III, 211.	Westminster. Feb. 13, 1312.		"Premunientes." "Ad faciend. et consenciend."		
Int. Rep., pp. 68–9. Rep. Dig., III, 214.	Lincoln. July 23, 1312.		"Premunientes." "Ad faciend. et consenciend."		
Int. Rep., pp. 68–9. Rep. Dig., III, 218.	Westminster. Aug. 20, 1312.		"Premunientes." "Ad faciend. et consenciend."		
Int. Rep., pp. 68–9. Rep. Dig., III, 221.	Westminster. March 18, 1313.		"Premunientes." "Ad faciend. et consenciend."		
Int. Rep., pp. 68–9. Rep. Dig., III, 224–5. Int. Rep., pp. 68–9.	Westminster. July 8, 1313. Sept. 23, 1313.		"Premunientes." "Ad faciend. et consenciend." "Premunientes." "Ad faciend. et consenciend."		
Int. Rep., pp. 68–9. Rep. Dig., III, 232.	Westminster. April 21, 1314.		"Premunientes." "Ad faciend. et consenciend."		
Int. Rep., pp. 68–9. Rep. Dig., III, 240.	York. Sept. 9, 1314.		"Premunientes." "Ad faciend. et consenciend." Provincial writ to Abp. of Cant.		

Results.	Matters Treated concerning the Clergy.	Clerical Composition or use of "Premunientes."	Assemblies and Great Councils.	Parliaments. Place and Date.	Sources.
Grant of a tenth by the clergy of Province of Canterbury.	Grant by clergy of Province of Canterbury.	"Premunientes." "Ad faciend. et consenciend." Provincial writs to Abps. of York and Canterbury. Chapter of Carlisle and clergy of Carlisle sent Proctors.		Westminster. Jan. 20, 1315.	Int. Rep., pp. 70–1. Rep. Dig., III, 243, 246.
	Articles presented by the clergy and considered by Parliament. Cf. Appendix A in this year for assembly in Lincoln Cath.	"Premunientes." "Ad faciend. et consenciend." Provincial writs to Abps. Abp. of Cant. summons the clergy before him on Jan. 26 in the cathedral church of Lincoln.		Lincoln. Jan. 27, 1316.	Int. Rep., pp. 70–1. Rep. Dig., III, 252. Statutes of the Realm, I, 171–4.
		"Premunientes." "Ad faciend. et consenciend."		(Lincoln.) (Jan. 27, 1318.)	Int. Rep., pp. 70–1. Rep. Dig., III, 273.
		"Premunientes." "Ad faciend. et consenciend."		(Mar. 12, 1318.)	Int. Rep., pp. 70–1. Rep. Dig., III, 275–6.
		"Premunientes." "Ad faciend. et consenciend."		(June 19, 1318.) Revoked.	Int. Rep., pp. 70–1. Rep. Dig., III, 278–9.

Sources.	Parliaments. Place and Date.	Assemblies and Great Councils.	Clerical Composition or use of "Premunientes."	Matters Treated concerning the Clergy.	Results.
Int. Rep., pp. 70–1. Rep. Dig., III, 290.	York. Oct. 20, 1318.		"Premunientes." "Ad faciend. et consenciend."	Grant by clergy of Province of York.	Grant of tenth by clergy of York Province.
Cal. C.R. (1318–1323), 13 E. II, 156, 203. Reg. Halton, C. and Y. Soc., II, 235.	York. May 6, 1319.		"Premunientes." "Ad faciend. et consenciend." Clergy of Carlisle sent Proctors.	Grant by clergy of Province of Canterbury.	Grant of twelfth by clergy of Province of Cant. To be superseded if the Pope should impose a tenth. (It was superseded.)
Int. Rep., pp. 70–1. Rep. Dig., III, 291.	York. Jan. 20, 1320.		No "Premunientes."		
Int. Rep., pp. 70–1. Rep. Dig., III, 299.	Westminster. October 6, 1320.		No "Premunientes."		
Int. Rep., pp. 70–1. Rep. Dig., III, 306, 309. Reg. Reynolds (Cantuar.), fol. 299.	Westminster. July 15, 1321.		"Premunientes." "Ad faciend. et consenciend." Provincial writ to Abp. of Cant. "Rogantes quatinus ... ad tractand et consenciend."		
Int. Rep., pp. 70–1. Rep. Dig., III, 318–19. Reg. Reynolds (Cantuar.), fol. 304. Reg. Halton, II, 235.	York. May 2, 1322.		"Premunientes." "Ad faciend. et consenciend." Provincial writ to Abp. of Cant. Clergy of Carlisle sent Proctors.		

Sources.	Parliaments. Place and Date.	Assemblies and Great Councils.	Clerical Composition or use of "Premunientes."	Matters Treated concerning the Clergy.	Results.
Int. Rep., pp. 70-1. *Rep. Dig.*, III, 327.	(Ripon.) York. Nov. 14, 1322.		*No* "Premunientes."		
Int. Rep., pp. 70-1. *Rep. Dig.*, III, 346. Reg. Reynolds (Cantuar.), fols. 235, 236. Reg. Halton, II, 235.	Westminster. Feb. 23, 1324.		"Premunientes." "Ad faciend. et consenciend." Provincial writ to Abps. of Cant. and York. Clergy of Carlisle sent Proctors.		
Int. Rep., pp. 70-1. *Rep. Dig.*, III, 351.	(Salisbury.) Westminster. Oct. 20, 1324.		*No* "Premunientes."		
Int. Rep., pp. 70-1. *Rep. Dig.*, III, 363. *Int. Rep.*, pp. 70-1. *Rep. Dig.*, III, 366. Wake, *State*, p. 277. (Ex Capit. Lib. Act, Lincoln, I, fol. 5.)	Westminster. June 25, 1325. Westminster. Nov. 18, 1325.		"Premunientes." "Premunientes." "Ad faciend. et consenciend." Church of Lincoln sent Proctors.		
Int. Rep., pp. 70-1. *Rep. Dig.*, IV, 369. Reg. Reynolds (Cantuar.), fol. 313v. Wake, *State*, pp. 277-8. (Ex Acta Capit. Eccl. Cath. Lichfield in Mus. Ashmol.; Lib. Mem. H. Burghersh Linc., fol. 152.)	Westminster. (Dec. 14, 1326.) Jan. 7, 1327.		"Premunientes." "Ad consenciend." Lincoln & Lichfield sent instructions for Proctors.		

Sources.	Parliaments. Place and Date.	Assemblies and Great Councils.	Clerical Composition or use of "Premunientes."	Matters Treated concerning the Clergy.	Results.
Int. Rep., p. 108. Rep. Dig., IV, 376. Reg. Reynolds (Cantuar.), fol. 207. Wake, State, p. 278. (Ex Reg. Melton Ebor., fol. 468.)		Lincoln. Sept. 15, 1327.	"Et premuniatis." "Ad faciend. et consenciend." Provincial writs to Abps. of Cant. and York.		York clergy refuse to go out of their Province.
Int. Rep., pp. 72–3. Rep. Dig., IV, 328–9.		York. Feb. 7, 1328. Sessions Feb. 7–Mar. 5.	"Premunientes." "Ad faciend. et consenciend." Provincial writs to Abp. of York and Keeper of Spiritualities of Cant.		Grant of tenth by clergy of Province of Cant. Rec. Nor. Convoc., p. 74 (Reg. Jo. Kirkby, fol. 321). [Probably Leicester aid.]
Int. Rep., pp. 72–3. Rep. Dig., IV, 381.	Northampton. April 24, 1328. Sessions of Commons, Apr. 24–May 14.		"Et premuniatis." "Ad faciend. et consenciend." Provincial writs to the Abps. of Cant. and York.		
Int. Rep., p. 108.		York. July 31, 1328.	"Et premuniatis." "Ad faciend. et consenciend." Provincial writs to Abp. of York and Keeper of Spirit. of Cant.		

Sources.	Parliaments, Place and Date.	Assemblies and Great Councils.	Clerical Composition or use of "Premunientes."	Matters Treated concerning the Clergy.	Results.
Int. Rep., pp. 72–3. Rep. Dig., IV, 386, 389.	Salisbury. Oct. 16, 1328. Commons in session, Oct. 16–31.		"Et premuniatis." "Ad faciend. et consenciend." Provincial writs to Abp. of York and Keeper of Spirit. of Cant.		Prelates refuse an aid in the absence of the Archbishop of Cant, but will give an answer in a convocation. Cf. Appendix A in this year for Assembly of the Clergy.
Int. Rep., pp. 72–3. Rep. Dig., IV, 389.	Adjourned to Westminster. Feb. 9, 1329.				
Int. Rep., pp. 72–3. Rep. Dig., IV, 391–2.	Winchester. Mar. 11, 1330. Sessions of Commons, March 11–23, 1330.		"Premunientes." "Ad faciend. et consenciend." Provincial writs to Abps. of Cant. and York. N.B. Abp. of Cant. summons clergy to Winchester Cathedral.		
Int. Rep., pp. 72–3. Rep. Dig., IV, 397.	Westminster. Nov. 26, 1330. Sessions of Commons. Nov. 26–Dec. 9.		"Et premuniri faciatis." "Ad faciend. et consenciend."		
Int. Rep., pp. 72–3. Rep. Dig., IV, 400.	Westminster. (April 15, 1331.)		No "Premunientes."		
Int. Rep., pp. 72–3. Rep. Dig., IV, 402, 406.	Sept. 30, 1331. N.B. Not held.		No "Premunientes."		
Int. Rep., pp. 72–3. Rep. Dig., IV, 408.	Westminster. Mar. 16, 1332.		"Et premuniatis." "Ad faciend. et consenciend."	Proctors of the clergy go apart to consult.	Clergy have leave to go on Saturday, March 21.

Sources.	Parliaments. Place and Date.	Assemblies and Great Councils.	Clerical Composition or use of "Premunientes."	Matters Treated concerning the Clergy.	Results.
Rot. Parl., II, 656, no. 11.	Sessions of Commons. Mar. 16–21, 1332.		Provincial writs to the Abps. of Cant. and York.		
Int. Rep., pp. 72–3. Rep. Dig., IV, 411.	Westminster. Sept. 9, 1332. Sessions of Commons. Sept. 9–12,		No "Premunientes."		
Int. Rep., pp. 72–3. Rep. Dig., IV, 416.	York. Dec. 4, 1332. Sessions of Commons. Dec. 4–11.		No "Premunientes."		
Int. Rep., pp. 72–3. Rep. Dig., IV, 418.	York. Jan. 20, 1333. Sessions of Commons. Jan. 20–26.		No "Premunientes."		
Int. Rep., pp. 72–3. Rep. Dig., IV, 423, 425. Rot. Parl., II, Appendix, p. 376, no. 9.	York. Feb. 21, 1334. Sessions of Commons. Feb. 21–Mar. 2.		"Premunientes." "Ad faciend. et consenciend." Provincial writs to Abp. of York and Keep. of Spirit. of Cant.	Petitions presented by the clergy.	

Sources.	Parliaments, Place and Date.	Assemblies and Great Councils.	Clerical Composition or use of "Premunientes."	Matters Treated concerning the Clergy.	Results.
Int. Rep., pp. 72-3. Rep. Dig., IV, 427-8, 430.	Westminster. Sept. 19, 1334. Sessions of Commons. Sept. 19-23.		"Premunientes." "Ad faciend. et consenciend." Provincial writs to Abps. of Cant. and York.	Abp. of Cant. executes "Premunientes" by calling clergy to S. Paul's, Sept. 19. Cf. Appendix A in this year for the Assembly of the Clergy at this time.	
Reg. Orleton Winchester, pt. I., fol. 7v. Int. Rep., pp. 72-3. Rep. Dig., IV, 443-4, 446. Cal. C.R. (1333-1337), 9 E. III, p. 425.	York. May 26, 1335. Sessions of Commons. May 26-June 3.		"Premunientes." "Ad faciend. et consenciend." Provincial writs to Abps. of Cant. and York.	Abp. of York testifies that the tenth granted by the clergy is according to the New Taxation—not otherwise.	
Int. Rep., pp. 72-3. Rep. Dig., IV, 454, 456. Cal. C.R. (1333-1337), 10 E. III, p. 660. Reg. Orleton, Winchester, pt. I, fols. 33-33v. Rep. Dig., IV, 460-1, 462.	Westminster. Mar. 11, 1336. Sessions of Commons. Mar. 11-20.		"Premunientes." "Ad faciend. et consenciend." Provincial writs to Abps. of Cant. and York. Abp. of Cant. executes calling clergy to S. Paul's.	Grant by clergy of Province of Canterbury.	Grant of a tenth by the clergy of the Province of Canterbury. Cf. Appendix A in this year for the Assembly of the Clergy at this time.

Sources.	Parliaments. Place and Date.	Assemblies and Great Councils.	Clerical Composition or use of "Premunientes."	Matters Treated concerning the Clergy.	Results.
Int. Rep., p. 108.		Nottingham. Sept. 23, 1336.	"Et premuniatis." "Ad faciend. et consenciend." Provincial writs to Abps. of Cant. and York.		
Int. Rep., pp. 72–3. Rep. Dig., IV, 467.	(York. Jan. 13, 1336–7.)		"Premunientes." "Ad faciend. et consenciend."		
Int. Rep., pp. 72–3. Rep. Dig., IV, 467.	(York. Feb. 9, 1337.)		"Premunientes."		
Int. Rep., pp. 72–3. Rep. Dig., IV, 470, 473.	Westminster. Mar. 3, 1337. Sessions of Commons. Mar. 3–13.		"Ad consenciend." Provincial writs to Abps. of Cant. and York.		
Int. Rep., p. 108. Rep. Dig., IV, 479.		Westminster. Sept. 26, 1337.	"Premunientes." "Ad consenciend."		
Int. Rep., pp. 72–3. Rep. Dig., IV, 488–9.	Westminster. Feb. 3, 1338		"Premunientes." "Ad consenciend."		
Int. Rep., p. 108. Rep. Dig., IV, 492–3.		Northampton. July 26, 1338.	"Et premuniatis." "Ad faciend. et consenciend."		
Int. Rep., pp. 72–3. Rep. Dig., IV, 492–8, 500.	Westminster. Jan. 14, 1339. Westminster. Feb. 3, 1339.		"Premunientes." "Ad consenciend."		

Sources.	Parliaments. Place and Date.	Assemblies and Great Councils.	Clerical Composition or use of "Premunientes."	Matters Treated concerning the Clergy.	Results.
Int. Rep., pp. 72–3. Rep. Dig., IV, 500–1. Ibid, IV, 503.	Sessions of Commons. Feb. 3–14, 1339.		Provincial writs to Abps. of Cant. and York. "Premunientes." "Ad consenciend."		
Int. Rep., pp. 72–3. Rep. Dig., IV, 503–4. Rot. Parl., II, 105, no. 16, 106, no. 24.	Westminster. Oct. 13, 1339. Sessions of Commons. Oct. 13–28.		Provincial writs to Abps. of Cant. and York. "Premunientes." "Ad consenciend."		Accorded and agreed that letters should be sent to the Abp. & clergy of Province of York to excite them to make a grant similar to that made by the Province of Canterbury.
Int. Rep., pp. 72–3. Rep. Dig., IV, 507, 509.	Westminster. Jan. 20, 1340. Sessions of Commons. Jan. 20–Feb. 19.		"Premunientes." "Ad consenciend." Provincial writs to Abps. of Cant. and York. "Et premuniatis." "Ad consenciend."		Memoranda for convocations of both provinces.
Int. Rep., pp. 72–3. Rep. Dig., IV, 515.	Westminster. Mar. 29, 1340.			A grant by the clergy of the Province of Canterbury.	Charter given by the King to the clergy. Clergy paying the tenth not held to pay the ninth.

Sources.	Parliaments. Place and Date.	Assemblies and Great Councils.	Clerical Composition or use of "Premunientes."	Matters Treated concerning the Clergy.	Results.
Rot. Parl., II, 112. Reg. Grandisson, II, 937–8.	Sessions of Commons. Mar. 29–May 10, 1340.		Provincial writs to Abps. of York and Cant.		Tenth granted by the clergy of the realm of England. Cal. C.R. (1339–1341) 14 E. III., p. 530.
Int. Rep., pp. 74–5. Rep. Dig., IV, 521–2.	Westminster. July 12, 1340. Sessions of Commons. July 12–26.		"Et premuniatis." "Ad consenciend."		
Int. Rep., pp. 74–5. Rep. Dig., III, 529. Rot. Parl., II, 129–30.	Westminster. April 23, 1341. Sessions of Commons. April 23–May 18.		"Et premuniatis." "Ad consenciend."	Petitions submitted by the clergy complained especially of the levy of the ninth.	Responses given to clergy's petitions.
Int. Rep., p. 108. Rep. Dig., IV, 542.		Westminster. Oct. 16, 1342.	"Premunientes." "Ad consenciend."		
Int. Rep., pp. 74–5. Rep. Dig., IV, 546.	Westminster. April 28, 1343.		"Et premuniatis." "Ad consenciend."		
Int. Rep., pp. 74–5. Rep. Dig., IV, 551. Rot. Parl., II, 149, 151–2, 153.	Westminster. June 7, 1344. Sessions of Commons. June 7–20.		"Premunientes."	Commons pray that no petitions by the clergy be granted until tried by the King and Commons. Petitions submitted by Abp. and clergy.	Charter given to clergy. Responses to petitions.

Sources.	Parliaments. Place and Date.	Assemblies and Great Councils.	Clerical Composition or use of "Premunientes."	Matters Treated concerning the Clergy.	Results.
Int. Rep., pp. 74–5. Rep. Dig., IV, 558. Rot. Parl., II, 163, no. 46. Wake, State, Appendix, p. 68. (Reg. Zouch Ebor., fol. 258.)	Westminster. Sept. 11, 1346. Sessions of Commons. Sept. 11–20.		"Premunientes." "Ad consenciend." ["Premunientes" not sent to Abp. of York in writ, Rep. Dig., IV, 560.]	Commons request that all benefices of aliens be taken into the King's hands. Request also that Abps. and Bps. should be commanded to hand in the names of benefices held by aliens and the value before the convocation of the clergy.	
Int. Rep., pp. 74–5. Rep. Dig., IV, 572–3. Rot. Parl., II, 218.	Westminster. Jan. 14, 1348. Sessions of Commons. Jan. 14–Feb. 12, 1348.		"Premunientes." "Ad consenciend."	Petition of Prior of S. John Jerusalem against coming to parliaments and convocations (made in this parliament or the following year).	
Int. Rep., pp. 74–5. Rep. Dig., IV, 575.	Westminster. March 31. Sessions of Commons. Mar. 31–Apr. 13, 1348.		"Premunientes." "Ad consenciend."		
Int. Rep., pp. 74–5. Rep. Dig., IV, 577–8. Int. Rep., pp. 74–5. Rep. Dig., IV, 580–1.	(Westminster. Jan. 19, 1349.) (Westminster. Apr. 26, 1349.) Sine die because of the Black Death.		"Premunientes." "Ad faciend. et consenciend." "Premunientes." "Ad consenciend."		

Sources.	Parliaments. Place and Date.	Assemblies and Great Councils.	Clerical Composition or use of "Premunientes."	Matters Treated concerning the Clergy.	Results.
Int. Rep., pp. 74-5. Rep. Dig., IV, 587-8.	Westminster. Feb. 9, 1351. Sessions of Commons.		"Premunientes." "Ad faciend. et consenciend."		
Int. Rep., pp. 74-5. Rep. Dig., IV, 590-1.	Westminster. Jan. 13, 1352. Sessions of Commons. Jan. 13–Feb. 11.		"Premunientes." "Ad faciend. et consenciend."	Abp. of Cant. & Bps. of his Prov. present petitions for the whole clergy.	Privileges confirmed for the clergy.
Rot. Parl., II, 244. Reg. Islep, fol. 54.		Westminster. Aug. 16, 1352. (Int. Rep., p.108.)			
Cal. C.R. (1349–1354), 26 E. III, p. 449.		Westminster. Sept. 23, 1353. (Int. Rep., p.108.)	"Premunientes." "Ad faciend. et consenciend."		
Int. Rep., pp. 74-5. Rep. Dig., IV, 603-4.	Westminster. April 28, 1354. Sessions of Commons. Apr. 28–May 20. (Westminster, Nov. 12, 1355.)		"Premunientes." "Ad faciend. consenciend."		
Int. Rep., pp. 74-5. Rep. Dig., IV, 607.	Prorogued to Westminster, Nov. 23, 1355. Sessions of Commons. Nov. 23–Dec. 30, 1355.		"Premunientes." "Ad faciend. et consenciend."		
Int. Rep., pp. 74-5. Rep. Dig., IV, 611.	Westminster. April 17, 1357.		"Premunientes." "Ad faciend. et consenciend."		

Sources.	Parliaments. Place and Date.	Assemblies and Great Councils.	Clerical Composition or use of "Premunientes."	Matters Treated concerning the Clergy.	Results.
Wake, *State*, Appendix, p. 69. (Reg. Decani et Capit. Ebor ab anno 1352, fol. 22.)	Sessions of Commons. Apr. 17–May 16.			Chapter of York sent Proctors.	
Int. Rep., pp. 74–5. *Rep. Dig.*, IV, 614.	Westminster. Feb. 5, 1358. Sessions of Commons. Feb. 5–27.		"Premunientes." "Ad faciend. et consenciend."		
Int. Rep., pp. 74–5. *Rep. Dig.*, IV, 622. Wake, *State*, p. 300. (Reg. Decani et Capit. Ebor. ab anno 1352, fol. 33.)	Westminster. May 15, 1360. Sessions of Commons. May 15 to ?		"Premunientes." "Ad consenciend."	Chapter of York sent Proctors.	
Int. Rep., pp. 74–5. *Rep. Dig.*, IV, 624.	Westminster. Jan. 24, 1361.		"Premunientes." "Ad faciend. et consenciend."	Chapter of York sent Proctors.	
Wake, *State*, p. 300. (Reg. Dec. et Capit. Ebor. ab anno 1352, fol. 37.)	Sessions of Commons. Jan. 24–Feb. 18.				
Int. Rep., pp. 74–5. *Rep. Dig.*, IV, 631.	Westminster. Oct. 13, 1362. Sessions of Commons. Oct. 13–30.		"Premunientes." "Ad consenciend."		

Sources.	Parliaments, Place and Date.	Assemblies and Great Councils.	Clerical Composition or use of "Premunientes."	Matters Treated concerning the Clergy.	Results.
Int. Rep., pp. 74-5. Rep. Dig., IV, 634.	Westminster. Oct. 6, 1363. Sessions of Commons. Oct. 6-30.		"Premunientes." "Ad consenciend."		
Int. Rep., pp. 74-5. Rep. Dig., IV, 636.	Westminster. Jan. 20, 1365. Sessions of Commons. Jan. 30-Feb. 28.		"Premunientes." "Ad consenciend."		
Int. Rep., pp. 74-5. Rep. Dig., IV, 639.	Westminster. May 4, 1366. Sessions of Commons. May 4-11.		"Premunientes." "Ad consenciend."		
Int. Rep., pp. 74-5. Rep. Dig., IV, 641-2.	Westminster. May 1, 1368. Sessions of Commons. May 1-21.		"Premunientes." "Ad consenciend."		
Int. Rep., pp. 76-7. Rep. Dig., IV, 644.	Westminster. June 3, 1369. Sessions of Commons. June 3-10.		"Et Premunientes." "Ad consenciend."		
Int. Rep., pp. 76-7. Rep. Dig., IV, 646-7.	Westminster. Feb. 24, 1371. Sessions of Commons. Feb. 24-Mar. 29.		"Premunientes." "Ad consilend. et consenciend."		
Int. Rep., p. 108.		Winchester. June 8, 1371.			

Sources.	Parliaments. Place and Date.	Assemblies and Great Councils.	Clerical Composition or use of "Premunientes."	Matters Treated concerning the Clergy.	Results.
Int. Rep., pp. 76-7. Rep. Dig., IV, 653.	Westminster. (Oct. 13, 1372.)		"Premunientes." "Ad consenciend."		
Int. Rep., pp. 76-7. Rep. Dig., IV, 655-6.	Nov. 3, 1372. Sessions of Commons. Nov. 3-27.		"Premunientes. "Ad faciend. et consenciend."		
Int. Rep., pp. 76-7. Rep. Dig., IV, 659-60.	Westminster. Nov. 21, 1373. Sessions of Commons. Nov. 21-Dec. 10.		"Premunientes." "Ad consenciend."		
Int. Rep., pp. 76-7. Rep. Dig., IV, 662-3.	(Westminster.) (Feb. 12, 1376.)		"Premunientes." "Ad consenciend."		
Rep. Dig., IV, 665-6. Rot. Parl., II, 357-8, nos. 199-208.	Westminster. Apr. 28, 1376. Sessions of Commons. Apr. 28-July 10.		"Premunientes." "Ad consenciend."	Petitions presented by the clergy of the Province of Canterbury.	
Int. Rep., pp. 76-7. Rep. Dig., II, 669. Rot. Parl., II, 373, nos. 80-5; also in Reg. Sudbury (Cantuar.), fol. 42.	Westminster. Jan. 27, 1377. Sessions of Commons. Jan. 27-Mar. 2.		"Premunientes." "Ad consenciend."	Petitions presented by the prelates & clergy of the Province of Canterbury.	

Results.	Matters Treated concerning the Clergy.	Clerical Composition or use of "Premunientes."	Assemblies and Great Councils.	Parliaments. Place and Date.	Sources.
	Petitions presented in the name of the prelates and clergy of the Provinces of Canterbury and York.	"Premunientes." "Ad consenciend." The Prior and Chapter of Ely sent one Proctor.		Westminster. Oct. 13, 1377.	Int. Rep., pp. 76–7. Rep. Dig., IV, 673.
				Sessions of Commons. Oct. 13–Dec. 2.	B.M. Add. MS. 41612, fol. 22v. Rot. Parl., III, 25–7, nos. 112–25.
		"Premunientes." "Ad consenciend." Proctors sent by the Dean and Chapter of York.		Gloucester. Oct. 20, 1378.	Int. Rep., pp. 76–7. Rep. Dig., IV, 676.
				Sessions of Commons. Oct. 20–Nov. 16, 1378.	Wake, State, p. 311. (Reg. Dec. et Capit. Ebor. ab anno 1352, evidently the source.)
				Westminster. April 24, 1379.	Int. Rep., pp. 76–7. Rep. Dig., IV, 679–80.
		"Premunientes." "Ad consenciend." Lincoln diocese taxed for Proctors in Parliament as well as in Convocation.		Apr. 24–May 27.	Wake, State, p. 311. (Reg. Dec. et Capit. Ebor. ab anno 1352, fol. 137a.) Wake, State, p. 311. (Lib. Mem. Jo. Bokingham, Linc., fol. 184.)

Sources.	Place and Date. Parliaments.	Assemblies and Great Councils.	Clerical Composition or use of "Premunientes."	Matters Treated concerning the Clergy.	Results.
Int. Rep., pp. 76-7. Rep. Dig., IV, 682-3.	Westminster. Jan. 16, 1380. Sessions of Commons. Jan. 16-Mar. 3.		"Premunientes." "Ad consenciend."	Grant from the clergy of the Province of Canterbury.	16d. in the mark granted to the King by the clergy of the Province of Canterbury. [Cal. C.R. (1377-1381) 4. R. II, p. 464.] This grant was made in the convocation on February 28 (cf. Appendix A). It was evidently reported in Parliament.
Int. Rep., pp. 76-7. Rep. Dig., IV, 686.	Northampton. Nov. 5, 1380.		"Premunientes." "Ad consenciend."	The Commons offered the King £100,000 if the clergy would bear a third part. The clergy replied that their grants were never made in Parliament.	The clergy said that they might be depended upon to do their part if the laity did theirs.
Rot. Parl., III, 89-90, nos. 12, 13. Wake, Appendix, p. 76. (Reg. Magnum Prior, et Capit. Wigorn, fol. 306b.)	Nov. 5-Dec. 5.		The Parliamentary Proctors of the Prior and Chapter of Worcester were different from those for Convocation on December 1.		

Sources.	Parliaments. Place and Date.	Assemblies and Great Councils.	Clerical Composition or use of "Premunientes."	Matters Treated concerning the Clergy.	Results.
Int. Rep., pp. 76–7. Rep. Dig., IV, 688–9.	Westminster. (Sept. 16, 1381.)		"Premunientes." "Ad faciend. et consenciend."	Ordained that preachers of heresies shall be arrested. Chancellor to make commissions.	
Int. Rep., pp. 76–7. Rep. Dig., IV, 691–2.	Nov. 3, 1381. Sessions of Commons. Nov. 3–Dec. 13.				
Int. Rep., pp. 76–7. Rep. Dig., IV, 694–5.	Westminster. May 7, 1382. Sessions of Commons. May 7–22.		"Premunientes." "Ad consenciend."		
Int. Rep., pp. 76–7. Rep. Dig., IV, 698.	Westminster. Oct. 6, 1382. Sessions of Commons. Oct. 6–24.		"Premunientes." "Ad consenciend."		
Int. Rep., pp. 76–7. Rep. Dig., IV, 700–1.	Westminster. Feb. 23, 1383. Sessions of Commons. Feb. 23–Mar. 10.		"Premunientes." "Ad consenciend."		
Int. Rep., pp. 76–7. Rep. Dig., IV, 704.	Westminster. Oct. 26, 1383. Sessions of Commons. Oct. 26–Nov. 26.		"Premunientes." "Ad consenciend."	Commons made a grant on condition that the clergy will make a proportionate grant.	

Sources.	Parliaments. Place and Date.	Assemblies and Great Councils.	Clerical Composition or use of "Premunientes."	Matters Treated concerning the Clergy.	Results.
Rot. Parl., III, 151, no. 13. Int. Rep., pp. 76–7. Rep. Dig., IV, 707–8. Rot. Parl., III, 176, nos. 4, 5.	Salisbury. April 29, 1384. Sessions of Commons. Apr. 29–May 27.		"Premunientes." "Ad consenciend."	Commons made a grant on condition that the clergy would make a proportionate grant. Petitions presented by the clergy (either in this Parliament or the preceding one).	
Int. Rep., pp. 76–7. Rep. Dig., IV, 711. Reg. Courteney, I., fol. 81v.	Westminster. Nov. 12, 1384. Sessions of Commons. Nov. 12–Dec. 24, 1384.		"Premunientes." "Ad consenciend."	Abp. Courteney made a famous protest when the laity announced that they would give two fifteenths if the clergy would give two tenths.	

Sources.	Parliaments. Place and Date.	Assemblies and Great Councils.	Clerical Composition or use of "Premunientes."	Matters Treated concerning the Clergy.	Results.
Int. Rep., pp. 76-7. Rep. Dig., IV, 717.	Westminster. Oct. 20. Sessions of Commons. Oct. 20–Dec. 6.		"Premunientes." "Ad consenciend."	Walsingham (Hist. Ang., II, 139–40), recounts a protest made by the Abp. of Cant. in this Parliament against proposals by the laity concerning a grant from the clergy. This may have been confused with that of the preceding year.	
Int. Rep., pp. 76-7. Rep. Dig., IV, 721.	Westminster. Oct. 1, 1386. Sessions of Commons. Oct. 1–Nov. 28.		"Premunientes."		
Int. Rep., pp. 78-9. Rep. Dig., IV, 724. Rot. Parl., III, 236, 247, no. 27.	Westminster. Feb. 3, 1388. Sessions of Commons. Feb. 3–Mar. 20.		"Premunientes." "Ad consenciend."	Commons pray that the two half tenths due from the clergy of Prov. of York be paid. If they do not pay, that they be put outside of the realm. Protest of Abp. of Cant. against the clergy taking part in certain matters to be discussed.	

Sources.	Parliaments. Place and Date.	Assemblies and Great Councils.	Clerical Composition or use of "Premunientes."	Matters Treated concerning the Clergy.	Results.
Int. Rep., pp., 78–9. Rep. Dig., IV, 729–30.	Cambridge. Sept. 9, 1388. Sessions of Commons. Sept. 9–Oct. 8.		"Premunientes." "Ad consenciend."		
Int. Rep., pp., 78–9. Rep. Dig., IV, 732–3.	Westminster. Jan. 17, 1390. Sessions of Commons. Jan. 17–Mar. 2.		"Premunientes." "Ad consenciend."		
Int. Rep., pp., 78–9. Rep. Dig., IV, 735–6.	Westminster. Nov. 12, 1390. Sessions of Commons. Nov. 12–Dec. 3.		"Premunientes." "Ad consenciend."		
Int. Rep., pp., 78–9. Rep. Dig., IV, 738.	Westminster. Nov. 3, 1391. Sessions of Commons. Nov. 3–Dec. 2.		"Premunientes." "Ad consenciend."		
Int. Rep., pp., 78–9. Rep. Dig., IV, 741.	(York. Oct. 14, 1392. Prorogued sine die.)		"Premunientes." "Ad consenciend."		
Int. Rep., pp., 78–9. Rep. Dig., IV, 746.	Winchester. Jan. 20, 1393. Sessions of Commons. Jan. 20–Feb. 10.		"Premunientes." "Ad consenciend."		
Int. Rep., pp., 78–9. Rep. Dig., IV, 749.	Westminster. Jan. 27, 1394. Sessions of Commons. Jan. 27–Mar. 6.		"Premunientes." "Ad consenciend."		

Sources.	Parliaments. Place and Date.	Assemblies and Great Councils.	Clerical Composition or use of "Premunientes."	Matters Treated concerning the Clergy.	Results.
Int. Rep., pp. 78–9. Rep. Dig., IV, 752–3.	Westminster. Jan. 27, 1395. Sessions of Commons. Jan. 27–Feb. 15.		"Premunientes." "Ad consenciend."		
Int. Rep., pp. 78–9. Rep. Dig., IV, 755–6.	Westminster. Jan. 22, 1397. Sessions of Commons. Jan. 22–Feb. 12.		"Premunientes." "Ad consenciend."	Abps. of Cant. and York for themselves and their Prelates protest against any ordinances. assented to by the King & lords temporal for power & authority of Parliament touching the provisions of the Court of Rome.	
Int. Rep., pp. 78–9. Rep. Dig., IV, 758–9. Rot. Parl., III, 348, no. 9.	Westminster. Sept. 17, 1397. Sessions of Commons. Sept. 17–29.		"Premunientes." "Ad consenciend."	Abps. of Cant. & York appoint Sir Thomas Percy as the Proctor for the clergy.	
Int. Rep., pp. 78–9. Rep. Dig., IV, 762. Rot. Parl., III, 359, no. 50.	Adjourned to Shrewsbury. Jan. 27, 1398. Sessions of Commons. Jan. 27–31.			Prelates & clergy appoint William le Scrop, Earl of Wiltshire as their Proctor.	

Sources.	Parliaments. Place and Date.	Assemblies and Great Councils.	Clerical Composition or use of "Premunientes."	Matters Treated concerning the Clergy.	Results.
Int. Rep., pp. 78–9. Rep. Dig., IV, 765.	Westminster. Sept. 30, 1399. Sessions of Commons. Sept. 30.		"Premunientes." "Ad consenciend."		
Int. Rep., pp. 78–9. Rep. Dig., IV, 768.	Westminster. Oct. 6, 1399. Sessions of Commons. Oct. 6–Nov. 19.		"Premunientes." "Ad consenciend."		

APPENDIX D

LITERA excusacionis domini directa domino nostro Regi
quod dicta conuocacio non potest fieri citra tempus in
dicto breui limitatum.

Tresexcellent et tresredoute Seigneur Je me reco-
manka vostre tres noble seigneurie come vostre assiduel
chapellain humblement signifiaunt a vostre benignitee
que ie receu vostre honourable briefe[2] lendemayn de la
purificacion nostre dame en la quiel vostre hautesse mad
prie et commaunde de faire vne nouele conuocacion des
prelatz et le clergie de ma prouince entrecy et la
dymange en demye qaresme donnt mesmes les prelatz
et clergie porroient resonablement merueiller si ie le
feisse coment que ils estoient si tard ensemblez eu le
temps de vostre darrein parlement et lors ils safforce-
rent de vous grantier por la defense de vostre roialme et
de seint eglise quantz ils poient et si auannt que si toute
la summe grauntee por vostre viage serent leuee deinz
cest an as termes assigneez apein le busoigne se ferra
sannz tres graunde disease de eux qy por lour graund
pouert a mesme lour congregacion refusent de grauntier
vn petit subsidie en eide, socour, et defense de nostre
tres seint piere le pape et de toute seinte eglise, pour
quiel il lour maunda se lettres bulleez ove graundez
priers et requestz, as queux ils vssent obeiez (fol. 82v.)
de bone volontee, si ne fusse graund charge quils
avoient touchant la defense du votre roialme et de
seinte eglise, come desus est dit Auxi come mes frieres

[1] Reg. Courteney, I, fols. 82—82v.
[2] The king's writ was dated January 15, eighth year of his reign.
Cal. C.R. (1381—1385), 8 Richard, II, p. 605.

et autres prelatz le savount bien. Isint que si ie duisse
faire execucion de vostre brief susdit, eiaunt regard al
effect et noueltee dycele, it tournereit al plus greuous
et importable domage de clergie auauntdit et arerisse-
ment de seinte eglise et de ses libertees que unques ne
lour aviendroient en les temps de voz nobles progenitours. Et porceque iespoir que vous, mon tres redoute
seigneur a nulle informacion ne mettrez seinte eglise en
plus greindre seruage que vos nobles progenitours ne
ount fait en lour temps, mes que vous serez, si dieu
plest, en apres menteignour et defendour de franchises
et libertees de mesme eglise, sicome vous auez este tout
foiz deuaunt ces heures, auxi come beneit et christien
roy dust estre, de tres humble cuer non tres honourable
seigneur ie vous requer, que eiaunt regard al pouert del
clergie et la bone uoluntee quil porte envers vostre
excellence pour lamour de dieu et en eoure le charitee
vous luy vuillez a cest foiz auoir pour excuse et estre
content del summe a vous grauntee oue lour priers.
Entendaunt, sil vous plest, que puis que vous estez eu
vostre honourable viage pour la defense de vostre
roialme, si come vous biez oue leide de dieu vous
trouerez mesmes les prelatz et clergie si bien veillauntz
et naturels de vous socourer solonc lour poiar, come
ascun clergie de mounde poureit estre a lour seigneur
lige. Et endroit si vous vous assiez dentier cuer en lour
seintz priers, et de vostre poeure people, iespoir a luy
tutpuissant, qul vous deignera oftroier bone et honor-
able exploit en vostre dit viage. Et tres redoute
seigneur, si askun conuocacion serreit faite pour la
cause auantdite me semble sil plerreit a vostre hautesse
que depuis les termes du graunt de la darrein disme
sonnt a les quinszimes de Paske et de seint John pros-
chein aueuir il ne sereit my affaire densembler le clergie
deinz les termes qar toutz les causes, perils et meschiefs
que sonnt comprisz en le dit brief et plus autres queux

moi termes frieres sauoiems penser ou deuiser, furent declareez al darein conuocacion auxi pleniement, come ils pourroient estre declareez au present et leffect de quilez ce que serreit graunte si nul y serreit ne pourreit estre leue tanque mes les termes furrent passeez et adonques tout le clergie serreit en greindre voluntee de performer vos desires que au present.

BIBLIOGRAPHY

I. BIBLIOGRAPHIES, GUIDES, DICTIONARIES, MANUALS AND ALMANACKS.

A. BIBLIOGRAPHIES:

Gross, Charles, *The Sources and Literature of English History*. London, 1915.

Paetow, L. J., *Guide to the Study of Medieval History*. Revised Edition (Mediæval Acad. of America). New York, 1931.

B. GUIDES:

Giuseppi, M. S., *A Guide to the Manuscripts preserved in the Public Record Office*. 2 vols., London, 1923—4.

Hardy, T. D., *Descriptive Catalogue of materials relating to the history of Great Britain and Ireland to the end of the reign of Henry VII*. 3 vols. in 4, Rolls Series. London, 1862—71.

James, Montague Rhodes and Jenkins, Claude, *Lambeth Palace*. A Descriptive Catalogue of the Manuscripts in the Library. 1 vol. in 5 parts. Cambridge, 1930—2. In progress.

C. DICTIONARIES:

A Dictionary of English Church History, edited by S. L. Ollard, assisted by Gordon Crosse. 2nd edition, London, 1919.

Dictionary of National Biography, edited by Sir L. Stephen and S. Lee. 68 vols. London, 1885—1904.

Du Cange, C. du Fresne, *Glossaire françois*. 2 vols. Niort, 1879.

Du Cange, C. du Fresne, *Glossarium ad Scriptores mediæ et infimæ Latinitatis*. 6 vols. Paris, 1733—36.

D. MANUALS:

Capelli, Adriano, *Dizionario di Abbreviature Latine ed Italiane*. Milano, 1899.

Giry, A., *Manuel de Diplomatique*. Paris, 1894.

Jenkinson, Hilary, *Palæography and the Practical Study of Court Hand*. 2 vols. Cambridge, 1915.

Johnson, Charles and Jenkinson, Hilary, *English Court Hand A.D. 1066 to 1500, illustrated chiefly from the public records*. Oxford, 1915.

Prou, Maurice, *Manuel de Paléographie,* 4e Edition Refondue avec la Collaboration de Alain de Bouard Accompagnée d'un album de 24 planché. Paris, 1924.

Waltherus, J. L., *Lexicon Diplomaticum*. Göttingen, 1745.

E. ALMANACKS:

Bond, John James, *Handy-book of Rules and Tables*. London, 1869.

Fry, Edward Alexander, *Almanacks for Students of English History*. London, 1915.

II. MANUSCRIPT SOURCES.

A. MANUSCRIPTS PRESERVED IN THE BRITISH MUSEUM:

B.M. Additional Charter 36449.

" Charter of B(enedict) Bishop of Rochester, setting forth the circumstances attending his consecration of Eustace de Faukumberg, Bishop of London; St. Mark's day (25th April) in St. Katharine's chapel, Westminster, 1st year after the Translation of St. Thomas the Martyr (1221)."

B.M. Additional Manuscript 24062.

" A large collection of forms of documents passing under the Privy Seal, consisting of copies of letters and warrants, tempp. Ric. II—Hen. V, chiefly in French, compiled by Thomas Hocclyf or Occleve, the poet, Clerk of the Privy Seal, and almost wholly in his writing."

B.M. Additional Manuscript 41612.

A Cartulary of Ely Priory.

B.M. MS. Cotton, Cleopatra, F II., fols. 52—53v.

" Catalogus Convocationum ab anno 1296 sub Roberto de Winchelsea, Archiep. Cantuar. ad ann. 1580 sub Edmundo Grindallo."

B.M. MS. Cotton, Cleopatra, F II, fols. 52—53v.

" Epistola circularis cujusdam archiepiscopi Cantuar. ad prelatos clerumque provinciæ Cantuariensis; ut Lincolniæ conveniant, regi opem Laturi, tempore R. Edward II quo Scoti cum exercitu Angliam invasissent, et omnia illic ferro et igne vastassent."

B.M. MS. Cotton, Faustina, A V, fol. 3.

" Petitiones et supplicationes abbatum priorum, ecclesiarum cathedralium, decanarum, archidiacanorum, capitulorum et cleri provinciæ Cantuar. quas porrigant instanti congregationi apud Lincolniam."

B.M. MS. Cotton, Faustina, A V, fol. 4.

" Petitio a clero Cantuariensis provinciæ, super remedio contra Scotos inimicos regis et regni."

B.M. MS. Egerton, 2031—2034.

" Indexes to the registers in the Episcopal Registry of Winchester, 1282—1555, by William Turner Alchin. Four volumes."

B. MANUSCRIPTS PRESERVED IN THE ARCHIVES AT LAMBETH PALACE:

The Register of John Pecham, Archbishop of Canterbury (1279—92).

The Register of Robert Winchelsey, Archbishop of Canterbury (1293—1313).

The Register of Walter Reynolds, Archbishop of Canterbury (1313—27).

The Register of Simon Islep, Archbishop of Canterbury (1349—66).

The Register of Simon Langham, Archbishop of Canterbury (1366—68).

The Register of William Witlesey, Archbishop of Canterbury (1368—74).

The Register of Simon Sudbury, Archbishop of Canterbury (1375—81).

The Register of William Courteney, Archbishop of Canterbury (1381—96). Two Parts.
The Register of Thomas Arundel, Archbishop of Canterbury
(1396—1414). Two Parts.

C. MANUSCRIPTS PRESERVED IN THE PUBLIC RECORD OFFICE:
Ancient Correspondence (Class S.C. 1), vols. I—LXV.
Chancery Records.
Chancery Miscellanea (Class C 47):
Bundle 18. File 9. Nos. 7, 9, 10, 11, 12, 16, 17, 20,
21, 23, 24, 30.
Bundle 30. File 6. No. 8d.
Chancery and Parliamentary Proceedings (Class C 49):
File 4. No. 1.
File 5. No. 19.
File 33. No. 6.
File 45. No. 2.
File 46. No. 4.
File 53. No. 16.
Close Rolls (Class C 54):
10 Edward III.
11 Edward III, Pt. 1.
12 Edward III, Pt. 3.
8 Richard II.
13 Richard II, Pt. 1.
Patent Rolls (Class C 66):
18 Henry III.
4 Edward II, Pt. 2.
Exchequer Records.
Exchequer K.R. Ecclesiastical (Class E 135):
Bundle 10. Nos. 11, 13, 14, 15, 16, 18.
K.R. Memoranda Rolls (Class E 159):
4 Edward III. Roll nos. 106, 107.
5 and 6. Edward III. Roll no. 108.
7 Edward III. Roll no. 109.
11 Edward III. Roll. no. 113.
12 and 13. Edward III. Roll no. 114.
13 Edward III. Roll no. 115.
19 Edward III. Roll no. 121.
L.T.R. Memoranda Rolls (Class E 368):
13 Edward III. Roll III.
Subsidy Rolls (Class E 179):
Nos. 3/6, 8/2a, 8/2aa, 11/2, 11/3, 11/7, 11/8, 11/9a,
15/7, 15/8c, 15/11, 24/2, 24/7, 24/9, 30/4, 58/4,
67/11, 67/15, 68/4, 68/45, 68/49, 278/69, 279/15,
279/51.

D. MANUSCRIPTS PRESERVED IN THE ARCHIVES OF THE DIOCESAN
REGISTRY AT WINCHESTER:
The Register of Adam de Orleton, Bishop of Winchester
(1333—1345). Two Parts.
The Register of William of Edyndon, Bishop of Winchester
(1342—1366). Two Parts.
The Register of William of Wykeham, Bishop of Winchester
(1367—1404). Four Parts in two volumes.

E. MANUSCRIPTS PRESERVED IN THE LIBRARY OF THE DEAN AND
CHAPTER OF WINCHESTER CATHEDRAL:
The Chartulary of Winchester Cathedral.

III. PRINTED SOURCES.

    A. NARRATIVE SOURCES :

Adam Murimuth, *Chronica Sui Temporis, Cum Eorundem Continuatione A Quodam Anonymo,* edited by Thomas Hog. English Historical Society. London, 1846.

Continuatio Chronicarum, edited by Sir Edward Maunde Thompson. Rolls Series. London, 1889.

Annales Monastici, vol. I, *Annales de Margan. Annales monasterii de Theokesberia. Annales monasterii de Burton.* Vol. II, *Annales monasterii de Wintonia. Annales monasterii de Waverleia.* Vol. III, *Annales prioratus de Dunstaplia.* Vol. IV, *Annales monasterii de Oseneia. Chronicon Thomae Wykes. Annales prioratus de Wigornia,* edited by Henry Richards Luard. 5 vols. Rolls Series. London, 1864—69.

The Anonimalle Chronicle, edited by V. H. Galbraith. Manchester, 1927.

Bartholomæus de Cotton, *Historia Anglicana,* edited by Henry Richards Luard. Rolls Series. London, 1859.

Benedict of Peterborough, *Gesta Regis Henrici Secundi* (1169—1192), edited by William Stubbs. 2 vols. Rolls Series. London, 1867.

Chronica Monasterii de Melsa, edited by Edward A. Bond. 3 vols. Rolls Series. London, 1866—68.

Chronicles of the Reigns of Edward I and Edward II, edited by William Stubbs. 2 vols. Rolls Series. London, 1882—83.

Chronicles of the Reigns of Stephen, Henry II and Richard I, edited by Richard Howlett. 4 vols. Rolls Series. London, 1884—89.

The Chronicle of the Monastery of Abingdon (1218—1304), edited by James Orchard Halliwell. Berkshire Ashmolean Society. Reading, 1844.

Chronicon Abbatiæ Rameseiensis, edited by W. Dunn Macray. Rolls Series. London, 1886.

Chronicon Angliæ, edited by Edward Maunde Thompson. Rolls Series. London, 1874.

Chronicon Angliæ Petriburgense, edited by John Allen Giles. Caxton Society. London, 1845.

Chronicon Monasterii de Abingdon, edited by Joseph Stevenson. 2 vols. Rolls Series. London, 1858.

Chronicon Petroburgense, edited by Thomas Stapleton. Camden Society. London, 1849.

Eadmer, *Historia Novorum in Anglia,* edited by Martin Rule. Rolls Series. London, 1884.

Florence of Worcester, *Chronicon ex Chronicis,* edited by Benjamin Thorpe. 2 vols. English Historical Society. London, 1848—49.

Flores Historiarum (Matthew of Westminster attributed author), edited by Henry Richards Luard. 3 vols. Rolls Series. London, 1890.

Gervase of Canterbury, *Historical Works,* edited by William Stubbs. 2 vols. Rolls Series. London, 1879—1880.

Henry of Huntingdon, *Historia Anglorum,* edited by Thomas Arnold. Rolls Series. London, 1879.

John of Oxenedes, *Chronica,* edited by Sir Henry Ellis. Rolls Series. London, 1859.

Matthew Paris, *Chronica Majora,* edited by Henry Richards Luard. 7 vols. Rolls Series. London, 1872—83.

Ordericus Vitalis, "Historia Ecclesiastica," *Patrologia Latina,* edited by J. P. Migne. (221 vols. Paris, 1844—1905.) Vol. 188, Paris, 1855.

Ralph de Diceto, *Opera Historica,* edited by William Stubbs. 2 vols. Rolls Series. London, 1876.

Roger of Howden, *Chronica,* edited by William Stubbs. 4 vols. Rolls Series. London, 1868—71.

Roger of Wendover, *Chronica, sive Flores Historiarum,* edited Henry O. Coxe. 4 vols. English Historical Society. London, 1841—42.

Symeon of Durham, *Opera Omnia,* edited by Thomas Arnold. 2 vols. Rolls Series. London, 1882—85.

The Saxon Chronicle with an English Translation, edited by J. Ingram. London, 1823.

Two of the Saxon Chronicles Parallel (787—1001), with supplementary extracts from others. A revised text edited by Charles Plummer. 2 vols. Oxford, 1892—99.

Venerabilis Bædæ Opera Historica, edited by Charles Plummer. 2 vols. Oxford, 1896.

Walsingham, Thomas, *Gesta Abbatum Monasterii Sancti Albani,* edited by Henry Thomas Riley. 3 vols. Rolls Series. London, 1867—69.

Historia Anglicana, edited by Henry Thomas Riley. 2 vols. Rolls Series. London, 1863—64.

Walter of Coventry, *Memoriale,* edited by William Stubbs. 2 vols. Rolls Series. London, 1872—73.

Walter de Hemingburgh, *Chronicon de Gestis Regum Angliæ,* edited by Hans Claude Hamilton. 2 vols. English Historical Society. London, 1848—49.

William of Malmesbury, *De Gestis Regum Anglorum. Historiæ Novellæ,* edited by William Stubbs. 2 vols. Rolls Series. London, 1887—89.

De Gestis Pontificum Anglorum, edited by N. E. S. A. Hamilton. Rolls Series. London, 1870.

B. RECORD SOURCES :

(1) General Collections.

An Exact Abridgement of the Records in the Tower of London from the Reign of Edward II and Richard III, collected by Sir Robert Cotton, Knight and Baronet, revised by William Prynne, Esq. London, 1657.

Cartularum Saxonicum: a collection of Charters relating to Anglo-Saxon history, edited by Walter de Gray Birch. 3 vols. London, 1885—93.

Cole, H., *Documents illustrative of English History.* (Record Commission.) London, 1844.

Die Gesetze der Angelsachsen, hrsg. im Auftrage der Savigny-Stiftung von F. Liebermann. 3 Bände, Halle a.S., 1903—16.

Diplomatarium anglicum ævi Saxonici, edited by Benjamin Thorpe. London, 1865.

Quadripartitus, ein Englisches Rechtsbuch von 1114. Herausgegeben von F. Liebermann. Halle a.S., 1892.

Regesta Regum Anglo-Normannorum (1066—1154), edited by H. W. C. Davis with the assistance of R. J. Whitwell. Vol. I (1066—1100). Oxford, 1913.

Royal and other Historical Letters illustrative of the Reign of Henry III, edited by Walter Waddington Shirley. 2 vols. Rolls Series. London, 1862—66.

Rymer, T., *Fœdera* (1101—1654), 20 vols. (XVIff. by R. Sanderson.) London, 1704—35. 3rd edn. The Hague, 1739—45. New edn. (1069—1383) by A. Clarke, F. Holbrooke and J. Caley. 4 vols. in 7 pts. (Record Commission.) London, 1816—69.

Stubbs, William, *Select Charters and other illustrations of English Constitutional History to the reign of Edward I.* 9th edn., edited and revised by H. W. C. Davis. Oxford, 1921.

The Laws of the Earliest English Kings, edited and translated by F. L. Attenborough. Cambridge, 1922.

The Laws of the Kings of England from Edmund to Henry I., edited and translated by A. J. Robertson. Cambridge, 1925.

(2) Chancery.

Calendar of the Close Rolls preserved in the Public Record Office. Edward I 1272-(1307). 5 vols. London, 1900—1908.

Calendar of the Close Rolls preserved in the Public Record Office. Edward II 1307-(1327). 4 vols. London, 1892—98.

Calendar of the Close Rolls preserved in the Public Record Office. Edward III 1327-(1377). 14 vols. London, 1896—1913.

Calendar of the Close Rolls preserved in the Public Record Office. Richard II. 6 vols. London, 1914—27.

Calendar of the Patent Rolls preserved in the Public Record Office. Edward I 1272-(1307). 4 vols. London, 1893—98.

Calendar of the Patent Rolls preserved in the Public Record Office. Edward II 1307-(1327). 5 vols. London, 1894—1904.

Calendar of the Patent Rolls preserved in the Public Record Office. Edward III 1327-(1377). 16 vols. London, 1891—1916.

Calendar of the Patent Rolls preserved in the Public Record Office. Richard II 1377-(1399). 6 vols. London, 1895—1909.

Close Rolls of the Reign of Henry III preserved in the Public Record Office. 1227-(1259). 10 vols. London, 1902—32.

Patent rolls of the reign of Henry III preserved in the Public Record Office. 1216-(1272). 6 vols. (Vols. 3—6 have title *Calendar of the Patent Rolls.*) London, 1901—13.

Rotuli Litterarum Clausarum, edited by T. D. Hardy. 2 vols. (Record Commission.) London, 1833–44.

Rotuli Litterarum Patentium, edited by T. D. Hardy. (Record Commission.) London, 1835.

(3) Records of Parliamentary History.

Dugdale, William, *A Perfect Copy of all summons of the Nobility to the Great Councils and Parliaments of this Realm from XLIX of King Henry the III*[d] *until these present times.* London, 1685.

The Parliamentary Writs and Writs of military Summons, together with Records and muniments, collected and edited by Sir Francis Palgrave. 2 vols. in 4. London, 1827—34.

Prynne, William, *The First-Fourth Part of a brief Register, Kalendar and Survey of the several kinds, forms of all Parliamentary writs.* 4 vols. in 5. London, 1659—64.

Reports (Brought from the Lords) on the Dignity of a Peer of the Realm. 4 vols. London, 1820—26.

Rotuli Parliamentorum ut et Petitiones et Placita, edited by J. Strachey and others. 6 vols. London, 1767—77. Index. (Record Commission.) London, 1832.

Statutes of the Realm. 11 vols. and Index (Record Commission). London, 1810—28.

(4) Ecclesiastical Records.

(a) General.

A Roll of the Household Expenses of Richard de Swinfield, Bishop of Hereford during part of the years 1289 and 1290, edited by John Webb. Camden Society. Vols. 59, 62. London, 1854—55.

Beati Lanfranc Cantuariensis Archiepiscopi et Angliæ Primatis, ordinis S. Benedict, Opera Omnia quæ reperiri potuerunt, evulgavit Dominus Lucas Dacherius, Benedictinus Congregationis S. Mauri in Gallia. Venetiis. 1745.

Beati Lanfranc Opera Quæ supersunt Omnia, edited by J. A. Giles. 2 vols. *(Patres Ecclesiæ Anglicanæ.)* Oxford, 1844.

Calendar of the Manuscripts of the Dean and Chapter of Wells. (Prepared and edited by W. H. B. Bird.) Historical Manuscripts Commission. 2 vols. London, 1907—14.

The Cartulary of the Abbey of Old Wardon, edited by G. Herbert Fowler. Publications of the Bedfordshire Historical Record Society, vol. XIII., 1930.

Charters and Documents illustrating the History of the Cathedral, City, and Diocese of Salisbury, selected by W. Rich Jones and edited by W. Dunn Macray. Rolls Series. London, 1891.

Chartulary of Winchester Cathedral, edited in English by A. W. Goodman. Winchester, 1927.

Chapters of the Augustinian Canons, edited by H. E. Salter. Canterbury and York Society. London, 1922.

Concilia, Decreta, Leges, Constitutiones in Re Ecclesiarum Orbis Britannici (1066—1531), compiled by Sir Henry Spelman. 2 vols. (Vol. II. edited by Sir William Dugdale.) London, 1639—64.

Concilia Magnæ Britanniæ et Hiberniæ edited by David Wilkins. 4 vols. London, 1737.

Councils and Ecclesiastical Documents relating to Great Britain and Ireland, edited after Spelman and Wilkins, by Arthur West Haddan and William Stubbs. 3 vols. Oxford, 1869—73.

Documents illustrating the Activities of the General and Provincial Chapters of the English Black Monks, edited by William Abel Pantin. 2 vols. Royal Historical Society (Camden Third Series, vol. XLV, XLVII), London, 1931—33.

Episcopacy Ancient and Modern, edited by Claude Jenkins and K. D. MacKenzie. London, 1930.

Godolphin, John, *Repertorium Canonicum.* 3rd edn. London, 1687.

Hefele, Charles Joseph and Leclerq, Dom Henri, *Histoire des Conciles d'apres les Documents Originaux.* Nouvelle Traduction française faite sur la deuxième édition allemande corrigée et augmentée de notes critiques et bibliographiques par un Religieux Benedictin de l'abbaye Saint-Michael de Farnborough. (Dom Henri Leclerq.) Paris, 1907, etc. In progress.

The Historians of the Church of York and its Archbishops, edited by James Raine. 3 vols. Rolls Series. London, 1879—94.

Johnson, John, *A Collection of All the Ecclesiastical Laws, Canons, Answers or Rescripts, with other Memorials concerning the Government, Discipline, and Worship of the Church of England.* 2 vols. London, 1720. New edn., Oxford, 1850.

"Letters of Cardinal Ottonboni," edited by Rose Graham. *English Historical Review* XV (1900), 87—120.

Lyndwood, William, *Provinciale.* Oxford, 1679.

Regesta Pontificum Romanorum ab condita Ecclesia ad annum post Christum natum MCXCVIII. Edidit Philippus Jaffé Editionem secundam correctam et auctam auspiciis Gulielmi Wattenbach . . . curaverunt. S. Loewenfeld, F. Kaltenbrunner, P. Ewald. 2 vols. Lipsiæ, 1885—88.

Regesta Pontificum Romanorum inde ab anno 1198 ad annum 1304, edited by A. Potthast. 2 vols. Berlin, 1874—75.

Registrum: sive Liber irrotularius et consuetudinarius Prioratus Beatæ Mariæ Wigorniensis, with introduction and notes by William Hale Hale. Camden Society. London, 1865.

Roberti Grossteste Epistolæ, edited by Henry Richards Luard. Rolls Series. London, 1861.

Sacrorum Conciliorum Nova et Amplissima Collectio, in quo præter ea quæ Labbeus et Cossartius et novissime Nicolaus Coleti in lucem edidere ea omnia insuper exhibentur, quæ J. D. Mansi evulgavit. 31 vols. Venice, 1759—98.

Statutes of Lincoln Cathedral. Arranged by Henry Bradshaw, edited by Chr. Wordsworth. 2 Pts. in 3 vols. Cambridge, 1892—97.

The Bishops' Register. Introd. and notes by Clifford J. Offer. London, 1929.

The Liber Albus of the priory of Worcester, edited by James Maurice Wilson. Parts I and II, Worcestershire Historical Society. London, 1919.

The Records of the Northern Convocation, edited by George W. Kitchin. Surtees Society, vol. 113. Durham, 1907.

The Registrum Antiquissimum of the Cathedral Church of Lincoln, vol. I edited by C. W. Foster. Lincoln Record Society, vol. 27. Hereford, 1931.

The Valuation of Norwich, edited by W. E. Lunt. Oxford, 1926.

Vetus Registrum Sarisberiense alias Dictum Registrum S. Osmundi Episcopi, edited by W. H. Rich Jones. 2 vols. Rolls Series. London, 1883—4.

(b) Archiepiscopal and Episcopal Registers.

Bath and Wells.

The Registers of Walter Giffard, Bishop of Bath and Wells (1265—66) and of Henry Bowett, Bishop of Bath and Wells (1401—7), edited by Thomas Scott Holmes. Somerset Record Society. London, 1899.

Calendar of the Register of John de Drokensford, Bishop of Bath and Wells (1309—29), edited by E. Hobhouse. Somerset Record Society. London, 1887.

*The Register of Ralph of Shrewsbury, Bishop
of Bath and Wells (1329—63),* edited by
Thomas Scott Holmes. 2 vols. Somerset
Record Society. London, 1896.

Canterbury.

*Registrum Epistolarum Fratris Johannis
Peckham, Archiepiscopi Cantuariensis,* edited
by Charles Trice Martin. 3 vols. Rolls
Series. London, 1882—85.
*Registrum Johannis Pecham, Archiepiscopi
Cantuariensis (1279—92),* edited by Claude
Jenkins. Pts. I, II. Canterbury and York
Society. London, 1908. In progress.
*Registrum Roberti Winchelsey, Archiepiscopi
Cantuariensis (1294—1308),* edited by Rose
Graham. Parts I—IV. Canterbury and
York Society. London, 1917. In progress.

Carlisle.

*The Register of John de Halton, Bishop of
Carlisle (1292—1324),* transcribed by W. N.
Thompson, with an introduction by T. F.
Tout. 2 vols. Canterbury and York
Society. London, 1913.

Chichester.

Register of Robert Rede (1397—1415), edited
by C. Deedes. Two parts. Sussex Record
Society. London, 1908—10.

Coventry and Lichfield.

The Register of Roger de Norbury, an abstract
of contents and remarks by E. Hobhouse.
William Salt Archæological Society. Col-
lections for a History of Staffordshire.
Vol. I, pp. 241—88. Birmingham, 1880.
*The Register of the Guardians of the Spiritual-
ities during the Vacancy of the See and the
First Register of Bishop Robert De Stretton
(1358—85),* an abstract of the contents by
Rowland A. Wilson. William Salt Archæ-
ological Society. Collections for a History
of Staffordshire. Vol. X, Part 2. New
Series. London, 1907.
*The Second Register of Bishop Robert De
Stretton (1360—85),* an abstract of the
contents by Rowland A. Wilson. William
Salt Archæological Society. Collections for
a History of Staffordshire. Vol. VIII New
Series. London, 1905.

Durham.

*Registrum Palatinum Dunelmense, The
Register of Richard de Kellawe,* edited by
Sir Thomas Duffus Hardy. 4 vols. Rolls
Series. London, 1873—78.

Ely.

"Ely Episcopal Registers," a series of extracts from the Bishops Registers by J. H. Crosby. *Ely Diocesan Remembrancer.* November, 1889—December, 1914. Cambridge.

"Simon de Montacute (1337—45)." *Ibid.* November 1889—June, 1892.

"Thomas Lisle (1345—61)." *Ibid.*, to October—November, 1894. (Registers of Langham and Barnet are wanting.)

"Thomas de Arundel (1374—88)." *Ibid.*, to March—April, 1897.

"John de Fordham (1388—1425)." *Ibid.*, to May—June, 1902.

Ely Episcopal Records. A calendar and concise view of the Episcopal records preserved in the muniment room of the palace at Ely, compiled by A. Gibbons. Lincoln, 1891 (contains extracts from registers 1375—1587).

Exeter.

The Registers of Walter Bronescombe, Bishop of Exeter (1257—80) and Peter Quivil, Bishop of Exeter (1280—91), with some records of the episcopate of Bishop Thomas de Bytton (1292—1307); also the Taxation of Pope Nicholas IV, 1291 (diocese of Exeter), edited by F. C. Hingeston-Randolph. London, 1889.

The Register of Walter de Stapledon, Bishop of Exeter (1307—26), edited by F. C. Hingeston-Randolph. London, 1892.

The Register of John de Grandisson, Bishop of Exeter (1327—69), edited by F. C. Hingeston-Randolph. Three parts. London, 1894—99.

The Register of Thomas de Brantyngham, Bishop of Exeter (1370—94), edited by F. C. Hingeston-Randolph. Two parts. London, 1901—6.

The Register of Edmund Stafford, Bishop of Exeter (1395—1419), an index and abstract by F. C. Hingeston-Randolph. London, 1886.

Hereford.

Registrum Thome de Cantilupo, Episcopi Herefordensis (1275—82), transcribed by R. G. Griffiths, with an introduction by W. W. Capes. Cantilupe Society and Canterbury and York Society. London, 1907.

The Registrum Richardi de Swinfield, Episcopi Herefordensis (1283—1317), transcribed and edited by William W. Capes. Canterbury and York Society. London, 1909.

Registrum Ade de Orleton, Episcopi Herefordensis (1317—27), transcribed and edited by A. T. Bannister. Canterbury and York Society. London, 1908.

Registrum Thome de Charlton, Episcopi Herefordensis (1327—44), edited by William W. Capes. Canterbury and York Society. London, 1913.

Registrum Johannis de Trillek, Episcopi Herefordensis (1344—61), transcribed and edited by Joseph Henry Parry. Canterbury and York Society. London, 1910—12.

Registrum Ludowici de Charltone, Episcopi Herefordensis (1361—70), edited by Joseph Henry Parry. Canterbury and York Society. London, 1914.

Registrum Willelmi de Courtenay, Episcopi Herefordensis (1370—75), edited by William W. Capes. Canterbury and York Society. London, 1914.

Registrum Johannis Gilbert, Episcopi Herefordensis (1375—89), transcribed and edited by Joseph Henry Parry. Canterbury and York Society. London, 1915.

Registrum Johannis Trefnant, Episcopi Herefordensis (1389—1404), edited by W. W. Capes. 2 vols. Canterbury and York Society. London, 1916.

Lincoln.

Rotuli Ricardi Gravesend, Diocesis Lincolniensis (1258—79), edited by F. N. Davis, C. W. Foster and A. Hamilton Thompson. Canterbury and York Society. London, 1925.

London.

Registrum Radulphi Baldock, Gilberti Segrave, Ricardi Newport, et Stephani Gravesend Episcoporum Londoniensium (1304—38), transcribed and edited by R. C. Fowler. Canterbury and York Society, 1911.

Registrum Simonis de Sudbiria, Episcopi Londoniensis (1362—75), transcribed and edited by R. C. Fowler. Canterbury and York Society. London, 1916—29.

Rochester.

Registrum Hamonis Hethe, Episcopi Roffensis (1319—52), edited by Charles Johnson. Canterbury and York Society. Parts I—IV. London, 1914. In progress.

Salisbury.

Registrum Simonis de Gandavo, Episcopi Saresbiriensis (1297—1315), edited by Cyril T. Flower and M. C. B. Dawes. 2 vols. Canterbury and York Society. London, 1914—32.

Winchester.

Registrum Johannis de Pontissara, Episcopi Wyntoniensis (1282—1304), edited by Cecil Deedes. 2 vols. Surrey Record Society, with Canterbury and York Society. London, 1913—24.

The Registers of John de Sandale and Rigaud de Asserio, Bishops of Winchester (1316—23), edited by Francis Joseph Baigent. Hampshire Record Society. London, 1897.

Wykeham's Register, edited by T. F. Kirby. 2 vols. Hampshire Record Society. London, 1896—99.

Worcester.

The Register of Bishop Godfrey Giffard (1268—1301), edited by J. W. Willis Bund. 2 vols. Worcestershire Historical Society. Oxford, 1898—1902.

The Register of William de Geynesburgh, Bishop of Worcester (1302—7), edited by J. Willis Bund, with an introduction by Rowland Alwyn Wilson. Worcestershire Historical Society. Oxford, 1907—29.

The Register of Walter Reynolds, Bishop of Worcester (1308—13), edited by Rowland Alwyn Wilson. Dugdale Society and Worcestershire Historical Society. London, 1928.

The Register of Thomas De Cobham, Bishop of Worcester (1317—27), edited by Ernest Harold Pearce. Worcestershire Historical Society. London, 1930.

The Register of the diocese (of Worcester) during the vacancy of the see usually called "Registrum Sede Vacante," edited by John William Willis Bund. Four parts in 5. Worcestershire Historical Society. Oxford, 1893—97.

York.

Register of Walter Giffard, Lord Archbishop of York (1266—79), edited by W. Brown. Surtees Society, no. 109. Durham and London, 1904.

Register of William Wickwane, Lord Archbishop of York (1279—85), edited by W. Brown. Surtees Society, no. 114. Durham and London, 1907.

Register of John le Romeyn, Lord Archbishop of York (1286—96), edited by W. Brown. Two parts. Surtees Society, nos. 123, 128. Durham and London 1913—17.

Register of Thomas Corbridge, Lord Archbishop of York (1300—4), edited by A. Hamilton Thompson. Two parts. Surtees Society, nos. 138, 141. Durham and London, 1925—28.

Register of William Greenfield, Lord Arch-
bishop of York (1306—15). Part I transcribed and annotated by William Brown,
edited by A. Hamilton Thompson. Surtees
Society, no. 145. Durham and London,
1931. In progress.
Historical Papers and Letters from the
Northern Registers, edited by James Raine.
Rolls Series. London, 1873.

(5) Miscellaneous.

The Doctor and the Student or Dialogues between a
Doctor of Divinity and a Student in the Laws of
England. Revised and corrected by William
Muchall. Cincinnati, 1874.

IV. MODERN WORKS.

A. GENERAL:

Freeman, Edward A., *The History of the Norman Conquest*.
6 vols. Oxford, 1867—79.
The Collected Papers of Frederic William Maitland, edited
by H. A. L. Fisher. 3 vols. Cambridge, 1911.
Searle, William George, *Onamasticon Anglo-Saxonicon: a*
list of Anglo-Saxon proper names from the time of Beda
to that of King John. Cambridge, 1897.

B. STUDIES ON SPECIAL SUBJECTS:

(1) Constitutional and Administrative.

Freeman, Edward A., *William the Conqueror*.
London, 1903.
Interim Report of the Committee on House of
Commons Personnel and Politics, 1264—1832.
London, 1932.
Jacob, E. F., "England: Henry III," *Cambridge*
Medieval History (Cambridge, 1929), vol. VI,
chap. VIII, pp. 253—83.
Johnstone, Hilda, "England: Edward I, and
Edward II." *Cambridge Medieval History*
(Cambridge, 1932), vol. VII, chap. XIV, pp.
393—433.
Legg, J. Wickham, *Three Coronation Orders*. Henry
Bradshaw Society. Vol. XIX. London, 1900.
Liebermann, F., *The National Assembly in the Anglo-*
Saxon period. Halle a.S., 1913.
Lowry, Edith Clark, "Clerical Proctors in Parliament
and Knights of the Shire, 1280—1374." *English*
Historical Review, vol. XLVIII (1933), pp.
443—55.
McIlwain, Charles Howard, *The High Court of*
Parliament. New Haven, 1910.
"Medieval Estates." *Cambridge Medieval History*
(Cambridge, 1932), vol. VII, chapter XXIII,
pp. 664—715.
Manning, Bernard L., "England: Edward III and
Richard II." *Cambridge Medieval History*
(Cambridge, 1932), vol. VII, chapter XV,
pp. 434—85.
Mitchell, Sydney Knox, *Studies in Taxation under*
John and Henry III. New Haven, 1914.
Morris, William Alfred, *The Constitutional History*
of England to 1216. New York, 1930.

Parry, Charles Henry, *The Parliaments and Councils of England.* London, 1839.

Pasquet, D., *An Essay on the Origin of the House of Commons,* translated by R. G. D. Laffan, with a preface and additional notes by Gaillard Lapsley. Cambridge, 1925.

Petit-Dutaillis, Charles, *Studies and notes supplementary to Stubbs' Constitutional History down to the great Charter,* edited by J. Tait and F. M. Powicke. Vol. I, translated by W. E. Rhodes; vol. II, translated by W. T. Waugh; vol. III, by Ch. Petit-Dutaillis and Georges Lefebre, translated by M. I. E. Robertson and R. F. Treharne. Manchester, 1908—29.

Pollock, F. and Maitland, F. W., *The History of English Law before the time of Edward I.* 2 vols. 2nd edn. Cambridge, 1898.

Pollard, A. F., *The Evolution of Parliament.* 1st edn. London, 1920.

Redlich, Josef, *The Procedure of the House of Commons,* translated from the German by A. Ernest Steinthal, with an introduction and supplementary chapter by Sir Courtenay Ilbert. 3 vols. London, 1908.

Richardson, H. G. and Sayles, George, " The Early Records of the English Parliaments," *Bulletin of the Institute of Historical Research.* Vol. V (1928), pp. 129—54; vol. VI (1928—9), pp. 71 —88, 129—55.

Richardson, H. G. and Sayles, George, " The Parliaments of Edward III." *Bulletin of the Institute of Historical Research.* Vol. VIII (1930), pp. 65—82; vol. IX (1931), pp. 1—18.

" The King's Ministers in Parliament, 1272—1377." *English Historical Review.* Vol. XLVI (1931), pp. 529—50; vol. XLVII (1932), pp. 194—203, 377—97.

Richardson, H. G., " The Origins of Parliament." *Transactions of the Royal Historical Society.* 4th series. Vol. XI (1928), pp. 137—83.

Stenton, Frank Merry, *William the Conqueror and the rule of the Normans.* New York and London, 1908.

The First Century of English Feudalism. Oxford, 1932.

Stubbs, William, *The Constitutional History of England.* Vol. I, sixth edn., 1897; vol. II, 4th edn., 1896; vol. III, 5th edn., 1896. Oxford.

Tout, Thomas Frederick, *Chapters in the Administrative History of Mediæval England.* 6 vols. Manchester, 1920—33.

Turner, G. J., " The St. Albans Council of 1213." *English Historical Review.* Vol. XXI (1906); pp. 297—99.

Viollet, Paul, *Histoire des Institutions Politiques et Administratives de la France.* 3 vols. Paris, 1890—1903.

White, Albert Beebe, *The Making of the English Constitution.* 2nd edn. New York, 1925.

(2) Ecclesiastical.

Atterbury, Frances, *The Rights, Powers and Privileges of an English Convocation.* London, 1700.

Ayer, Joseph Cullen, " Church Councils of the Anglo-Saxons." *Papers of the American Society of Church History.* 2nd series. Vol. VII (1923), pp. 91—107.

Barker, Ernest, *The Dominican Order and Convocation.* Oxford, 1913.

Böhmer, Heinrich, *Kirche und Staat in England und in der Normandie.* Leipzig, 1899.

Burn, Richard, *Ecclesiastical Law.* 2 vols. London, 1763. New Edition, 4 vols. London, 1842.

Brooke, Z. N., *The English Church and the Papacy.* Cambridge, 1931.

Capes, W. W., *The English Church in the Fourteenth and Fifteenth Centuries.* London, 1900.

Cheney, C. R., *Episcopal Visitation of Monasteries in the Thirteenth Century.* Manchester, 1931. " The Papal Legate and English Monasteries in 1206." *English Historical Review.* Vol. XLVI (1931), pp. 443—52.

Chew, Helena Mary, *The English Ecclesiastical Tenants-in-chief and Knight Service, especially in the thirteenth and fourteenth centuries.* Oxford University Press, 1932.

Churchill, Irene Josephine, *Canterbury Administration: The Administrative Machinery of the Archbishopric of Canterbury.* 2 vols. Church Historical Society. London, 1933.

Crozals, J. de, *Lanfranc Archevêque de Cantorbéry.* Paris, 1877.

Dansey, W., *Horæ decanicæ rurales.* 2nd edn. 2 vols. London, 1844.

Duchesne, Louis, *Early History of the Christian Church from its foundation to the end of the fifth century,* rendered into English from the 4th edn., 3 vols. Vol. III, translated by Claude Jenkins. London, 1909—24.

Duchesne, L., *Histoire Ancienne de l'Église.* 3 vols., 3rd edn. Paris, 1907—10.

Dodd, John Theodore, *Convocation and Edward Dodd's Share in its Revival.* London, 1931.

Dugdale, William, *Monasticon Anglicanum.* New edition by John Caley, Henry Ellis, Bulkeley Bandinal. 6 vols. in 8. London, 1817—30.

Fasti Ecclesiæ Anglicanæ, compiled by J. Le Neve, corrected and continued from MDCCXV to the present time by T. D. Hardy. 3 vols. Oxford, 1854.

Fowler, R. C., *Episcopal Registers of England and Wales.* (Helps for Students of History, S.P.C.K.) London, 1918.

Gabel, Leona C., " Benefit of Clergy in England in the Later Middle Ages." *Smith College Studies in History.* Vol. XIV, nos. 1—4, Oct. 1928—July 1929. Northampton, Mass.

Gibson, Edmund, *Codex Juris Ecclesiastici Anglicani.*
 London, 1761.

Graham, Rose, *English Ecclesiastical Studies.* London,
 1929.

Graves, E. B., "Circumspecte Agatis." *English
 Historical Review.* Vol. XLIII (1928), pp. 1—20.

Hodgkin, Thomas, *The History of England from the
 Earliest Times to the Norman Conquest.* London,
 1920.

Hody, Humphrey, *A History of English Councils and
 Convocations.* London, 1701.

Hunt, William, *The English Church from its
 Foundation to the Norman Conquest.* London,
 1899.

Jacob, E. F., "Wilkins' 'Concilia' and the Fifteenth
 Century." *Transactions of the Royal Historical
 Society.* (London, 1932.) Vol. XV. (Fourth
 Series), pp. 91—131.

Jenkins, Claude, "Some Thirteenth Century
 Registers." *Church Quarterly Review.* Vol.
 XCIX (1924), pp. 69—115.

 Ecclesiastical Records. London, S.P.C.K. (Helps
 for Students of History), 1920.

 *The Monastic Chronicler and the early School of
 St. Albans.* London, 1922.

Johnstone, Hilda, "Archbishop Pecham and the
 Council of Lambeth of 1281." *Essays in
 Medieval History presented to Thomas Frederick
 Tout,* edited by A. G. Little and F. M. Powicke
 (Manchester, 1925), no. 14, pp. 171—88.

Joyce, James Wayland, *England's Sacred Synods.*
 London, 1855.

Kennett, White, *Ecclesiastical Synods and Parliamentary Convocations in the Church of England.*
 London, 1701.

Lathbury, Thomas, *A History of the Convocation of
 the Church of England.* London, 1842.

Lunt, William E., "Clerical Tenths Levied in Eng-
 land by Papal Authority During the Reign of
 Edward II." *Anniversary Essays in Mediæval
 History* by Students of Charles Homer Haskins,
 edited by C. H. Taylor and John L. La Monte.
 Boston and New York, 1929, no. 8, pp. 157—82.

 "The Consent of the English Lower Clergy to
 Taxation during the Reign of Henry III."
 *Persecution and Liberty. Essays in honor of
 George Lincoln Burr* (New York, 1931), pp.
 117—69.

Macdonald, A. J., *Lanfranc; a study of his life,
 work and writing.* Oxford, 1926.

Maitland, Frederic William, *Roman Canon Law in
 the Church of England.* London, 1898.

Makower, Felix, *Die Verfassung der Kirche von
 England.* Berlin, 1894.

 *The Constitutional History and Constitution of the
 Church of England,* translated from the German.
 London, 1895.

Oughton, Thomas, *Ordo Judicorum.* 2 vols. London,
 1738.

Parker, Matthew, *De Antiquitate Britannicæ Ecclesiæ et Privilegiis Ecclesiæ Cantuariensis,* edited by Samuel Drake. London, 1729.

Powicke, F. M., *Stephen Langton.* Oxford, 1928.

Reichel, Oswald J., *The Canon Law of Church Institutions.* London, 1922.

Robertson, E. William, *Historical Essays in connexion with the land, the Church, etc.* Edinburgh, 1872.

Robinson, J. Armitage, "Convocation of Canterbury: its early History." *Church Quarterly Review.* Vol. LXXXI (1915), pp. 81—137.

Gilbert Crispin, Abbot of Westminster. Cambridge, 1911.

St. Oswald and the Church of Worcester. British Academy. London, 1919.

The Saxon Bishops of Wells. British Academy. London, 1918.

Somerset Historical Essays. British Academy. London, 1921.

The Times of Saint Dunstan. Oxford, 1923.

Smith, Arthur Lionel, *Church and State in the Middle Ages.* Oxford, 1913.

Stenton, F. M., *The Early History of the Abbey of Abingdon.* Reading, 1913.

Stephens, W. R. W., *The English Church from the Norman Conquest to the Accession of Edward I.* London, 1901.

Stubbs, William, *On Convocation.* A letter to the Archbishop (Benson) of Canterbury and a Speech in the Upper House of Convocation of the Southern Province. Prepared for publication with a Preface by W. H. Hutton. London, 1917.

"Historical Appendices I, V." *Report of the Commissioners appointed to inquire into the Constitution and working of the Ecclesiastical Courts.* (2 vols. in one. London, 1883.) Vol. I, pp. 21—51, 142—162.

Registrum Sacrum Anglicanum, edited by William Stubbs. 2nd edn. With appendix by E. E. Holmes. Oxford, 1897.

Tillmann, Helene, *Die päpstlichen Legaten in England bis zur Beendigung der Legation Gualas* (1218). Bonn, 1926.

Trevor, George, *The Convocations of the Two Provinces.* London, 1852.

Troeltsch, Ernst, *The Social Teaching of the Christian Church,* translated by Olive Wyon, with an introduction by Charles Gore. 2 vols. London, 1931.

Wake, William, *The Authority of Christian Princes.* London, 1697.

The State of the Church and Clergy of England. London, 1703.

Watson, Edward William, *The Church of England.* London, 1914.

" The Development of Ecclesiastical Organization and its Financial Basis." *Cambridge Medieval History* (Cambridge, 1929). Vol. VI, chap. XVI, pp. 528—58.

Willard, J. F., " The English Church and the Lay Taxes of the Fourteenth Century." *University of Colorado Studies,* IV, pp. 217—25. Boulder, 1907.

Wordsworth, Chr., *The Precedence of English Bishops: and the Provincial Chapter.* Cambridge, 1906.

York Minster Historical Tracts, edited by A. Hamilton Thompson. London, 1927.

(3) Political Theory.

Carlyle, R. W. and Carlyle, A. J., *A History of Mediæval Political Theory in the West.* 5 vols. Edinburgh and London, 1903—28.

Gierke, Otto, *Political Theories of the Middle Age,* translated with an introduction by Frederic William Maitland. (Reprinted) Cambridge, 1922.

McIlwain, Charles Howard, *The Growth of Political Thought in the West.* New York, 1932.

The following books and essays, which are pertinent to a study of Convocation appeared too late to be used in the writing of this book. It was possible, however, to include in one of the charts certain data from Mr. C. R. Cheney's article, " Legislation of the Medieval English Church," in regard to the councils of 1258, 1261 and 1342 for which due acknowledgment has been given.

PRINTED SOURCES :

Registrum Henrici Woodlock Episcopi Wintoniensis, transcribed and edited by A. W. Goodman. Parts I—II. Canterbury and York Society. London, 1934—6. In progress.

Registrum Hamonis Hethe Episcopi Roffensis, transcribed and edited by Charles Johnson. Part V. Canterbury and York Society. London, 1934. In progress.

The Register of William Greenfield, Lord Archbishop of York (1306—15). Part II. Edited by the late William Brown and A. Hamilton Thompson. Surtees Society, no. 149. Durham and London, 1934. In progress.

MODERN WORKS :

Cheney, C. R., " Legislation of the Medieval English Church." *English Historical Review,* vol. L (1935), pp. 193—224, 385—417.

Clarke, M. V., *Medieval Representation and Consent.* London, 1936.

Darlington, R. R., " Ecclesiastical Reform in the Late Old English Period." *English Historical Review,* vol. LI (1936), pp. 385—428.

Gibbs, Marion and Lang, Jane, *Bishops and Reform* (1215—72). Oxford, 1934.

INDEX

PRINTED IN GREAT BRITAIN BY THE FAITH PRESS, LTD., LEIGHTON BUZZARD

Date Due
